RETHINK
GAMIFICATION

RETHINKING GAMIFICATION

Edited by
**Mathias Fuchs, Sonia Fizek,
Paolo Ruffino, Niklas Schrape**

μ meson press

IMPRINT

A collaboration between the Gamification Lab and the Hybrid Publishing Lab
at Leuphana University of Lüneburg, Germany
http://cdc.leuphana.com/structure/gamification-lab/
http://cdc.leuphana.com/structure/hybrid-publishing-lab/

Editors Sonia Fizek, Mathias Fuchs, Paolo Ruffino, Niklas Schrape
Editorial Assistance and Project Management Fabian Lehmann
Proofreading and Editorial Assistance Jacob Watson
Layout, Design, and Artwork Laleh Torabi
meson press Mercedes Bunz, Marcus Burkhardt, Andreas Kirchner

Bibliographical Information of the German National Library
The German National Library lists this publication in the Deutsche Nationalbibliografie
(German National Bibliography); detailed bibliographic information is available online at
http://dnb.d-nb.de.

Published by meson press, Hybrid Publishing Lab, Leuphana University of Lüneburg, Germany
www.meson-press.com

The paperback edition of this book is printed by Lightning Source, Milton Keynes,
United Kingdom.
The digital editions can be downloaded freely at www.meson-press.com.

ISBN (Print): 978-3-95796-000-9
ISBN (PDF): 978-3-95796-001-6
ISBN (EPUB): 978-3-95796-002-3

Funded by the EU major project Innovation Incubator Lüneburg

CONTENTS

Introduction 7

RESETTING BEHAVIOUR

Niklas Schrape
Gamification and Governmentality 21
Paolo Ruffino
From Engagement to Life, or: How to Do Things with Gamification? 47
Maxwell Foxman
How to Win Foursquare: Body and Space in a Gamified World 71
Joost Raessens
The Ludification of Culture 91

REPLAYING HISTORY

Mathias Fuchs
Predigital Precursors of Gamification 119
Felix Raczkowski
Making Points the Point: Towards a History of Ideas of Gamification 141

REFRAMING CONTEXT

Fabrizio Poltronieri
Communicology, Apparatus, and Post-History: Vilém Flusser's
Concepts Applied to Videogames and Gamification 165
Thibault Philippette
Gamification: Rethinking 'Playing the Game' with Jacques Henriot 187
Gabriele Ferri
To Play Against: Describing Competition in Gamification 201

RECLAIMING OPPOSITION

Daphne Dragona
Counter-Gamification: Emerging Tactics and Practices Against the Rule
of Numbers 227
Matthew Tiessen
Gamed Agencies: Affectively Modulating our Screen and App-Driven
Digital Futures 251

REMODELLING DESIGN

Sonia Fizek
Why Fun Matters: In Search of Emergent Playful Experiences 273
Scott Nicholson
Exploring the Endgame of Gamification 289
Sebastian Deterding
Eudaimonic Design, or: Six Invitations to Rethink Gamification 305

APPENDIX

Authors 333
Index 337

INTRODUCTION

This book is about gamification, and much more. The publication intends to explore the concept of gamification, its history and applications, its implications for theory and practice. It also aims at doing more than simply mapping a trend, or providing guidelines for the design of gamification apps. In this book the concept of gamification will be rethought, through several distinct approaches and a multitude of questions.

But first, what is gamification? Gamification can be approached in at least two ways. First, as a general process in which games and playful experiences are understood as essential components of society and culture. From this perspective we could look at how practices and rituals, belonging to different historical and cultural contexts, might take the form of or resemble a game. Roger Caillois, while drawing on anthropology, biology and the study of myths, has shown how the playful might in fact belong to living beings of any kind, and not be limited to the human sphere. It might also be less of a process of rationalisation, and more of an instinctive reaction to the surrounding environment, a form of adaptation that connects life and death into one single thing (Caillois 1960, 1961 and 1964). Before him, Johan Huizinga had already argued that play is an essential component in the formation of societies and civilisation (1949/1938). From this perspective, gamification may be viewed as a much broader phenomenon, and as a concept not nearly as novel as many would have us believe.

More recently, however, gamification has also been used to describe a much more limited practice. This second and more widely-known meaning has been brought forward by marketing gurus and designers over the last few years. It is this latter sense that has led to a great number of definitions on gamification. It is also this second meaning that drives us to discuss gamification in the context of this publication. Sebastian Deterding, Rilla Khaled, Lennart Nacke and Dan Dixon have proposed a tentative history of the term: "'gamification' as a term originated in the digital media industry. The first documented use dates back to 2008, but gamification only entered widespread adoption in the second half of 2010" (Deterding et al. 2011, 1).

In other publications we can read that extensive use of the term has been reported from 2010, but its origins are probably to be found in a British consultancy company, Conundra Ltd., founded in 2003 by Nick Pelling, a game designer, who claimed to be specialising in gamification (Werbach and Hunter 2012). The no longer active Conundra Ltd. focused on helping "manufacturers evolve their electronic devices into entertainment platforms" (Conundra Ltd. 2014). Its core business focused on advising companies interested in attracting new customers on the implementation of game features into the companies' products and services. This type of activity was called "gamification" on Conundra's website (ibid.). More recently the idea of "gamifying" a business seems to have re-emerged, not necessarily directly as a result of Pelling's first attempt but in a very similar vein.

Over the last few years the marketing and consultancy sectors have been promoting gamification as a potential source of revenue. This period has also witnessed the emergence of several events and publications that have contributed to defining gamification. Gabe Zichermann's and Cristopher Cunningham's book *Gamification by Design: Implementing Game Mechanics in Web and Mobile Apps* (2011) is one of the most popular in the business context, as is Zichermann's website *Gamification.co* and the associated annual conference Gamification Summit held annually in San Francisco since 2011. Jane McGonigal's work, expounded in her contribution at the TED Talk series in 2010, is also concerned with "selling" gamification to corporations. In her book *Reality is Broken: Why Games Make Us Better and How*

They Can Change the World (2011) she mostly looks at her own work as a consultant for McDonald's, the Olympic Games organising committees, and other companies for whom she organised marketing campaigns based on alternate reality games. In McGonigal's view, gamification is not only a new goldmine for designers and business people; it is also a tool that has the power to change the world.

In her understanding, gamification is a concept that describes a new age where gamers can collectively use their problem-solving skills not only to solve puzzles within a digital game but also to approach social and political issues in the real world. Gaming, according to McGonigal's vision, could and should play a redeeming role. Game designers could become the new social entrepreneurs, and citizens become gamers. From this perspective, gamification thus becomes a technique for enabling greatly ambitious change. Reporter Alex Konrad on the Fortune segment of *CNN Money* described gamification as a sort of new "Wild West" on the 17th of October 2011: "gamification is the *hot* new business concept, with many of the world's most admired companies signing on" (Konrad 2011).[1] On the 10th of October Rachel Emma Silverman of the *Wall Street Journal* also declared that companies all over the world were already jumping onto the gamification bandwagon (Silverman 2011).

It seems that gamification is now the keyword for a generation of social entrepreneurs and marketing experts, in perfect and timely combination with the re-evaluation of participatory practices (as also recorded in the art and cultural sector, see Bishop 2012) and the trends of quantification and self-governance (often categorised under the label of the Quantified Self movement). Thus, the question remains: Does gamification need to be rethought? Is there something wrong with it? Or to put it differently, why do we need this book in the first place?

Let us start by saying that, according to its many promoters and "evangelists", there is nothing wrong with gamification at all. Quite on the contrary, although the keyword might now be a bit more rusty than a few years ago, consultancies and workshops on this topic are still popular, as well as academic courses and training programmes. In the blogs, workshops, and

---

1   Konrad's emphasis.

publications on the topic it seems that gamification is working so well that the last thing it needs is second guessing. Consumer loyalty, issues related to finance and governance, workers' productivity, training and development – these are only some of the areas that are allegedly being positively revolutionised by the emergence of gamification.

However, if we have to summarise why gamification needs to be rethought in a sentence, it would be: Precisely because it "works". The number of statements produced in support of the rise of gamification and the wide adoption of this concept, in both private and public sectors, force us, thinkers and players, to consider what exactly is at stake in its emergence. What could it possibly be that makes such an enthusiastic narrative apparently fulfil itself so perfectly? How come the ideas surrounding gamification happened to confirm themselves with no need for further discussion?

The number of critiques of gamification is in fact already quite large. As outlined by Ian Bogost in several contexts (2011a, 2011b), gamification has little to do with the design of games (or an allegedly salvific process), and much more with the exploitation of consumers. It frustrates the practice of game design and reduces playing to a stimulus-response experience; whereas, games, and video games in particular, have been trying to differentiate and complicate the meanings of play in a digital culture. Gamification so far has been a bad word for those involved in the study and understanding of video games, as it has been associated with a process of appropriation of the values of digital gaming by marketing and business interests. It seems that gamification "works" only in the eyes of those who have been inventing and promoting it in the first place. In other words, gamification needs to either disappear or be rethought, if it wants to gain the respect of those who have been working with games over the last decades.

This book proposes to keep the word, but change its meanings and the ideas associated with it. While gamification might work just fine as it is now for those who have been evangelising about its redeeming properties, it is also too limiting a concept for conveying political statements, artistic values, educational content or any sort of unconventional message through games.

The first section of this book is a collection of articles that try to grasp how gamification appears to be rooted in a specific understanding of the concept of behaviour, as something to be affected through the design of a game-like environment. Behaviour has been extensively discussed in numerous texts on gamification. Niklas Schrape proposes looking, through Foucault, at how gamification might work as a method to regulate individuals and their social lives. It also works as a pleasant regulator of behaviour because it offers positive feedback (rewards, leaderboards, etc.) rather than negative penalties (fines, prison, etc.). Schrape first looks at how airline frequent-flyer programmes operate. Extrapolating this example, he sketches a libertarian and dystopian society that would result from the domestication of human beings via governance mechanisms modelled on customer loyalty programmes, putting the very concept of democracy in crisis. In such a scenario, the very concept of free will can be disputed and questioned.

Paolo Ruffino looks instead at engagement, another keyword in the studies on gamification, and proposes to rethink the models underpinning the discourses on gamification and its capacity to affect the behaviour of players. Ruffino looks at the work of Tim Ingold and his reading of Bergson and Heidegger and argues that participation, dwelling and co-existence could be seen as alternative ways of thinking about engagement: less as a transitive process that goes from games to their players and more as an intransitive status that needs to be narrated in order to be of any value. He then proposes recuperating, from the theoretical perspective he offers, the notion of life itself, a topic rarely debated in relation to gamification, which could instead help us in the invention of a creative way of approaching games both in our playing and research practices. Ruffino explores the implications of switching the focus from the idea that games "affect us" on the possibilities offered by thinking of games as things we live with and within. He concludes by showing how some artistic projects could be seen as examples of different ways of being engaged with both video games and gamification.

Life and movement are also relevant in the following contribution by Maxwell Foxman, who provides a deep look at one of the most notorious gamified applications, Foursquare. The author's main concern is to explore what it is that drives players to engage with an app like Foursquare, and how it affects the ways in which movement and body presence are understood. He argues that Foursquare alters the experience of moving about on the streets of a city and establishes a form of communication based on bodily proximity. It is a form of expenditure, as Bataille would put it, which preserves competition and rivalry, but now entirely based on movement.

Joost Raessens examines how gamification could be seen in the context of a more general "ludic turn", which affects society and culture at many different levels. This century, Raessens notes, has seen several different kinds of "turns": We have seen the linguistic turn, the digital, followed by the material one and many others. To what extent could we say that we are now experiencing a playful turn – in the sense of a cultural shift that brings playful experiences to the centre of the use, design, and study of media and technologies? Raessens argues that this perspective could in fact be useful in understanding contemporary Western culture, drawing on several examples from a variety of contexts. Gamification could then be understood as another example of this more general process. The ludification of culture, as Raessens puts it, thus becomes a strategic concept for understanding and making sense of current changes in contemporary culture.

The second part of the book looks at the history of games as a potential source for formulating different definitions of gamification. Similarly to Raessens, Mathias Fuchs intends to put gamification into a cultural-historical context. Fuchs offers a retrospective on the use of games in various spheres of social life, including religion and economy. The ways in which games permeate these aspects of culture is not, according to Fuchs, a prerogative of the digital era. It is in fact an ongoing and continuous influence, which also generates similar forms of hysteria towards the ludicisation of society in different ages. Gamification becomes, through the historical overview offered by Fuchs, the name of a relatively recent development in a much longer process, whose origins are difficult to trace, but which nonetheless presents interesting similarities with the hopes and concerns raised today in the discourses surrounding gamification.

Points and rankings, another oft-debated part of gamification, are the subject of Felix Raczkowski's contribution. The author perceives this aspect as a legacy of behaviourism and psychiatry as these disciplines developed during the 1960s. He then argues that a critique of gamification has to deal with this theoretical heritage, which is not always made explicit but indeed nevertheless informs a great many of the current discourses on the topic. The author proposes, for instance, that the enthusiastic views on the effects of gamification and gamified apps might in fact be consistent with this background. The complex position of the player, who is mostly expected to follow precise guidelines in order to win the game, also raises issues about the value of these kinds of playful practices since they appear to be capable of altering the user's behaviour. Raczkowski also suggests that gamification can and should be critiqued from an historical perspective, looking at the intricacies of its origins and the ideas that have made it possible, at one point in history, to institutionalise the practice of making games with the purpose of affecting players' behaviours.

The third section of the book looks at gamification in relation to the contexts of making and playing. This area is approached in different ways by the authors. Fabrizio Poltronieri brings to video games and gamification the concepts of communicology, apparatus, technical images, and post-history, as initially proposed by Vilém Flusser. An historical overview is presented from Flusser's perspective in order to argue that gamification might represent a phase in a post-historical era, one where the projection of realities on the natural world plays a dominant role. Poltronieri's proposal shows the potential for studying digital games in general by applying Flusser's theories, which he brilliantly presents and introduces to the readers in all their complexity. In this paper the context in which games are played and understood moves radically from the usual understanding of both video games and gamification, opening up many potential consequences for game studies.

Gabriele Ferri looks instead at competition and antagonism in gamification, at how these are usually presented in the apps and systems that rely on gamification techniques and how they have been understood thus far. Ferri proposes a semiotic perspective on the issue of competition, re-evaluating concepts such as the actant and the semiotic square. He also proposes distinguishing between what he calls "interstitial" and "exclusive" gamification; the former being an activity that is carried out simultaneously to other activities, and the latter being instead a text that completely absorbs the player. From this theoretical background, Ferri establishes some crucial distinctions in the varied field of gamification and explores how competition could become a key element in understanding the different values and meanings at stake while rethinking gamification.

Thibault Philippette offers a reading of gamification based on the work of Jacques Henriot and his *sciences du jeu* or "play studies", whose work, according to Philippette, could be used to reconsider some of the basic concepts of gamification as proposed by designers and gurus of the concept. The main problem Philippette is concerned with is the arbitrary distinction between games and non-games, a distinction implied in the definition of gamification as the use of game elements in a non-game context. While this distinction is arbitrary, it also reveals a rather static view of games, which could instead become more interesting if opened up to other kinds of definitions. Philippette suggests the very idea that games that can influence the non-game context could be re-interpreted following Henriot's theories on play.

Daphne Dragona introduces the fourth section of the book, which is focused on forms of antagonism and opposition to gamification. Dragona illustrates what she defines as "counter-gamification". Counter-gamification is not a precise practice; it is not defined in guidebooks, workshops, or tutorials. It is instead a form of appropriation of playful elements by artists in order to promote radical and oppositional values. Dragona comments on several projects, less known than the marketed apps that strongly rely on gamification techniques, but still based on a game-like environment. Dragona's ambition is to map the territory outside the most well-known forms of gamification and expand it by including alternative practices of political disobedience that come to be organised as games. Dragona expresses the need to oppose the current trends of gamification and to expand what could potentially be defined as an alternative use of games. Dragona's main focus is on the effects of gamification on social networking sites and on the process of "datafication", which generates forms of resistance from users and artists.

Matthew Tiessen expands Dragona's perspective by asking to what extent gamification can be viewed as desirable by players and society in general. To what extent are gamification apps to be "played" rather than accomplished and fulfilled to receive pre-established rewards? How much enjoyment is expected from playing with gamified apps? If gamification is mostly about directing players' behaviour then it also results, Tiessen suggests, in the objectification of human agency and in the elimination of choice in the practices of playing. Gamification risks leaving players in a passive condition rather than giving them an active role in choosing how to change themselves and the worlds surrounding them.

The final part of the book explores issues related to design, with three important contributions that offer original ways of thinking about how to use gamification. The authors have in fact explored those techniques and reinvented them in order to forge a new approach to the creation of playful environments. None of them offer a proper step-by-step guide, as might be expected in a typical gamification textbook. Instead, they discuss their experience and practice as a way of reimagining the use of games in a non-game context, and as a theoretical contribution to the debates on gamification.

Sonia Fizek looks at how gamification might look like in the "post-bullshit" era, when the focus on points, leaderboards and more generally on the one-size-fits-all approach will be over. Fizek argues that emergent playfulness, a concept she elaborates by drawing on the work of Eric Zimmerman mostly, might be a more interesting concept to look at, rather than the design techniques proposed so far by gamification experts. However, it is also a much more complex concept, difficult to grasp and yet more capable of capturing the interest of the players. Gamification gurus themselves, Fizek says and as has emerged in some of the most recent conferences on this topic, are not completely satisfied with the practice they are supporting and contributing to establish. There is a shared feeling that gamification, as it is now, might be missing the point, and be successful only in very precise and much more limited circumstances than what originally had been proclaimed possible. Fizek's proposal is to expand the concept of play and fun and to introduce new forms of engagement in the practice of gamification.

Scott Nicholson turns to the relation between "grinding", a concept mostly used in massively multiplayer online role-playing games, and gamification. Grinding consists of accumulating points and improving the player's statistics. Nicholson argues that many gamification apps and systems tend to re-purpose a similar approach in a different context. However, these specific types of role-playing games also have an "endgame" component, where players, once all has been achieved that could be possibly accomplished, continue to exploit the game's open-worldness, caring less for game tasks and focusing more on non-progression-motivated play. If the endgame approach were applied to gamification, Nicholson argues, we could see very different ways of designing and playing. The author explores these alternative modes of gamifying things through a text that offers both a theoretical understanding of gamification and exceptionally useful suggestions for designers.

Last but not least, Sebastian Deterding closes the publication with a re-interpretation of his original definition of gamification as the "use of game design elements in non-game contexts", as formulated with colleagues

Dixon, Khaled, and Nacke in 2011. Here he presents six critiques of the current dominant models for the understanding of gamification, starting from the deterministic models of game design that he considers to be replicated in this new context. Deterding proposes an optimistic view of gamification, that still preserves its transformative and critical values but from a more complex, relational, and emergent perspective. He names this new form of design "eudaimonic", an autotelic practice which is equivalent, in Aristotle's original view, to the "good life". The instrumental element that gamification all too often brings to games and work risks perpetuating a "bad life" instead, one where self-discovery and pleasure rarely happen. Instead, an eudaimonic view of gamification could bring a "good" way of living and playing, one where joy and satisfaction are at the centre of a responsible practice. Gamification, according to Deterding, could become the name of a play practice that truly helps human beings in fulfilling their own lives and those of others, but it needs to change in order to do this – it needs to be "rethought". His text can be read as a final and conclusive manifesto for anyone who is involved in gamification, from a theoretical or practical standpoint.

In conclusion, we hope this publication will revamp the debate on gamification as a much more general concept for the study and adoption of games, or game-like environments, and their influences in contemporary life. This is also the ambition and goal of our research centre, the Gamification Lab, where we have just started to investigate the many implications of game technologies, and their ethical, political, artistic, and educational values. We believe that gamification has the potential to become a common term for thinking about and doing games – both practices seen as dependent on and in communication with one another. We hope this book will raise questions on this subject and contribute to further innovative research directions for gamification.

BIBLIOGRAPHY

BISHOP, CLAIRE. 2012. *Artificial Hells: Participatory Art and the Politics of Spectatorship.* London: Verso Books.

BOGOST, IAN. 2011a. "Persuasive Games: Exploitationware." *Gamasutra*, May 3. http://www.gamasutra.com/view/feature/6366/persuasive_games_exploitationware.php.

BOGOST, IAN. 2011b. "Gamification Is Bullshit! My Position Statement at the Wharton Gamification Symposium." *Ian Bogost Blog*, August 8. http://www.bogost.com/blog/gamification_is_bullshit.shtml.

CAILLOIS, ROGER. 1964. *The Mask of Medusa.* New York: C.N. Potter.

CAILLOIS, ROGER. 1961. *Man, Play and Games.* New York: Free Press of Glencoe.

CAILLOIS, ROGER. 1960. *Man and the Sacred.* New York: Free Press of Glencoe.

CONUNDRA LTD. 2014. "Conundra." Accessed April 26. http://www.nanodome.com/conundra.co.uk/.

DETERDING, SEBASTIAN, DAN DIXON, RILLA KHALED AND LENNART NACKE. 2011. "From Game Design Elements to Gamefulness: Defining Gamification." In *Proceedings of the 15th International Academic MindTrek Conference: Envisioning Future Media Environments,* 9–15. New York: ACM.

ESCRIBANO, FLAVIO. 2012. "Gamification as the Post-Mortem Phalanstere: Is the Gamification Playing with Us or Are We Playing with Gamification?" In *The Video Game Industry: Formation, Present State, and Future,* edited by Peter Zackariasson and Timothy L. Wilson, 198–219. New York and London: Routledge.

HUIZINGA, JOHAN. 1949 / 1938. *Homo Ludens: A Study of the Play-Element in Culture.* London: Routledge and Kegan Paul.

KONRAD, ALEX. 2011. "Inside the Gamification Gold Rush." *CNN Money*, October 17. Accessed April 26, 2014. http://tech.fortune.cnn.com/2011/10/17/gamification/.

McGONIGAL, JANE. 2011. *Reality is Broken: Why Games Make Us Better and How They Can Change the World.* New York: Penguin Press.

SILVERMAN, RACHEL EMMA. 2011. "Latest Game Theory: Mixing Work and Play." *The Wall Street Journal*, October 10. Accessed April 26, 2014. http://online.wsj.com/news/articles/SB10001424052970204294504576615371783795248.

WERBACH, KEVIN AND DAN HUNTER. 2012. *For the Win: How Game Thinking Can Revolutionize your Business.* Philadelphia: Wharton Digital Press.

ZICHERMANN, GABE AND CRISTOPHER CUNNINGHAM. 2011. *Gamification by Design: Implementing Game Mechanics in Web and Mobile Apps.* New York: O'Reilly Media.

RESETTING
BEHAVIOUR

GAMIFICATION
AND GOVERNMENTALITY

by **Niklas Schrape**

INTRODUCTION

This article suggests a research perspective that investigates the techniques of gamification as a symptom for an emerging new mode of *governmentality* (Foucault 2007 / 2004 and 2008 / 2004) that depends on the global infrastructure of digital computer-networks. Together with choice architectures (Thaler and Sunstein 2008) and big data techniques (Mayer-Schönberger and Cukier 2013; Paharia 2013), gamification belongs to a set of methods that aim to regulate individuals and society in ways, hailed as *libertarian paternalism* by its proponents (Thaler and Sunstein 2008). This mode of regulation takes Michel Foucault's concept of a liberal governmentality to the extreme. Within it, the subject is constructed as a free player in a defined rule-space. So far, the biopolitically appropriate behaviour of the players had to be ensured by negative feedback-techniques like punishment and deterrence. Now, gamification allows for effective behaviour regulation via positive feedback. Points, badges and leaderboards are more pleasant than prisons and executions. The carrot beats the stick. The only price to pay is total surveillance.

However gamification did not start out as a dystopian control technique but rather a marketing ploy. Many of its techniques were invented in order to foster brand loyalty. So let's start at the beginning.

BRAND LOYALTY

Gamification originally was – and predominantly still is – a marketing buzzword. Several definitions exist but in its broadest sense scholars like Deterding et al. (2011), Fuchs[1] and Escribano (2012) agree: Gamification describes the permeation of non-game contexts with game elements. Several different understandings of this concept exist, but the most common one is to understand gamification as a set of techniques to regulate behaviour via game rules for strategic purposes. At least this is the dominant usage of the notion in marketing discourse. This becomes evident in the whitepaper Gamification 101 by the company Bunchball, one of the most successful proponents of gamification techniques: "At its root, gamification applies the mechanics of gaming to non-game activities to change people's behavior" (Bunchball 2010, 2).

In the marketing context, gamification techniques do not aim to change the way people think, but how they behave. The importance of this fact cannot be overstated: many traditional marketing techniques, like advertising, aim to influence the thoughts, attitudes, and beliefs of the consumer. In this, they follow the paradigm of classical rhetoric. Aristotle distinguished three categories of rhetorical means in his *The Art of Rhetoric* (1991): *logos* (rational argumentation), *pathos* (emotional appeal) and *ethos* (the image and the expression of the orator). Rhetorical persuasion, therefore, cannot only be achieved by appealing to the mind, but also to emotions and to pre-existing notions about the speaker. But regardless of the means of persuasion, changing the mindset of the listener is always the objective.

---

1 Mathias Fuchs in his presentation from March 8, 2013 at the Serious Games Conference in Hannover, titled "Einführung in das Phänomen Gamification" (Introduction to the Gamification Phenomenon). See also: http://www.biu-online.de/de/presse/newsroom/newsroom-detail/datum/2013/03/13/serious-games-conference-2013-erfolgreiches-comeback-nach-einjaehriger-pause.html (accessed February 27, 2014).

Most modern advertising techniques share the same goal: they aim to influence the consumer's attitudes, beliefs, and feelings about products. The classic four steps to describe the intended consumer reaction to an advertisement are attention, interest, desire, and action (AIDA) (cf. Kotler et al. 2011, 808). The acronym was coined as early as 1921 by C.P. Russell. While this idealised process has been reframed, condensed, and complemented several times in the history of marketing, its general characteristics have persisted. Persuasion is understood as a process in which the intended consumer behaviour (the action) is the result of a previous cognitive and affective processing: First, the consumer has to notice the advertisement. Then his or her interest in the product has to be raised by promises of advantages, features or qualities. If successful and if the consumer can connect the characteristics of the products to his or her own needs, a desire arises. This desire can be understood as a cognitive and affective complex, it encompasses a rational understanding and evaluation but also emotional components (e.g. attraction to the model on the poster). Only if there is a desire and if the consumer is capable of attaining the product, may he or she actually perform the purchase.

Even if persuasion cannot be limited to a linear process, there is no doubt about the objective of the advertisers: they want the consumers to think and feel about products just they way they planned it. They want to create and to communicate a desirable image. In advertising, the behaviour of a consumer (e.g. to regularly buy a specific brand and not another) can be interpreted as deriving from an instilled attitude towards a product.

A predictable behavioural tendency towards purchasing a specific brand is interpreted as "consumer loyalty" or "brand loyalty" in marketing literature.[2] Commonly, brand loyalty is understood as the commitment of a consumer to a certain brand. This concept is perfectly illustrated by the memorable dialogue between George Clooney's character Ulysses Everett

---

2   Both terms are in use. The online-dictionary of the American Marketing Association (2014) defines brand loyalty as: "1. The situation in which a consumer generally buys the same manufacturer-originated product or service repeatedly over time rather than buying from multiple suppliers within the category. 2. The degree to which a consumer consistently purchases the same brand within a product class."

McGill and a salesman in the Coen Brothers' adaption of Homer's *Odyssey*, titled *O Brother Where Art Thou?* (Coen and Coen 2000).

> Pomade Vendor: [. . .] here's your pomade [. . .]
> Ulysses Everett McGill: Hold on, I don't want this pomade. I want Dapper Dan.
> P.V.: I don't carry Dapper Dan, I carry Fop.
> U.E.M.: Well, I don't want Fop, goddamn it! I'm a Dapper Dan man!

The attitude that Ulysses Everett McGill shows towards his favourite brand of pomade can be considered the epitome of brand loyalty – he connects his very identity as a man and human being to the brand of pomade. Thus, loyalty becomes a matter of the heart, a question of defining oneself via the use of specific products. The loyal consumer of a branded product partakes of its image.

GAMIFIED LOYALTY

Gamification processes, however, promise a far more direct way to getting at the behaviour and therefore the loyalty of the consumer. Simple examples are the frequent-flyer programs, described in Bunchball's whitepaper (2010) as a primal form of gamification.

The most successful of these is the Miles & More programme by Lufthansa and other airlines of the so-called Star Alliance.[3] Here, aircraft passengers can gather points through their flights, appropriately labelled as miles. There exist two kinds of miles: "award miles", which can be invested in various upgrades and benefits, and "status miles" that can be collected in order to climb up in a hierarchy of levels: 35,000 miles are rewarded with the "frequent-flyer status" (level 1), represented by a silver card, giving access to the business lounges as well as several smaller benefits. 100,000 miles lead to a golden card, the so-called "senator status" (level 2), and access to the senator lounges as well as an exclusive telephone service hotline for instance. Finally, after collecting the unlikely amount of 600,000 miles in two years, the passenger is allowed to call him or herself a member of the elected

---

3   More information under: http://www.miles-and-more.com (accessed May 8, 2014).

HON-circle (level 3), and is granted a card in pure black, a personal assistant and limousine service in selected airports (and access to an even more exclusive telephone service hotline). The tangible benefits of the levels are quite small, but the promise of status and exclusiveness itself seems to work as a driving force of motivation.

Recently, Lufthansa and Star Alliance even added a kind of badge system in the form of so-called "status stars" on the frequent-flyer, senator, and HON-circle cards. Like military emblems, these stars are printed directly on the card for all to see.[4] This public visibility of status and loyalty rewards is one of the decisive characteristics of gamification as Zichermann and Cunningham emphasise:

> In the old days (pre-2008) if a person preferred Cuisinart over KitchenAid, for example, how was that bias expressed? How did she get her friends to understand this loyalty choice? First, her friends needed to be standing in the kitchen near the product itself. Then, a conversation would have to introduce the subject. This process was called word-of-mouth marketing [. . .] Loyalty is no longer private. It is no longer a matter of standing in a kitchen next to your favorite mixer. It is public, and millions are viewing it. (Zichermann and Cunningham 2011, 9)

The traditional way to publicly demonstrate loyalty to a certain brand was to repeatedly use a product or service for all the world to see (e.g. sitting with an Apple MacBook in a coffee shop). The brand preferences are visible in the very act of use. But gamification techniques allow it to monitor product usage, to memorise this information, and to compress it into publicly visible signs (like badges, levels or status stars). Thus, brand loyalty and preferences become apparent, independent from the actual use of the product or service. Consequently, every partaker in gamification programmes attains a visible history of product usage. In the case of the frequent-flyer programmes, the status cards are the carriers and visual displays of this personal history with the brand. The individual status of every passenger, measured in miles and

---

4   See: http://www.miles-and-more-promotion.com/statusstars/en/index.html (accessed May 7, 2014).

materialised in cards and stars, derives from his or her memorised history with the brand. Suddenly, consumption transforms from a momentary action to a process that carries its own history and displays it publicly.

According to Bunchball, the promise of status makes all the difference: Brand loyalty does not depend on a company's image anymore. Gamification techniques like the frequent-flyer programmes can be understood as strategic instruments to manipulate the behaviour of people towards products and services while circumventing their very attitudes towards them. The personal history with a brand creates a commitment that is independent from its image or the consumer's satisfaction: "And they'll [the passengers] go out of their way to stick with the vendor where they have the most points and status – even when disappointed with the actual service" (Bunchball 2010, 3).

Another film with George Clooney illustrates the power of such a gamified loyalty: *Up in the Air* (Reitman and Turner 2009) by director Jason Reitman. In this movie, Clooney plays Ryan Bingham, a travelling "downsizer" who is basically hired by companies to fire their employees. Ryan Bingham is a frequent flyer and a participant in the frequent-flyer programme of American Airlines (AAdvantage).[5] He dearly loves his status and feels a deep sense of loyalty towards the airline, and also to the Hilton hotel chain, which participates in the programme. In fact, his main life goal consists in gathering miles, as this dialogue with his young assistant Natalie Keener (Anna Kendrick) attests:

> Ryan Bingham: I don't spend a nickel, if I can help it, unless it somehow profits my mileage account.
> Natalie Keener: So, what are you saving up for? Hawaii? South of France?
> R.B.: It's not like that. The miles are the goal.
> N.K.: That's it? You're saving just to save?
> R.B.: Let's just say that I have a number in mind and I haven't hit it yet.
> N.K.: That's a little abstract. What's the target? [. . .]
> R.B.: It's ten million miles.

---

5 See: https://www.aa.com/AAdvantage/aadvantageHomeAccess.do?anchorLocation=DirectURL&title=aadvantage (accessed May 1, 2014.)

N.K.: Okay. Isn't ten million just a number?
R.B.: Pi's just a number [...] I'd be the seventh person to do it. More people have walked on the moon.
N.K.: Do they throw you a parade?
R.B.: You get lifetime executive status.

If frequent-flyer programmes can be considered prototypical gamification techniques then the character of Ryan Bingham exemplifies how gamification can foster a new kind of loyalty. Such gamified loyalty might motivate a certain sense of identity, but its immediate object is not the brand as such, but rather the point system attached to its consumption. Ryan Bingham's life-goal is to gather miles. The primary object of his desire therefore is the frequent-flyer programme itself and the status it promises. But because of that he develops a behaviour pattern that he retrospectively interprets as loyalty. This becomes apparent in a romantic conversation with his future casual relationship Alex Goran about his new status card:

Alex Goran: Oh, my God. I wasn't sure this actually existed. This is the American Airlines...
Ryan Bingham: It's a Concierge Key, yeah.
A.G.: What is that, carbon fibre?
R.B.: Graphite.
A.G.: Oh, I love the weight.
R.B.: I was pretty excited the day that bad boy came in [...]
A.G.: This is pretty fucking sexy.
R.B.: Hope it doesn't cheapen our relationship.
A.G.: We're two people who get turned on by elite status. I think cheap is our starting point.
R.B.: There's nothing cheap about loyalty.

Ryan Bingham feels rewarded for his loyalty and draws his self-esteem from this recognition. His one life-goal is to gather more than 10 Million miles as one of just seven persons in the world. In fact, his sense of identity stems to a certain degree from his understanding himself to be being loyal. Ryan Bingham believes in gamified loyalty.

Ryan Bingham's concept of loyalty is a product of the gamified marketing programmes of airlines and hotel chains. For him, loyalty can be measured in points. It is a variable in a game, something that can be calculated and fed into computational models. His attitudes towards brands seem to be the result of a behaviour pattern, motivated by a formal system of game rules – because of gamification, the very concept of loyalty transformed for keeps.

AIRPORT POLITICS

But gamification does not only transform crucial concepts of our society like loyalty. It holds the potential to transform the very social space itself. The frequent-flyer programmes might be symptomatic in this regard.

The structure of status signs (different cards, status stars), exclusive areas (the various lounges), and privileges (special service-hotline and limousine service) creates an artificial hierarchy within the social space of the airport. This hierarchy is the precondition for the experience of status: the access to the exclusive lounges and the privileges has to be restricted – otherwise it would be worthless. In reverse the hierarchy has to be protected through means of surveillance and discipline: Star Alliance's economy class passengers without Miles & More cards may not enter the senator lounges. They have to be excluded, in order to protect the exclusiveness for the privileged. Therefore, the lounges are separated from the rest of the airport through borders, guarded by friendly personnel in uniform. Like in a border control of a nation-state, the crosser has to present the correct ID-card in order to attain access.

But the status cards differ in one crucial aspect from the ID-cards of the nation-states: an ID-card does not memorise data beside what is printed on it. In contrast, the frequent-flyer card functions as an externalised memory of a person's past as passenger – condensed into a number of miles, an attained level (type of card), and visible badges (status stars). While the customs officers at a nation-state border-control cannot attain much knowledge about a traveller's past by looking at his or her ID-card, the employee of the airline has immediate insight into the passenger's past.

This reliance on history and the past marks the crucial difference between the hierarchies imposed by the frequent-flyer programmes and the traditional class system of the airport (the distinction of first class, business class, and economy class). While the class system is actualised in the moment of the purchase, the frequent-flyer hierarchies persist over time. Any passenger can decide to spend all of his or her money at once to experience first-class comfort for one single time. Thus, the affiliation to a class is realised in the moment of transaction. It is ahistorical, not depending on the former decisions of the passenger but only on his or her willingness to invest. In contrast, it is impossible to buy oneself into to the senators lounge. One has to earn the right to climb up one step in the frequent-flyer hierarchy. This hierarchical belonging is completely dependent on an individual's past-decisions and personal history with the airline.

The existence of memorised and publicly visible individual histories marks a tremendous transformation of the very nature of the social space of the airport. In 1992 Marc Augé published the original French version of *Non-Places. Introduction to an Anthropology of Supermodernity* (1995), in which he presented the airport as prime example for his thesis. According to him, our contemporary society is more and more saturated with non-places, places devoid of social relations and history from which a sense of identity could stem.[6] Airports, motorways, train stations, chain hotels and many other such non-places are somewhat artificial, anonymous, and governed by rules that dictate behaviour (e.g. "wait in line"). They are no places to stroll around but simply to pass through – logistically organised as effective as possible.

Just one year later, in 1993, Lufthansa started the Miles & More programme and changed the nature of the non-place for good. The programme became a tremendous success: in 2011, it counted more then twenty million participants worldwide (Lufthansa 2011). In a certain way, the programme can be interpreted as answer to the lack of history and identity that Augé described. For the enthusiastic participants of the Miles & More programme, the airport is no longer an ahistorical place devoid of social relations. Quite the contrary, it is a deeply hierarchical field for social contests about status and privilege. The airport is the very source of identity. But these identities

---

6 "If a place can be defined as relational, historical and concerned with identity, then a space which cannot be defined as relational, or historical, or concerned with identity will be a non-place. The hypothesis advanced here is that supermodernity produces non-places [. . .]" (Augé 1995 / 1992, 77–78).

and histories are products of strategic designs. Moreover, they are automatically generated through tracking and monitoring techniques, put into numbers, and stored and processed by computers. They are pure data. And the citizens of the airport are living within these data structures.

Airlines are not the only ones who collect and store data about their subjects. States do it too – a well-known fact since the Roman census in the times of Jesus. But this kind of data is concerned with statistical social demographics and does not involve evaluations of individuals. States do keep track of the deeds of their subjects, however this should only encompass information about the transgression of legal boundaries – at least in democratic ones: it should be about what a subject did wrong, not about what it did right. Not all state officials need to know how much tax money an individual generated, how many children he or she conceived, or to what extend he or she has been otherwise a particularly good citizen. What they do need to know, however, is if the person in front of them is a danger to society and its laws. This information is stored in the crime record, a record about former punishments.

Punishment can be considered to be a *negative feedback technique.* Through punishments, states try to discourage their subjects from committing crimes – the logic of deterrence. Punishment diminishes unwanted behaviour. In contrast, gamification techniques, like those implemented in the frequent-flyer programmes, exploit *positive feedback.* They aim to enforce actions that are considered to be favourable. They amplify desired behaviour.

GAMIFICATION AND BIG DATA

What becomes obvious at this point is that the frequent-flyer programmes are not only amongst the earliest examples of successful gamification but that they also are symptomatic for a novel mode of behaviour regulation. This regulative technique is dependent on constant monitoring and data-collection. Only the existence and accessibility of this data allow for the implementation of positive-feedback mechanisms. The frequent-flyer programmes and gamification techniques in general are therefore intrinsically linked to another common buzzword of today: big data.

The term big data emerged in the early 2000s in the context of sciences like astronomy and genomics that collected unprecedented amounts of data about their subject and were forced to develop new computerised methods to process it (cf. Mayer-Schönberger and Cukier 2013, 6–7). Since the late 2010s the term dissipated as a buzzword into marketing and economics. There exists no consensual definition but most practitioners agree on the following characteristics:

> Big data refers to things one can do at a large scale that cannot be done at a smaller one, to extract new insights or create new forms of value, in ways that change markets, organizations, the relationship between citizens and governments and more. But this is just the start. The era of big data challenges the way we live and interact with the world. Most strikingly, society will need to shed some of its obsession for causality in exchange for simple correlations: not knowing *why* but only *what*. This overturns centuries of established practices and challenges our most basic understanding of how to make decisions and comprehend reality. (Ibid.)

According to these authors, big data revolutionises society in the most fundamental way. This may be typical Silicon Valley hype but the concept nevertheless highlights some important shifts: the computer technology permits us to store and process information in a way that was simply not possible before, allowing for novel ways to analyse it. Most importantly, today's computing power makes it a lot easier to base decisions on stochastically stable correlations between factors without knowing the underlying causal relations and principles. To some degree, the manager of an airline does not need to know what the customers expect and why they choose the one airline and not the other. What he or she does need to know, however, is whether a certain bonus or badge in the frequent-flyer programme correlates with a higher use of their airline.

Gamification is a symptom of our contemporary society in which every aspect is being captured and processed by computers and digital networks. It relies on a specific techno-historical situation, characterised by global pervasions of nearly every fibre of the society's body with networked computer technology. This development has recently been described by several theoreticians as cybernatisation (cf. Tiqqun 2001, Mersch 2013). According to the German media philosopher Erich Hörl (2011) it even led to a new kind of "environmentality": The omnipresent digital technology merged into the background of society. We are embedded within it. It became our environment.

The new state of nature is a cybernetic one. The existence of such a seemingly self-evident, unquestioned and apparently natural cybernetic environment is the precondition for gamification and big data techniques. The opportunities to gather huge amounts of data, to track movements and behaviour patterns, to award points for deeds and tasks, and to compare them in social networks, they all are only made possible by the pervasiveness of digital networks and computational processes.

Only because of the omnipresent information technology, companies like Bunchball can sell universal gamification engines to be implemented in various businesses. In his book *Loyalty 3.0. How to Revolutionize Customer and Employee Engagement With Big Data and Gamification* (2013), Rajat Paharia, the CEO of Bunchball, describes the new condition of ubiquitous mediation and data generation as great opportunity:

> [. . .] we're now living our lives online – community, entertainment, work, finances – everything we do is being mediated by technology and, as a result, is throwing off reams of data (big data) about our activity. Smart companies, forward-thinking companies, are feeding this user-activity data into gamification systems, which use data-driven motivational techniques [. . .] to drive engagement, high-value activity, and loyalty. (Ibid., 5)

Paharia advises using data mining techniques, including predictive modelling, in order to forecast the behaviour of groups, and sentiment analysis to extract and to filter out information from natural language communication. The picture he is painting might seem dystopian for many readers, but for him as a professional marketer, the new world of permanent and ubiquitous data-generation is a dream come true: "With big data, a business can learn a lot about what you do, where you do it, when you do it, and what you like" (ibid., 40–41).

The use of big data in gamification reveals itself as deeply linked to the issue of surveillance. This becomes obvious in Paharia's description of outlier detection, meaning statistical deviators from norms, that would help to "expose bad behaviour" (2013, 48). He hails big data as opportunity to monitor one's own personnel in order to attain a "360-degree view" of every individual and to "use this data to predict such things as which employees are at risk for leaving, who are going to be top and bottom performers, who is likely to get injured and file for workers' compensation [. . .]" (ibid., 59–61).

But Paharia does not want to regulate the employees' behaviour through negative feedback techniques like punishment. He strives for an effective regulation through motivation by the means of points, badges, and leaderboards – the positive-feedback mechanisms of gamification. For him, the existence of big data is the precondition for an effective use of gamification mechanics:

> [. . .] *gamification,* is *motivating people through data* [. . .] Streams of big data on user activity are sent to the business, and in real time, the business feeds that data to a *gamification engine* that processes the data, feeds it through a set of rules, updates all the necessary statistics, and then responds to users with real-time feedback and other data-driven motivational techniques. (Ibid., 68)[7]

Paharia's concept of gamification is far removed from romantic idealisations of playfulness. This gamification is a technique for behaviour regulation. It is not achieved through disciplinary means (e.g. loan-reductions for employees who cannot reach target productivity) but via codified positive-feedback mechanisms. The feedback is conceptualised to be anonymous: Paharia does not imagine a manager who personally praises the work of an employee, he envisions an automated feedback-system based on the computer evaluation of measured performance. Such a feedback-system can easily be up-scaled to fit the needs of large workforces or to address huge target groups.

Paharia extends the logic of the frequent-flyer programmes to all market sectors. In his view, the behaviour of the customers and employees of any given company should be monitored in the same way that passengers' are. The 360-degree profile of consumers and staff takes the place of the status card in the airport. All decisions shall be tracked in order to identify patterns of behaviour and in order to influence it with motivational techniques. These techniques derive from a specific understanding of management. He clearly envisions the manager as a panoptic governor of workforces and

---

7   Paharia's emphasis.

consumers. While the big data techniques are the governor's tools to watch over the subjects, the gamification mechanisms are the means to regulate their behaviour.

GAMIFICATION AND LIBERTARIAN PATERNALISM

Mayer-Schönberger and Cukier (2013, 7) make the claim that big data demands we think in correlations not causalities. This mirrors the observation that gamification techniques aim to influence the behaviour and not the attitudes of their target group. In the age of big data and gamification, analysts do not have to ponder why something is the case, and no one cares what the consumers think about brands and products. Reasons are not as important anymore. Questions of "why?" and "how?" are sealed in black boxes. The new primary focus is on the quantifiable outcomes of a process: the correlation between factors and the behaviour of consumers.

see also
Raczckowski
p. 147, 155

With its black-boxing and its focus on outcomes and behaviour, gamification appears to be a resurrection of the psychological school of behaviourism. Its techniques do not stand in the tradition of advertising as they do not aim to change consumers' attitudes. Instead they can be considered as advancements of behavioural marketing and management techniques. A simple example of such a technique is the placement of a product in a super market: high-price products are placed at eyelevel in the shelves, low-priced products at the bottom. The reason being that it is more convenient for buyers to see and to grasp what is right in front of their nose than to bend down. For a similar reason, milk and butter are always put at the very opposite ends of the multideck cabinet: thus buyers have to pass by a lot of tempting products in order to get to the essentials. In both cases, products are strategically positioned in space in order to influence the behaviour of consumers.

Such behavioural marketing techniques have recently been described as "choice architectures" by the behavioural scientists Richard Thaler and Cass Sunstein in *Nudge. Improving Decisions about Health, Wealth and Happiness* (2008). They even invent a job description for persons who design such choice architectures: "A choice architect has the responsibility for organizing the context in which people make decisions" (ibid., 3). For them architectures of choices are inevitable: "[. . .] there is no such thing as a 'neutral' design" (ibid.), they claim, and therefore the design should be made consciously with an eye on the intended effect. Their prime example is a school canteen.

Here, the healthy food should be put in eye-high and right next to the cash point – not the sweets. They admit that the children would basically be tricked into buying the intended food. But for Thaler and Sunstein every other organisation of the shelves would also be a choice architecture –

"Fitter, healthier and more productive,
A pig in a cage on antibiotics."
- *Radiohead (Fitter Happier)*

so why should the owner of the canteen not consciously make "the right" decision that improves the wellbeing of the children?[8]

Gamification systems often involve the conscious creation of choice architectures: frequent-flyer programmes e.g. comprise options for participants to invest their award miles in services and products of partner companies. Award miles work much like a currency. But they differ from money in at least two fundamental regards: on the one hand, they cannot be spent anonymously and each investment will create new data that marketers can monitor. On the other, they cannot be spent for everything but only for the products and services that have been selected. The award miles can only be invested in a strategically designed micro-economy of business partners. The participants can only choose between the options given to them. And these options are embedded within a carefully built choice architecture. Gamification and choice architectures are concerned with the same task: to influence people's behaviour in intended ways. Both techniques aim not to change mindsets but only visible and measurable performance and conduct.

Thaler and Sunstein deduce a political style of governance from their behaviouristic reasoning: *libertarian paternalism*. While the concept might seem paradoxical at first glance it follows neatly from their observation that it is impossible not to design choices in any given social situation. Libertarian paternalism implies that, for example, the state grants its subjects the freedom of choice, but designs all possible options in such a way that they will decide in an intended way. The subjects should feel free but their behaviour is regulated. This principle is familiar to all players of computer games: the choices at hand are quite limited in most games but some do a good

---

8   Of course, the question arises what qualifies as "the right" architecture of choices. What are the criterias behind our judgments about right and wrong? Surprisingly, Thaler and Sunstein don't ask these questions.

job of hiding the limitations, thus giving the player the illusion of freedom. In a similar way, the children in the canteen are free to choose whatever food they want, but they can decide between the given options, and the proclaimed healthy one is positioned in the most convenient way. For Thaler and Sunstein there exists no contradiction between freedom and regulation:

> The libertarian aspect of our strategies lies in the straightforward insistence that, in general, people should be free to do what they like – and opt out of undesirable arrangements if they want to do so [. . .] We strive to design policies that maintain or increase freedom of choice [. . .] The paternalistic aspect lies in the claim that it is legitimate for choice architects to try to influence people's behavior in order to make their lives longer, healthier and better. In other words, we argue for self-conscious efforts, by institutions in the private sector and also by government, to steer people's choices in directions that will improve their lives. (Ibid., 5)

Thaler and Sunstein's political ambitions are much more than mere boasting: In 2010, the British Prime Minister David Cameron set up a Behavioural Insight Team[9], commonly called the "nudge unit", in order to explore the potentials of Thaler and Sunstein's concepts for governance. According to an article in The New York Times, the Whitehouse is currently considering to set up a similar programme in the United States (cf. Bennhold 2013).

Like choice architectures, gamification is envisioned by its proponents as universal remedy to make the world a better place, as made especially obvious in the talks and writings of Jane McGonigal: "What if we decided to use everything we know about game design to fix what's wrong with reality?"(2011, 7) For McGonigal, gamification holds the potential to motivate every individual to behave more responsibly, to cope better with problems, to feed on better nutrition, to be less messy etc. But most of the gamification techniques entail surveillance. Evgeny Morozov mentions a particularly striking example in *To Save Everything, Click Here* (2013, 2): BinCam, the gamified trash can that takes pictures of dumped waste, posts them online,

---

9   For more information see: https://www.gov.uk/government/organisations/behavioural-insights-team (accessed May 1, 2014).

and awards points for correct separation while exposing unwanted behaviour. For Morozov (ibid, 1–6), this and other gamification techniques are examples of what he calls "solutionism" – the belief that technological innovations would not only solve all possible problems but more importantly the tendency to identify all possible situations and states as problems in the need of solving.

In the eyes of Morozov, David Cameron and his nudge unit must appear as wonderful examples of solutionism. But the European Commission jumped on the same bandwagon in their current Horizon2020 programme, when they decided to set up a call for research and innovation called "Advanced Digital Gaming/Gamification Technologies". Here, consortia of academic institutions and commercial enterprises are invited to hand in proposals for joined innovation programmes regarding "digital games and gamification mechanics in non-leisure contexts" (European Commission 2014). The text explains that "digital games can [. . .] make a real change in the life of a large number of excluded groups, enhancing their better integration in society" (ibid.) thus praising games and gamification mechanics as tools for political means. The call draws heavily from an issue of the European Commision's in-house science-service Joint Research Centre's "JRC Scientific and Policy Reports". It describes the political values of "digital game-based approaches" encompassing gamification and concludes that these techniques "show potential in addressing issues of policy concern including wellness and aging, education and employability of poor learners, improved quality of training and skill development in industry, and civic participation" (Centeno 2013, 11).

As honourable as these goals might be, it becomes obvious that in the eyes of the European Commission, gamification is a tool for Foucauldian biopolitics: a way to reduce the statistical average of people dying from diseases related to obesity, to increase the percent of citizens with appropriate skills in reading, writing, arithmetic, or IT that suffice the needs of the market, etc (Foucault 2008/2004). The enthusiasm of nation-states and supra-national organisations to make use of techniques like choice architectures and gamification might indicate that there is more in play than mere solutionism. These techniques could indeed be harbingers of a novel style of governance.

GAMIFICATION AND GOVERNMENTALITY

Behind the EU's interest in gamification lies the same reasoning as in Thaler and Sunsteins book (2008). Gamification and choice architectures both are examples of governance techniques that are actually quite accurately described by liberal paternalism. Drawing on Foucault, both emergent techniques can be analysed as signs of a shift in the dominant mode of governmentality.

With "governmentality" Foucault described specific, historically situated rationalities of governing (2007/2004 and 2008/2004). He invented the concept independently and probably unaware of the one of governance in the political sciences, as defined here by Mark Bevir:

> [G]overnance refers [. . .] to all processes of governing, whether undertaken by a government, a market, or network, whether over a family, tribe, formal or informal organization, or territory, and whether through laws, norms, power, or language. Governance differs from government in that it focuses less on the state and its institutions and more on social practices and activities. (Bevir 2012, 1)

Broadly speaking, governmentalities could be described as paradigms of governance in the sense of Kuhn (1962). A historically specific governmentality does not only encompass particular governance techniques but also the underlying principle, idea, or model behind them.

Foucault originally coined the term to characterise a specific type of governance aimed at the statistical regulation of a state's population through biopolitics, specifically:

> the attempt, starting from the eighteenth century, to rationalize the problems posed to governmental practice by phenomena characteristic of a set of living beings forming a population: health, hygiene, birth rate, life expectancy, race [. . .]. (Foucault 2008/2004, 317)

Later, he used the concept in a much broader way, which allowed him to distinguish different historical modes of governmentality. He discerns today's governmentality from the Christian and medieval concept of "pastoral power" (cf. Foucault 2007/2004, 161–185). In those cases, the ruler was considered analogous to a shepherd and conversely the subjects as members of a flock that had to be taken care of by worldly and religious means (e.g. by confession, penance, and indulgence). This differs vastly from the political rationality of the "reason of state", which developed in early modernity. In this Machiavellian doctrine, ruling was conceptualised as rational calculation of advantages against competing European powers. Every state's goal was to maximise its economic and military power at the cost of the others, while preserving internal security through disciplinary means. In reverse, every subject's duty was to maximise the wellbeing of the state. And in order to guarantee this appropriate behaviour, the subjects had to be under the control of the police.

With the rise of modern economics and liberal thought, a different rationality of what it meant to rule emerged: the idea that economic power stems from a growing, healthy, and educated population with a strong work ethic. The wellbeing of the state suddenly depended much more than before on the size of its population and the conditions they live in. In consequence, the management and administration of population became a fundamental part of governance – the birth of biopolitics. In stark contrast to the medieval feudal lords in the time of pastoral power, the individual citizen is now unknown to the rulers: not the single subject is the object of regulation but the statistically determined collectives of citizens.

Moreover, the "discovery" of seemingly natural market laws in economic theory led to the conviction that the optimisation of state power via economic prosperity could paradoxically be realised through a limitation of regulatory activities. The logic of liberalism demanded that the state guarantees the free play of the market to maximise its gains. But in order to let the market dynamic unfold, the state's subjects had to be granted freedoms. Thus, the state re-defined its function. It became, in fact, the *game master* and *rule keeper* of the free play of the market and its citizens. Fittingly, Foucault describes this concept of a natural and beneficiary economy as an "economic game":

> This is the idea that the economy is basically a game, that it develops as a game between partners, that the whole of society must be permeated by this economic game, and that the essential role of the state is to define the economic rules of the game and to make sure that they are in fact applied.

> What are these rules? They must be such that the economic game is as active as possible and consequently to the advantage of the greatest possible number of people [. . .] (Foucault 2008/2004, 201–202)

For Foucault, this mode of liberal governmentality is still dominant. It is not restricted to actual political institutions like legislative, executive, and judiciary organs. It encompasses all institutions and discourses that regulate the behaviour of the subjects. The order and prosperity of a state is obviously not only dependent on some laws and their enforcement by the police, courts, and prisons. It is equally dependent on schools, universities, hospitals, and much more. The state does not control all of these institutions directly but it creates the conditions and the legal boundaries for them, in which they are free to act. All its regulatory techniques can be described as the definition of game rules. Thus liberal governmentality gives rise to a very specific kind of society:

> [. . .] a society in which there is an optimization of systems of difference, in which the field is left open to fluctuating processes, in which minority individuals and practices are tolerated, in which action is brought to bear on the rules of the game rather than on the players, and finally in which there is an environmental type of intervention instead of the internal subjugation of individuals. (Ibid., 259–260)

It is the paradox of liberal governmentality that it has to enforce disciplinary means in order to not only guarantee but to produce the very freedom that is its necessary precondition of existence. Freedom might be the precondition for prosperity but an excess of freedom can endanger it. For instance, the freedom to grow as a company can become dangerous for the free play of the market if a monopoly is established. Thus freedom is bound to surveillance and discipline.

As in his study *Discipline and Punish* (1977/1975) about disciplinary techniques, Foucault refers in his work on governmentality to the liberal philosopher Jeremy Bentham (1748–1832) and his "panopticon" as epitome of disciplinary means – a visionary architecture that allows for perfect surveillance of inmates in prisons. But Bentham did not want to restrict the use of this panopticon to the penal system. As the subtitle of his book *Panopticon;*

or the Inspection-House shows, the panopticon should be implemented in various institutions of the state, from mental institutions and factories to schools:

> [. . .] a New Principle of Construction Applicable to Any Sort of Establishment, in Which Persons of Any Description Are to Be Kept Under Inspection; and in Particular to Penitentiary-Houses, Prisons, Houses of Industry, Work-Houses, Poor-Houses, Lazarettos, Manufactories, Hospitals, Mad-Houses, and Schools [. . .]. (Bentham 1995 / 1787)

Omnipresent surveillance might appear contradictory to the idea of liberalism for many contemporaries. But not for Bentham, one of the fathers of liberal thought, and one of the earliest proponents of universal human rights and gender equality. For him, ultimate transparency of everyone to everyone is the precondition for the prevention of crimes, the guarantee for civilized behaviour, security and thus for freedom. In the Benthamian philosophy, surveillance and freedom are inextricably linked.

Contrary to his older interpretations, Foucault (2008 / 2004, 67–68) therefore interprets the panopticon in his work on governmentality not only as a disciplinary technology but also as one to produce freedom. For Bentham, only omnipresent surveillance of all subjects guarantees security, and only security guarantees freedom. The responsibility of the state would be to intervene wherever the freedom (as free play within defined rules) is endangered. Thus Bentham dreamed of a spy system in order to monitor all the citizens, to prevent them from crimes, and to encourage them to exhibit righteous behaviour (cf. Bentham 1843).

In Bentham's time, perfect surveillance of all the state's subjects was utterly impossible. But today, the situation has changed. His vision of the panopticon is obviously similar to Paharia's praise of the potential of combined big data and gamification techniques. Both are advocating a technology that allows monitoring and tracking individuals in order to regulate their behaviours. Moreover, most of the information about every individual would be made public in the form of high scores in social networks, badges, leaderboards or frequent-flyer status cards – with the public transparency for every individual thus achieved competition is then fostered. Bentham and Paharia both aim to create a surveillance infrastructure to secure the free play of market mechanics and the efficiency of the workforce.

There is, however, a crucial difference between Bentham's and Paharia's visions: the means of regulation. Bentham and also Foucault concentrate on direct or indirect disciplinary means, but Paharia dreams of establishing a motivational system. Disciplinary techniques like punishment or deterrence can be considered to be negative feedback: Behaviour that is out of line is punished, a given collective is normalised within a defined range of allowed differences. Gamification techniques, in contrast, are positive-feedback techniques – they encourage desired behaviour via points, badges, and leaderboards.

The fundamental difference can be exemplified with the frequent-flyer programme discussed above: In airports like in liberal societies, the space is structured by borders, separating public from non-public areas, including or excluding individuals. But the separated areas in the liberal society exist mostly to confine the excluded and the punished, thereby posing deterrence to everyone else. They are materialisations of negative feedback. But the exclusive areas in the airport exist to privilege the elite, motivating the excluded to strive for access. The passengers in the senator lounges are not dangerous individuals to be jailed or unwilling workers that have to be locked-up in the factory, they are privileged customers who are granted status and exclusiveness for being loyal to their airline. They are not disciplined to behave correctly or punished because they did not behave so, they are rewarded for their past behaviour – thus motivated to continue. The senators lounge is a materialisation of positive feedback.

A NEW GOVERNMENTALITY

Gamification and choice architectures are hailed as universal remedies by their proponents. This surely is hype. The use of points, badges and leaderboards has always been common in the military, schools, and to some degree even at the workplace (cf. Nelson 2012). Tasks have been transformed into games for centuries, as Mathias Fuchs demonstrates. Point systems and token economies as control methods were already tested in mental institutions in the 1960s. What is new, however, is the degree to which such techniques can be put to use today. Until recently, the dominant technique of behaviour regulation was negative feedback. Now, big data and gamification allow the

see also
Fuchs
p. 119–140
and
Raczckowski
p. 150–153

42

broad implementation of positive-feedback techniques in various sectors of society. This could foreshadow a new mode of governmentality, characterised by the constant monitoring of every individual's behaviour and its regulation through designed options and positive-feedback mechanisms. It could be the fulfilment of liberalism.

The possibility to monitor nearly every move, action, and decision of any given subject is not only a blessing for companies who want to manage their customer relations, secure their brand loyalty, and maximise the effectiveness of their workforce – it also allows for seemingly humane techniques of governance. Gamification makes it possible to effectively motivate intended behaviour in a pleasant way, without the need to appeal to the mind or reason. It aims at the regulation of behaviour while circumventing attitudes. A passenger does not have to appreciate the image or reliability of an airline in order to be loyal, as long as status cards and senator lounges are promised. But if that is the case in marketing, it is also true for governance techniques: If someone is motivated to choose carrots over bacon by badges and leaderboards, he or she does not need to know why carrots are healthier but only that they give more points. It might no longer be necessary to teach children the value of eating healthy food in order to attain the biopolitical goal of a healthy population. Insight is no longer relevant, if all that is tracked and regulated is behaviour. The age of reason finally comes to an end.

This, however, could deeply transform our understanding of a democratic and free society. The Habermasian notion of a deliberate democracy might always have been illusionary. But this ideal has been powerful and performative over centuries. From Jesus to the proponents of Enlightenment to Marxist activists, the education of people was always considered to be a venerable goal. Individual insight promised a change in behaviour and thus the potential for change in society. Now it seems that people do not have to be illuminated but simply regulated by points and badges in order to make them fitter, happier, and more productive. In fact, the world could be transformed into an airport.

BIBLIOGRAPHY

AMERICAN MARKETING ASSOCIATION. 2014. "Dictionary." Accessed March 3.
https://www.ama.org/resources/Pages/Dictionary.aspx?dLetter=B&dLetter=B.

ARISTOTLE. 1991. *The Art of Rhetoric*. London: Penguin Books.

AUGÉ, MARC. 1995/1992. *Non-Places. Introduction to an Anthropology of Supermodernity*. London, New York: Verso.

BENNHOLD, KAREN. 2013. "Britain's Ministry of Nudges." *The New York Times*, December 7. Accessed March 5, 2014.
http://www.nytimes.com/2013/12/08/business/international/britains-ministry-of-nudges.html?pagewanted=1.

BENTHAM, JEREMY. 1995/1787. "Panopticon; or the Inspection-House: Containing the Idea for a New Principle of Construction Applicable to Any Sort of Establishment, in Which Persons of any Description Are to Be Kept Under Inspection; and in Particular to Penitentiary-Houses, Prisons, Houses of Industry, Work-Houses, Poor-Houses, Lazarettos, Manufactories, Hospitals, Mad-Houses, and Schools." In *The Panopticon Writings*, edited by Miran Bozovic, 29–95. London: Verso.

BENTHAM, JEREMY. 1843. "Of Indirect Means of Preventing Crimes." In "Principles of Penal Law" In *The Works of Jeremy Bentham, Vol. 1, Principles of Morals and Legislation, Fragment on Government, Civil Code, Penal Law*, edited by John Bowring. Edinburgh: William Tait.

BEVIR, MARK. 2012. *Governance: A Very Short Introduction*. Oxford: Oxford University Press.

BUNCHBALL. 2010. "Gamification 101: An Introduction to the Use of Game Mechanics to Influence Behavior." Accessed April 29, 2014.
http://www.bunchball.com/sites/default/files/downloads/gamification101.pdf.

CENTENO, CLARA. 2013. *JRC Scientific and Policy Reports: The Potential of Digital Games for Empowerment and Social Inclusion of Groups at Risk of Social and Economic Exclusion: Evidence and Opportunity for Policy*. Luxembourg: Publications Office of the European Union.

COEN, ETHAN AND JOEL COEN. 2000. *O Brother Where Art Thou?* Directed by Joel Coen. Burbank: Buena Vista Pictures Distribution.

DETERDING, SEBASTIAN, RILLA KHALED, LENNART NACKE AND DAN DIXON. 2011. "Gamification: Toward a Definition." Accessed May 1, 2014.
http://gamification-research.org/wp-content/uploads/2011/04/02-Deterding-Khaled-Nacke-Dixon.pdf.

ESCRIBANO, FLAVIO. 2012. "Gamification as the Post-Modern Phalanstère: Is the Gamification Playing with Us or Are We Playing with Gamification?" In *The Video Game Industry: Formation, Present State, and Future*, edited by Peter Zackariasson, and Timothy L. Wilson, 198–219. New York: Routledge.

EUROPEAN COMMISSION. 2014. "Founding Opportunities." Accessed March 5.
http://ec.europa.eu/research/participants/portal/desktop/en/opportunities/h2020/topics/90-ict-21-2014.html.

FOUCAULT, MICHEL 2008/2004. *The Birth of Biopolitics: Lectures at the Collège du France, 1978–79*. New York: Palgrave Macmillan.

FOUCAULT, MICHEL. 2007/2004. *Security, Territory, Population: Lectures at the Collège du France, 1977–78*. New York: Palgrave Macmillan.

FOUCAULT, MICHEL. 1977 / 1975. *Discipline and Punish: The Birth of the Prison.* New York: Pantheon Books.

HOMER. Around 800 BC. *Odyssey.* Ancient Greece.

HÖRL, ERICH. 2011. *Die Technologische Bedingung.* Frankfurt am Main: Suhrkamp.

KOTLER, PHILIP, GARY ARMSTRONG, VERONICA WONG AND JOHN SAUNDERS. 2011. *Grundlagen des Marketing.* München: Pearson.

KUHN, THOMAS S. 1962. *The Structure of Scientific Revolutions.* Chicago: University of Chicago Press.

LUFTHANSA. 2011. "Rekord bei Miles and More: 20 Millionen Teilnehmer." Accessed March 3, 2014.
http://www.lufthansagroup.com/de/presse/meldungen/view/archive/2011/february/11/article/1875.html.

MAYER-SCHÖNBERGER, VIKTOR AND KENNETH CUKIER. 2013. *Big Data: A Revolution That Will Transform How We Live, Work, and Think.* Boston, New York: Eamon Dolan Book, Houghton Mifflin Harcourt.

MCGONIGAL, JANE. 2011. *Reality is Broken: Why Games Make Us Better and How They Can Change the World.* New York: Penguin Books.

MERSCH, DIETER. 2013. *Ordo ab Chao – Order from Noise.* Zürich: Diaphanes.

MOROZOV, EVGENY. 2013. *To Save Everything, Click Here: Technology, Solutionism and the Urge to Fix Problems That Don't Exist.* London, New York: Penguin.

NELSON, MARK J. 2012. "Soviet and American Precursors to the Gamification of Work." In *Proceedings of the 16th International Academic MindTrek Conference,* 23–26. New York: ACM.

PAHARIA, RAJAT. 2013. *Loyalty 3.0: How to Revolutionize Customer and Employee Engagement with Big Data and Gamification.* New York: McGraw Hill.

REITMAN, JASON AND SHELDON TURNER. 2009. *Up in the Air.* Directed by Jason Reitman. Los Angeles: Paramount Pictures.

RUSSELL, C.P. 1921. "How to Write a Sales-Marketing Letter." Printers' Ink June 2, 49–56.

THALER, RHICHERT AND CASS SUNSTEIN. 2008. *Nudge: Improving Decisions About Health, Wealth and Happiness.* New Haven: Yale University Press.

TIQQUN. 2001. "The Cybernetic Hypothesis." Accessed May 1, 2014.
http://theanarchistlibrary.org/library/tiqqun-the-cybernetic-hypothesis.pdf.

ZICHERMANN, GABE AND CHRISTOPHER CUNNINGHAM. 2011. *Gamification by Design.* Sebastobol: O'Reilly Media.

FROM ENGAGEMENT TO LIFE, OR: HOW TO DO THINGS WITH GAMIFICATION?

by **Paolo Ruffino**

INTRODUCTION: WHAT IS THE PROBLEM WITH "ENGAGEMENT"?

Let us first outline the meaning of engagement, as it is presented in the literature on gamification. In those texts, engagement is one of the most used keywords. One of the best known texts about gamification, *Gamification by Design* (Zichermann and Cunningham 2011) starts precisely with a definition of the notion of engagement:

> The term "engagement", in a business sense, indicates the connection between a consumer and a product or service. Unsurprisingly, the term is also used to name the period in a romantic couple's relationship during which they are preparing and planning to spend the rest of their lives together. Engagement is the period of time at which we have a great deal of connection with a person, place, thing or idea. (Ibid., xvi)

However, for Zichermann and Cunningham, this definition is problematic as it is too vague and difficult to apply in a marketing context. Therefore, they propose to create a metric to break down engagement:

> We would be better off thinking of engagement as being comprised of a series of potentially interrelated metrics that combine to form a whole. These metrics are: recency, frequency, duration, virality, ratings. Collectively, they can be amalgamated as an 'E' (or engagement) score. (Ibid., xvi)

Engagement is presented here as a "score". The need to count, number and evaluate appears quite often in gamification. It is frequently brought forward in order to record data and compare results. In one of the most often mentioned examples of gamification, what comes to be quantified is "life" itself. This is in fact what NikeFuel (2012), a recent development of the (2006) series of sport applications developed by Nike, states in its advertisement:

> Our minds, our bodies and our experience all tell us that movement is life and that the more we move the more we live. It's something athletes have understood from the beginning. The kind of movement it takes to improve your game is the kind of movement it takes to improve your life. But unlike sport, life doesn't come with convenient ways of measuring movement. So we developed one. NikeFuel: a single universal unit uniquely designed to measure the movement of the entire human body for the entire human race, whatever your weight, whatever your gender, whatever your activity. It's that simple and that revolutionary. So get out there, find what fuels you and get moving. (Nike Inc., 2013)

NikeFuel is a service based on a wearable technology that counts, via an accelerometer, how much the body moves during its daily activities. In so doing it provides a number, which is supposed to quantify movement – and life, which is allegedly the same thing. Again, what can be seen here is an attempt to engage sport practitioners, and potentially beginners, through a service that quantifies what would be otherwise difficult or problematic to quantify.

In this paper I will suggest that this specific idea of engagement, as it is presented in the books on gamification and its applications, has in fact a problem with the notion of life. Participation and involvement of the players should have an impact, in the theories of gamification, on their daily lives. However the ways in which this impact is performed brings about a rather limiting concept of life, one that remains static rather than being *in movement*.

What sort of notion of life and movement is performed by gamification apps? Nike+, for instance, connects to a mobile device and records, via GPS, and an accelerometer the path and pace of a runner. Nike+ is a system that is designed to receive and record already predicted signals; it rewards precise events, which are already expected by the simulation. It works as a system for recording and reviewing runners' performances, and compares them with each other, on a local or global scale. The runner/player of Nike+ is brought to comply with a frame of rules, which works as a regulatory frame, where only specific events are expected, saved, calculated, and evaluated. Through this practice of compliance, the runner/player of Nike+ is normalised, and regulates him or herself in order to maintain and progress in a process of constant self-normalisation. As Foucault notes (1977), disciplinary practices tend to optimise the body and stimulate its submissiveness. A mobile application such as Nike+ produces docile bodies while disciplining their sport activity and punishing their eventual failure. Failure here comes to be defined not only as failure to improve the body's performance, but more subtly as failure to produce the expected data, to update the system as frequently as possible and to provide information about the body. Nike+ is not a game to play, but mostly to update.

There are many other examples of gamification apps that propose to motivate the player in sport and fitness practises. On a similar note, the game SuperBetter (2012), designed by Jane McGonigal, works in a similar fashion, while attempting to regulate physical and mental health. The goals to achieve (losing weight, running a marathon, connecting with friends and relatives and similar ones), and the tasks offered to reach such goals, prescribe a limited set of possibilities for improving one's life. Games such as Nike+ and SuperBetter tend to limit the possibilities of play, and can also be seen as conservative images of a way of living. Both games, or gaming platforms, offer a unique path to the achievement of well being, where what is defined as good for the body is catalogued and presented as necessarily positive.

It is from these considerations about the conservative visions of life that come to be performed by gamification apps that I propose to rethink our own possibilities for critical participation. I will suggest that reconsidering

49

life and movement can be crucial in rethinking engagement, gamification, and more generally the performativity of video games. I will do so through the work of anthropologist Tim Ingold, who has been closely inspired by Bergson's notions of intuition, creativity, and vitalism. Bergson's idea of life as movement, strikingly similar to Nike's slogan, will be presented in its radical difference to what Nike and the gamification gurus have been proposing so far. Before going through the theories of Ingold and Bergson, I will look at how different perspectives on what gamification supposedly is and does have been expressed in the academic field. I will conclude the final section by pointing out how a certain idea of the performativity of video games, of their agency and effects, could be seen as replicated in ways that are not too greatly dissimilar from what gamification gurus have been promoting.

CRITIQUES OF GAMIFICATION

As a response to the emergence of gamification, one of the reactions in the academic world interested in digital gaming has been to propose a more moderate understanding of this newly emerging phenomenon, possibly eliminating the marketing aspects involved. It is from this context that Sebastian Deterding and colleagues have proposed a relatively simple definition of gamification: "gamification is the use of game design elements in non-game contexts" (Deterding et al. 2011, 2). The above quote has been accepted in the academic discourse over the last couple of years as a good description of the term gamification.

As reported by Deterding and colleagues, gamification is not the only term used to label the practice of adopting game design techniques in a non-game experience:

> Parallel terms continue being used and new ones are still being introduced, such as "productivity games", "surveillance entertainment", "funware", "playful design", "behavioral games", "game layer" or "applied gaming". Yet "gamification" has arguably managed to institutionalize itself as the common household term. (Ibid., 1)

The paper by Deterding and colleagues helps to define gamification beyond the enthusiastic talk that usually transpires in the uses of the term since Jane McGonigal made it popular through a series of TED talks and her book

Reality is Broken: Why Games Make Us Better and How They Can Change the World (2011). However, gamification has received a relatively large number of more or less consistent definitions and studies of the origin of the term and its political implications (Nelson 2012; Fuchs 2012; Jacobs 2012; Mosca 2012). This is partly due to the concept's background. Gamification is in fact mostly a marketing concept, developed and promoted by designers and business consultants. In this context a clear and simple definition soon became a necessity in order to sell gamification to existing businesses (and sometimes also to public institutions). It is for this reason, probably, that most texts on gamification take the form of guidelines and instructions on *how to gamify* a certain experience. The term has been further defined in the academic context as well, simply replicating the how-to approach of many publications (e.g. "Gamification" module at Pennsylvania University, held by prof. Kevin Werbach, also seen in Werbach and Hunter 2012) or, occasionally, articulating what else could be involved in the phenomenon ("Rethinking Gamification" workshop at Centre for Digital Cultures, Leuphana University, May 2013).

Deterding and colleagues attempt to define gamification, but say little of what gamification does and what it could do, which I believe are much more relevant questions. These are in fact questions more directly challenging the discourse on the potential effects of digital games, which is what the promoters of gamification insist on. The attempts to further elaborate what could be at stake with gamification are not many, and the present paper aims precisely at addressing this point. New definitions of gamification, in fact, would not yet tell us why we should be interested in it, and what we could make of it.

Ian Bogost has attempted to address a more nuanced question about gamification, firstly by saying that, from what we have seen so far, the technique should be renamed "exploitationware" (2011a) – or elsewhere, and more explicitly, "bullshit" (2011b) – and secondly by exploring the potential uses of video games in his text *How to do Things with Videogames* (2011c). His first argument can be summarised as follows. Gamification has little to do with the design of games, as it tends to reduce them to a predictable series of mechanisms to attract players / customers. Such mechanisms include the use of leaderboards, rankings, and badges to award the best players, as well as quick and unchallenging tasks to encourage players and make them feel gratified. However, Bogost argues game design (or at least "good" game design) has been trying to complicate such techniques by introducing more varied tasks, demanding a variety of skills from the players and possibly questioning the experience of playing through complex narratives. Gamification does not attempt to achieve any of these goals, as it is uniquely interested in maximising the activity of the users, and potentially turning them into "better" customers, or unpaid contributors to their business. Therefore, according to Bogost, it should not be embellished by the word "game", and should be more correctly called "exploitationware".

Bogost also adds that "serious games" is instead a much fairer nomenclature than gamification. Bogost has supported on several occasions those games that show a political or activist agenda (for instance, in his work on "persuasive" games, 2007). Serious games, in fact, combine two apparently contradictory words to describe a challenge to the design of games through which players are supposed to question their own knowledge and beliefs. The serious aspect serves to distinguish these emerging kinds of video games from more facetious forms of entertainment (Bogost 2011a, 2011b). Bogost expands his view on serious games in the text *How to do Things with Videogames* (2011c). Here the reference to Austin's *How to do Things with Words* (1962) is explicit, and so is the attempt to introduce a debate on the potential of video games from a perspective that is possibly more nuanced than the one seen in the context of gamification. This means, according to Bogost, that a better understanding of the potential of digital games entails an expansion of the number of things attainable from them: not only to be used as entertainment tools, or as part of marketing campaigns and self-help applications, as proposed in gamification, but also as objects with an artistic value, or as elements of social and political campaigns, and much more.

In *How to do Things with Videogames*, Bogost lists and analyses some of the possible uses for digital games that have recently emerged, including games with political content, promotional games displaying in-game advertisements, games used for propaganda or activism and those with artistic purposes. He also discusses, through several short chapters, how games could provoke "empathy", "reverence", "relaxation", "disinterest" and "drill", among many other effects. Bogost argues that we can understand the relevance of a medium by looking at the variety of things it does: "we can think of a medium's explored uses as a spectrum, a possibility space that extends from purely artistic uses at one end [. . .] to purely instrumental uses at the other [. . .]" (2011c, 3).

Bogost's answer to the debates on the potential of the medium of the video game is to avoid binaries and oppositions between serious and superficial technologies. He proposes instead what he calls an ecological understanding of the medium, inspired by McLuhan and Postman's theory of media. In this view, according to Bogost, media affect the environment where they are introduced at a variety of levels, not necessarily to be evaluated in positive or negative terms. Bogost's response to gamification, and more broadly to the idea that video games can be used for achieving specific effects, contests the institutionalisation and appropriation from the side of the marketing context of the alleged transformations of the medium currently happening through the emergence of gamification. However, it does not yet tell us how the binaries he evokes could be further complicated and possibly surpassed, and therefore does not propose a way of thinking about video games that could be seen as radically different from what McGonigal, Zichermann and colleagues evangelise about.

The question of what we can do with video games receives a more varied response from Bogost, when compared with any of the gamification gurus. However, what persists is the idea that the medium of the video game has a certain impact on its users – an impact which could be more or less predicted and channelled through design.

While this and similar approaches to the study and design of video games can work well for specific purposes,[1] I would like to propose different questions, and not just for the sake of proposing something different, or because different is "good for its own sake". I think instead that a process of rethinking gamification, while maybe not urgently needed in the marketing sector, is quite indispensible for the debates about the medium of the video game, where the performativity of games (and the theories about them) has yet to be investigated properly.

---

1   See for example how the theories by Ian Bogost have been discussed in the debates on what is known as procedurality; seen as a method for both the critic and the design of video games that want to "communicate messages to players" through "rhetorical strategies" and arguments, each allegedly deriving from a specific component of a video game (Treanor et al., 2011).

In the following section, I will consider the question of gamification as proposed by both its gurus and detractors, and as rephrased by Bogost, with reference to Austin: as "how to do things with video games?" I will discuss how the anthropological perspective proposed by Tim Ingold (2010, 2011) can suggest how to rethink gamification, and not necessarily against the current proposals originating from the non-academic contexts. The reason why Ingold's perspectives could prove useful in this context is that they directly address how objects and things (the distinction soon to be debated) come to be constituted, and with what implications. I will argue, via Ingold, that the discourses on gamification tend to produce objects (gamified apps) allegedly composed of identifiable parts that can each potentially affect players. The theories against gamification contribute to this process of objectification by expanding it to the entire medium of the video game. I will now discuss how we could think differently about gamification in particular and video games in general.

GAMIFICATION AND THE LIFE OF THINGS

I will be addressing this issue through the contribution provided by Tim Ingold, whose work, although not explicitly related to games or video games, questions the concept of performativity from an anthropological perspective. In the discourses about gamification the focus is on the agency of games: games can "do something" to their players, they have a certain power to affect players in a more or less predictable way. As Ingold would put it, agency is a term often brought into a debate in order to resuscitate the concept of materiality. In this view, objects have a certain material presence that does something to us; they have a certain agency with regard to the surrounding environment. However, Ingold suggests, while thinking in this way we tend to be suffocated by "the dead hand of materiality" (Ingold 2011, 28). Ingold here means that agency and materiality are not only forms of abstraction that overshadow the nuanced relations between human beings and the surrounding environment, but, as concepts, they also actively produce this distinction. The distinction remains even when agency and materiality are nuanced and complicated and this is why they (metaphorically!) strangle our thinking. Through Ingold, I will question how this distinction is also replicated in the discourses on gamification, and I will attempt to articulate a different reading of gamification by re-imagining the relation between human beings (players or game scholars) and video games.

In Ingold's perspective a crucial role is played by the distinction between objects and things, which he draws on Martin Heidegger's essay "The Thing" (1971). The distinction is useful in the context of my work because it helps to move from understanding *engagement* as the result of a cause-and-effect relation (one in which video games do something to us or us to them). While drawing on Heidegger's essay he comments:

> The object stands before us as a fait accompli, presenting its congealed, outer surfaces to our inspection. It is defined by its very "overagainstness" in relation to the setting in which it is placed (Heidegger 1971, 167). The thing, by contrast, is a "going on", or better, a place where several goings on become entwined. To observe a thing is not to be locked out but to be invited in to the gathering. (Ingold 2010, 4)

Ingold follows from this that things are constantly in contact with each other through their surfaces. This contact is what makes it possible for "things" to "gather" and participate in each other's presence. Imagining the environment to be populated by objects suggests the image of an excavated world, similar to a piece of Swiss cheese (Ingold 2011, 24). Objects are seen here to be separated and abstracted from the environment. In this view, objects need to be "resuscitated" by what is commonly called "agency". Instead, Ingold argues, things fill the environment and are entangled with one another, in "a meshwork of interwoven lines of growth and movement" (Ingold 2010, 4). Things are alive, as much as we are. The perspective offered by Ingold is more than an attempt to avoid a sort of horror *vacui* of an environment where objects are "cut" and surrounded by an empty space. There is still, for Ingold, the need to make sense of our own participations, as "things" ourselves, participating in the world. He sums up his point saying, "[i]n effect, to render the life of things as the agency of objects is to effect a double reduction, of things to objects and of life to agency" (ibid., 7).

It is not my purpose to consider what Ingold names a "double reduction" to be necessarily negative, strangling, or a "dead hand". It can in fact be said to be working fine in those contexts where engagement is intended as an effect, something that video games can do to their players. However, I

find Ingold's theory interesting for the ways in which it thinks about participation as "living" with and "within", as a sort of co-existence, which I see as
radically different from thinking in terms of engagement as "doing something to someone". Through Ingold, we no longer pose the question of what
video games (and gamified apps) can do to us, but of what it means to participate and live in a world populated by video games.[2]

Life is here a crucial concept for Ingold, and he explicitly mentions
Bergson and his *Creative Evolution* as one of the major influences for his
work (ibid., 13). From Bergson, Ingold develops the notion of life as movement and duration. Bergson argues that we, as humans, tend to capture the
things around us intellectually, interrupting the flow of life to freeze, control, and transform things into forms. However, this process loses sight of
movement. The intellectual faculty of our mind is accompanied by the intuitive faculty, which we rarely exercise but which persists and occasionally
comes through. Intuition, for Bergson, originates from the "vital impulse"
shared by all living species. While intelligence is analytical, in that it divides
and recomposes things in order to give us the knowledge we need to satisfy
our needs, intuition instead gives us the knowledge of how things are in
constant movement and always in the process of becoming other (Bergson
1914/1907).

Creativity is that which accounts for the continuity of life, the movement of things, and at the same time for the discontinuity of such things, the

---

2   Which is not the same question that Bogost proposes in *Alien Phenomenology, Or, What
    It's like to Be a Thing* (2012). Bogost proposes an analysis of how objects, or things, expe-
    rience the world surrounding them. In his attempt to reflect on what experience could
    be like outside of an anthropocentric view, and how this could lead to different morals
    and ethics, Bogost does not eliminate the essential alien quality of the objects/things he
    uses as examples. To interrogate ourselves on the "ethics of the spark plug, the piston, the
    fuel injector, or the gasoline" (Bogost 2012, 75) when looking at the engine of a car, can
    indeed be a different question from seeing how a car engine is entangled with human ac-
    tivities. However, it is not yet telling us much about how the plug, piston, injector and gas-
    oline "happen to us", how come they have been divided as such, as separate and abstracted
    objects, and how such process of "cutting" the environment makes sense to us, what is at
    stake in it, and how it could be otherwise: In other words, we do not yet know from such an
    analysis of "aliens" how we are participating in the analysis itself, how we are in contact –
    physically, intellectually, or intuitively – with the engine of a car, or any other system.

diversity of matter that we tend to intellectually fixate in time and space. Our task, for Bergson, is to reconnect with the intuitive faculty and participate in the life of things, in order to reach absolute knowledge. What does it mean, then, for us, to creatively participate in such a "flow of life"? It means, first of all, that the very idea of the agency of objects of any sort (words, technologies, human beings, etc.) has to be rethought as being less a transitive action (doing something to someone else) and more a dynamic state of being, a property that allows things "to be alive" in the world.

BRINGING LIFE INTO GAMIFICATION (AND GAME STUDIES)

But what does it mean *to be alive*? More importantly, how can this be helpful for a study of gamification, or the study of video games more generally? In this section I will further articulate these questions through the work of Tim Ingold, Patrick Crogan and Henry Bergson. First I will discuss how Ingold sees the "world" or environment as composed of "materials", and how this aspect recuperates a narrative side of theory as that which makes sense (and in fact constitutes) the properties of the things around us. With Crogan I will connect this way of looking at our engagement and presence in the world with a study of video games (and of what we can do with them). I will then investigate, through Bergson (in fact, a main reference in Ingold's work), how this ultimately brings to the notions of movement and freedom as necessarily connected to the ways in which we engage with the world.

What I have addressed thus far as a problem of rethinking our engagement with games is formulated by Ingold in different terms, as a problem of understanding life. The meanings of being alive, and ways of bringing things to life, are the main concerns of Ingold's anthropological endeavour. He argues that the question of "life" is inherently connected to the physical presence of things in the environment, and that this question is hindered by the theories of materiality. Ingold argues that materiality is a concept derived from a sort of "academic perversion" (2011, 20). Ingold draws on Gibson's theory of perception to suggest that it is in the problem of the boundary that materiality demonstrates its inconsistency. If we consider objects to be in contact, physically, with the external environment, to be immersed in different "materials", then the boundary appears to be artificial. However, the problem, for Ingold, is not really in the artificiality of the boundary, but rather in what it offers in the understanding of our presence in the world, and what it eliminates: "[M]aterials do not present themselves as tokens of some common essence – materiality – that endows every worldly entity with its inherent 'objectness' rather they partake in the very processes of the world's ongoing generation and regeneration [. . .]" (ibid., 26).

Shifting the focus to materials, rather than materiality, is what allows Ingold to re-evaluate the human presence in the environment, an aspect he finds to be articulated, in the theories of agency, in a distinction human versus matter. He takes the example of a stone, which can become wet by being dropped in water. After a certain amount of time, water will evaporate and the stone will be dry. The appearance of the stone has indeed changed, and so have its properties. The wet stone will feel and sound different from the dry one. What can we say then of the "materiality" of the stone? Has the dry stone more "stoniness" than the wet stone? Ingold argues:

> There is no way in which its stoniness can be understood apart from the ways it is caught up in the interchanges across its surface, between medium and substance [. . . T]he stone has actually changed as it dried out. Stoniness, then, is not the stone's "nature", in its materiality, nor is it merely in the mind of the observer or practitioner. Rather, it merges through the stone's involvement in its total surroundings – including you, the observer – and from the manifold ways in which it is engaged in the currents of the lifeworld. (Ingold 2011, 32)

If the observer is also considered to be part of that same "lifeworld" of the things around him or her, then the distinction in quality and hierarchy between subject and object comes into dispute. Ingold ultimately proposes a different narrative of engagement, one that does not have much to share with the narrative that has been emerging in contemporary video game culture thus far, but that could tell us something about how we engage, also, with digital games. What he offers is indeed a different way of thinking about our own immersion in the world, as thinkers, doers, scholars, producers, and consumers. These practices, however, are thought less as transitive actions and more as what results from a co-presence of live materials.

The crucial aspect in Ingold's theory that I would like to bring into the debate on gamification is that what ultimately comes to re-evaluation is the narrative aspect of theory. Rather than looking for the essential properties of objects and their supposed effects, Ingold encourages the creation of narratives of those same properties in which different forms of participation are presented. However, those same narratives are immediately revealed as necessarily strategic and partial. They in fact actively constitute, each time they are per-

What if we consider gamified systems to be part of that same world that it is claimed they are affecting?

formed, the properties of which they talk about, by cutting a series of lines (as Ingold, 2007, puts it) to form new things. In this way Ingold recuperates the performative potential of theory, as that which is capable of bringing things to life through a narrative of our participation with them.

How can this perspective prove useful when rethinking gamification, and how can it contribute to the study of digital games in general? Drawing on Ingold's approach to theory can prove useful when trying to counter the conservative side of gamified applications, as discussed earlier. In fact, Ingold does not simply propose a way of looking at things, but also to narratively rethink those same things and bring about new ones, possibly more interesting and, if needed, less conservative. Gamified systems, of which Nike+ and SuperBetter are examples, can in fact be seen as conservative tools, where unexpected and original ways of thinking about a specific practice are ruled out. But also, possibly, they are inevitably so. The struggle to eliminate uncertainty appears in the very origin of cybernetics and digital simulations. This is what Patrick Crogan argues in his text *Gameplay Mode: War, Simulation and Technoculture* (2011) through an analysis of the historical and ideological relations between the video game industry and military developments.

Crogan's text can be seen as creating a link (although not intended by the author) between the Ingold's theory and the field of game studies. Crogan in fact, while trying to reconsider the foundations of the approaches to the study of video games, similarly concludes in favour of a re-evaluation of the performative aspect of theory and its capacity to bring about specific realities. Crogan points out that the study of video games has tended towards an uncritical acceptance of the ideology of cybernetics (Crogan 2011, 145). In Espen Aarseth's (1997) original proposal for a study of "cybertexts" this meant the dismissal of a semiotic approach in the study of computer games in favour of a study of the interpretation of "cybernetic signs", arbitrarily determined by the relation between a coded, invisible level and an expressive, visible level (ibid., 24–41). From Aarseth's approach, computer programming determines not only the ways in which cybertexts, including computer games, are structured but also their interpretation: "[T]he concept of cybertext focuses on the mechanical organization of the text, by positing the intricacies of the medium as an integral part of the literary exchange" (ibid., 1). However, Crogan argues that the "intricacies of the medium", as Aarseth puts it, derive from a specific ideology. It is the same ideology that has been framing military research and the study of simulations, as systems for the pre-emption of possible future events. His proposal is to counter, from an academic and artistic perspective, what he describes as:

> [The] overarching tendency of the program industries to standardize and predetermine the nature of access and utilization of their products. Nevertheless one can play, and design and co-create [. . .] or becoming the bugs, artifacts, mods, critical and creative readings and appropriation, and other accidental becomings that alter what we can do with games, what games do with us, and what they give us to think about what we are doing with them now and tomorrow. (Crogan 2011, 174–175)

Similarly to Ingold, Crogan also proposes to bring the focus on our possibilities for reading creatively. Crogan's contribution to the recurring question of how to do things with games, and of what they do to us, which I have argued is also the basis of the discourses surrounding gamification, is useful and relevant for a variety of reasons. First, Crogan highlights how the logic of the "war on contingency" subsumed by the military-industrial complex is not only important in the development of forms of digital entertainment, but is also present in the ways we (gamers and scholars) tend to make sense of these entertainment forms. Second, he proposes that one possible way of thinking outside of such *weltanschauung* is to rethink the physical presence of the players and the materiality of games and game technologies. The problem of materiality and of our physical and intuitive participation is seen by Crogan in the light of an historical and ideological background that shapes both the medium of the video game and the theory about it.

I would like to expand on these suggestions and connect Crogan's analysis of the medium of the video game with Ingold's proposal for an anthropological rethinking of the concepts of performativity, materiality, and agency. I believe that these two perspectives, distant from each other with regard to the objectives they aim to achieve, can in fact contribute by saying something different about gamification.

I think that what calls for some alternative modes of thinking is the rather unproductive dead-end into which gamification and its critique have confined themselves. Drawing on the introduction to this paper, the statement "movement is life", presented by Nike in the advertisement of Nike-Fuel, is interpreted by the sport company as if being alive could somehow be a problem: "[L]ife doesn't come with convenient ways of measuring movement", says the advertisement (Nike Inc., 2013). Nike's response to this problem is that each singular activity of the body should come to be quantified and counted by the application. In doing so NikeFuel disregards movement as a process of knowledge, as wayfaring (in Ingold's terms), and applies instead a notion of movement as homogenous, and divisible into homogenous unities. In this sense, movement is spatialised here, as the notion of scientific time introduced by Bergson in his *Time and Free Will: an Essay on the Immediate Data of Consciousness* (2001 / 1889). Bergson proposed that to account for duration we cannot limit ourselves to the scientific time but also allow an intuitive understanding of time and space. Scientific time, the kind of time we measure and quantify, is expressed through numbers. As such, it is based on the idea of a homogenous space as it implies the presence of a unit of measure, which is juxtaposed to the next unit, as if temporal units were linearly disposed. Spatialised time also brings the notions of determinism and causation, as individual moments are seen as one being the effect of the other, following one another in a cause-effect relation.

The production of a "single universal way to measure all kinds of activities [. . . to track] your active life" (Nike, Inc., 2013) is another way of regulating movement, and in fact also performatively produce, in a Foucaltian sense, a notion of life as measurable and traceable through data. By tracing, measuring and quantifying, NikeFuel, and gamification in general, freeze movement and life through the separation and invention of fixities, through what Bergson would define as an intellectual approach, and replicating the notion of time that Bergson identifies as belonging to ancient Greek philosophy (and Zeno's conception of time and space in particular). Bergson's contribution is highly relevant in the context of this paper because it is ultimately concerned with the possibility of freedom within such a notion of time.

By introducing a question about life, rather than engagement, in the discourses about the things that we can do with games (and gamification) I have tried precisely to propose that we have freedom, that is, a multitude of possibilities of movement (not only physical but intuitive and creative). In the final part of this paper, I will attempt to map some possible ways for such forms of intervention which exemplify how a different way of "doing things with games" might take form. In these examples, taken mostly from the art context, our engagement with video games is understood through a different configuration, which inquires – rather than merely replicating – the dualities and separations that tend to frame the processes of understanding of digital games. These proposals investigate the materials which video games are made of, and the significance of dwelling and playing in a world of materials. Yet, they also propose temporary fixities, cuts in an ongoing process of mediating our presence in such a world.[3]

GAZIRA BABELI AND GAME ARTHRITIS: GAME STUDIES BY DIFFERENT MEANS

The works I would like to introduce are by the artist Gazira Babeli (an avatar in the game Second Life) and a piece by Matteo Bittanti and the collective IOCOSE. In these investigations, conceived and presented mostly within the context of art galleries and festivals, I believe a suggestion can be found as to what else game studies could be, and on what is at stake in finding an alternative.

The work by Babeli that I would like to introduce is a piece she made in 2006, entitled *Come to Heaven*. I will propose to look at this performance as a potentially different perspective on the relationship between digital games

---

3   The perspective I propose while looking at these two examples is strongly inspired by Sarah Kember and Joanna Zylinska's work *Life After new Media: Mediation as Vital Process* (2012). I do not articulate this reference much further in this context, for the sake of brevity, but I encourage exploring their approach. Kember and Zylinska look at possible ways for "doing things" with media, as a form of invention and scholarly critique. The theoretical foundation for their intervention is also strongly inspired by Bergson's vitalism, although much more fully developed in their text than in this paper.

and the materials they are made of, the ways in which games are played and how they can be understood to reach unexpected results. I suggest that thinking about video games in the terms proposed by Babeli entails, possibly, looking less at the performativity of games and more at games as "performers". In the example I will now introduce I believe this happens in quite an interesting way. I propose that this artistic investigation explores the materials of which video games are made, and our co-existence with these materials, in a way, which is radically alternative (although not intentionally, considering its date of publication) to the ways in which the question of performativity is currently debated with regard to gamification.

Babeli was a code performer, and avatar in Second Life (2003) – her artistic career was intentionally stopped a few years ago, so it is appropriate to talk about her in the past tense, as a dead artist. Her work investigated the possibility of performing in a digital online environment such as Second Life. In *Come to Heaven* (2006), one of the pieces I find to be most relevant to her career, Babeli lets her avatar (her "body" in the digital simulation) fall from a very high point in the sky of Second Life. While falling, the 3D model of the avatar tends to lose its integrity, and generates a series of unpredictable glitches.[4]

Babeli's work centres on one essential property of digital simulations. That is, digital simulations, by participating in the "war on contingency" (as proposed by Crogan), will replicate the same script with the same identical results, regardless of the spatial and temporal context where the script is performed. Babeli's intervention consists in allowing her avatar to automatically repeat the same script, which forces the avatar to fly up to the highest point in the digital simulation and then freefall down to the ground. She repeated the same script on different computers, with different hardware and at different times of day (i.e. with different Internet connection speeds and traffic).

The outcome of her work is a series of still images of the falls. The performance stresses the graphic engine of the game and the graphic capabilities of each of the computers on which the same code is performed (or, rather, "performs"). Babeli highlights the unpredictability of the engine

---

4   Documentation of Babeli's *Come to Heaven* is available online at: http://www.gazirababeli.com/cometoheaven.php (accessed May 6, 2014).

itself, which mixes the textures of the 3D model in different ways each time it is run. At stake here is not only a way of playing with the logic of the script. Babeli, more interestingly, questions the iterability of the code, which makes it reliable and worthwhile, through the material from which the computers are made.

Babeli's crucial move is that she does not play the video game Second Life, but rather sets it up to perform itself. She is not producing, or consuming the game. Babeli's intervention is not, simply, a form of re-appropriation of the game product, or a form of "active consumerism". Indeed, she had to program the script beforehand, take the screenshots and so on, but the interesting part of the work is when the hardware performs such a script, when the game plays itself and makes itself visible for the materials from which it is made. It becomes crucial, in Babeli's concept, to document and report not only the screenshots of the performance but also the precise hardware that has been performing in each instance. Graphic cards, CPUs, and RAMs are the performers, communicating with the Second Life servers in California, and unpredictably generating graphic deformations while overheating and "crashing". As Babeli comments, "[. . .] millions of meters away, at a very high speed. The effect obtained on the graphic card of the computer is hard to anticipate and it depends on the creativity process of the card itself. Yes, cards go bananas [. . .]" (Gazira Babeli 2006).

Letting cards go bananas is, potentially, one of the many ways to investigate how the narrative of pre-emption (as Crogan would put it), which underlies the computer script, can be narrated otherwise. Babeli's work does not offer an answer, neither it does crystallise into a technique for "doing things with games". It rather offers a temporary perspective on what else scripts, and video games, are, what they are made of, and how our ideas about them can be challenged by inquiring into such material presence. Babeli offers what Crogan, through Samuel Weber, has defined as a "theatrical" gesture (Crogan 2011, 141), which questions our participation in the video game Second Life, looks at what this participation is made of and how does it happen rather than, too simply, framing the answer on a cause-effect or producer-consumer binary.

Another example that similarly inquires about the ways in which we live and co-exist with video games is *Game Arthritis*. Game Arthritis is an art project presented at the Venice Biennale in 2011 by Matteo Bittanti, adjunct professor at the California College of the Arts, and the collective IOCOSE, of which I have myself been a member since its inception in 2006. *Game Arthritis* (2011) is a photographic documentation of a "systemic study of video game induced diseases".[5] It investigates the topic of the alleged effects of video games, particularly from the angle of medical and scientific discourse. Moreover, it questions the ways in which we tend to narrate what video games do to us, and us to them. The project is inspired by, and directly refers to, a series of publications that, until the early 2000s, claimed that video games would affect an entire generation of teenagers by altering their bodies due to prolonged use of video game interfaces. From a Foucaultian perspective, game arthritis and the other differently named disorders (the "3D Optical Disorder", "Playstation Thumb", "Wii Shoulder Dislocation" and so on) could be seen to have been brought about by authoritarian statements, such as articles in medical journals on the evidence of their emergence, and reinforced by mainstream newspapers and video game magazines. However, game arthritis and other disabilities are also symptomatic of a deterministic narrative, which permeates both the scientific and mainstream discourse. According to this view, video games can harm people – a narrative not necessarily dissimilar, in its logic, when reverted through a positive connotation (as in Jane McGonigal's "video games will save the world" slogan). *Game Arthritis*, the art project, displayed in 2011, what should have been the scientific evidence of the studies published in the early 2000s. No evidence has ever been found, despite the diseases being analysed in peer-reviewed scientific journals. The photographic "documentation" shocks the viewer with its disturbing images, which should appear familiar (as this is what we have been told video games can do to our bodies) and yet unfamiliar at the same time, as an actual image to prove the alleged effects of digital games has never been provided. Also, the images of *Game Arthritis* do not match the current trend of describing video games through positive and celebratory narratives as an art form, or as good for health and in preparing the professional class of the next generation (as enthusiastically argued, in the first

---

5 Documentation of the artwork by Bittanti and IOCOSE is available at http://gamearthritis. org (accessed May 6, 2014). More information and references are available on IOCOSE's website at http://www.iocose.org/works/game_arthritis (Accessed May 6, 2014).

consistent study, by Beck and Wade 2004). It proposes what appears to be a sort of conspiracy narrative, according to which the game industry has been hiding evidence that would have proved the concerns of the scientific community.

Game Arthritis summarises, through a series of images, a potential narrative of our physical relation with the hardware of the medium. At the same time, however, it disputes our tendency to abstract such a relation, allowing deterministic discourses to become institutionalised interpretations. It mocks the ways in which video games are transformed into "objects" with clear and identifiable effects. *Game Arthritis'* move is to ridicule such abstraction proposing occurrences, examples of players actually affected by their continuous contact with the materials of which video games are made. Yet, it is precisely by switching the focus from an abstract discourse to the contingent embodiments of which the various "game arthritides" are made that game arthritis, the disease that officially existed until about a decade ago, is revealed to be a rather uncanny and probably biased narrative.

Game Arthritis is not only a project about the properties of the materials from which video games are made; it is mostly about the narratives that we (both scholars and gamers) tend to formulate to make sense of our engagement with such materials. The focus is on the human, on the ways in which we participate in an environment populated by things, and how we tend to abstract them as objects and then resuscitate them by giving them agency, or a "sparkle of life", as Ingold puts it. In *Game Arthritis* the question is about (and the joke is on) us.

When we start thinking about the properties of the materials of video games as narratives, then we can also imagine stories, which are intentionally false. However, their falsity sheds light on what video games are for us and what else they could be. In conclusion, I believe that an approach similar to the one proposed by these two examples could also be adopted more extensively in the study of games, rather than being exclusively undertaken in the artistic context. It would mean focusing less on the alleged effects of video games and the ways in which we can channel those effects through design, instead concentrating more on what sort of "things" we could bring about by living with and through video games. Following Bergson's notion of creativity as that which reconnects to the intuitive faculty of the mind and participate in the life of things, I propose to name this potential detour in the study of the medium of the video game as "creative game studies" – a proposal that needs, however, to be articulated more extensively in a separate context.

BIBLIOGRAPHY

AARSETH, ESPEN. 1997. *Cybertext: Perspectives on Ergodic Literature.* Baltimore: Johns Hopkins University Press.

AUSTIN, JOHN LANGSHAW. 1962. *How to Do Things with Words.* Cambridge, MA: Harvard University Press.

BECK, JOHN C. AND MITCHELL WADE. 2004. *Got Game: How the Gamer Generation Is Reshaping Business Forever.* Boston: Harvard Business School Press.

BERGSON, HENRY. 2001/1889. *Time and Free Will: An Essay on the Immediate Data of Consciousness.* Mineola: Dover Publications.

BERGSON, HENRY. 1914/1907. *Creative Evolution.* London: MacMillan.

BOGOST, IAN. 2012. *Alien Phenomenology, Or, What It's Like to Be a Thing.* Minneapolis: University of Minnesota Press.

BOGOST, IAN. 2011a. "Persuasive Games: Exploitationware." *Gamasutra,* May 3. http://www.gamasutra.com/view/feature/6366/persuasive_games_exploitationware.php.

BOGOST, IAN. 2011b. "Gamification Is Bullshit! My Position Statement at the Wharton Gamification Symposium." *Ian Bogost Blog,* August 8. http://www.bogost.com/blog/gamification_is_bullshit.shtml.

BOGOST, IAN. 2011c. *How to do Things with Videogames.* Minneapolis: University of Minnesota Press.

BOGOST, IAN. 2007. *Persuasive Games: The Expressive Power of Videogames.* Boston: MIT Press.

CROGAN, PATRICK. 2011. *Gameplay Mode: War, Simulation and Technoculture.* Minneapolis: University of Minnesota Press.

DETERDING, SEBASTIAN, DAN DIXON, RILLA KHALED AND LENHART NACKE. 2011. "From Game Design Elements to Gamefulness: Defining 'Gamification'." In *Proceedings of the 15th International Academic MindTrek Conference: Envisioning Future Media Environments (MindTrek '11),* 9–15. New York: ACM.

FOUCAULT, MICHEL. 1977. *Discipline and Punish: The Birth of the Prison.* London: Pantheon Books.

FUCHS, MATHIAS. 2012. "Ludic Interfaces: Driver and Product of Gamification." *GAME Journal* 1(1).
 http://www.gamejournal.it/ludic-interfaces-driver-and-product-of-gamification/.
HEIDEGGER, MARTIN. 1971. *Poetry, Language, Thought*. New York: Harper and Row.
INGOLD, TIM. 2011. *Being Alive: Essays on Movement, Knowledge, Description*. London and New York: Routledge.
INGOLD, TIM. 2010. "Bringing Things to Life: Creative Entanglements in a World of Materials." Accessed April 7, 2014.
 http://www.socialsciences.manchester.ac.uk/morgancentre/realities/wps/15-2010-07-re-alities-bringing-things-to-life.pdf.
INGOLD, TIM. 2007. *Lines: A Brief History*. London and New York: Routledge.
JACOBS, MELINDA. 2012. "Click click click click: Zynga and the Gamification of Clicking." *GAME Journal* 1(1).
 http://www.gamejournal.it/click-click-click-click-zynga-and-the-gamification-of-click-ing/#.Uui-q3lZC2w.
KEMBER, SARAH AND JOANNA ZYLINSKA. 2012. *Life After New Media: Mediation as a Vital Process*. Cambridge, MA: MIT Press.
McGONIGAL, JANE. 2011. *Reality is Broken: Why Games Make Us Better and How They Can Change the World*. New York: Penguin Press.
MOSCA, IVAN. 2012. "+10! Gamification and deGamification." *GAME Journal* 1(1).
 http://www.gamejournal.it/plus10_gamification-and-degamification/#.Uui-6nlZC2w.
NELSON, MARK J. 2012. "Soviet and American Precursors to the Gamification of Work." In *Proceedings of the 16th International Academic MindTrek Conference*, 23–26. New York: ACM.
NIKE INC. 2013. "What Is Fuel." Accessed December 18.
 http://nikeplus.nike.com/plus/what_is_fuel/.
TREANOR, MIKE, BOBBY SCHWEIZER, IAN BOGOST AND MICHAEL MATEAS. 2011. "Proceduralist Readings: How to Find Meaning in Games with Graphical Logics." In *Proceedings of Foundations of Digital Games – FDG 2011*, 115–122. New York: ACM.
WERBACH, KEVIN AND DAN HUNTER. 2012. *For the Win: How Game Thinking Can Revolutionize Your Business*. Philadelphia: Wharton Digital Press.
ZICHERMANN, GABE AND CHRIS CUNNINGHAM. 2011. *Gamification by Design: Implementing Game Mechanics in Web and Mobile Apps*. New York: O'Reilly Media.

LUDOGRAPHY

NIKE+. 2006. Nike, Inc.
    https://secure-nikeplus.nike.com/plus/.
NIKEFUEL. 2012. Nike, Inc.
    https://secure-nikeplus.nike.com/plus/what_is_fuel/.
SECOND LIFE. 2003. Developed by Linden Lab. Windows, OS X. Linden Lab.
SUPERBETTER. 2012. Jane McGonigal.
    https://www.superbetter.com.

ARTWORKS

BABELI, GAZIRA. 2006. *Come to Heaven.* Video game performance.
    http://www.gazirababeli.com/cometoheaven.php.
BITTANTI, MATTEO AND IOCOSE. 2011. *Game Arthritis.* Photographs.
    http://gamearthritis.org.

HOW TO WIN FOURSQUARE:
BODY AND SPACE IN A GAMIFIED WORLD

by **Maxwell Foxman**

I desired to do something truly unprecedented for our housewarming. The festivities began Saturday morning at Artichoke Pizza. We called it "The Alphabetical Tour of Alphabet City". The goal was simple: in twenty-four hours, traverse twenty-six restaurants and bars throughout the lower Manhattan neighbourhood, in alphabetical order.

I rarely sat and only spoke briefly to the ever-increasing group of guests at each locale. Instead, I was preoccupied typing out the name of each venue we entered on my smartphone. I "checked-in" to each spot using the social media application Foursquare, which utilised GPS to verify my location and allowed me to compete with friends and strangers over how many places we frequented.

Each check-in, furthermore, was linked to other social media platforms, namely Facebook and Twitter, enabling other users online to meet up with us even as we progressed at our frantic pace. I relished each check-in as the software awarded me points.

The next day, we were joined by a few celebrants for brunch at our final destination, Zum Schneider. Recovering over German sausages in the beer hall, we three stalwarts who made it to every venue bragged and congratulated each other, in awe of our achievement. Through the bounty of the social media applications employed, our exuberant adventure and the spoils of our social competition had been recorded for all to envy. At some point, I recall thinking to myself not so much that the Alphabetical Tour was just a great party and a social success, but that I had won. I wasn't sure what I had won, but I certainly had the score to prove it.

1   GETTING INTO THE GAME

The Alphabetical Tour was not particularly unique in a city like New York where bars abound and crawls between them are commonplace. Atypical was the extravagant amount of time, money, calories and brain cells I expended for a bit of merriment, and the role the then year-old program Foursquare (2009) played in shaping our adventure. Its presence punctuated moments throughout the day and evening, and not only broadcasted where I was along the route, but also became a topic of conversation during the event itself.

Foursquare, in many ways, has become the corporate embodiment of gamification. Its use of location-based technology and mobile media makes Foursquare the perfect target for admonishments about the exploitation of users through game-like elements, the facility for surveillance and the promotion of conspicuous consumption. We realised such apprehensions during the tour. However, knowing full well its potential ramifications, why did I, like millions of others, use Foursquare? The sheer zealousness of the celebration highlights how I was willing to disregard concerns about manipulation for reasons that are at once difficult to define yet fundamentally important to that day. The desire for a glorious experience outweighed any rational judgments.

While much of the research surrounding the proliferation of gamification into non-playful settings and the design of Internet applications has centred on either the potential effects of game elements on the populace, or the growing cultural acceptance of games and play, the experience of gamification has been less explored. As the Alphabetical Tour illustrates, this phenomenon is subtle yet distinctive, involving new forms of communication, and exploits some of our most elemental urges: to compete, to win, to forge a path to glory.

This article will deal with the experience of gamification, specifically through the lens of Foursquare. After first situating the application within the larger discourse of gamification, it will become evident that, while Foursquare has never purported itself to be a game, it remains a quintessential example of a tool that capitalises on user behaviour through the employment of explicit and implicit game-like functions.

Superficially, Foursquare appears to reduce a user's environment to a series of icons and locations that flaunt capitalism and a culture of "cool" within primarily urban and suburban settings and constituencies. This perception also intensifies claims that Foursquare is merely a waste of time.

I will argue instead that Foursquare rescripts ordinary experience into one of expenditure and glory by allowing its users to bring an ethos of competition into their existence. Through Foursquare, life becomes a conduit for fierce play, communicated less through words than through presence, a kind of "proximal communication".

Because the application maintains a constant presence within everyday life, this form of communication becomes as much part of the bodily experience as an outwardly communicated act. Through a phenomenological approach, along with personal anecdotes to support it, I will show how Foursquare engenders what I call a "state of play" in which the motivating forces of play are not only felt in the virtual space of a "magic circle", but also punctuate and pervade mundane activities, ultimately characterizing the experience of gamification more generally.

2 GAMIFICATION AND ITS DISCONTENTS

Gamification might have been a rhetorical inevitability with the ascension of digital and video games in the beginning of the twenty-first century. Game Studies scholars, such as Jesper Juul and Eric Zimmerman, endeavoured to carve out a distinct field for the study of games, connecting them to the realm of play, or "ludology" (Frasca 1999), a term attributed to Johan Huizinga, who attempted to track the pervasiveness of play in society in *Homo Ludens: A Study of the Play-Element in Culture*. As a consequence, at its theoretical roots, Game Studies underscores play's potential universality and its broader application to cultural contexts.

The study of gamification has helped to disclose the discontinuities between perceptions of games and play and their impact on society. Advocates foresee games helping to mitigate adverse social conditions (McGonigal 2011; Zichermann and Cunningham 2011). For instance, current projects make weight loss (Block 2012) and the awareness of climate change (Fox 2013) a game. Others assail the insidious and unbridled enthusiasm to capitalise on "game elements" for corporate greed.

While the potential societal effects of play and gamification deserve much attention, the experience of the player and what motivates him to engage with gamified programs remains a less travelled frontier. If the invocation of gamification opened up a Pandora's box of predictions about a gameful world, it is worth asking what it is like to live in it.

3   WHY STUDY FOURSQUARE?

Founded in 2009 by Dennis Crowley and Naveen Selvadurai, Foursquare has developed along with the proliferation of gamification, becoming the quintessential example for academics interested in both gamification and mobile media (de Souza e Silva and Frith 2012; Deterding et al. 2011; Frith 2012; Frith 2013; Glas 2013; Whitson 2013). The premise of the application is simple: Users check in primarily with smartphones to various venues, ranging from their homes to bars, restaurants, stores, parks and other public settings. Venues are assigned both by the company and created by users. Users are rewarded for checking-in with points posted on a virtual "leaderboard" of friends. They may also achieve "mayorships" and badges on rarer occasions.

The foremost reason for using Foursquare as a case study is to examine the paradoxical relationship between the systems that make up the application and the experiences of the user. That the application fosters competition over leisure appears not only to be impractical in a utilitarian sense, but also blatantly exploitative due to the company's knowledge of users' locations. The by-product of Foursquare is a valuable commodity: a record of the whereabouts of users, including the timing and frequency of their every excursion, which has recently enabled Foursquare to offer businesses the ability to advertise to users when in close proximity to their establishments (Tate 2013). However, the experience of the user remains somewhat divorced from this capitalist ploy. Users willingly volunteer information, submitting to "Big Brother", while revelling within the constraints of the system. Public disclosure and control are produced from the bottom up.

Foursquare, like other gamified applications, lies provocatively on the border between being a game and social media. Games are defined by Katie Salen and Eric Zimmerman, in *Rules of Play: Game Design Fundamentals*, as "a system in which players engage in an artificial conflict, defined by rules, that results in a quantifiable outcome" (Salen and Zimmerman 2003, 83). Although their definition is meant to be functional, it emphasises the game-like quality of the application. Foursquare encourages competition through rewards while retaining the basic components of social networking sites, which "(1) construct a public or semi-public profile within a bounded system, (2) articulate a list of other users with whom they share a connection, and (3) view and traverse their list of connections and those made by others within the system" (boyd and Ellison 2007, 211).

Even as it sets the stage for friendly competition, the program is marketed as a singular tool to connect people throughout cities via location-based technologies, offering coupons and deals for those who frequent participating restaurants and bars. This somewhat prosaic goal neither explains Foursquare's appeal to at least 40 million users (Foursquare 2013), nor its growing ubiquity among retailers throughout cities in the United States. The essential functions of the program, the check-in and the subsequent rewards, provide a peephole into the application's appeal.

4   FUN-CTIONS OF FOURSQUARE

While comments, the uploading of photos and other social elements commensurate with social media like Facebook have been added since the end of 2010 (Van Grove 2010), the primary function of Foursquare has always been the check-in with corresponding rewards. This is the causation that drives the Foursquare experience. Upon close observation, the check-in function is tinged with both implicit and explicit means of feeling a sense of glory; the user competes and potentially wins by performing the act.

The check-in is not an inherently competitive act. In Foursquare, once recognised, the user is informed of his successful check-in and rewarded. The importance of the check-in is not only related to registering the user's presence at the venue, but also the value ascribed to the act of registering. Users only receive rewards, points and trophies when the GPS software on their phones traces them to the vicinity of the particular venue.

Since the majority of places where the user checks in are retail establishments and public venues (Bawa-Cavia 2010), Foursquare is frequently associated with consumption, underscoring its business/marketing model.

Check-in restrictions can be circumnavigated by users with few consequences. They can check in from a mobile internet browser version of the application, or emulate a GPS signal on a computer.[1] These practices invoke a kind of "cheating" that is somewhat unusual within the context of social interaction.[2] Rather than being innocuous, the check-in is actually a playful and competitive act, the standard by which rewards are given fairly or illicitly.

Foursquare's rewards adhere to Salen and Zimmerman's game definition, providing a quantifiable outcome for particular actions. Each prize is appropriated toward competitive ends, bestowing bragging rights and promoting a kind of glory. Jordan Frith describes users cultivating their activities around cities in order to obtain particular badges and mayorships (Frith 2013, 251), which are prominently displayed on the profile page of each user. Badges, which are given for specific sets of check-ins such as registering in the same place three times in one week, or checking-in to five different Mexican restaurants, define the achievements of a user and the breadth of his activity, or the type of player he is. Foursquare's reward system expanded in 2011 with the addition of levels to specific badges (Parr 2011). The repetitive completion of the same task now garners even more benefits.

A mayorship is granted to a user for frequenting and achieving an abundance of check-ins at a particular venue, more than any other user within a 60-day period. The glory that comes from a mayorship is highly localised. Particularly in cases where friends frequent the same venue, they become cognisant of each other's mayorships and can vie over them. Mayorships garner other tangible and intangible awards. Both mayors and friends of mayors receive extra points for their check-ins at establishments for which they are mayor, as well as occasional mayoral perks from venues. In the case of restaurants, often a free drink or appetizer is the mayor's reward for each check-in, a fair honorarium for a loyal patron who, at any time, is in danger of losing his position.

---

1   It should be noted that if a user checks in with the browser version of the application, they are able to receive points and badges, but not mayorships.

2   The most notorious case of cheating in Foursquare can be found in the case of Indonesian "Jumpers" who gained notoriety by checking-in to venues in the United States, en masse, from Indonesia (Glas 2013).

The most constant form of competition and reward is the leaderboard, which appoints a numerical score, seen only among friends, for the user's check-ins over the prior week. Users receive points for a variety of prescribed reasons, ranging from bonus points for checking in to new venues, to attaining a mayorship, to checking in over multiple days or weeks at a particular type of establishment. Other points are awarded completely arbitrarily, such as extra points for the inauguration of the Year of the Dragon on the lunar calendar, or on a user's anniversary of joining Foursquare. Accumulation of points does not lead to achieving any specific reward; points are only significant because the leaderboard is built into the overall structure of the program. Like the high scores in an arcade game, the leaderboard tally records and perpetuates the overall glory of the user. Furthermore, because the score reflects only the past week's activity, it constantly resets, establishing perpetual competition among users. Since the scores on the leaderboard are only shared among friends, the entire reason for its existence is localised glory and competition. The leaderboard seems to be Foursquare's most "game-like" feature with obvious allusions to scoreboards and video game scoring systems.

As can be seen from this brief synopsis of Foursquare, the possibility for competition and play is explicitly fostered, in the case of the leaderboard and mayorships, or potentially, in the case of badges and the check-in itself. More than anything, like other gamified systems, these rewards are meant to motivate users, to induce them to play. However, both the consequences and experiences of these functions for the user are lacking in this analysis.

5 CONCEPTIONS, CONSUMPTION AND CONTESTS

Foursquare activity appears to stem more from the act of checking-in than the rewards received. Publicizing a particular space at a particular time, especially in an urban setting, automatically carries socio-economic connotations. The software promotes a certain kind of conspicuous consumption, allowing users, as hackneyed as it may sound, to appear cool.

The desire to be seen at particular places is popular in urban settings, where knowing the trendiest spot is often competitive. Historically, the data about Foursquare showed that the primary locales checked-into were commercial establishments, such as restaurants, bars and art galleries

(Bawa-Cavia 2010).[3] This evinces a natural inclination that the average Foursquare user wants to be seen and "in-the-know" more generally. In a July 2010 Urbagram study, check-ins were concentrated in areas where restaurant culture and high retail consumption thrived, such as downtown areas of Manhattan, Williamsburg, and Park Slope. In other cities, such as London and Paris, this same study found similarly that "Nightlife" and "Food" venues were the primary places where users were checking in, with Paris also having slightly more frequent check-ins at both art galleries and parks (ibid.).

However, Carnegie Mellon's "Livehoods" project, started in 2012, both updated and complicated the findings of the Urbagram study (Livehoods 2013). The project visualised the activity of Foursquare users in different US and Canadian cities with fascinating results. In different neighborhoods, distinctly diverse activity occurred. For instance, while a number of groceries made up the most checked-in sites of New York's predominantly residential Upper West Side, Brooklyn's hipster enclave Williamsburg featured two bars in its most popular check-ins. In other words, the check-ins mirrored the particular demographics of each neighbourhood, rather than being homogenous throughout New York City (ibid.).

Livehoods contradicted the preconceived notions of conspicuous consumption associated with the check-in, describing different ends based on the users' locales. Users may choose to forego some check-ins in favour of being seen at others. For instance, I rarely see users check in at home. This is supported by Frith's determination that players predominantly check in "to score points, earn badges, present themselves to others, and remember where they have been" (Frith 2012, 189).

Foursquare's activity, consequently, is prompted by personal use, for personal reasons. Furthermore, this personal choice drives Foursquare's economic model. After all, Foursquare generates its revenue through advertising; its software is free. Foursquare's existence is sustained by the continued use of its players, whom it must stimulate in order to maintain an audience for advertisements and from which to collect information. Users must ex-

---

3   As of 2013, the most popular check-in spot within the United States was airports (Shankman 2013).

pend on behalf of the program. Such exertion has led PJ Rey to describe the activity as "playbor". The term, which he derived from Julian Kücklich's 2005 study of the modding of video games, means making "productive activity an end in-itself (namely, fun) . . . The object of production is no longer to create value; instead value becomes a mere by-product of play" (Rey 2012).

Certainly, the activity in Foursquare encompasses this definition. The play of the check-in belies the effort people expend on behalf of the program. Rey partially invokes playbor to dissolve the traditional notions of economy in capitalist systems, in which work and play are separate. Rather than simply a device to promote frivolous conspicuous consumption, within the context of playbor, Foursquare becomes an outlet for work, causing play to lose "its innocence" (ibid.). However, Rey acknowledges that the experience of play has its own value, including the symbolic capital of intangible rewards. What motivates "playborers" (ibid.) then does not derive from traditional capital models, but instead from intrinsic incentives that come from play itself, namely personal choice and competition. If not driven by capitalism, an ontological investigation of exchange within society may explain the motivation for such competition: glory.

6   COMPETITION AND GLORY

Becoming mayor in Foursquare can be associated with a certain amount of boasting. Mayorships allow users to compete over their favourite haunts. So strong was my desire to obtain mayorships, that I sought them from any number of places. I became mayor of my grandmother's condo, as well as the "gym" in my mother's basement (actually just a stationary bicycle). Many friends were similarly mayors of their local delicatessens, bagel shops and apartment buildings, rather than the hippest restaurant or nightclub. These trumped up mayorships still had value, with a friend complaining if another had pre-empted the mayorship of their apartment. In fact, when I was nearing the assumption of the mayorship at the completely fictitious "Arsenal HQ" (the Foursquare title given to the bar where Arsenal FC fans met to watch soccer games), the head of the supporters' group half-seriously threatened me if I overtook his mayorship. His sincerity was enough for me to abandon my quest for that position.

Playbor certainly characterises my pursuit for mayorships. Mayorships require persistent checking-in to venues, and as described in the above account, the additional labour of making up both factual and fictional places in which to check in. The reasons for the effort are related to competition.

Since competition is so prominent within Foursquare, its importance and nature warrant further exploration. This analysis will begin to position Foursquare within the realm of game play and to substantiate user participation. It explains, not only how people play Foursquare, be it as playbor or otherwise, but also why they put so much effort into the program.

Salen and Zimmerman refer to the importance of conflict as both "intrinsic" to the game and the means by which players achieve their goals within the confines of the game (Salen and Zimmerman 2003, 265). Johan Huizinga indicates in *Homo Ludens*, "[t]hus competitions and exhibitions as amusement do not proceed from culture, they rather precede it" (Huizinga 1971, 47). Huizinga sees the contest as a prescribed event, not dissimilar from play: "Like all other forms of play, the contest is largely devoid of purpose. That is to say, the action begins and ends in itself, and the outcome does not contribute to the necessary life-processes of the group" (Ibid., 49).

The desire for glory, to win at the contest, remains a part of the economy of play, motivating play, as well as proffering a result when play occurs. It is a means of rethinking the "value" of Foursquare. Users will check in to more places for renown as opposed to receiving some tangible economic boon. The users' check in is rewarded with glory, for bragging rights, the "exalted phenomena that we can never fully understand but can only experience" (Leibovitz 2013, 75).

The goal of the Foursquare user therefore diverges from capitalist economic purposes in the competition for glory. Expenditure, the dispensing of time and energy into the Foursquare experience, with no economic value in return, galvanises the Foursquare user and is implicit within Rey's playbor model. Participation in Foursquare, in regard to traditional economic models, is to some degree a bona fide waste of time. As in any game, its economy is dictated by the rules of and desire to play, rather than any rational capitalist motivation.

This expenditure echoes Georges Bataille's analysis in "The Notion of Expenditure" that:

> A certain excitation, whose sum total is maintained at a noticeably constant level animates collectivities and individuals. In their intensified

form, the states of excitation, which are comparable to toxic states, can be defined as the illogical and irresistible impulse to reject material or moral goods that it would have been possible to utilise rationally (in conformity with the balancing of accounts). (Bataille 1985, 128)

Excitement is then caused when the user expends. Interaction with the software, for the sake of glory and competition, exposes the user to more activities. The user does not react to the software as a promotional tool. Foursquare has created a mode of consumption that marries advertising and traditional marketing with anti-productive activity, namely competition and glory.

Bataille's expenditure also explains the reasons why users play, a kind of economy of competition, independent of capitalist models. As he puts it:

[T]he creation of unproductive values; the most absurd of these values, and the one that makes people the most rapacious, is *glory*. Made complete through degradation, glory, appearing in a sometimes sinister and sometimes brilliant form, has never ceased to dominate social existence; it is impossible to attempt to do anything without it when it is dependent on the blind practice of personal or social loss. (Ibid.)

Glory, according to Bataille, is inherently a part of human interaction and culture.

6.1 The Potlatch

Bataille, Huizinga and foundational anthropologist Marcel Mauss all mention glory in their dissection of the potlatch ceremony. The potlatch was one of the first tribal systems of exchange studied by anthropologists. While based partially on economics, the practice permeated all aspects of society including "initiations, marriages, [and] funerals" (Bataille 1985, 121).

The potlatch was a ceremony of competition and expenditure, with the goal of "humiliating, defying, and *obligating* a rival" (ibid.) through the giving of gifts and the sacrificing of wealth. The goal of the potlatch was to give away one's excesses with the expectation that some day a gift of greater value would be returned, and by receiving that gift, another of even greater value was obligated.

Bataille states that the potlatch "is linked to the possession of a fortune, but only on the condition that the fortune be partially sacrificed in unproductive social expenditures such as festivals, spectacles, and games" (ibid., 123). This sacrifice of excesses and expenditures relates to Foursquare in that users are ranked by how much they give in excess to the game. In this way, Foursquare mimics the potlatch gift culture when friends turn their daily activities into spectacles of expense.

The reasons for the potlatch were entwined in a society of self-perpetuated loss and destruction, endemic to the human condition, what Bataille believes to be the "reckless, discharge, and upheaval that constitutes life . . ." (ibid., 128). Glory came from the much more intrinsic need to humiliate, to win and ultimately expend excesses. Bataille further expounds that all forms of "order" and "reserve" in society are merely temporary states to facilitate glorious expenditure (ibid.).

Foursquare's software, by Bataille's estimations, serves a natural need: when seeking glory wherever he can, the user needs order and meaning to freely expend. Foursquare supplies an ordered pattern to everyday life, so that the user may find the means to compete and potentially feel the sense of liberty afforded by his expense. This begins to rationalise Bataille's "states of excitation" in the excessive "play" of Foursquare.

Competition can be incorporated into just about anything, and potlatch interaction enveloped numerous aspects of daily life. Bataille and Mauss state that the potlatch was woven into all forms of exchange. It was "reserved for forms which, for archaic societies, are not distinguishable from exchange" (ibid., 123). For Mauss, all of these systems of giving, of glory and sacrifice are integrated. They are part of what makes up these early anthropological societies (Mauss 2000/1950). For Bataille, expenditure extends to the entire biosphere, which he characterises in terms of "a play of energy that no particular end limits: the play of *living matter in general*, involved in the movement of light of which it is the result. On the surface of the globe, for *living matter in general*, energy is always in excess" (Bataille 1991/1949, 21).

Foursquare taps into something quite fundamental if it is indeed making use of excess and expenditure. The expenditure on behalf of Foursquare is not explicit, however – and the rewards bestowed are intangible. The competition between players acts as a kind of public sacrifice between users.

Mauss also broadens the scope of the potlatch to a wider gift culture, which he argues persisted in a subdued manner into nineteenth century Europe, long before the current interest in the "gamification" of everyday life. Citing an exchange among the Maori people, Mauss states that the gifts given are "a tie occurring through things, is one between souls, because the thing itself possesses a soul, is of the soul" (Mauss 2000/1950, 12). In relation to Foursquare, such an atmosphere pervades and capitalises on the structures of the program. The application's architecture allows the competition to expose users' lived experience, where they went and what they did, thereby making their expenditure on the game's behalf, at least rhetorically, of the soul. The everyday becomes the gift that the users sacrifice and exchange. The giving, rewarding and playing for the sake of Foursquare is based upon everyday existence. The result of these exchanges, in Mauss' perspective, was a frenzy of excitement.

Bataille, clearly acquainted with Mauss, refers to the state of excitement in his own models and Huizinga, also aware of such a state, pronounces "the potlatch spirit is akin to the thoughts and feelings of the adolescent" (Huizinga 1971, 60). In the same text, Huizinga considers the study of the potlatch as both a social and religious experience, similar to Mauss, and, as such, places the potlatch within the realm of what he calls the "magic circle".

6.2 The Real Shape of the Magic Circle

The magic circle acts as a bridge in explaining the spiritual and societal worlds in which competition and the gift economy exist. The theoretical basis of the magic circle lies within the work of Huizinga, who manufactured the term when studying the play element in culture. For Huizinga, the circle represents the place of comfort, which one enters to play. Huizinga enumerates several important points in describing this circle: first, the circle provides a sense of freedom. Second, Huizinga identifies play (the state of entering the magic circle) as "distinct from 'ordinary' life both as to locality and duration" (Huizinga 1971, 9). While this view has been faulted for too narrowly defining the act of play (Zimmerman 2012) and has been amended and redrawn by game studies scholars (Juul 2008; Zimmerman 2012), the potency of the hypothesis lies in the fact that the magic circle "creates order, is order" (Huizinga 1971, 10). Huizinga explains further: "For archaic man, doing and daring are power, but knowing is magical power. For him all particular knowledge is sacred knowledge—esoteric and wonder-working wisdom, because any knowing is directly related to the cosmic order itself" (ibid., 105).

The magic then partly derives from what is known. Huizinga connects this to the feast and competition, glory and, implicitly, the potlatch (ibid.). The magic circle becomes, within this context, the landscape of what is known, a moment in space where things can be predictable.

The power of knowing, and in the case of Foursquare, knowing about particular venues, knowing where friends are, knowing where one is in relation to friends, is predicated by the compulsion to enter the magic circle. Control of that order, to some degree, through contest and competition might be seen as the desired goal of the game. But it remains dissonant with the experience of the user, who must learn how to play through their proper experience of the game. This notion aligns with phenomenologist Hubert Dreyfus' theory of "maximal grip" (Dreyfus 2002, 367), in which the body naturally acquires proficiency at skills and tasks to the point where players are no longer cognisant of the necessary skills to perform / play. In explaining the phenomenon of games, Dreyfus explains that expertise, or knowledge of a game, is achieved when a player reaches maximal grip. Thus, the delight of games comes from the developing level of knowledge, which a player experiences each time he engages with the game.

The "magic" of the magic circle can then be defined by the experience of the players, who engage with a game, not rationally comprehending what has occurred, but "knowing" the experience through their bodies, their lived experience, which is not static, but ever-changing. As Foursquare now reveals itself to be part of the magic circle, providing an order to life congruent with gift economies and expenditure, a study of this inexplicable bodily engagement, this magic, brings to light a theory behind the user experience within this particular social network.

7   PROXIMAL COMMUNICATION

As my workload steadily increased during my Master's career and with my free time limited, I felt obligated to decline friends' invitations to spend time with them. I soon developed a new ritual to steal moments of relaxation. After a full day immersed in academia, I would inevitably reach a burnout point in the evening and use the opportunity to sneak out for a quick, low-key dinner with my girlfriend, now wife.

Meanwhile, each time my girlfriend and I would surreptitiously visit a restaurant or bar, I instantly wondered how I could check in to Foursquare. Since many of my friends use the social network, I feared my log of check-ins would offend their social sensibilities. With the flick of a virtual switch on my smartphone, I would check in "off the grid", a private check-in option that allowed me to acquire the same points as if I checked-in publicly.

I kept at it, noting my standing on the leaderboard within the top 10 of my friends. However, my score dropped precipitously after Foursquare revised its policy to one point per off-the-grid check-in, as opposed to the 5 to 10 points per public check-in, with the claim that this change would encourage "friendly competition" (Foursquare 2012). My leaderboard score slipped, inciting surprise from my friends and incurring a blow to my ego. Suddenly, the choice to check in off the grid became a decision I had difficulty making, and indeed my off-the-grid check-ins were reduced to nearly zero after the policy change. I felt a mixture of guilt and resentment each time I checked-in off the grid, stemming not only from hiding my whereabouts from friends, but also for not getting credit for my illicit excursions.

While the "magic" of playing Foursquare is linked to competition and glory, it also embraces its antithesis, defeat. The experience of Foursquare is felt rather than contemplated, coupled to the competition of play and the personal and social components of everyday life. The check-in becomes absorbed into daily experience, becoming part of one act: registering one's presence in a particular location, and along with it the frenetic competition and glory of the magic circle.

This begins to explain the individual experience of Foursquare: the user gets lost in play throughout his daily activity. That this activity is perpetual also makes the experience different from that of ordinary gameplay. The player of a video game or board game has a rarefied experience, while the user of Foursquare has an experience ultimately integrated into ordinary life.

Expenditure and reward through Foursquare allow the experiences of the user to be of service to him, by bringing these aspects of play into his daily routines. This interpretation implies that Foursquare has the potential to change our most mundane actions from meaningless to meaningful by furnishing the tools to understand them within a larger set of involvements.

This playfulness extends beyond personal achievement to interaction with others through Foursquare's social network. Socialising through Foursquare is not based primarily on comments or even text-based conversation of any kind, which would be the norm within a social network. Although friends in Foursquare do not usually "chat" back and forth through text, nonverbal interaction regularly occurs. This communication is based on presence and gathering in relation to users' proximity. This form of "proximal communication" should be defined as communicating through a user's presence within a particular space and time.

My first awareness of proximal communication occurred a number of years ago, when I noticed my growing jealousy over my friends' check-in routines. I would watch their activity as I worked at home. As groups of my friends successively checked-in to the same place, I would take note of it. They would not necessarily advertise their goings-on through other social media outlets, such as commenting on Twitter or Facebook. Rather, they would merely check in as each of them arrived. No verbal or written communication was necessary. The opposite of my decision to check in off the grid, the act conveyed a specific meaning of friends congregating and interacting at a given moment, of which I was not a part.

Foursquare transforms play from a moment in life to an ever-present state.

Proximal communication, however, is not confined to social sniping or jealousy. Its spirit is much more basic. A perfect example was a habit of my former roommate, who would often stop by unannounced to say hello when I was out on a date with my girlfriend. In these casual visits, a complex series of proximal communications were articulated. By checking-in, I was stating that I was available, present and wanting to socialise, without saying any of those things specifically.

Proximal communication is not merely communication over a virtual network with text, but a communication of time and space. Communication and interaction are physical and active, based on the check-in. This communication is also contingent upon a number of factors, including gathering, relationship to space and the meaning that space may have to other users and friends. Proximal communication embodies these relationships and relays them silently. Most significantly, proximal communication points to the importance of real-world location within the context of Foursquare. Space and gathering here shapes the platform. The experience of proximal communication is further sustained by notions of glory and competition, which provide an easy means of "knowing" within this non-verbal communication.

To understand Foursquare is to comprehend the experience of using it and the mediating role of engaging with the platform, which teeters provocatively along the edges of games and play. As a consequence, the experience often pervades everyday life in unexpected ways that deviate from both the paradigms of fun and games, as competition encounters everyday life.

Users remain in a state of anticipation for punctuated moments of glory, which both can be premeditated and arrive when least expected. The frenetic excitement conjured within the magic circle, when extended beyond a singular bounded moment in time and place, when it appears unexpectedly at any moment and time, becomes a potent force. As such, the presence of proximal communication lies at the very foundation of the Foursquare experience, transforming life from a moment of play to an ever-present state of play.

8   STATE OF PLAY

Foursquare is not strictly a game. It neither provides the boundaries of a game, nor does it correspond with the feelings of safety or order, the rarefied experience, that might be perceived in a game. Paradoxically, Foursquare does impart a sense of magic by creating a state of play within mundane activities. I use the term state due to the nature of the program itself. Its use of proximal, as opposed to written or verbal communication, renders an experience that is felt within the real world. The term play is purposely selected to counter the critiques of gamification, which rightfully argue that providing rewards and badges to anything is merely a superficial exercise in the utilisation of game elements.

The key to Foursquare's success is more elemental. The use of the software for the sake of expenditure (for the sake of play) causes a state of play that has less to do with engendering productive activity and more with transforming mundane activity and chaos into play. The experience within this platform furnishes structure and meaning in our lives through the same means as the magic circle.

Foursquare then not only enacts a state of play, but also a "state of magic", not a circumscribed or rarefied magic circle, but the experience of the "knowing" found inside it, within the script of our everyday life. Furthermore, unlike the magic circle, there is no skill set required to understand the rules of the state of magic or the need to experience it with the expertise of maximal grip. It can be entered into and almost immediately understood.

Foursquare operates, unabashedly, as a promotional tool through which it creates a state of play for the sake of advertising and consumption. By designing the program around a very ordinary and unproductive activity, simply where we go, Foursquare has found a perfect arena in which a state of play can be enacted. The user is aware of the intentions of the company, but uses the application because of the state of play it creates, not because of its overt manipulation. This state of play is not exclusive to Foursquare. While other gamified platforms comprise other types of interaction, covering a wide spectrum of daily activity, the state of play and proximal communication discussed here are often present as well. While such states might not be as obvious, they are drawn out of us by the software itself. As a consequence, when exploring the pervasive effects of gamification on the populace, and even play more generally, as this article and personal accounts highlight, there is the need to unearth what is deep within us when we play and fathom the power of play on our daily experiences.

BIBLIOGRAPHY

BATAILLE, GEORGES. 1991 / 1949. *The Accursed Share: An Essay on General Economy, Vol. 1: Consumption*. Cambridge, MA: Zone Books.

BATAILLE, GEORGES. 1985. *Visions Of Excess: Selected Writings, 1927–1939*. Minneapolis: University of Minnesota Press.

BAWA-CAVIA, ANIL. 2010. "Archipelago." Accessed April 7, 2012.
http://www.urbagram.net/archipelago/.

BLOCK, JONATHAN. 2012. "Insurers Are Plugging Into 'Gamification,' But Are Only Beginning to See Its Potential." *AISHealth*, April 23. Accessed February 17, 2014.
http://aishealth.com/archive/nhpw042312-03.

BOYD, DANAH M. AND NICOLE B. ELLISON. 2007. "Social Network Sites: Definition, History, and Scholarship." *Journal of Computer Mediated Communication* 13(1): 210–230.

DETERDING, SEBASTIAN, RILLA KHALED, LENNART NACKE AND DAN DIXON. 2011. "Gamification: Toward a Definition." Accessed March 27, 2014.
http://gamification-research.org/wp-content/uploads/2011/04/02-Deterding-Khaled-Nacke-Dixon.pdf.

DREYFUS, HUBERT L. 2002. "Intelligence without Representation – Merleau-Ponty's Critique of Mental Representation. The Relevance of Phenomenology to Scientific Explanation." *Phenomenology and the Cognitive Sciences* 1(4): 367–383.

FOURSQUARE. 2013. "About Foursquare." Accessed December 17.
https://foursquare.com/about.

FOURSQUARE. 2012. "Why Am I Not Getting Points for Being Mayor?" Accessed April 7.
http://support.foursquare.com/entries/20513187-why-am-i-not-getting-points-for-being-mayor.

FOX, ZOE. 2013. "Al Gore Gamifies the Climate Change Conversation." *Mashable*, February 28.
http://mashable.com/2013/02/28/reality-drop/.

FRASCA, GONZALO. 1999. "Ludology Meets Narratology: Similitude and Differences Between (Video)Games and Narrative." Accessed March 27, 2014.
http://www.ludology.org/articles/ludology.htm.

FRITH, JORDAN. 2013. "Turning Life into a Game: Foursquare, Gamification, and Personal Mobility." *Mobile Media & Communication* 1(2): 248–262.

FRITH, JORDAN. 2012. "Constructing Location, One Check-in at a Time: Examining the Practices of Foursquare Users." Accessed March 27, 2014.
http://www.lib.ncsu.edu/resolver/1840.16/8064.

GLAS, RENÉ. 2013. "Breaking Reality: Exploring Pervasive Cheating in Foursquare." Accessed March 27, 2014.
http://www.digra.org/digital-library/publications/breaking-reality-exploring-pervasive-cheating-in-Foursquare/.

HUIZINGA, JOHAN. 1971. *Homo Ludens: A Study of the Play-Element in Culture*. Boston: The Beacon Press.

JUUL, JESPER. 2008. "The Magic Circle and the Puzzle Piece." In *Conference Proceedings of the Philosophy of Computer Games 2008*, edited by Stephan Günzel, Michael Liebe, and Dieter Mersch, 56–67. Potsdam: Universitätsverlag Potsdam.

LEIBOVITZ, LIEL. 2013. "Playing to Lose: On Video Games, Excess, and Expenditure." *The Velvet Light Trap* 72(1): 75–76.

LIVEHOODS. 2013. "Home." Accessed December 18.
http://livehoods.org/.

MAUSS, MARCEL. 2000 / 1950. *The Gift: The Form and Reason for Exchange in Archaic Societies*. New York: W. W. Norton & Company.

McGONIGAL, JANE. 2011. *Reality Is Broken: Why Games Make Us Better and How They Can Change the World*. New York: Penguin Books.

PARR, BEN. 2011. "Foursquare Badges Now Level Up." *Mashable*, November 14.
http://mashable.com/2011/11/14/Foursquare-badges-now-level-up/.

REY, PJ. 2012. "Gamification, Playbor and Exploitation." *Cyborgology*, October 15.
http://thesocietypages.org/cyborgology/2012/10/15/gamification-playbor-exploitation-2/.

SALEN, KATIE AND ERIC ZIMMERMAN. 2003. *Rules of Play: Game Design Fundamentals*. Cambridge, MA: The MIT Press.

SHANKMAN, SAMANTHA. 2013. "10 Most Checked Into U.S. Places on Foursquare Are Airports." *Skift*, December 13.
http://skift.com/2013/12/13/airports-are-the-most-frequently-checked-into-u-s-places-on-Foursquare/.

DE SOUZA E SILVA, ADRIANA AND JORDAN FRITH. 2012. *Mobile Interfaces in Public Spaces: Locational Privacy, Control, and Urban Sociability*. New York: Routledge.

TATE, RYAN. 2013. "The Brilliant Hack That Brought Foursquare Back From the Dead." *Wired*, September 12.
http://www.wired.com/business/2013/12/the-brilliant-Foursquare-hack/

VAN GROVE, JENNIFER. 2010. "Foursquare Adds Photos and Comments." *Mashable*, December 20.
http://mashable.com/2010/12/20/foursquare-photos/

WHITSON, JENNIFER R. 2013. "Gaming the Quantified Self." *Surveillance & Society* 11(1/2): 163–176.

ZICHERMANN, GABE AND CHRISTOPHER CUNNINGHAM. 2011. *Gamification by Design: Implementing Game Mechanics in Web and Mobile Apps*. Sebastopol: O'Reilly Media.

ZIMMERMAN, ERIC. 2012. "Jerked Around by the Magic Circle – Clearing the Air Ten Years Later." *Gamasutra*, February 7.
http://www.gamasutra.com/view/feature/6696/jerked_around_by_the_magic_circle_.php.

LUDOGRAPHY

FOURSQUARE. 2009. Dennis Crowley and Naveen Selvadurai.
http://www.foursquare.com.

THE LUDIFICATION OF CULTURE

by **Joost Raessens**

1   INTRODUCTION

Most of you, including those who do not engage in media studies, are familiar with the subject of this article: the concept of play.[1] Just open your newspaper and see how this concept imposes itself, both in word and image. Take for example the Dutch cabinet formation in 2010: "Formation Rules Out of Date" *de Volkskrant* announces (Voermans 2010). And *NRC Next* points out that the "formation game is not played properly" and that the process shows signs of "rough play" (Peters 2010). Imagery in *de Volkskrant* similarly uses the play metaphor to denote the political situation. Dutch politician Geert Wilders is depicted as a puppeteer pulling the strings at whim while the political arena is reduced to his playground. Rules: no Muslims, no leftist elite and no judges. Closing time – or how long will this cabinet stay in power? – ask Mr Wilders.

---

1   This article is based upon my inaugural lecture, delivered in 2010 and published by Utrecht University in 2012 (Raessens 2012).

Figure 1: Puppeteer Wilders, 2010. [2]

A second example – this time from the field of media studies – is offered by the film *Slumdog Millionaire* (Beaufoy 2008). It is remarkable that this particular film was the big winner at the Academy Awards – the Oscars – in 2009. Suspense in the film largely depends on the format of a major television genre, the game show, and more specifically the quiz show: the Indian version of *Who Wants to Be a Millionaire?* (Big Synergy 2000). At the beginning of the film, we have an opening ritual that introduces protagonist Jamal Malik, which is followed by the actual game, the quiz, while the film ends with a closing ritual showing how the winner Jamal is congratulated by the presenter and handed a check with the amount of money he has won. Media scholar John Fiske calls this format of "ritual-game-ritual" (1987, 265) an enactment of capitalist ideology. The suggestion is made that – regardless of

2   Jos Collignon's drawings were published in *de Volkskrant*, September 9, 2010 and October 7, 2010. I am grateful to Jos Collignon for providing both drawings. Collignon had foresight; as of April 21, 2012 the government fell because Wilders withdrew his support.

Figure 2: Playground Wilders, 2010.

the differences – everyone would have the same opportunities. That differences in the standard of knowledge are often associated with differences in social backgrounds would thus be hidden from view. This is indeed how the film could be interpreted. The *people in the film* who in increasing numbers follow the show watch in amazement as Jamal correctly answers each new question yet again. But director Danny Boyle plays a double game. Ingeniously he interweaves the storyline of the quiz with the narrative of Jamal's life. By thus addressing Jamal's social background he manages to show the *film's audiences* how this bum from the slums gleaned his superb knowledge from the streets to win the quiz show.[3]

These two examples highlight most of the features of the play concept that I want to discuss in this article: the importance of rules, the idea that rules can be changed, the playful nature of cultural domains such as politics and media, the understanding that play is often less open than it looks (it

---

3   For a fuller analysis of *Slumdog Millionaire*, see Raessens (2009a).

is Mr Wilders's playground), the worldwide popularity of game shows, in other words: the cultural significance of play. To study and understand these features, we need a playful turn in media theory as I will argue in this article.

Since the 1960s, when the word *ludic* became popular to denote playful behaviour and fun objects – think for example of the Dutch counterculture movement Provo and the Situationist International of founding member Guy Debord – playfulness has gradually become a central category of our culture. The popularity of computer games is a striking example in this respect. A lot of people play games, young and old, male and female.[4] The game industry plays an increasingly important role in the Netherlands, as it does in other countries. The city of Utrecht is gradually changing into the gaming capital of Europe, hosting the Festival of Games, the Dutch Game Garden as a boost to the Dutch game industry, and U-GATE, the Utrecht Center for Game Research and Technology.[5] Although computer games draw a lot of attention, they are not the only manifestation of this ludification process. Play is not only characteristic of leisure, but also turns up in those domains that once were considered the opposite of play, such as education (e.g. educational games), politics (playful forms of campaigning, using gaming principles to involve party members in decision-making processes, comedians-turned-politicians)[6] and even warfare (interfaces resembling computer games, the use of drones – unmanned remote-controlled planes – introducing war à la PlayStation). Such playfulness can also be witnessed in the surge of using mobile phones and the playful communication resulting from this – think of texting and twittering. As linguist Andrea Lunsford argues, "writing has become amazingly creative. It is playful and experimental" (Houtekamer 2009, 4).

---

4   See www.theesa.com (accessed May 6, 2014).

5   For an overview of the Dutch gaming ecosystem, see van Grinsven and Raessens (forthcoming). For more information, see these websites: www.festivalofgames.nl, www.dutch-gamegarden.nl and www.u-gate.nl (all accessed May 6, 2014).

6   The German Pirate Party and Beppe Grillo's 5 Star Movement (*Movimento 5 Stelle*) are two examples. For an analysis of the German Pirate Party, see the German blog Carta (carta. info), in particular the contributions of Bieber (2009) and Lange (2012). For the 5 Star Movement, see Turner (2013).

I have described this development earlier as the "ludification of culture" (Raessens 2006). One specific part of this more general process is referred to by the term *gamification* (Deterding et al. 2011): the integration of game elements in products and services with the aim to advance user involvement.[7] The economist Jeremy Rifkin refers to this development as follows: "Play is becoming as important in the cultural economy as work was in the industrial economy" (Rifkin 2000, 263). And the sociologist Zygmunt Bauman argues that playfulness in our ludic culture is no longer confined to childhood, but has become a lifelong attitude: *"The mark of postmodern adulthood is the willingness to embrace the game whole-heartedly, as children do"* (Bauman 1995, 99).[8]

It's important to address the question whether the "ludification of culture" refers to, or is meant to be interpreted as, an ontological or an epistemological claim. The claim would be ontological if it would refer to a "new phase of history characterized so much by play that we can deem it a *play world*" (Combs 2000, 20).[9] Or, as Eric Zimmerman and Heather Chaplin claim in their *Manifesto for a Ludic Century*: "the 21st century will be defined by games" (Zimmerman and Chaplin 2013).[10] To me, their claim seems difficult to prove because it is too general a statement. One thing we should do is focus on more specific questions, such as whether today's cinema is more (or less) playful than it was, say, ten years ago. In this article my claim is on

---

7   We in the Netherlands have known this phenomenon of *gamification* since 1959, when the amusement park De Efteling introduced the figure Holle Bolle Gijs that rewards children for cleaning up their waste. Dutch Supermarket chain Albert Heijn mined the 2012 European football championships to create a "men against women" pool on Facebook. Participants could predict the results of matches. Winners received a discount on AH products. For more examples, see: www.gamification.org (accessed May 6, 2014).

8   Bauman's emphasis.

9   Combs' emphasis.

10   Taking Zimmerman and Chaplin's claim serious that "the ludic century is an era of games", would mean that also their manifesto should be considered to be a game, or as Dutch theorist Jan Simons puts it in relation to the manifesto of Dogma 95: "as a 'move' in the game" of, in the case of Lars von Trier, competing modes of film making (Simons 2007, 25). Such an approach would transform the field of media theories into an agonistic domain within which manifesto's (such as *Manifesto for a Ludic Century*) and articles (such as this one) are part of a (theoretical) battle of all against all. My article for this book can be considered to be a counter-move in the game we media theorists play.

the other hand foremost epistemological. I argue that the concept of *play* can be used as a heuristic tool to shed new light on contemporary media culture, as a lens that makes it *possible* to have a look at new objects and study them in a particular way. The concepts of play, and the ludification of culture play a crucial role in what I call the "ludic turn in media theory" (Raessens 2012). Both concepts enable me as a theorist to identify specific aspects of today's culture, and to construct a specific conceptual perspective on today's media culture. Zimmerman and Chaplin's claim is both too broad and too narrow: it is too broad because it has as its focus the twenty-first century, it is too narrow because it starts from a games perspective. My approach is just the opposite, I specifically focus on media (theory) and the ludic or playful turn that is taking place in that specific field.

2   THE STUDY OF PLAY

Considering man and his world as playful certainly is no recent phenomenon; it is of all times and all cultures. In 1795 Friedrich Schiller, for example, emphasized the importance of the play instinct for mankind. Well-known is the dictum from his *On the Aesthetic Education of Man*, one of the most important philosophical works of early German romanticism: "Man only plays when he is in the fullest sense of the word a human being, and *he is only fully a human being when he plays*" (Schiller 1967/1795, 107).[11] Schiller expects no salvation from politics; only play, especially the game of art, can be expected to humanise society. Next to reasoning (*homo sapiens*) and crafting (*homo faber*) it is playing (*homo ludens*) that takes up the centre of attention. Philosophers such as Nietzsche, Wittgenstein, Heidegger, Gadamer, Marcuse, Derrida, Deleuze and Guattari – most of whom are considered as precursors or representatives of postmodern thought – follow Schiller in their appreciation for the notion of play.[12] Not only philosophy, however, but also the (natural) sciences, social and behavioural sciences, geosciences

---

11 Schiller's emphasis.

12 See the special issue "Gaming and Theory" of the journal *symplokē* 17(1-2) from 2009. The issue contains contributions that "engage the various intersections of the idea and practice of digital gaming and critical theory" (page 5). The work of Gilles Deleuze and Felix Guattari is particularly alluded to.

and the full width of the humanities have in recent years testified to an every growing interest in the notion of play.

Strikingly, the conceptual framework of play used to meet with little systematic research in media studies. Four developments at the end of the last century changed this, however: socio-cultural changes, changes in the media themselves, changes in media studies, and institutional changes in education and research. The first change made it *possible* to envisage research into the concept of play, the second made it *desirable*, and with the third and fourth it became a matter of *reality*.

Let us start with the socio-cultural changes. In his article "Play and (Post)Modern Culture" Lourens Minnema (1998) offers an interesting explanation for the growing interest in play in nineteenth- and twentieth-century culture. Minnema points to the fact that, since modernity, Western culture has come to consist of many sub-domains – such as politics, economics, law, education, science, technology, and art – each possessing relative autonomy and a specific set of rules. We see our contemporary (post)modern culture "as a game without an overall aim, as play without a transcendent destination but not without the practical necessity of rules agreed upon and of (inter)subjective imagination; as a complex of games each one having its own framework, its own rules, risks, chances, and charms" (ibid., 21). It is this type of social-cultural change that made it possible to envisage research into the conceptual framework of play.

Second, we are witnessing changes in the media themselves, for example in the areas of film, TV, and new media. Since the 1990s, a new type of playful film narrative has enjoyed great popularity. Play is central to so-called puzzle films (Buckland 2009) such as *Lost Highway* (Lynch and Gifford 1997), *Run Lola Run* (Tykwer 1998) and *Memento* (Nolan 2000). The films feature plots of such intricacy that viewers feel they are solving a puzzle.[13] New developments in the field of TV such as the online video sharing website YouTube enable users to "play" or mimic television, and to look like a professional (Feely 2006). Not only do YouTube users play the

---

13 In their analysis of contemporary film, Simons (2007) as well as Leschke and Venus (2007) similarly employ the concept of play. Also see "Playing Games With Story Time" in Bordwell and Thompson (2008) and Juul (2008).

television game, but conversely the broadcasting companies play the You-Tube game by launching websites such as Uitzending Gemist[14], an internet protocol based replay service which enables viewers to watch shows they have missed on television. As I will argue below, mimicry is an important feature of play. Another example of what could be called the gamification of television is offered by second screen applications and apps such as the Heineken Star Player app, which enables viewers of Champions League matches to gamble on the outcome of an attack on Facebook. New media appear to exemplify this process of ludification: think of both commercial and serious computer games, playful communication via mobile phones, or social media like Facebook where identities are constructed in a playful way. Creating and maintaining communities form the core of these sites, which offer users the possibility to playfully express who they think they are and, more importantly, how they can be seen as more attractive in the eyes of fellow users. Following the view that it is the rules that constitute game worlds, one could conclude that this process of ludic identity construction can only take place within the formats developed and controlled by Facebook: a kind of multiple-choice test with a limited number of possible responses, little free play or improvisation (*paidia*), despite the suggestion of otherwise, and, on closer inspection, a lot of rule-governed discipline (*ludus*).[15] All in all, these changes in media – in film, television, as well as new media – made it *desirable* to investigate the conceptual framework of play.

Third, as I suggested above, play until recently occupied only a modest position in media studies. This is changing, however, which has to do with the alterations in the way game and media studies relate to one another. That relation has three forms, which for the major part can be situated historically in terms of three stages. At its incipience, game studies emphatically sought a position outside media studies, clearly searching for an identity of

---

14 See www.uitzendinggemist.nl (accessed May 6, 2014).

15 The terms and *paidia* and *ludus* are further explained below. The idea that Facebook as a sort of Big Brother closely monitors our purchasing behaviour (data mining) so as to enable advertisers to target users specifically is perhaps balanced by the fact that the very formats Facebook uses enable user groups to lie more convincingly about the selves they present, making it harder to figure out what individual users really, actually like. This might be the paradox of Facebook.

its own. Any overtures from the part of film or literary studies were seen as an attempt to colonise this new domain. In 2001, Espen Aarseth in his editorial for the new online magazine *Game Studies* stated that computer games had an aesthetics of their own and could not be reduced to a type of film or literature, and that the "colonising attempts" of both film and literature studies at absorbing computer games would continue until game studies have established itself as an independent academic field (Aarseth 2001). And for its part, media studies merely tolerated the newcomer. In the second stage, game studies and media studies opened up to one another. Within the Digital Game Research Association (DiGRA), for example, the special interest group Digital Games and Film was set up, creating a platform where game and film scholars could collaborate.[16] Leading publications such as *Screen-Play: Cinema/Videogames/Interfaces* (King and Krzywinska 2002) would have been unthinkable or merely marginal only a few years before: in this book the authors explore the ways in which film and computer games are related to one another. The third stage is the one we are in now and also the one that particularly is of interest to me here. Not only is game studies gradually becoming an integral part of media studies, but play is also increasingly seen "as a tool for the analysis of the media experience" (Silverstone 1999, 59). Play is increasingly regarded as a central notion for understanding media culture (Neitzel and Nohr 2006; Thimm 2010).[17] In this third stage, research into the conceptual framework of play has become a matter of *reality*.

Fourth, this is also reflected in the institutional changes in education and research. New disciplines, such as new media studies and computer game studies, are being established in art and media departments (academic as well as vocational education), which invest a lot of their research and teaching into the theory of play. Take for example the activities going on within the GAP Center for the Study of Digital Games and Play, which is

---

16 See www.digra.org (accessed May 6, 2014). In 2003 Utrecht University hosted "Level Up", the first DiGRA conference (Copier and Raessens 2003).

17 In recent issues of *ToDiGRA* (Physical and Digital in Games and Play), *G.A.M.E.* (Reframing Video Games in the Light of Cinema), and *Media Fields* (Playgrounds), we see this focus on the concept of play: researchers refer to "playful media", they want to answer the question "what is ludic at the cinema" and study what they call "mediated play spaces".

affiliated with Utrecht University.[18] And also knowledge institutions such as the Netherlands Organisation for Scientific Research NWO, the independent research organisation TNO, the Royal Netherlands Academy of Arts and Sciences KNAW, and the Netherlands Study Centre for Technology Trends STT are involved in either researching play or facilitating such research. Game studies thus have gradually become an integral part of the Dutch academic community.[19]

To sum up then, changes in culture and society, in media, in the relation between game studies and media studies, as well as in the educational and knowledge institutions have each in turn made it *possible* to envisage research into the conceptual framework of play, have made such research *desirable*, and have made it become a matter of *reality*.

3 PLAY

Having situated the state of affairs regarding research into the conceptual framework of play, there are three remaining questions to address: what is play, which forms does play take up in contemporary media culture, and what do I mean to say when I refer to the ludic, playful turn in media theory? Let us begin with the concept of play.

To capture this concept, I want to focus on one of the most important books in the current debate about play: Johan Huizinga's *Homo Ludens*. This book was first published in 1938 and since then has been translated into many languages. It is considered the most influential modernist exposition of play and continues to remain – mind you, more than seven and a half decades after the first edition – the inevitable reference point for any "serious" discussion of play. Undeniably, the book's on-going impact has to do with

---

18 See www.gamesandplay.nl (accessed May 6, 2014).

19 See for example three studies investigating so-called serious games: the TNO report *Serious Gaming* (van Kranenburg et al. 2006), and the explorative reports *Serious gaming: Vergezichten op de Mogelijkheden* (van Uden 2011) and *Play On: Serious Gaming for Future Seniors* (Bakkes et al. 2012), a study on healthy ageing, by the Netherlands Study Centre for Technology Trends STT. The impact of playful media on the construction of identities was central to the NWO-funded research project Playful Identities (2005–2010, led by Valerie Frissen, Jos de Mul and Joost Raessens). This article builds on the results of this project. Also see note 21.

its large ambition and scope. As the subtitle "A Study of the Play-Element of Culture" makes clear, it was Huizinga's ambition to demonstrate that the rise and evolution of culture occurs in and as play.[20] In the first chapter Huizinga offers a definition of the phenomenon of play, which has since been quoted in almost any book on play. Play is:

> [. . .] a free activity standing quite consciously outside "ordinary life" as being "not meant", but at the same time absorbing the player intensely and utterly. It is an activity connected with no material interest, and no profit can be gained by it. It proceeds within its own proper boundaries of time and space according to fixed rules and in an orderly manner. It promotes the formation of social groupings. (Huizinga 1955 / 1938, 13)

Let us examine the six elements of this definition. Play first of all expresses the freedom of humanity, because as a free act it is disinterested and has no practical utility. For Huizinga, play belongs to symbolic culture, which he refers to as "holy earnest" (ibid., 23) and which in his view contrasts with ordinary life, the realm of what we as fragile beings need to survive: food, clothing, housing, etc. We could call the latter instances of "profane earnest" in line with Huizinga's reasoning; play is not meant and refers to an activity of make belief or "pretence" (ibid., 47). In play, you know that the game you play belongs to a different category from ordinary life; you can be immersed in play, be completely lost in it, experience excitement and joy; play is characterised by specific boundaries in space and time and the game you play can always be repeated; crucial to play are the rules that constitute the world of the game, which are absolutely binding and indisputable; finally, play creates order in an imperfect world and a confused life. Play is essential for community engagement.

---

20 Part of the confusion in the reception of *Homo Ludens* is due to unfortunate translations. For example, the subtitle of the English translation (Boston: Beacon Press, 1955) - reads "A Study of the Play Element *in* Culture" (own emphasis), which obviously is a substantial mistranslation of the Dutch subtitle: "Proeve eener Bepaling van het Spel-Element *der* Cultuur" (own emphasis). In Huizinga's definition of play, the Dutch "'niet gemeend'" is also wrongly translated as "not serious", it should have been: "not meant".

Huizinga's definition of play has met with three major types of critique. First, his definition would be universalist and essentialist in the sense that it claims to cover the immense variety in games and play. This could be countered however by understanding the six elements I have distinguished in Huizinga's definition as a set of criteria that together constitute a family resemblance in the Wittgensteinian sense. An activity belongs to the family of play when it meets at least some of these characteristics, the number of which then determines the degree of "playfulness" of that activity.

The second type of critique asserts that Huizinga discusses play merely in general terms. Roger Caillois (2001 / 1958) proposes to further develop Huizinga's play concept by distinguishing four different categories of play: (1) *mimicry* (make believe or pretence), which ranges from the imitation games of children or the above-mentioned "playing television" on YouTube to the plays staged in the theatre; (2) *agôn* (competitive games), which covers competitive sports like football or the quiz show; (3) *alea* (games with a luck factor) referring to games like the lottery; and (4) *ilinx* (games in which vertigo is central), which includes entertainments like bungee jumping or the rollercoaster. Besides these four categories Caillois distinguishes the poles *paidia* and *ludus*, with in each of the four categories the specific types of games taking up a relative position between these poles: Paidia refers to free play, improvisation, spontaneity and impulsiveness, while ludus enriches paidia by adding forms of discipline and refers to more explicit forms of rule-driven games.

While the first two points of critique can be read in supplement to Huizinga, the third is more fundamental. By defining play as he does, Huizinga upholds a distinction between play and non-play that is far too strict. This entails that playful activities share at least some of the characteristics which I outlined above; while non-play is exclusively situated in the opposite domain of reality, utility, coercion, seriousness, etc. As a consequence Huizinga fails to do justice to the ambiguity of play that according to play theorists such as Brian Sutton-Smith (1997) is precisely its defining characteristic. Huizinga's strict distinction can be understood in terms of his adherence to modernist dichotomies, which is why I explicitly referred to his *Homo Ludens* concept as the most important "modernist" exposition of play. For modernist thought, including that of Huizinga, leaves no room for ambiguities and seeks to dispel them. As a result, however, Huizinga becomes entangled in insoluble conceptual tensions. He denotes play as reality at one moment, but as appearance at another; it constitutes a core di-

Culture arises and unfolds in *and as play.*

mension of human life (reality), yet stands outside it (appearance) because of its make believe element; play is freedom and then again it is another form of coercion; play celebrates human freedom, but the player can be completely lost in his game; the rules of the game are absolutely binding, but players can also bend the rules; games lack utility yet are useful; play is a purposeless interlude, yet it also creates order and community, and so on.

The solution is to do justice to these ambiguities, because they are so typical for play. The player for example is both part of the ordinary world and immersed in the world of the game: this is where the ludic experience matches the aesthetic experience. When we play we plunge enthusiastically into the world of the game, while at the same time we maintain a certain distance in relation to our own behaviour in play; this is why we can call that behaviour playful. This duality allows us to maintain less or more critical distance with respect to the rules; it allows us to see those rules as just the rules of the game, which are always open to adaptation. Taken together, Huizinga's ideas about play along with the three amendments discussed here form a good starting point for the analysis of the ludification of contemporary media culture, as we shall see in the next section.

A final remark on *Homo Ludens*. Although Huizinga argues that all culture arises and evolves in and as play, he also claims that not every culture continue to play. According to Huizinga, the Romantic period was the last in our culture to exhibit a playful spirit. In the nineteenth century the play factor much recedes into the background. And in the dark final chapter – on the play element of the twentieth century – Huizinga proposes that the element of play has largely lost its meaning. There is hardly any play in modern culture. A major reason for the demise of play, he argues, is the rise of technology. Here I would defend the thesis – stepping up in time – that, from an ontological perspective, digital information and communication technologies have precisely enabled new forms of play.

The first of the three questions – what is play? – has now been answered. The remaining two – which forms do play take up in contemporary media culture, and what do I mean to say when I refer to the ludic, playful turn in media theory? – will be addressed presently. Let us begin with tracing play in contemporary media culture.

4 PLAYFUL MEDIA CULTURE

In our contemporary media culture, digital technologies and play are closely linked. In order to better understand the impact this has, we need to further specify the concept of play. It is important to emphasise the distinction between *play* and *game*. How do the two concepts relate to each other? *Play* is the overarching category. It refers to all activities of play, including both games and non-game activities such as playful communication. *Games* are the formalised parts of *play* (cf. Salen and Zimmerman 2004, 301–311). This distinction allows us to focus our attention not only on computer games, but also on the impact of play on media culture as such.

Huizinga's concept of play – to which I confine myself in this article – seems like a good starting point for the analysis of our media experience, because our experiences in media and play have a great deal of ambiguities and characteristics in common. Or, to put it differently, the media – each in their own medium-specific way – offer users new possibilities – "affordances" – to play. Let us briefly consider the six elements of the play concept distinguished above, taking into account the associated ambiguities.[21] This discussion makes clear that the process of ludification is not necessarily a positive development: freedom goes hand in hand with coercion, fun with annoyance.

To start with the first element, media use may initially look like harmless, disinterested fun. Think of all the creative adaptations of *Star Wars* (Lucas 1977) on YouTube. It can also, however, become involved in political ends. Think of the Turkish court blocking access to YouTube because it allegedly hosted videos that attacked Ataturk, the founder of the Republic of Turkey; the element of make believe refers to the dual nature of media. Like play, our media culture consists of accepting the "as-if-ness of the world" (Silverstone 1999, 59). According to the philosopher Gianni Vattimo, it is

---

21 For a detailed analysis of the playfulness of digital media, see Cermak-Sassenrath (2010) and the book resulting from the Playful Identities project: Frissen et al. (forthcoming). Also see note 19.

becoming increasingly difficult to imagine a single reality, due to the current proliferation of digital media. He therefore reasons that if media cause us to lose our "sense of reality", this is a liberation rather than a great loss (Vattimo 1992, 8). In line with this, he argues that media realities are just versions of how the world works, subject to the "game of interpretations" (Vattimo 1998, 19). The impact of this debate – is it possible that media show us an objective reality, or do they merely offer versions of this reality – can be witnessed when considering the current reorganisation of news shows within the Dutch public broadcasting system: some shows are assigned the role of broadcasting news from a specific angle or perspective, whereas others such as *Nieuwsuur* should maintain strict objectivity.

Considering the other elements, it is worth pointing out that digital media offer forms of pleasure and annoyance resulting from the interactive aspect: there is frustration when the computer does not perform what you want it to do and pleasure involved in surrendering to the rules or conversely opposing them; the specific boundaries of space and time appear to be under heavy pressure when considering the culture of constant accessibility that arose with mobile phone usage. Yet, the boundaries become clear when we focus on the aspect of safety. On social media like Facebook, users can playfully construct identities that do not necessarily have any implications for real life; the element of order and community engagement returns in the formation of web-based social groups: green blogs like *sustainablog*[22] unite users who are committed to a better environment and oppose the existing social order.

As for the rules of the game, I would like to discuss this sixth element of play a bit more in depth. Rules can be either accepted or transformed or bent, both at an individual level and at the media system's macro level. In order to achieve a better understanding of the way we can deal with rules, we must consider the interaction between, on the one hand, levels of playability enabled by different media (Kücklich 2004) and, on the other hand, individual users' ludoliteracy or play competence (Zagal 2010). With respect to television, the aforementioned John Fiske addresses the playfulness that arises from the relationship between a medium and its user. Fiske makes a

---

22 See sustainablog.org (accessed May 6, 2014).

distinction between two types of play. First, a text (e.g. a movie) "has 'play' in it, like a door whose hinges are loose" (Fiske 1987, 230). Play here is "free movement within a more rigid structure" (Salen and Zimmerman 2004, 304). Second, such "play" enables viewers to play with the text, i.e. playfully develop an interpretation of their own. Think of the film I mentioned at the beginning of this article, *Slumdog Millionaire*. Is it a form of poverty porn (exploitation of poverty) or a critical reflection on Jamal's social background? What is distinct about new media is that they enable multiple forms of participation and thus playability, and that they therefore are not limited to the game of interpretations (Raessens 2005).

Playability can have four different levels. First, there is the player who accepts that "the rules of a game are absolutely binding and allow no doubt" (Huizinga 1955/1938, 11). Such a player voluntarily submits himself to the rules that govern the world of the game. The cheater who "pretends to be playing the game" (ibid.) operates on the second level. This player – for example the one who uses cheat codes in computer games – is aware of the explicit and implicit rules of the game and tries to deploy them (against the rules) to his own gain. At the third level we have the spoilsport, "the player who trespasses against the rules or ignores them" (ibid.). An example is the so-called *modder*, the player who modifies the computer game if the system allows for it. The fourth and final level is that of "the *outlaw*, the revolutionary" (ibid., 12) who in digital culture takes the shape of the programmer. Where the player (level 1), the cheater (level 2) and the spoilsport (level 3) still operate within the boundaries of the game or oppose these, the programmer (level 4) creates "a new community with rules of its own" (ibid., 12), his own game world, in other words, thus driving a system's playability over the edge to discover new forms (Rushkoff 2010 and 2012).[23]

I will offer three examples to show that such an approach to play can be fruitful for the analysis of contemporary media culture. The first example concerns the study of serious games, the second example expands on this,

---

23 The fact remains that programmers are bound by certain codes and protocols, which by definition preclude absolute freedom. This is an important theme in critical software studies. See Galloway (2004 and 2006). The rules of ludo-capitalism provide additional limitations (Dibbell 2006 and 2008).

approaching digital media and digital media experience as something play-ful, and the third addresses the debate surrounding the concept of media literacy.

Serious games are computer games, which are not only played for enter-tainment but also for educational purposes. These games are often designed as ideological spaces, as worlds that aim to convince players of certain ideas. Think for instance of Food Force (2005) developed by the United Nations' World Food Programme which sets out to convince players that humanitar-ian aid, possibly involving military intervention – preferably by the UN – is of great importance to solve conflicts worldwide. At first sight a purely noble cause. But closer inspection yields that such games are built on the metaphor of the West as the helping parent, on the premise that emergencies, conflicts, or local wars, all originate from within while the conflict can only be defined or solved by external forces. From this perspective, these games are not really that much different from commercial war games like Call of Duty (2003) or Medal of Honor (1999) which are based on a similar analysis of the nature of conflicts, suggesting that their solution is possible only through external mili-tary intervention. In other words, serious games that appeal to our sympathy are by no means innocent, because they shape the paradigms of guilt and re-sponsibility in a very particular way. This raises the ethical-political question of what game developers, game researchers, and game players should do. Try-ing to make games more effective by allowing players to become completely immersed in the game world is an option, although allowing for a measure of critical distance in the design of the game is quite recommendable, as I have argued elsewhere using the term gaming apparatus. If that condition is met, serious games incorporate "a moment of disavowal – of distancing . . . We [i.e. players] perform actions in the full knowledge that we are doing this within the constraints set by someone else" (Raessens 2009b, 26). This distinction between immersion and critical distance – which I previously described as a game ambiguity – is based on the above-mentioned forms of playability. Within such serious games, players will normally subject them-selves to the prevailing ideological lines of the game world, while from an ethical-political perspective the awareness of (and where necessary resist-ance against) these rules is important. This is where the programmer in-volved in the creation of activist computer games – such as independently

107

produced "critical computer games" or "games of multitude"[24] – attempts to do something different (Flanagan 2009; Dyer-Witheford and De Peuter 2009).

The second example concerns the playability of digital media in general. At first glance, it seems that these media increase users' room for play. That is, all software-based products can be modified and adapted to users' personal needs (level 3 of playability). Think of the hacking and further development of Sony's robot dog Aibo. When Sony launched this dog in 1999, users soon wanted it to have more functionalities. One of them, hacker Aibopet, designed a program to make the dog dance and made it available on his own website. As media scholar Mirko Schäfer shows, Sony initially did not appreciate these forms of "play beyond the manual" (Schäfer 2006) and threatened with lawsuits, but soon changed track. Sony realised that these hacks could also be integrated into new versions of Aibo. Such playful forms of product modification are characteristic of the major changes taking place in contemporary cultural industries. This example demonstrates – note: within certain limits – the disintegration of the traditional distinction between consumer and producer. In today's "bastard culture" (Schäfer 2011), media users can become active participants in the process of the creation and evolution of media products. On the other hand, present-day Web 2.0-optimism suggests that we – the consumers – are the ones who are in power. This optimism "urgently begs for deconstruction" (van Dijck and Nieborg 2009, 855). For example, *Time Magazine* elected as person of the year 2007: "You. Yes you. You control the information age. Welcome to your world". Yet research into the online game World of Warcraft (2004) shows for example that although negotiations take place between players and Blizzard Entertainment, the game company (game scholar René Glas calls these negotiations very appropriately "a battlefield", 2013), the extent to which players can claim room for play to do their own thing is mainly determined by Blizzard. Here too, the principle remains unaltered that one should buy the game, pay monthly

---

24 Think of more casual games like McDonald's Video Game (2006) by the collective of media activists Mollindustria (www.molleindustria.org, accessed May 6, 2014) and September 12th: A Toy World (2003) and MADRID (2004) by newsgaming.com (accessed May 6, 2014). On the basis of Jesper Juul's notion of casual games (2010) new media scholar Alex Gekker labels such forms of playful activism as "casual politicking" (2012).

subscription fees, and thus remain part of a system that you could designate as ludo-capitalism.

The third example concerns media literacy. How to behave in this media culture, which appears to be characterised on the one hand by autonomy and emancipation and on the other hand by being determined by media (technology)? The ability to be immersed in, yet at the same time maintain critical distance to media, as well as the ability to address the arbitrary nature and mutability of rules (two of the aforementioned ambiguities), are components of what I would call ludoliteracy or play competence, which is in fact a specific form of what is called media literacy (Zagal 2010). Where media literacy in general terms is defined as "*the totality of knowledge, skills, and attitudes needed to operate as critically aware and active citizens in a complex, changing and fundamentally mediated world*" (Raad voor Cultuur [the Dutch Arts Council] 2005, 2),[25] the distinction between game and play and between different forms of playability facilitate a more precise definition of civic participation. Game competence or "gaming literacy" (Zimmerman 2009) relates in particular to playing computer games and involves skills and knowledge related to using games, critically interpret them and design and produce them. Ludoliteracy, however, is applicable across the full spectrum of media. It involves playing by the rules, bending and adjusting the rules in order to move easily through the system, or where necessary and possible, adjusting the system or playing the system. Or as French philosopher Gilles Deleuze once put it: trace and where necessary create lines of flight, allow for leaks in the system (Rabinow and Gandal 1986). Considered as such, the term play is not only suitable for characterising our contemporary media culture (playful) but also for defining the knowledge and skills (ludoliteracy or play competence) required to function in media culture.

5   THE PLAYFUL TURN IN MEDIA THEORY

This leaves us with the question whether we could speak of a ludic turn in media theory. Let us put things in perspective. In recent years the claims of yet another turn followed each other in rapid succession. We already had the linguistic turn, and then supposedly a digital turn, a material turn, a visual

---

25   Emphasis by Raad voor Cultuur.

turn, a pictorial turn, an experiential turn, a spatial turn, a cultural turn, a mediamatic turn, and so on. Is this a clear case of concept inflation, or are these changes really all taking place? Speaking in terms of turns could also stem from the all too human tendency to overestimate the significance of their own times, perhaps even from the irresistible need of researchers delivering articles to accentuate the significance of their own research.

Considering the above, I do indeed claim we are witnessing a ludic turn and that this turn in the field of media studies combines two elements. On the one hand, the notion that media are playful opens up new objects of study: computer games (including serious games), playful aspects of media use (such as product modifications), and the competence to deal playfully with the systems you are part of (ludoliteracy). On the other hand, there is a ludic turn in media theory itself, a turn to which this article hopes to contribute. This allows for considering these media objects in a particular way. A new interpretative framework arises from using new concepts and conceptual dichotomies from game and play studies, a specific focus to deploy in the theoretical study of media and their use. Think of concepts such as playability, gaming apparatus, play competence or ludoliteracy, battlefields of negotiation, and casual games-casual politicking, and of conceptual dichotomies or ambiguities such as: rules (constitutive, limiting, closure) and variability thereof (openness, freedom); immersion (surrender) and critical distance (monitoring); disinterestedness versus social criticism; depicting reality or only versions thereof; the pleasure of being either in control or not. I believe that these concepts and conceptual dichotomies are useful in bringing to light the important characteristics of and issues in the field of digital media culture and to prepare the ground for new perspectives and action plans. Think for example of the power game fought between producers, distributors, and consumers, with the industry trying to set the rules of the game while certain user groups aim to maintain a degree of openness by transforming these rules.

Three perspectives should be united in this: the political analysis of media, paying attention to the struggle for power between producers and consumers and the impact of ludo-capitalism; the analysis of the "digital material" aspects of media such as they are studied in critical code studies and software studies (van den Boomen et al. 2009), and the philosophical analysis of play and media, the lines of flight and leaks in the system. The ludic turn in media theory expounded here seems very fruitful, as I hoped to have shown in this article. Now I do not just want to study the ludic turn but actually bring it about, as an example of what Henry Jenkins once called "intervention analysis" (Tulloch and Jenkins 1995, 238). Intervention analysis is not just interested in describing and explaining the existing orders of knowledge, but wishes to change these. For this we at Utrecht University are busy with bringing together our research and teaching activities in this area to set up a collaborative community of researchers and students (from inside and outside our university). We christened this community as the Center for the Study of Digital Games and Play, abbreviated GAP. If we do our work well, you will soon associate GAP no longer with what Huizinga would call the "profane earnest" of GAP clothing, but with the "holy earnest" of games and play.

BIBLIOGRAPHY

AARSETH, ESPEN. 2001. "Computer Game Studies, Year One." *Game Studies* 1(1). www.gamestudies.org/0101/editorial.html.

BAKKES, SANDER, ELLIS BARTHOLOMEUS, THOMAS GEIJTENBEEK, JACCO VAN UDEN, SABINE WILDEVUUR. 2012. *Play On. Serious Gaming for Future Seniors.* Den Haag: Stichting Toekomstbeeld der Techniek.

BAUMAN, ZYGMUNT. 1995. *Life in Fragments. Essays in Postmodern Morality.* Oxford: Blackwell.

BEAUFOY, SIMON. 2008. *Slumdog Millionaire.* Directed by Danny Boyle. Paris: Pathé.

BIEBER, CHRISTOPH. 2009. „Kampagne als ‚Augmented Reality Game': Der Mitmachwahlkampf der Piratenpartei." *Carta*, September 25. www.carta.info/15450.

BIG SYNERGY. 2010-2014. *Kaun Banega Crorepati.* Culver City: Sony Pictures Television International.

BORDWELL, DAVID AND KRISTIN THOMPSON. 2008. *Film Art: An Introduction.* Boston: McGraw-Hill.

BUCKLAND, WARREN. 2009. *Puzzle Films. Complex Storytelling in Contemporary Cinema.* Oxford: Wiley-Blackwell.

CAILLOIS, ROGER. 2001 / 1958. *Man, Play and Games.* Chicago: University of Illinois Press.

CERMAK-SASSENRATH, DANIEL. 2010. *Interaktivität als Spiel. Neue Perspektieven auf den Alltag mit dem Computer.* Bielefeld: transcript.

COMBS, JAMES E. 2000. *Play World. The Emergence of the New Ludenic Age.* Westport: Praeger Publishers.

COPIER, MARINKA AND JOOST RAESSENS. 2003. *Level Up. Digital Games Research Conference.* Utrecht: Universiteit Utrecht.

DETERDING, SEBASTIAN, DAN DIXON, RILLA KHALED AND LENNART NACKE. 2011. "From Game Design Elements to Gamefulness: Defining Gamification." In *Proceedings of the 15th International Academic MindTrek Conference: Envisioning Future Media Environments*, 9–15. New York: ACM.

DIBBELL, JULIAN. 2008. "The Chinese Game Room. Play, Productivity, and Computing at Their Limits." *Artifact* 2(3): 1–6.

DIBBELL, JULIAN. 2006. *Play Money. Or, How I Quit My Day Job and Made Millions Trading Virtual Loot*. New York: Basic Books.

DYER-WITHEFORD, NICK AND GREIG DE PEUTER. 2009. *Games of Empire. Global Capitalism and Video Games*. Minneapolis: University of Minnesota Press.

FEELY, JIM. 2006. "Lights! Camera! Vodcast! How to Make Your Own Viral Hit." *Wired*, May 14. www.wired.com/wired/archive/14.05/howto.html.

FISKE, JOHN. 1987. *Television Culture*. London: Routledge.

FLANAGAN, MARY. 2009. *Critical Play. Radical Game Design*. Cambridge, MA: The MIT Press.

FRISSEN, VALERIE, SYBILLE LAMMES, MICHIEL DE LANGE, JOS DE MUL AND JOOST RAESSENS. Forthcoming. *Playful Identities: The Ludification of Digital Media Cultures*. Amsterdam: Amsterdam University Press.

GALLOWAY, ALEXANDER R. 2006. *Gaming. Essays on Algorithmic Culture*. Minneapolis: University of Minnesota Press.

GALLOWAY, ALEXANDER R. 2004. *Protocol. How Control Exists After Decentralization*. Cambridge, MA: The MIT Press.

GEKKER, ALEX. 2012. *Gamocracy: Political Communication in the Age of Play*. MA-thes., Utrecht University.

GLAS, RENÉ. 2013. *Battlefields of Negotiation. Control, Agency, and Ownership in World of Warcraft*. Amsterdam: Amsterdam University Press.

HOUTEKAMER, CAROLA. 2009. "Taal is Speelser Geworden." *NRC Next*, September 28.

HUIZINGA, JOHAN. 1955 / 1938. *Homo Ludens. A Study of the Play-Element in Culture*. Boston: The Beacon Press.

JUUL, JESPER. 2010. *A Casual Revolution: Reinventing Video Games and Their Players*. Cambridge, MA: The MIT Press.

JUUL, JESPER. 2008. "The Magic Circle and the Puzzle Piece." Accessed April 1, 2014. http://opus.kobv.de/ubp/frontdoor.php?source_opus=2455&la=de.

KING, GEOFF AND TANYA KRZYWINSKA. 2002. *ScreenPlay. Cinema / Videogames / Interfaces*. London: Wallflower Press.

KÜCKLICH, JULIAN. 2004. "Play and Playability as Key Concepts in New Media Studies." Accessed April 1, 2014. http://citeseerx.ist.psu.edu/viewdoc/download?doi=10.1.1.94.4169&rep=rep1&type=pdf.

LANGE, ANDREAS. 2012. "LiquidFeedback: Gamification der Politik?" *Carta*, March 14. http://www.carta.info/42081/.

LESCHKE, RAINER AND JOCHEN VENUS. 2007. *Spielformen im Spielfilm. Zur Medienmorphologie des Kinos nach der Postmoderne*. Bielefeld: transcript.

LUCAS, GEORGE. 1977. *Star Wars*. Directed by George Lucas. Los Angeles: 20th Century Fox.

LYNCH, DAVID AND GIFFORD, BARRY. 1997. *Lost Highway*. Directed by David Lynch. London: October Films.

MINNEMA, LOURENS. 1998. "Play and (Post)Modern Culture. An Essay on Changes in the Scientific Interest in the Phenomenon of Play." *Cultural Dynamics*, 10(1): 21–47.

NEITZEL, BRITTA AND ROLF F. NOHR. 2006. *Das Spiel mit dem Medium. Partizipation – Immersion – Interaktion*. Marburg: Schüren Verlag.

Nolan, Christopher. 2000. *Memento*. Directed by Christopher Nolan. Universal City: Summit Entertainment.

Peters, Jit. 2010. "Formatiespel Wordt Niet Zo Netjes Gespeeld." *NRC Next*, September 10.

Raad voor Cultuur. 2005. *Mediawijsheid. De Ontwikkeling van Nieuw Burgerschap*. Den Haag: Raad voor Cultuur.

Rabinow, Paul and Keith Gandal. 1986. "The Intellectual and Politics (an Interview with Gilles Deleuze)." *History of the Present* 2(1–2): 20–21.

Raessens, Joost. 2012. *Homo Ludens 2.0. The Ludic Turn in Media Theory*. Utrecht: Utrecht University.

Raessens, Joost. 2009a. "Homo ludens 2.0." *Metropolis M* 5 (October/November): 64–69, 85–88.

Raessens, Joost. 2009b. "Serious Games From an Apparatus Perspective." In *Digital Ma-terial. Tracing New Media in Everyday Life and Technology*, edited by Marianne van den Boomen, Sybille Lammes, Ann-Sophie Lehmann, Joost Raessens and Mirko Tobias Schäfer, 21–34. Amsterdam: Amsterdam University Press.

Raessens, Joost. 2006. "Playful Identities, or the Ludification of Culture." *Games and Culture* 1(1): 52–57.

Raessens, Joost. 2005. "Computer Games as Participatory Media Culture." In *Handbook of Computer Game Studies*, edited by Joost Raessens and Jeffrey Goldstein, 373–388. Cambridge, MA: The MIT Press.

Rifkin, Jeremy. 2000. *The Age of Access. The New Culture of Hypercapitalism, Where All of Life Is a Paid-for Experience*. New York: Jeremy P. Tarcher/Putnam.

Rushkoff, Douglas. 2012. "Monopoly Moneys. The Media Environment of Corporatism and the Player's Way Out." PhD diss., Utrecht University.

Rushkoff, Douglas. 2010. *Program or Be Programmed: Ten Commands for a Digital Age*. New York: OR Books.

Salen, Katie and Eric Zimmerman. 2004. *Rules of Play: Game Design Fundamentals*. Cambridge, MA: The MIT Press.

Schäfer, Mirko Tobias. 2011. *Bastard Culture! How User Participation Transforms Cultural Production*. Amsterdam: Amsterdam University Press.

Schäfer, Mirko Tobias. 2006. "Spielen Jenseits der Gebrauchsanweisung. Partizipation als Output des Konsums Software-Basierter Produkte." In *Das Spiel mit dem Medium. Partizipation – Immersion – Interaktion*, edited by Britta Neitzel and Rolf F. Nohr, 296–312. Marburg: Schüren Verlag.

Schiller, Friedrich. 1967/1795. *On the Aesthetic Education of Man*. Oxford: Oxford University Press.

Silverstone, Roger. 1999. *Why Study the Media?* London: Sage.

Simons, Jan. 2007. *Playing the Waves. Lars von Trier's Game Cinema*. Amsterdam: Amsterdam University Press.

Sutton-Smith, Brian. 1997. *The Ambiguity of Play*. Cambridge, MA: Harvard University Press.

Thimm, Caja. 2010. *Das Spiel: Muster und Metapher der Mediengesellschaft*. Wiesbaden: VS Verlag.

Tulloch, John and Henry Jenkins. 1995. *Science Fiction Audiences. Watching Doctor Who and Star Trek*. London: Routledge.

Turner, Eric. 2013. "The 5 Star Movement and Its Discontents: A Tale of Blogging, Comedy, Electoral Success and Tensions." *Interface* 5(2): 178–212.

Tykwer, Tom. 1998. *Lola rennt*. Directed by Tom Tykwer. Geiselgasteig: Bavaria Media.

VAN DEN BOOMEN, MARIANNE, SYBILLE LAMMES, ANN-SOPHIE LEHMANN, JOOST RAESSENS AND MIRKO TOBIAS SCHÄFER. 2009. *Digital Material. Tracing New Media in Everyday Life and Technology*. Amsterdam: Amsterdam University Press.

VAN DIJCK, JOSÉ AND DAVID NIEBORG. 2009. "Wikinomics and Its Discontents: A Critical Analysis of Web 2.0 Business Manifestos." *New Media & Society* 11(5): 855–874.

VAN GRINSVEN, CHRISTEL AND JOOST RAESSENS. Forthcoming. "The Netherlands." In *Video Games Around the World*, edited by Mark J. P. Wolf. Cambridge, MA: The MIT Press.

VAN KRANENBURG, KARIN, MIJKE SLOT, MARTIJN STAAL, ANDRA LEURDIJK, JAN BURGMEIJER. 2006. "Serious Gaming. Onderzoek Naar Knelpunten en Mogelijkheden van Serious Gaming." Accessed April 1, 2014.
http://repository.tudelft.nl/view/tno/uuid%3A1c3e4a1f-b6b9-4a30-a8af-fb8b961b434f/.

VAN UDEN, JACCO. 2011. *Serious Gaming: Vergezichten op de Mogelijkheden*. Den Haag: Stichting Toekomstbeeld der Techniek.

VATTIMO, GIANNI. 1998. "Die Grenzen der Wirklichkeitsauflösung." In *Medien-Welten Wirklichkeiten*, edited by Gianni Vattimo and Wolfgang Welsch, 15–26. München: Wilhelm Fink.

VATTIMO, GIANNI. 1992. *The Transparent Society*. Malden: Polity Press.

VOERMANS, WIM. 2010. "Spelregels Formatie Uit de Tijd." *de Volkskrant*, September 9.

ZAGAL, JOSÉ P. 2010. *Ludoliteracy*. Pittsburgh: ETC Press.

ZIMMERMAN, ERIC. 2009. "Gaming Literacy: Game Design as a Model for Literacy in the Twenty-First Century." In *The Video Game Theory Reader* 2, edited by Bernard Perron and Mark J. P. Wolf, 23–31. New York: Routledge.

ZIMMERMAN, ERIC AND HEATHER CHAPLIN. 2013. "Manifesto for a Ludic Century." *Kotaku*, September 9.
http://kotaku.com/manifesto-the-21st-century-will-be-defined-by-games-1275355204.

LUDOGRAPHY

CALL OF DUTY. 2003. Developed by Infinity Ward. Windows. Activision.

FOOD FORCE. 2005. Developed by Deepend and Playerthree. Windows, OS X. United Nations World Food Programme.

HEINEKEN STAR PLAYER. 2011. AKQA.
http://www.akqa.com/#/work/heineken/star-player.

MADRID. 2004. Developed by Newsgaming.com. Browsergame. Newsgaming.com.

MCDONALD'S VIDEO GAME. 2006. Developed by Molleindustria. Browser game. Molleindustria.

MEDAL OF HONOR. 1999. Developed by DreamWorks Interactive. PlayStation. Electronic Arts.

SEPTEMBER 12TH: A TOY WORLD. 2003. Developed by Gonzalo Frasca. Browser game. Newsgaming.com.

WORLD OF WARCRAFT. 2004. Developed by Blizzard Entertainment. Windows, OS X. Blizzard Entertainment.

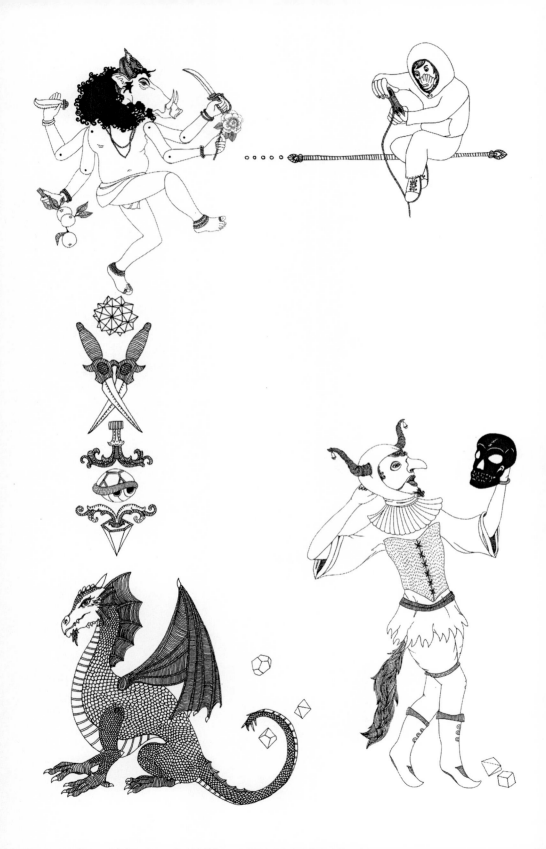

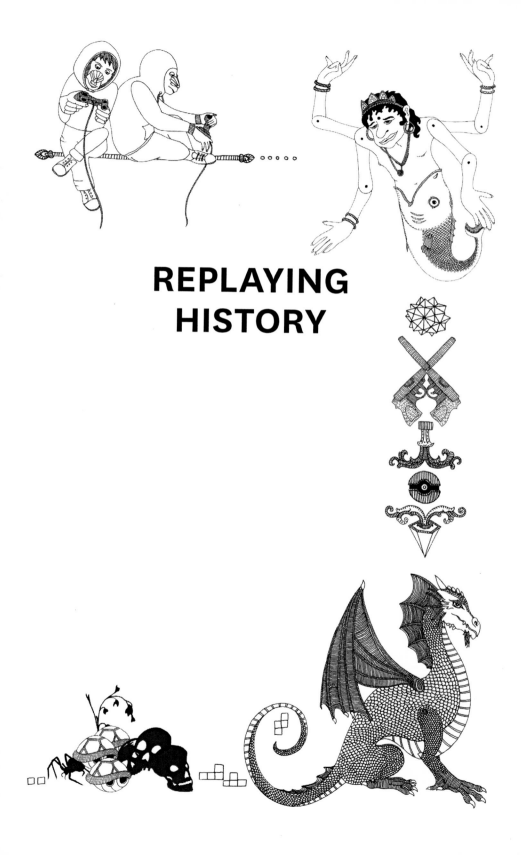

REPLAYING
HISTORY

PREDIGITAL PRECURSORS
OF GAMIFICATION

by **Mathias Fuchs**

INTRODUCTION

If we believe what renowned US-American market analysts tell us unanimously, then we have to accept that nothing will influence our lives as much as these: mobility, social media, and *gamification*. The latter is said to have the strongest impact: "Gamification is projected to be a $1.6 billion market by 2016" (Corry 2011). Other sources predict $2.8 billion for 2016 (Palmer, Lunceford, and Patton 2012) and $5.5 billion for 2018 (Markets and Markets 2013). In 2011 marketing analyst Gartner, Inc. said that "by 2015 more than 50 per cent of organizations that manage innovation processes will gamify those processes" (Gartner, Inc. 2011). Yet one year later Gartner, Inc. said, "Gamification is currently being driven by novelty and hype. By 2014 80% of gamification applications will fail to deliver" (Fleming 2012). But irrespective of whether gamification will change little, something or everything, no one can deny that it has become a buzzword that describes what many fear or hope to happen right now. The process of a total permeation of our society with methods, metaphors, values, and attributes of games (Fuchs

2011 and 2013)[1] was christened "gamification" in 2002 (Marczewski 2012) and has since been popularised by US marketing companies and their respective PR departments. Even though there have been attempts to differentiate between games-related and play-related phenomena, or processes that could be seen as either driven by *ludus* or *paidia* (Caillois 2001 / 1958), gamification has remained the buzzword. Greek, Italian, Spanish, Swedish and German terminological creations have been introduced and discussed in the scholarly world, but neither παιγνιδοποίηση, *ludicizzazione*, *ludificação*, *gamificación*, *ludización* nor the German-Latin *ludifizierung* could compete with the Anglo-American *gamification*. The reason for this might be that the Californian league of gamification evangelists such as Zichermann (2011), McGonigal (2011), and company have already been sowing on the semantic field at a time when European game scholars were not quite sure whether the ludification they observed was more of a curse than a gift. Flavio Escribano's terminological creation of a "ludictatorship" points in that direction.

The US politician Al Gore did not seem to be worried about what gamification might bring to our society when at the eighth annual Games for Change Festival in June 2013 he declared, "Games are the new normal". On the one hand this seems to be the Democrat's or even the democratic assumption that everybody should have the right to play. On the other hand, it declares total play with the hidden implication that those who cannot play society's games and those who do not want to play them are not to be considered normal. Even though 2002 is usually said to be the year when the term gamification was coined, it was only around the beginning of this decade that gamification became a buzzword. Deterding, Dixon, Khaled, and Nacke (2011), Schell (2010)[2], Reilhac (2010),[3] and others presented different flavours of gamification, some of them design-oriented, others psychological or judgemental. For Sebastian Deterding and his colleagues:

---

1   German original: "Gamification ist die Durchdringung unserer Gesellschaft mit Metaphern, Methoden, Werten und Attributen aus der Welt der Spiele" (Fuchs 2013).

2   "Gamification is taking things that aren't games and trying to make them feel more like games" (Schell 2010).

3   "There is no doubt that video games are the emergent form our times and that the process of gamification is transforming our world, contaminating it like never before" (Reilhac 2010).

[. . .] it is suggested that "gamified" applications provide insight into novel, gameful phenomena complementary to playful phenomena. Based on our research, we propose a definition of "gamification" as the use of game design elements in non-game contexts. (Deterding et al. 2011)

All of the definitions of gamification that have been proposed since 2002 are based on the idea that the digital computer and digital computer games are a reference without which gamification could not be conceived. There were, however, predigital predecessors of gamification long before digital computers became popular. A decade before programmable computers such as the Z3, Colossus or the ENIAC were introduced, a playful labour attitude had been mentioned and praised by the author Pamela Lyndon Travers. As early as in 1934 Travers' Mary Poppins character was developed to tell the following rhyme in the Disney movie:

In ev'ry job that must be done
There is an element of fun
You find the fun, and snap!
The job's a game! (Travers 1934)

This is obviously what we would nowadays call the gamification of labour. It is precisely the use of game elements in non-game contexts, as the definitions of Zichermann, Reilhac, Schell, Deterding et al. suggest.[4]

This article intends to present examples for gamification *avant la lettre* and compares these predigital forms of ludification with recent approaches that build heavily on the historic ideas, concepts, and gadgets. In particu-

---

4   I owe my colleague Paolo Ruffino thanks for the request for a clarification in regard to the "game elements" mentioned. In an email from January 21, 2014 Ruffino comments, "Deterding et al. talk about the use of game 'design' elements. They refer to a specific knowledge and practice: game design – a field mostly born with the emergence of video games as an industry." Ruffino has a point there. I acknowledge that I am trying to recontextualise gamification here not only in using predigital examples but also in looking at games before computer game design existed. Having said so, my understanding of gamification is close to what other authors label "playification" (Mosca 2012) or "ludification" (Raessens 2006).

lar the following fields of predigital gamification will be looked at: religious practice, music, magic, education, lifestyle, and styles for killing.

1 GAMIFYING RELIGIOUS PRACTICE

Gods from antique Greek myths knew how to play tricks on each other. Indian avatars experienced lust and joy and even the warrior gods from Nordic mythology had a lot of fun every now and then. The Loki character from Edda is a joker and a jester. Little fun however has been reported from the Christian God, Son of God, or the corresponding spirits. Protagonists in Jewish-Christian mythology never laugh, never make love, and they rarely play. Einstein is said to have commented on God's resistance to play with his famous phrase of "God doesn't throw the dice". If playing or gambling is reported of in the bible, it is usually the bad guys who do so. The maximum offence against piety and the example *par excellence* of how not to behave in the vicinity of Christ are the soldiers at the cross who dare to play when Christ is dying. Completely in line with the negative sanctioning of playfulness is the prohibition of any gambling practice in Christian culture. Play, that was felt to be the pastime of the gods in other religions, was associated rather with the devil in Christianity. Who could have invented such a nuisance as play? Reinmar von Zweter, a poet from the thirteenth century had no doubt about that when he wrote in a truly Christian spirit: "The devil created the game of dice":

> Der tuivel schouf das würfelspil,
> dar umbe daz er selen vil
> da mit gewinnen will (Wolferz 1916)

His anger about dice games is actually exemplifying a much wider rejection of play in general. Almost every century in Western European history has known legal sanctions on gambling, prohibition of certain games, and violent destruction of games (Ritschl 1884). On 10 August 1452 Capistrano, a travelling sermoniser, was said to have collected games that he labelled "sinful luxury items" and piled them up to an impressive mountain of 3640 board games, some 40,000 dice games and innumerable card games. The games were then burnt publicly (Dirx 1981, 82).[5]

It is frightening to see that game burning preceded book burning and that in both cases it was not the medium that was intended for destruction but a cultural practice and a practicing group.

In Western Europe gambling that involved monetary benefits was often prohibited. Reports about public houses that were accused of being gambling houses were used in many cases to shut down the pubs or to penalise the innkeepers. A class action from 1612 in Ernsdorf united the village mayor and members of the parish choir to sue an innkeeper who served alcoholic drinks in order to "attract gamblers and scallywags to visit his inn" (Schmidt 2005, 255).[6] In 1670 a list of all the inhabitants that were suspected of playing games was posted in the very same village of Ernsdorf. Nine years later the court usher was told to withdraw bowling pins from children on the day of their catechism classes (ibid.).

Yet real politics within Christian ethics developed ways and means to play and be pious at the same time. Gerhard Tersteegen can be called an eighteenth century gamification expert for religious practice. His Pious Lottery[7] (1769) was a card game consisting of 365 cards that contained words of wisdom and advice for the believers. By randomly selecting a card from the deck of cards the pious gambler would perform two activities at the same time: playing an aleatoric game of cards and practicing Christian-minded devotion. Tersteegen's gamified prayer book was successful because of the popularity of profane lottery practice of the eighteenth century that his game appropriated and adapted for Tersteegen's own purposes. The sermonist announces his game as a lottery with no danger of losing; however, if you hit the jackpot ("drawing the best lot"), your prize will be unsurpassable:

---

5   Translation by the author, German original: "Er errichtete einen Berg von 3640 Brettspielen, an die 40.000 Würfel, Kartenspiele ohne Zahl und 72 Schlitten und verbrannte dieses sündhafte Luxuswerk" (Dirx 1981, 82).

6   Translation by the author, German original: "so daß sich allerhand Gesinde bei ihm einfinde und spiele" (Schmidt 2005, 255).

7   Translation by the author, German original: Der Frommen Lotterie. The Pious Lottery was part of Tersteegen's Geistliches Blumengärtlein. This book included the Pious Lottery at latest in the fourth edition, published in 1769.

This is a lottery for Believers,
and nothing can be lost,
Yet nothing would be better,
then drawing the best lot (Tersteegen 1769, title)[8]

Not everybody was happy with Tersteegen's ludification of serious content. One of his contemporaries and critics, Heinrich Konrad Scheffler, mocked the pious lottery in his essay from 1734 on strange religious practice: "Praxis pietatis curiosa" (Brückner 2010, 261) as not pleasing to God.

The itinerant preacher Tersteegen was faced with a problem that is not unlike today's problems of selling products with low use-value as desirable – or boring work as fun. Common eighteenth century practice of prescribing a prayer per day must have been extremely fatiguing for the average believers. When the radical pietist Tersteegen introduced *alea* (Caillois 2001 / 1958) he achieved what today's gamification evangelists try to accomplish: increasing customer loyalty with fun elements. "Gamification is Driving Loyalty" (Goldstein 2013), "Motivation + Big Data + Gamification = Loyalty 3.0" (Paharia 2013), "Gamification = Recognition, Growth + Fun" (DeMonte 2013). More than 200 years before the notion of gamification had been introduced, similar practices were already in use: establishing loyalty by hiding the primary company's goal and offering "peripheral or secondary mechanics" (Ciotti 2013) that establish pseudo goals and re-direct the attention of the customers, a.k.a. gamers.

2 GAMIFYING MUSIC AND DANCE

Contemporaries of Gerhard Tersteegen, Johann Philipp Kirnberger, Carl Philipp Emanuel Bach, and Maximilian Stadler worked on something that

---

8 Translation by the author, German original: "Diß ist der Frommen Lotterie,/ wobei man kann verlieren nie,/ das Nichts darin ist all so groß,/ als wann dir fiel das beste Los".

could be called the gamification of music[9] when introducing a ludic generator for musical composition.[10] Kirnberger's Ever-Ready Minuet and Polonaise Composer[11] was first published in 1757 and then again in a revised version in 1783. The game preceded the *Musikalisches Würfelspiel*[12] from 1792 that dubitably has been attributed to Wolfgang Amadeus Mozart. If Mozart was the author of the Musikalisches Würfelspiel, his intention was most likely to present and sell another virtuosity stunt and not to question the nature of composition. It is probably also fair to say that Mozart was not particularly hesitant in appropriating material and concepts from fellow composers and to polish them in his personal way to make them a successful commodity. The idea of Kirnberger's gamified system of composition as well as that of Mozart's was to propose that music could be conceived as a game that follows certain rules and is affected by an element of chance, or "alea" as Caillois would name it (Caillois 2001 / 1958). This idea is completely anti-classical and anti-romantic, but was epistemically coherent with the eighteenth century thought. It is therefore not surprising that systems like the

---

9   When eighteenth century musicians used card games and dice to facilitate composition processes, they aimed at something that is similar to contemporary gamification attempts in the field of marketing: The former wanted to implement a layer of fun and entertainment and they wanted the audience to believe that they were composing. Actually the audience did not compose, they were just instrumental in starting algorithmic processes. The latter try to implement a layer of fun and entertainment above the functional level of marketing and they want the customers to believe that they desire what they are told to desire. In both cases rule-based ludic systems serve as persuasive devices for subject matter that is not play. That is why I speak of gamification in the context of music and in the context of recent marketing, even though the object of gamification differs in both cases.

10 The examples for aleatoric composition methods given here do not make claims about the earliest attempts to do so. There is a history of aleatoric composition in the eighteenth century, in the digital age (Nierhaus 2009) and much earlier than that. Already in the seventeenth century, composers had begun thinking of a piece of music as a system of units which could be manipulated according to chance processes. Around 1650, the Jesuit Athanasius Kircher invented the arca musurgica, a box filled with cards containing short phrases of music. By drawing the cards in combination, one could assemble polyphonic compositions in four parts.

11 Translation by the author, German original: Der allezeit fertige Menuetten- und Polonaisencomponist.

12 English: Musical Dice Game.

Ever-Ready Minuet and Polonaise Composer or the Musikalisches Würfelspiel have been devised by various eighteenth century composers.

In 1758 Carl Philipp Emanuel Bach's *A Method for Making Six Bars of Double Counterpoint at the Octave without Knowing the Rules*[13] introduced a game for short compositions as a demonstration of method and a tool for rule-based composition. It would not be appropriate to criticise Johann Sebastian Bach's son for a mediocre quality of the counterpoint compositions produced. The compositional spirit of the eighteenth century was different to classical musical thinking and for the late Baroque composer the main achievement was to produce something that fitted the rules of musical craftsmanship as effectively as possible. Aesthetic subtlety was not the point.

Maximilian Stadler was another composer who worked with a set of dice. His *Table for composing minuets and trios to infinity, by playing with two dice*[14] was published in 1780 and might well have been the inspiration for Mozart's Würfelspiel. Stadler was friend to Mozart, Haydn, and Beethoven and it would not be too surprising, if Mozart had picked up a few ideas from Stadler when meeting in Vienna. Innovative ideas were not protected by copyright at the time of Mozart, and Mozart was reported to have appropriated material, ideas, and concepts from fellow composers. But it is also possible that Haydn, another friend of Stadler's, might have influenced Stadler, Mozart, or both of them when presenting his Game of Harmony, or an Easy Method for Composing an Infinite Number of Minuet-Trios, without Any Knowledge of Counterpoint,[15] which was published in 1790 or in 1793 in Naples by Luigi Marescalchi. The piece, which is said to have been written in the 1780s, is very close in concept and terminology to Stadler's Table. *À la infinite* is what Stadler had in mind and Haydn, if he really wrote the Gioco himself, refers to it as "infinito numero". Once more, it was the

---

13 Translation by the author, German original: *Einfall, einen doppelten Contrapunct in der Octave von sechs Tacten zu machen ohne die Regeln davon zu wissen.*

14 Translation by the author, French original: *Table pour composer des minuets et des Trios à la infinie; avec deux dez à jouer.*

15 Translation by the author, Italian original: Gioco filarmonico, o sia maniera facile per comporre un infinito numero di minuetti e trio anche senza sapere il contrapunto : da eseguirsi per due violini e basso, o per due flauti e basso.

easy method – *maniera facile* – that served as key motivation for composers of the eighteenth century to use gamification for the compositional process.

Leonard Meyer observes that the practice of aleatoric and ludic methods in musical composition and in musical performance are for good reasons present in the eighteenth century but hard to find in nineteenth century musical practice:

> Eighteenth-century composers constructed musical dice games while nineteenth century composers did not [. . . W]hat constrained the choice of figures were the claims of taste, coherent expression and propriety, given the genre of work being composed, rather than the inner necessity of a gradually unfolding, underlying process [as in nineteenth century music]. (Meyer 1989, 193)

I would argue here that gamification provides methods for coherence and propriety in the context of music – as has been demonstrated by Meyer –, but also in other contexts such as learning (cf. the section below), religious practice (cf. the section above) and dance. That is why the eighteenth century is a time when examples of predigital gamification can be found in many cases. Processes that are driven by gradually unfolding underlying structures are much harder to be gamified. The ludic turn of the eighteenth century became apparent not only in the passion for games, in ludified social manners, in religious practice or in music. It also shaped the way people used to dance then. In her "Sociology of Dance on Stage and in Ballrooms"[16] Reingard Witzmann notices that dance was conceived as a game in Mozart's Vienna. At the end of the last act of *Le Nozze di Figaro* Mozart calls the actors of *Le Nozze* to reassemble on stage and proclaim what could be called the motto of the century: *"Sposi, Amici, al Ballo, al Gioco!"* (Witzmann 2006, 403).[17]

There are two points I want to make here by putting examples from the gamification of music and dance in close vicinity to the gamification of religious practice of the very same decades:

---

16 Translation by the author, German original: "[. . .] Zur Soziologie des Gesellschaftstanzes auf der Bühne und im Ballsaal."

17 English: "Beloved ones, Friends, lets Dance, lets Play!".

1.   I'd like to support the concept of gamification as "permeation of society with methods, metaphors, values and attributes of games" (Fuchs 2011, 2013) as opposed to the idea that gamification can fully be understood as the transfer of game design elements to non-game contexts with no regard to the historical and social framing. The latter is symptomatic for most of the scholarly attempts to define gamification (Deterding et al. 2011[18], Schell 2010[19], Werbach and Hunter 2012[20]). If I understand Deterding, Dixon, Khaled and Nacke, Shell, Werbach and Hunter correctly, then a single instance of adapting game design elements for non-game contexts could qualify as gamification. My understanding of gamification differs from that and I would be extremely hesitant to theorise societally isolated actions like convenience store marketing or flight sales optimisation as relevant for the phenomenon of gamification, if they are detached from a historical view and a social perspective that includes cultural analysis on a global scale. The way I want to use the notion of gamification is in line with various "fications" and "izations" that have been introduced in the social sciences over the past 20 years. *Globalization* (Robertson 1992, Ritzer 2011), *McDonaldization* (Ritzer 1993), *Californication* (Red Hot Chilli Peppers 1999)[21], *Ludification* (Raessens 2006), *Americanization* (Kooijman 2013) or *Disneyization* (Bryman 1999, Hartley and Pearson 2000) are all based on the assumption that we observe large societal changes that are driven by apparatuses that influence various sectors of society at a time. Of course, McDonaldization cannot be attributed to a society as a result of a few fast-food restaurants having been spotted in countries other than the USA. It is a way of living based on an economic structure, a power structure, a number of neologisms and changes in spoken language, introduction of a set of

see also Raessens p. 95

---

18 See introduction to this article.

19 "Gamification is taking things that aren't games and trying to make them feel more like games" (Schell, 2010).

20 "Gamification is the application of game elements and digital game design techniques to non-game problems, such as business [...]" (Werbach and Hunter 2012).

21 The video to the rock song *Californication* by the Red Hot Chilli Peppers is a perfect example for gamification of pop music.

manners and habits, and a perceptual shift that make McDonaldization what it is (Kooijman 2013). I would in analogy claim that game design elements applied to non-game contexts do not make a society gamified. It is the permeation of many societal sectors with methods, metaphors, and values that stem from the sphere of play that produce gamification.

2.   I want to show here that certain historical constellations have provided fertile ground for the process of predigital gamification. The second half of the eighteenth century certainly was one of those. The intention is also to explain why certain moments in history lent themselves to foster gamification, and to propose a few good reasons why our decade seems to be one of those as well.

3   GAMIFYING THE MAGIC ARTS

In 1762 Wolfgang Schwarzkopf published a book in the German city of Nuremberg that presented an enlightened and new take on what formerly has been said to be black magic or premodern sorcery. Schwarzkopf subtitled the book *Playground of Rare Sciences*[22] and combined a description of mathematical and mechanical skills with essays about card and dice games followed by an encyclopaedic section of prestidigitator tricks. This book was one of many scientific attempts of the eighteenth century to reclaim magic and enchantment as playful activities – and to separate it from any connotations to diabolic and irrational activities. In their book *Rare Künste* Brigitte Felderer and Ernst Strouhal lay out how the cultural history of magic took a dramatic turn in the eighteenth century and abandoned medieval black magic in favour of a ludic activity (Felderer and Strouhal 2006). This new form of edutainment was based on an enlightened concept of popular science, socially embedded empirical research and a post-religious belief in the fact that the new type of magic had much more in common with science then with ritualistic or obscure practices from the past. As James George Frazer put it in his *Golden Bough*:

---

22   Translation by the author, German original: *Spielplatz rarer Künste.*

Magic is much closer to Science than it is to Religion. Different to what religion tells us, Magic and Science both are based on the presupposition that identical causes result in identical effects. (Frazer 1989, 70)

As a consequence, it made a lot of sense for the eighteenth century publisher to talk about "natural magic" – as Schellenberg did in 1802[23] – or "the magic of nature" – as done by Halle in 1783[24]. The reappearing pattern of legitimation for the act of talking about magic as a game and as science is the rhetoric figure that magic is useful in societal daily life and that it is entertaining: "Revised to Take Account of Entertainment and Serious Applications" (Halle in Huber 2006, 335) or "Useful for Social Life" (Schellenberg in ibid.). This line of argumentation can be followed via Goethe's *bonmot* of "scientific games like mineralogy and the likes"[25] (Kaiser 1967, 37)[26] up to the present. This is probably not the place to develop the idea, but I would speculate that the notion of *serious games* can be followed back to the eighteenth century programmatic efforts to declare magic as a game, and in doing so introducing the idea that science can be entertaining and that entertainment can be scientifically relevant. Today we call this project *edutainment*.

---

23 The full title of Schellenberg's book is *A Glance / at / Döbler's and Bosko's / Magical Cabinet, / Consisting of / New Enchantment from the Field of / Natural Magic / that is Useful for Social Life.* (Translation by the author, German original: *Ein Blick / in / Döbler's und Bosko's / Zauberkabinet, / bestehend / in neuen Belustigungen aus dem Gebiete / der natürlichen Magie, / im gesellschaftlichen Leben anwendbar*, Huber 2006, 335).

24 Johann Sebastian Halle's book was published by Joachim Pauli in 1783 in Berlin as *Magic, / or / Magical Power of Nature, / Revised to Take Account of Entertainment and Serious Applications.* (Translation by the author, German original: *Magie, / oder, die / Zauberkräfte der Natur, / so auf den Nutzen und die Belustigung / angewandt worden, / von / Johann Samuel Halle, / Professor des Königlich=Preußischen Corps des Cadets / in Berlin*, Huber 2006, 335).

25 Translation by the author, German original "wissenschaftliche Spiele wie die Mineralogie".

26 Johan Wolfgang von Goethe's autobiographical *raisonnement* called *From my Life: Poetry and Truth* (German original: *Aus meinem Leben. Dichtung und Wahrheit*) was written between 1808 and 1831. It is said to be a reflection on Goethe's life in the 1750s to 1770s. The phrase about "scientific games" is quoted from Kaiser 1967.

4 GAMIFYING LIFESTYLE IN THE "CENTURY OF PLAY"

In 1751 Daniel Bernoulli tried to catch the zeitgeist of his century by saying, "The century that we live in could be subsumed in the history books as: Free Spirits' Journal and the Century of Play" (Bauer 2006, 377).[27] Bernoulli expressed an observation about the gamification of lifestyle that was based on observations in Vienna, but was valid for the main European capitals like Paris, Rome, London, the Haag, and Naples. The gaming culture was a pan-European phenomenon based on widely distributed types of games and game rules. *L'Hombre* (14th century), for example, was a game of cards originally developed in Spain, then picked up by Maria Theresia, the wife of Louis XIV, and was within a few years played in all European countries with only a few local variations.[28] This made it possible for a new travelling social class that extended beyond aristocracy to engage in gaming as a European lingua franca. Frequent travellers such as Mozart or Johann Wolfgang von Goethe could expect to find a gaming community in almost every city in Europe that they could share experiences and social skills with. Instructions for games like the mid-eighteenth century "Pleasant Pastime with enchanting and joyful Games to be played in Society" (ibid., 383)[29] were translated into most of the European languages and became popular among people of different social classes (ibid.). Lotteries could be found everywhere and became a source of income for some and a serious economic problem for others. Hazardous games or *jeux de contrepartie*, such as the *Pharo* (18th century) game or *Hasard* (14th century) were temporarily banned.

The eighteenth century was also the time when "*apartements pour le jeu*", or play rooms, were introduced in the houses of the aristocracy as well as in houses of the bourgeoisie. Special furniture was designed to both display

---

27 Translation by the author, German original: "Das gegenwärtige Jahrhundert könnte man in den Geschichtsbüchern nicht besser, als unter dem Titel: Das Freygeister=Journal und Spielsaeculum nennen".

28 In Spain the game was called "Juego del tresillo" and there was the Spanish set of cards used lacking the eights and nines.

29 Translation by the author, German original: "Angenehmer Zeitvertreib lustiger Scherz-Spiele in Compagnien" (anonymous 1757, quoted by Bauer 2006, 383).

well-designed games and to hide such games from view.[30] Social lifestyle evolved from the seventeenth to the eighteenth century through gamification: via the increased availability of games and gaming circles, trans-European distribution channels for gaming, and social acceptance that transcended class and social group. This is why Bernoulli's proposition to call the eighteenth century the "Century of Play" makes a lot of sense. Having said so, Bernoulli was unable to see how another wave of gamification would change another century; nevertheless, the twenty-first century is about to repeat the games craze of the eighteenth century. Today we see ubiquitous availability, transplanetary distribution channels, and an acceptance of computer games that transcends class and social group, and games no longer belong to any age group, ethnicity, gender, or subculture.

5 GAMIFYING LEARNING

In 1883 Samuel Langhorne Clemens, also known as Mark Twain, was trying to create an easy way for his daughters to remember the English monarchs and the dates when they commenced and finished ruling. Twain described the problem he was faced with in his notebooks: "It was all dates, they all looked alike, and they wouldn't stick" (Twain 2009). So Twain figured out a playful method of remembering dates, names, and numbers by mapping them to positions on a piece of land. He measured out 817 feet – each foot representing a year – and then put stakes in the ground where kings and queens started their reigns. His daughters remembered the dates by remembering spatial positions. "When you think of Henry III, do you see a great long stretch of straight road? I do; and just at the end where it joins on to Edward I. I always see a small pear-bush with its green fruit hanging down" (ibid.), he wrote.

When Twain's daughters learned the monarchs' dates in two days (they had been trying all summer), he knew he had discovered an efficient method for gamified learning. After a couple of years of tinkering, Twain patented the Memory Builder (1895): A Game for Acquiring and Retaining All Sorts of Facts and Dates. It consisted of a game board similarly divided by years.

---

30 See Salomon Kleiner's "apartements pour les jeu" from the first half of eighteenth century as found in Lachmayer 2006.

The game included straight pins, and players would stick a pin in the appropriate compartment to show that they knew the date of the event in question. Points were awarded based on the size of the event and how specific players could get on the date.

Mark Twain's invention introduced two elements of play into a teacher-learner relationship. On the one hand, he declared learning as an entertaining activity by framing it within a board game. On the other, he gamified historical data as spatial information. Information and knowledge about time and chronological order is reframed as spatial relationship. In terms of Derridean philosophy there is some type of play taking place (and taking time) on a semiotic level and the level of the very game's board. According to Derrida there is *différance*, an active movement involving spacing and temporalising. The presence of one element cannot compensate for the absence of the other. A gap or interval remains that escapes complete identity. "Constituting itself, dynamically dividing itself, this interval is what could be called spacing; time's becoming-spatial or space's becoming temporal (*temporalizing*)" (Derrida 1972 / 1968, 143). Mark Twain's board game therefore plays on two levels: The game is obviously a playful approach to teaching history as it differs from traditional and rather solemn forms of classroom lectures. The second level of play is a metalevel of spacing and temporalising, as described by Derrida. The instructions for the Memory Builder game state that:

1. The board represents *any* century.
2. Also, it represents *all* centuries.

This is what would have to be called dynamic spacing in Derrida's words or an ambiguous and playful potential for spatialisation of historical data. The player in this learning application encounters history as gamified and not as a solid body of knowledge based on numbers only.

6   GAMIFYING KILLING

In this section of the article, I want to present a rather small number of examples how the act of killing and the selection of victims can be gamified. I am not going to differentiate between military-action killing as the so-called legal procedure during war and illegal activity by gangs or individual gangsters.

It seems to me that it is impossible to differentiate between those two except on a cynical level. My intention is rather to show how the selection of victims can be influenced by a games system with proper rules and an outcome to the game played. The examples I would like to choose are the infrequent process of decimation in the Roman army and other military forces and an example taken from literature that is based on aleatoric gaming.

Roman praetor Marcus Crassus, when sent to the south of Italy in 71 BC during the Spartacan revolt, noticed that Mummius, one of Crassus' officers, had engaged the rebels in an early fight and lost. Many of his troops deserted the field instead of fighting. Crassus, in response to this embarrassment, ordered his legions decimated. The process of decimation is an aleatoric process that results in what Roman law would consider fair by selecting one out of ten accused to be killed. The logic in devising such an inhuman procedure, which seems completely unfair to us, is ludic. The rationale of random killing refers to a concept of Fortuna being both blind and just at the same time. Gamified mechanics of killing can therefore not be called unfair, a cheat, corrupt, or meaningless – if one believes in the apparatus of play, they must be seen instead as the ultimate form of game-inherent logic. I have tried to suggest in another publication that this circle of perfect logic makes gamification a perfect case of ideology in the sense of Sohn-Rethel's understanding of ideology, i.e. *necessary false consciousness* (Fuchs 2014).

> **"The century that we live in could be subsumed in the history books as . . . the Century of Play"**
>
> - *Daniel Bernoulli, 1751*

The idea to use alea is not an exclusively military accomplishment. Small crime can sometimes arrive at similar methods to solve problems. So did Anton Chigurh in *No Country for Old Men* (McCarthy 2005). Chigurgh forces his victims to have him toss a coin, and to be killed or left alive depending on the outcome of the coin toss. The perfidiousness of delegating a vital decision upon chance is in line with the rationale of Roman martial law to decimate the legions. Chigurh's motivation to allow for an escape from the fatal consequences of his manhunts has been speculated about at great length. Isabel Exner describes the killer as *"Homo aleator"* who introduces a de-individualised form of violence. (Exner 2010, 61) This "new man" is obviously a counter-concept to the traditional heroes of Western movies: The sheriff, the honest loner who is looking for revenge, and the intelligent gangster are both *"Homo faber"* type characters. They could solve their respective problems via individualised decision-making and action. Isabel Exner's proposition for the emergence of the *Homo aleator* in *No Country for Old Men* is not exclusively cinematic or related to the history of American movies and crime stories. Exner suggests that chance has become "the fundamental working principle of the prevailing order [. . .] that has already integrated Michel Serre's finding, that 'chance, risk, terror and even chaos have the potential to consolidate the system'" (ibid.).[31]

7 CONCLUSION

This article cannot provide the reader with a complete history of gamification and gamification-related historical documents to prove that something that we call gamification now has happened already in former centuries. Neither can I sum up all of the possible differences that might exist between games of former centuries and computer games of our days. My main hypothesis is that we can detect similarities in aspects of the games hype, games craze, seriousness of games, and of a process that transforms non-game contexts into playgrounds for ludic activities and of ludic experience across centuries. Such playgrounds could once be found in learning, religious practice, music, magic, dance, theatre, and lifestyle. Such playgrounds for ludic activities can be spotted equally well nowadays: When we look at theatre theory and find "Game Theatre" (Rakow 2013); when we look at religious blogs and find "Gamifying Religion" (Toler 2013); when we look at the information from health services and find "Fun Ways to Cure Cancer" (Scott 2013) or "Dice Game Against Swine Flu" (Marsh and Boffey 2009); or when we investigate collective water management and find "Games to Save Water" (Meinzen-Dick 2013).

It is the range of applications and not the individual examples that support the hypothesis that gamification takes place as a global trend, a new form of ideology – or as a *dispositif*, if you will. This is not exclusively

---

31 Translation by the author, German original: "das basale Funktionsprinzip einer herr-schenden Ordnung [. . .] die Serres' Erkenntnis längst integriert hat, dass 'Zufall, Risiko, Angst und selbst Unordnung ein System zu konsolidieren vermögen'". Exner quotes Michel Serres here from: *Der Parasit* (1987), page 29.

dependent on the digitalisation of society or the massive economic success of computer games. What I have tried to demonstrate here is a historic perspective on an understanding of gamification as a way of living (and dying), making music, selling and buying, engaging in economic processes and power structures, communicating, and introducing new manners and habits for a decade or a whole century. This can be the decade of the 2010s, but it can also be the eighteenth century, the "Century of Play" – *Spielsaeculum* – as Bernoulli called the century in which he was living in 1751.

The second half of the eighteenth century shared "pragmatic-relevant networking" (Lachmayer 2006, 35) with our days. The contemporaries of Wolfgang Amadeus Mozart, Schikaneder, Tersteegen, Casanova, Bernoulli, Schwarzkopf, and Stadler were deeply involved in a European "supra-nationality" (ibid.) that assembled a multiplicity of languages, lifestyles, games, and sources of knowledge; all of which somehow resembles our activities on the World Wide Web – without being worldwide then. Still powered by the naivety of a desire for unfiltered access to a variety of scientific, semi-scientific, popular, or superstitious forms of knowledge, the enlightened and the not-so-enlightened of the eighteenth century were striving for visions of progress. Playfulness on a personal level that included *mimesis*, *alea* and *ilinx* (Caillois 2001 / 1958) was a driver for *caprice* and virtuality rather than flat realism. The ludicity of the times was conducive to multifaceted identities and strictly contradictory to a monosequential development of character and career that later centuries required for social inclusion. It might be that we have returned to the state of Mozartesque playfulness and that the gamification of our society sets up a scenario for an intelligent plurality of expression, experience, and knowledge on a global level. Not completely serious, but myth-making and myth-breaking at the same time.

It might, however, also be true that our decade resembles the second half of the eighteenth century in a way that Doris Lessing once described with these words: "This country becomes every day more like the eighteenth century, full of thieves and adventurers, rogues and a robust, unhypocritical savagery side-by-side with people lecturing others on morality" (Fielding 1992, 762). Rococo culture developed a style that was jocular, florid, and graceful, while at the same time being full of sophisticated coarseness. And is this not identical to the state that our discourse on gamification is at. We want to be SuperBetter (2012) and want to enjoy "self-expansion escapism" (Kollar 2013).

We are slightly worried about it and we speculate about a forthcoming "revolution" (Zichermann 2013), yet we shout out loudly "Gamification is Bullshit!" (Bogost 2011). We finally discover that "gamification is transforming our world, contaminating it like never before" (Reilhac 2010).

That's so Rococo!

BIBLIOGRAPHY

BAUER, GÜNTHER. 2006. "Mozart, Kavalier und Spieler." In *Mozart: Experiment Aufklärung*, edited by Herbert Lachmayer, 377–388. Ostfildern: Hatje Cantz.

BOGOST, IAN. 2011. "Gamification Is Bullshit! My Position Statement at the Wharton Gamification Symposium." *Ian Bogost Blog*, August 8.
http://www.bogost.com/blog/gamification_is_bullshit.shtml.

BRÜCKNER, SHIRLEY. 2010. "Losen, Däumeln, Nadel, Würfeln." In *Spiel und Bürgerlichkeit: Passagen des Spiels I*, edited by Ernst Strouhal and Ulrich Schädler. Wien, New York: Springer.

BRYMAN, ALAN. 1999. "The Disneyization of Society." *Sociological Review* 47(1): 25–47.

CAILLOIS, ROGER. 2001 / 1958. *Man, Play and Games*. Urbana: University of Illinois.

CIOTTI, GREGORY. 2013. "Gamification and Customer Loyalty: The Good, The Bad, and The Ugly." *Help Scout*, May 1.
https://www.helpscout.net/blog/gamification-loyalty/.

CORRY, WILL. 2011. "Games for Brands Conference, Launching I London on October 27th." *TheMarketingblog Extra*, September 11.
http://wcorry.blogspot.de/2011_09_11_archive.html.

DEMONTE, ADENA. 2013. "What Motivates Employees Today?" Accessed February 25, 2014.
http://badgeville.com/2013/06/13/what-motivates-employees-today/.

DERRIDA, JACQUES. 1972 / 1968. *Differance, Speech, and Phenomena*. Evanston: Northwestern University Press.

DETERDING, SEBASTIAN, DAN DIXON, RILLA KHALED AND LENNART NACKE. 2011. "From Game Design Elements to Gamefulness: Defining Gamification." In *Proceedings of the 15th International Academic MindTrek Conference: Envisioning Future Media Environments*, 9-15. New York: ACM.

DIRX, RUTH. 1981. *Das Buch vom Spiel*. Gelnhausen: Burckhardthaus-Verlag.

EXNER, ISABEL. 2010. "Verbrechen Als Spiel? Aleatorik im Krimi (Jorge Luis Borges, Cormac McCarthy, Etan und Joel Coen)." In *Das Spiel und Seine Grenzen. Passagen des Spiels II*, edited by Mathias Fuchs and Ernst Strouhal, 47-66. Vienna, New York: Springer.

FELDERER, BRIGITTE AND ERNST STROUHAL. 2006. *Rare Künste: Zur Kultur- und Mediengeschichte der Zauberkunst*. Vienna, New York: Springer.

FIELDING, HENRY. 1992. *Tom Jones*. Ware, Hertfordshire: Wordsworth Classics.

FLEMING, NIC. 2012. "Gamification: Is It Game Over?" *BBC*, December 5. Accessed January 9, 2014.
http://www.bbc.com/future/story/20121204-can-gaming-transform-your-life.

FRAZER, JAMES GEORGE. 1989. *Der Goldene Zweig. Das Geheimnis von Glauben und Sitten der Völker*. Reinbek: Rowohlt.

FUCHS, MATHIAS. Forthcoming. "Subversive Gamification." In *Playing the System: The Playful Subversion of Technoculture*, edited by Daniel Cermak-Sassenrath, Chek Tien Tan and Charles Walker. Singapore: Springer.

FUCHS, MATHIAS. 2013. "Serious Games Conference 2013: Erfolgreiches Comeback Nach Einjähriger Pause." Accessed February 27, 2014.
http://www.biu-online.de/de/presse/newsroom/newsroom-detail/datum/2013/03/13/serious-games-conference-2013-erfolgreiches-comeback-nach-einjaehriger-pause.html.

FUCHS, MATHIAS. 2011. *Ludification: Ursachen, Formen und Auswirkungen der 'Ludification'*. Potsdam: Arbeitsberichte der Europäischen Medienwissenschaften an der Universität Potsdam.

GARTNER, INC. 2011. "Gartner Says By 2015, More Than 50 Percent of Organizations That Manage Innovation Processes Will Gamify Those Processes." Accessed January 9, 2014.
http://www.gartner.com/newsroom/id/1629214.

GOETHE, JOHAN WOLFGANG. 2001 / 1808–1831. *Aus Meinem Leben. Dichtung und Wahrheit*. Leipzig: Reclam.

GOLDSTEIN, MARK. 2013. "Reinventing Loyalty with Gamification." Accessed March 31, 2014.
http://de.slideshare.net/gzicherm/mark-goldstein-gamificationpresto.

HARTLEY, JOHN AND ROBERTA E. PEARSON. 2000. *American Cultural Studies: A Reader*. Oxford: Oxford University Press.

HUBER, VOLKER. 2006. "Magisch-Bibliographische Erkundungen." In *Rare Künste: Zur Kultur- und Mediengeschichte der Zauberkunst*, edited by Ernst Strouhal, and Brigitte Felderer, 313-338. Vienna, New York: Springer.

KAISER, WOLFGANG. 1967. *Kunst und Spiel. Fünf Goethe-Studien*. Göttingen: Vandenhoeck & Ruprecht.

KOLLAR, PHILIP. 2013. "Jane McGonigal on the Good and Bad of Video Game Escapism." *Polygon*, March 28.
http://www.polygon.com/2013/3/28/4159254/jane-mcgonigal-video-game-escapism.

KOOIJMAN, JAAP. 2013. *Fabricating the Absolute Fake. America in Contemporary Pop Culture*. Amsterdam: Amsterdam University Press.

LACHMAYER, HERBERT. 2006. *Mozart. Aufklärung im Wien des Ausgehenden 18. Jahrhundert*, Ostfildern: Hatje Cantz.

MARCZEWSKI, ANDRZEJ. 2012. *Gamification: A Simple Introduction & a Bit More*. Self Publishing.

Markets and Markets. 2013. "Gamification Market." Accessed January 9, 2014. http://www.marketsandmarkets.com/Market-Reports/gamification-market-991.html.

Marsh, Beezy and Daniel Boffey. 2009. "Fluedo: Health Chiefs Introduce Their Latest Weapon in the War Against Swine Flu... a Dice Game." *Dailymail*, August 30. Accessed January 15, 2014. http://www.dailymail.co.uk/health/article-1209974/Fluedo-Health-chiefs-introduce-latest-weapon-war-swine-flu.html.

McCarthy, Cormac. 2005. *No Country for Old Men*. New York: Alfred A. Knopf.

McGonigal, Jane. 2011. *Reality Is Broken. Why Games Make Us Better and How They Can Change the World*. New York: Penguin.

Meinzen-Dick, Ruth. 2013. "Playing Games to Save Water." *IFPRI*, March 22. http://www.ifpri.org/blog/playing-games-save-water.

Meyer, Leonard. 1989. *Style and Music: Theory, History, and Ideology*. Philadelphia: The University of Pennsylvania Press.

Mosca, Ivan. 2012. "+10! Gamification and deGamification." *GAME* 1(1). http://www.gamejournal.it/plus10_gamification-and-degamification/#.UwtTd_R5OA8.

Nierhaus, Gerhard. 2009. *Algorithmic Composition: Paradigms of Automated Music Generation*. Wien, New York: Springer.

Paharia, Rajat. 2013. "Loyalty 3.0: Big Data and Gamification Revolutionizing Engagement." http://de.slideshare.net/gzicherm/rajat-pahariag-summit2013.

Palmer, Doug, Steve Lunceford and Aaron J. Patton. 2012. "The Engagement Economy: How Gamification is Reshaping Businesses." *Deloitte Review* 11: 52–69.

Raessens, Joost. 2006. "Playful Identities, or the Ludification of Culture." *Games and Culture* 1(1): 52–57. London: SAGE Journals.

Rakow, Christian. 2013. "rePLAYCE:theCITY." Accessed January 15, 2014. http://www.trans4mator.net/styled-2/page9/index.html.

Red Hot Chilli Peppers. 1999. *Californication*. Warner Bros. Compact Disc.

Reilhac, Michel. 2010. "The Gamification of Life." *Power to the Pixel*, October 26. http://thepixelreport.org/2010/10/26/the-game-ification-of-life/.

Ritzer, George. 2011. *Globalization: The Essentials*. New York: John Wiley & Sons.

Ritzer, George. 1993. *The McDonaldization of Society*. London: SAGE Publications.

Ritschl, Albrecht. 1884. *Geschichte des Pietismus in 3 Bänden*. Bonn: Adolph Marcus.

Robertson, Roland. 1992. *Globalization: Social Theory and Global Culture*. London: Sage.

Schell, Jesse 2010. "When Games Invade Real Life." Accessed March 31, 2014. http://www.ted.com/talks/jesse_schell_when_games_invade_real_life.html.

Schmidt, Sebastian. 2005. *Glaube - Herrschaft - Disziplin. Konfessionalisierung und Alltagskultur in den Ämtern Siegen und Dillenburg (1538-1683)*. Paderborn: Ferdinand Schöningh.

Scott, Hilda. 2013. "Amazon, Facebook And Google Design Fun Way To Cure Cancer." *iTechPost*, March 1. http://www.itechpost.com/articles/5935/20130301/amazon-facebook-google-design-game-cure-cancer-research-uk.htm.

Serres, Michel. 1987. *Der Parasit*. Frankfurt am Main: Suhrkamp.

Tersteegen, Gerhart. 1729-1769. *Geistliches Blumen=Gärtlein Inniger Seelen. oder, Kurtze Schluß=Reimen, Betrachtungen und Lieder, Über Allerhand Wahrheiten des Inwendigen Christentums*. Frankfurt and Leipzig: G.C.B. Hoffmann.

Toler, Jonathan. 2013. "Gamifying Religion Part 1." Accessed January 15, 2014. http://www.jonathantoler.com/2013/01/gamification/gamifying-religion-part-1/.

Travers, Pamela Lyndon. 1934. *Mary Poppins*. London: HarperCollins.

Twain, Mark (Samuel Langhorne Clemens). 2009. "How to make History Dates Stick." Accessed March 31, 2014.
http://www.gutenberg.org/files/70/70-h/70-h.htm#link2H_4_0005.

Werbach, Kevin and Dan Hunter. 2012. *For The Win. How Game Thinking Can Revolutionize Your Business*. Philadelphia: Wharton Digital Press.

Witzmann, Reingard. 2006. "'Sposi, Amici, al Ballo, al Gioco!...' Zur Soziologie des Gesellschaftstanzes auf der Bühne und im Ballsaal." In *Mozart. Experiment Aufklärung*, edited by Herbert Lachmayer, 403-414. Ostfildern: Hatje Cantz.

Wolferz, Louis E. 1916. "The Rime Technique in the Poems of Reinmar von Zweter." PhD diss., Cornell University.

Zichermann, Gabe and Christopher Cunningham. 2011. *Gamification by Design: Implementing Game Mechanics in Web and Mobile Apps*. Sebastopol: O'Reilly.

Zichermann, Gabe and Joselin Linder. 2013. *The Gamification Revolution. How Leaders Leverage Game Mechanics to Crush the Competition*. New York: McGraw-Hill Professional.

LUDOGRAPHY

Der allezeit fertige Menuetten- und Polonaisencomponist. 1757. Developed by Johann Philipp Kirnberger. Musical game.

Der Frommen Lotterie. 1769. Developed by Gerhard Tersteegen. Card game.

Einfall, einen doppelten Contrapunct in der Octave von sechs Tacten zu machen ohne die Regeln davon zu wissen. 1758. Developed by Carl Philipp Emanuel Bach. Musical game.

Gioco filarmonico, o sia maniera facile per comporre un infinito numero di minuetti e trio anche senza sapere il contrapunto : da eseguirsi per due violini e basso, o per due flauti e basso. 1790 (or 1793). Probably developed by Joseph Haydn. Musical game. Luigi Marescalchi.

Hasard. 14th century (or earlier). Dice game.

L'Hombre. 14th century. Spain. Card game.

Memory-Builder: A Game for Acquiring and Retaining All Sorts of Facts and Dates. 1895. Developed by Mark Twain. Open-air game.

Musikalisches Würfelspiel. 1792. Developed by Nikolaus Simrock (or arguably Wolfgang Amadeus Mozart). Musical game.

Pharo. 18th century. Card game.

SuperBetter. 2012. Jane McGonigal.
https://www.superbetter.com.

MAKING POINTS THE POINT: TOWARDS A HISTORY OF IDEAS OF GAMIFICATION

by **Felix Raczkowski**

INTRODUCTION

Digital games are about points. Or so it seems, at least according to a constantly growing body of guidebook-like publications that inform us of the most important qualities of games and their potential to be of use in various fields. These books advocate gamification in one way or another, even though some of them avoid the term (Chatfield 2010; Dignan 2011), while others embrace it openly (Zichermann and Cunningham 2011, Werbach and Hunter 2012). Gamification, which is a problematic concept at best and remains highly contested and criticised (cf. Bogost 2011), is usually defined as a technique that seeks to apply game mechanics to non-game contexts (Graft 2011; Deterding et al. 2011), thereby aiming to "transplant" some of the motivational qualities of games into contexts that are not inherently leisure-focused or motivating in themselves. Thus, they are employed in marketing and PR (Zichermann and Linder 2010), consulting (Edery and Mollick 2009; Beck and Wade 2004), or self-optimisation (Dignan 2011). The theories informing these applications express certain assumptions about the nature and the potential of digital games. The following chapter will give a brief overview of some of the results of an extensive review of publications on gamification, especially focusing on the alleged qualities of digital games as they are mentioned by said publications. I will then attempt to develop a preliminary history of ideas for one of the core concepts of digital games according to gamification. By historically contextualising gamification and the assumptions it makes, it then becomes possible to develop a notion of what digital games are becoming and how this development is influenced by the way games are used by and positioned in modern society.

Points and scores appear to be the ultimate device for keeping track of the game state in digital games. As Juul (2005) asserts, one of the most obvious yet far-reaching results of the digitalisation of games is the fact that the management of the game state is accomplished by a computer and thus becomes automated. In these ludic environments, points feature prominently, be it as high-scores (indicating dominance over contenders) or as markers of progression (indicating player actions that are assigned some kind of value in the game). Even meta-gaming services like the Xbox or Playstation player profiles are largely built around points in the form of gamer-scores or trophy values. Small wonder, then, that points and scores are among the most frequently mentioned characteristics in gamification guidebooks. The popular literature[1] on gamification is very varied regarding the fields of application that are suggested, but shows great similarities in its views on digital games. Several assumptions concerning digital games can be singled out, three of which will be presented in the form of preliminary categorisations:

GAMES AS EXPERIMENTAL TECHNIQUES

Games have negotiable consequences. This feature of games is a prominent part of many definitions of digital games, as evidenced by Juul's literature review (2005, 29–36) and, while being controversial[2], it is part of an important argument in many guidebooks: digital games are presented as experimental environments in which certain tests, but also training, can be con-

---

1 The study focuses almost exclusively on popular publications instead of scientific research because they make up the bulk of publications on gamification and supposedly influence how gamification is actually implemented and, through this implementation, how digital games are perceived by those that gamify and those that participate in gamified systems.

2 Especially in debates on gambling, multiplayer games, or media harm, which often revolve around the question of the real-life consequence of gaming.

ducted in a less expensive way, without the fear of consequences beyond the game-world. Chatfield (2010) states that game-like systems are ideal training grounds for future soldiers (ibid., 193). Dignan (2011) similarly points out that games do not punish risky behaviour like non-game contexts would and that they are ideal for facing fears in the repetitive safety of simulated environments (ibid., 44, 45). Beck and Wade (2004) underline that "[g]ames are great practice for real life" (ibid., 75). Edery and Mollick (2009) directly refer to the capabilities of training games to induce experimentation that would otherwise be impossible (ibid., 126).

Interestingly, these perspectives tie into a strong and convincing argument that has become popular in game studies in recent years. The assumption that games can develop especially persuasive capacities because they can model systems (and their processes) through other systems (and processes) is commonly known as proceduralism and has been widely popularised through two consecutive books by Ian Bogost (2006; 2007). Although Bogost does not think of digital games in terms of experiments, but instead focuses on their similarities to simulations, some of his conclusions regarding the potential of digital games as a medium of persuasion (e.g. for advertising purposes) are very similar to the arguments proposed by gamification guidebooks.

GAMES AS SOURCES OF FLOW

A second aspect touched upon by many guidebooks concerns the psychological notion of flow, first described in 1975 by Mihaly Csikszentmihalyi, since which it has enjoyed an impressive career in game research. Csikszentmihalyi originally focused on the question of optimal experience and the actions and circumstances that afford it, demanding for work to be structured more like a game (Csikszentmihalyi 2008, 152). Specifically, he identified goal-orientation and rules as well as (among others) feedback and an altered sense of time (ibid., 49). Because of these characteristics,

Csikszentmihalyi proposes that even daily routines[3] could be transformed into optimal experiences by turning them into "personally meaningful games" (ibid., 51): "Mowing the lawn or waiting in a dentist's office can become enjoyable provided one restructures the activity by providing goals, rules and the other elements of enjoyment . . ." (ibid., 51). This leads to the reception of his theory in the context of gamification: the careful balance between challenge (through the task or environment) and ability (to meet said challenge) creates a particular state during which players feel challenged in just the right way, play extensively, and tend to forget their surroundings. As such, flow is a ubiquitous concept in gamification discourse. Especially its alleged effect of focusing attention is highlighted (Reeves and Read 2009, 182–184), among the advice to become one's own flow-designer through making a game of everyday chores (Dignan 2011, 6–8) and the ability of well-made games to absorb their players and circumvent boredom (Chatfield 2010, 43, 51). Of course, ultimately most guidebooks seek to "transplant" the flow caused by digital games into non-game activities, e.g. to structure business operations or work in general more like a game (Edery and Mollick 2009, 159).

GAMES AS GOVERNED BY POINTS AND HIGH-SCORES

The previously discussed aspects of digital games according to gamification are of a theoretical nature; they concern characteristics that are argued to be somehow connected to or adaptable by games without necessarily being game-intrinsic. The matter of high-scores is somewhat different in that (feedback) systems based on collecting and earning points are evidently featured in many games. The impact these systems have on actual gameplay varies, but they can be singled out as important arguments for the merits of games

---

3 Interestingly, it should be noted that Csikszentmihalyi at first concentrated his research efforts on very particular activities, such as performing surgery or climbing (Csikszentmihalyi 2008, 4). This would make flow in its original conception a supremely rare occurrence. Only later did he broaden the scope of his research to include, among others, assembly line workers. Thus flow became more common among different activities, though it still remained difficult to attain. The factory worker Csikszentmihalyi cites as one of his case studies has decades of experience and "mastered every phase of the plant's operation" (ibid., 148). This difficulty of actually meeting the requirements to attain flow is frequently disregarded by popular literature on gamification.

in gamification literature, according to which points and scores fulfil two main goals: they measure and they reward players. The former is evidenced by Chatfield, who enthusiastically points out: "[G]ame technologies excel at nothing so much as scoring, comparing and rewarding progress [. . .]" (Chatfield 2010, 199). Besides underlining the allure that points have as a scoring measure, Dignan describes their effect as "magical": "We see them as a reward, even when they're worthless, because they are a form of validation. Points represent an abstraction of value and so we often act irrationally when points are in the mix" (Dignan 2011, 155). This irrationality also forms the basis for Zichermann and Linder's advice for "making points the point" (2010, 68). Their gamified marketing strategies put high-scores and points in a central position because they can simulate value without actually granting benefits (ibid., 122–126), while at the same time sparking competition among customers through leaderboards (ibid., 55–64). This approach of assigning points to everything has not been criticised very often in the reviewed popular literature. Edery and Mollick point out that using points to make work feel like play could encourage cheating or power-gaming, decidedly undesirable behaviours in work environments (Edery and Mollick 2009, 168, 169).

Gamification guidebooks display ideological notions of what digital games are and how they work. The attributes mentioned above, compiled from groups of propositions, are not exhaustive and the list could be expanded in various levels of detail. This chapter is limited only to the most common of the features that were mentioned in relation to games in the reviewed literature. The next section of the chapter is concerned with contextualising these findings in what is to be the first sketch in a larger project on the history of ideas that pervades the discourse of gamification.

TOKEN ECONOMIES AND THE ALLURE OF SCORING

It has been shown that points and scores are paramount in today's popular theories on gamification. It seems opportune to discuss these systems in the light of their role in the media history of digital games, especially in the context of arcade gaming in the late 70s and 80s (cf. Kent 2001) and the first fan-driven attempts to develop nationwide leaderboards[4], thus adding additional social value to singular score. Instead, my approach is more in line with what gamification aspires to do. Point-based, closed systems are not to be seen as inherently ludic phenomena, but as arrangements of human motivation, measurement, and experimentation that can be traced to psychiatric experiments. The point systems of today, presented as formulas for the success of digital games that can be detached from said games and applied to marketing or consulting, are revisiting experimental approaches to behaviour modification that came to be known as token economies in the 1960s. Through reading the psychiatric method of the token economy against the backdrop of gamification discourse, the hierarchical and de-humanising structures both have in common will become apparent.

Token economies essentially were first conceived as a point- or token-based experimental rehabilitation treatment for long-term psychiatric patients. The first experiment began in 1961 at Anna State Hospital, Illinois, and was conducted by Teodoro Ayllon and Nathan Azrin. This pioneering effort still remains the best documented one. The token economy as developed by Ayllon and Azrin can be seen as an effort among a larger tendency to influence human behaviour through behavioural methods (Kazdin 1978). Generally, whenever a behaviour occurs that is to be strengthened (made to occur more often), reinforcement is made accessible to the patients, usually through an attendant. These reinforcements may range from handing out candy to offering intangible benefits such as praise. Tokens were a regular feature in many of the experiments, mostly because they guarantee a standardised and easily quantifiable way to control the reinforcement procedure (Ayllon and Azrin 1968, 77). The tokens are handed out and can be exchanged for tangible rewards later on. Token reward systems were used already at the end of the 1950s, for example in experiments with children with learning disabilities (Kazdin 1978, 253). The novelty of Ayllon and Azrin's approach is a matter of scope. Their goal was to create an effective "motivating environment" (Ayllon and Azrin 1968, 5) that would reinforce desirable behaviour and cause undesirable behaviour to become extinct. Thus, the

---

4   cf. Twin Galaxies: https://web.archive.org/web/20050613073727/http://www.twingalaxies.com/index.aspx?c=17&id=332 (accessed May 7, 2014).

experiment encompassed the whole closed psychiatric ward of Anna State Hospital and lasted for six years (ibid., 16), during which different series of experiments with varying parameters were conducted. The motivating environment of the token economy focuses on behaviour modification for long-term inmates, who are to be motivated and behaviouristically prepared for release from the ward. To achieve this, basically every desired activity (usually work assignments on the hospital grounds) earns the patients performing it a specific amount of tokens, while all items or activities that are coveted among the patients are assigned a specific cost of tokens. Only if the patients are able to pay the cost are they given the item or allowed to perform the activity. Patients have to pay tokens if they want private audiences with psychologists as well as for extra clothing, consumable articles, or even an additional religious service (Bandura 1969, 263).

Structurally, there are several similarities between how token economies handle their tokens and how points are treated in the gamification discourse. The general goal of a motivating environment seems almost identical, whether employees, customers, or psychiatric patients are to be motivated. The specific method of influencing or changing behaviour is what ties gamification approaches directly to behaviourism, as has already been shown (Deterding et al. 2011). The irrational actions that are ascribed to point-based games in gamification literature (cf. Zichermann and Linder 2010; Dignan 2011) in behaviouristic terms are nothing else than specific changes of behaviour that are the result of directed reinforcements. Token economies largely offer tangible rewards where gamification specifically labours to validate points through themselves. However, even the first major book on token economies already mentions the possibility of detaching the reinforcement from actual physical rewards: reading a mail-order catalogue without ordering anything is identified as a reinforcer to the patients (Ayllon and Azrin 1968, 69, 70). The same publication discusses the replacement of (tangible) tokens with (intangible) points or credits:

In addition, the points are standardized, have a simple quantitative dimension, and are not easily altered or destroyed since the record of the points or credits can be safeguarded. The disadvantages of points and credits are that they are intangible and hence are not in the individual's possession during the delay interval. Their intangibility also limits them as a medium of exchange and prevents their use for operation of automatic reinforcing devices. (Ibid., 78, 79)

The project of gamification has been already prefigured in considerations like these. The intangibility of points, perceived as a flaw by the behaviourists regarding their potential as an exchange medium, is precisely what predestines them for use in a ubiquitous digital motivation environment. In a gamified world, there is no delay interval between behaviour and reinforcement, because the devices and mechanics that are measuring players and awarding points are ubiquitous.[5] The same is true for points as a "medium of exchange", since the medial environments that gamification relies upon guarantee the value of points because of their interconnectedness – highscores and leaderboards only work if scores can be compiled and compared across different devices.

It is becoming clear now that the ideas driving gamification and through them the discursive knowledge amalgamating in the instrumentalisation of games are reaching beyond game-design theory or marketing strategy. The association of digital games and experimental techniques that has been identified as one of the central themes of gamification guidebooks is not a product of chance. Even more so than its strongest advocates may think, gamification is (re)creating experimental arrangements – gamified systems resemble laboratories that run experiments on normalisation and economic optimisation. The literature on token economies reveals the prevalence of considerations on automatisation and standardisation. The greatest risk for the motivational environment in the psychiatric ward seems to stem from the attendants:

One can easily excuse any laxity in administering rewards due to these factors by stating that the attendants are, after all, "only human". But that is just the point: One cannot rely upon the attendant's intentions as a measure of what she is doing. The attendant is too much influenced by predispositions, external events, and behaviours of the patient to be expected to

---

5   E.g. as envisioned in Jesse Schell's (2010) popular talks at the DICE conference.

administer rewards in and impartial, objective, and standardized manner.
(Ibid. 12)

Bluntly put, attendants are simply too unreliable; they are inconsistent in giving out rewards and their individual measure of what constitutes a desired behaviour varies. The solution in token economies is automatisation. The tokens function as chips and the actual rewards are handed out through vending machines. This system is implemented thoroughly and to the point where access to certain areas in the ward (e.g. the leisure room) is restricted by token-operated turnstiles (ibid., 141). Where vending machines cannot be employed, especially in the case of intangible rewards like social interaction or religious services, the procedure is strictly regulated through the measurement of duration. The experiments in general are designed for a minimum of human involvement: "The best way to eliminate the influence of a human in the recording and presentation of the reinforcer is to minimize his participation or to substitute some automated method" (ibid., 140). Token economies can be considered an attempt to implement a motivational environment that is largely automated, which is a procedure that inevitably is evoked as well in proposals concerning games in gamification discourse: "[G]ame technologies excel at nothing so much as scoring, comparing and rewarding progress . . ." (Chatfield 2010, 199). The environments envisioned by gamification could be called scoring economies; the problems posed by attendants in the experimental design of the token economy are solved through the automatisation provided by the structures of digital games. It is no longer necessary to develop a surrounding that is physically closed off or restricted, as long as the game design itself is not exposed.

Gamified systems are like laboratories running experiments on behavioural control.

This development towards scoring economies that are alluding to digital games is, for example, especially evident in Zichermann and Linder's account on frequent flyer miles. They laude the programmes as key inventions that single-handedly revolutionised the US airline business (Zichermann and Linder 2010, 115). The advantages of point-based FFPs (frequent flyer programmes) are described in a way that evokes the behaviouristic discourse around tokens:

Moreover, the technical cost of creating, implementing, and managing a point system, as pointed out in earlier chapters, may ultimately be much less than the alternative over the medium term. Once the infrastructure is in place, it's relatively easy to keep track of every actionable item, and this gives the FFP one of its core cost advantages over standalone promotions. (Ibid., 122)

The abilities to reduce costs and to keep track (of transactions and the people conducting them) seemed to be just as relevant in 1960s psychiatry as they are in today's marketing concepts, although the ideal goal of the latter is keeping the participants from actually spending their points and, by doing so, further reducing costs through unredeemed rewards. Gamification, as Zichermann and Linder bluntly put it (ibid., 68, 69), aims to make points the point. Beyond these intangible point-systems, FFPs also establish a hierarchical architecture in closed spaces that externalises an individual's "wealth of points" (or, simply, her score) in the form of status displays. Just as token economies enabled tiered access to different parts of the ward, so do the scoring economies of FFPs in airports: "From First Class lines to premium waiting areas, airports offer dozens of literal examples of the dividing lines between individuals of differing statuses" (ibid., 126). However, architectural arrangements in physical space like these gradually give way to purely digital structures in today's media environments. The tiered progression and status displays are even more emphasised; the scores become universal (cf. Xbox Live Gamerscore) – psychiatric architecture is translated to software and hardware architecture.

COSTS AND REWARDS

The token economy experiment, besides its already discussed therapeutic goals, revolves around efficiency. Long-term psychiatric patients are to be prepared for release, thus prepared to become functioning and efficient members of society. The experimental design for token economies showcases concern for efficiency as well: a core element of the therapeutic approach is having the patients work regularly in one of the jobs that usually have to be fulfilled on the ward. This leads to a substantial reduction in the costs for maintenance of the ward (Ayllon and Azrin 1968, 210). The ethical ramifications of having patients work regularly to maintain the ward they are confined in have been discussed extensively (for an overview, cf. Wexler 1973), while the idea of "generating" work as a by-product of other occupations prevails and flourishes in gamification literature. The vision of a gamified working environment turns the token economy on its head by focusing not on therapy, but instead directly on work and offering ludic involvement as the by-product. Whereas the token economy is about the gradual concealment of the psychiatric routine (in preparation for release), gamification aims to hide work (as another form of routine) behind mechanisms of play. The connection between work and (digital game) play is pointed out in several guidebooks, the scope of associations ranging from typical grinding in MMOs as work (Edery and Mollick 2009, 18) and gaming experiences as mediators for team-oriented thinking (ibid., 115–121; Beck and Wade 2004, 75; Reeves and Read 2009, 84) to speculations about how games can be used to "harvest" the knowledge of their players (Edery and Mollick 2009, 189). One could even go so far as to postulate that the core capabilities that can be called forward or taught by digital games according to gamification are very similar to those that the 1960s psychiatric wards tried to instil in their patients.[6] This connection cannot be explored in the scope of this chapter. I will instead focus on the outcome of working in the experimental design of token economies as compared to the game design of gamification.

The most distinct difference in ideology between the arrangements this paper seeks to compare seems to be regarding the rewards or incentives offered to the participants. Gamification specifically relies on "making points the point" (Zichermann and Linder 2010, 68); thus, positioning points at the core of its mechanics, but also doing so the ultimate intrinsic goal of every interaction with said mechanics. Additionally, the competition between participants (in the form of high-scores, leaderboards, or status displays) is regularly mentioned as a strong motivator (ibid., 34–37). Token economies, on the other hand, offer tangible rewards like cigarettes, sweets, or access to television, the tokens themselves merely figuring as a medium of

---

6   This assumption requires more research, but it is noticeable that some of the qualities that are praised as gamers' virtues like decision-making or sociability are those that at least some of the behavior-modifying treatment approaches relied upon as core competences that had to be conveyed to patients to prepare them for release (Fairweather as cited by Wexler 1973).

exchange without any official way for the inmates themselves to compare their wealth.[7] This comparison, however, neglects a fundamental structural similarity between token economies and gamification programs: both are multi-purpose applications. Gamification is presented as a ludic cure-all for the motivational and organisational problems of modern informational societies. It is applied to marketing (cf. ibid.), consulting (cf. Edery and Mollick 2009; Reeves and Read 2009), and self-optimisation (cf. Dignan 2011). Token economies are similar, since while they originated in 1960s behavioural psychiatry, there soon emerged various areas of application that ranged from educating citizens in ecological behaviour (Kazdin 1977, 229–236) and matters of military training (ibid., 243, 244) to the optimisation of job performance (ibid., 236–240).[8]

These later applications of the token economy system exhibit modifications and further developments that bring them closer to today's visions of gamified environments. A fairly common expansion of Ayllon and Azrin's original concept introduces official, public lists that display the participant's individual or general score. For example, a behaviouristic experiment to teach pollution control made use of a central scoreboard that was placed outside the venue where the experiment was conducted (Geller, Farris and Post 1973). The board prominently displayed two counters: one for customers who bought returnable bottles, the other for customers who bought throwaway bottles. The rules of the game, or, in the behaviourist's terms, the prompt, were given out as handbills to each customer and informed them about the advantages of returnable bottles. The customers were urged to "show concern" (ibid., 371) and were able to see how their individual purchase influenced the (manually adjusted) general score on the scoreboard. Other examples of individual, public scoring include an experimental community modelled after B.F. Skinner's utopian novel *Walden Two* (1948). The community members earned credits through work and community service

---

7   This, of course, excludes unofficial comparisons or even secondary economies between inmates, which largely remain undocumented.

8   Interestingly, token economies in their original form of behavioural modification programs for closed environments persist even today, often as motivational programs for children (e.g. http://tokenrewards.com/#Home, accessed May 7 2014).

and the amount of credits earned by each individual. Both examples illustrate a development towards public score-keeping and competition that is also reflected in the use of badges or patches in the fashion of boy-scout merit badges – which can be interpreted as the predecessors of achievements and trophies in digital games and gamification today. Token economies as a scientific motivational practice gradually evolve while at the same time staying true to their behaviouristic roots.

The range of applications for token economies already resembles a catalogue of desires that later on are to be satisfied through serious games and gamification. The token economy as a system stays the same at its core, wherever it is externally applied. It is this external application that puts token economies in line with later developments like large-scale bonus programs (e.g. frequent flyer miles), which in turn constitute the prime example for some marketing-oriented arguments (Zichermann and Linder 2010, 113–120) regarding the power of points and thus, of gamification, as has been shown above. The tangible incentives that token economies offer instead of "mere" points cannot be considered external benefits or "pay" for the participant's work. Token economies restructure the systems they are applied to and turn commodities everyone usually has access to into rewards that can be earned. In the case of the psychiatric wards, this means that access to luxury articles or recreational activities is usually possible, until the token economy purposefully restricts it. In an effort to discover which activities would work as reinforcers, patients on the ward were observed and the behaviour that was thought to occur frequently was restricted through the token economy. The restrictions cover a wide range, from trivial limitations like not being able to select one's chair to sit in (Ayllon and Azrin 1968, 61) to severe constraints of basic human rights, like being deprived of food or not being allowed to sleep in a bed (Wexler 1973, 87–89). Token economies in the 1960s do not (yet) use points as their ultimate motivational goal, but like gamification they aim to transform the systems they are applied to and to submit them to the rule of tokens or scores. They are both focused on measurement to the point of fetishising it. Anything can be distilled into points and scores – whether it is part of an effort to make human behaviour measurable in a scientific context or central to motivate players in a gamified system. If anything, the scores that replace tokens in today's digital motivating environments are becoming even more influential. Token economies were not built towards self-measurement; the tokens essentially served two different purposes for patients and psychiatrists: to the former, they provided the means to uphold a certain quality of life. To the latter, they measured the success of certain parts of the experiment or the experiment as a whole. When I talk about scoring economies today, this relationship blurs as well. Participants in gamified environments are not only measured and rewarded, they are expected to measure themselves and improve their performance. As such, scoring economies are as much about individual efficiency as token economies were about institutional efficiency.[9] A good example for this is the Attent program (2013) of US-based start-up Seriosity. Through what is described as an artificial economy derived from online games (Reeves and Read 2009, 113–127), the Attent program seeks to optimise electronic internal communication in businesses. Every participant (which in this case means everyone working at the company in question, since scoring economies are no less totalitarian than token economies) in the program gets a specific starting amount of an artificial currency named serios. These virtual points can then be attached to emails to highlight them as especially important. The higher the amount of serios attached to an email, the more important its contents are in the view of the sender. The email's recipient can then add the attached serios to her own account. While very similar to token economies in passing, the Attent program limits the amount of currency in circulation, thus creating artificial scarcity that is meant to reduce unnecessary emails. Attent can be interpreted in relation to classical tokens and rewards (they are a reward for reading some emails earlier or more precisely than others) as well as in relation to scores and evaluation (they make communication via email visible as a cascade-perceived relevance; they foster awareness of communication habits on an individual level). The employees

---

9   To this end, it seems productive to expand the concept of scoring economies to include not only gamification, but also related developments like the "quantified self movement" that aims to employ digital technologies to measure every measureable aspect of one's life, thus hoping to infer methods of personal improvement from the data. The quantified self movement (http://quantifiedself.com/, accessed May 7, 2014) marks a culmination of this tendency and exhibits several parallels to gamification, since it also employs gamified applications like Nike+ (2006) to measure life itself. For a more detailed account of Nike+ and the relationship between gamification and life, see Paolo Ruffino's text in this book.

see also
Ruffino
p. 49

are supposed to regularly consider their own score and work to improve it, which in the case of Attent means optimising their communication habits to reduce their serios spending. Compared to the token economy that is mainly concerned with measurement, institutional optimisation, and rewards, the scoring economy measures, rewards, encourages competition, demands self-optimisation, and functions self-sufficiently, without any incentives that stem from outside the system. This does lead to various developments, some of which demonstrate the alleged mutual relation with typical game-design elements, but also highlight one of the problems that today jeopardise gamified environments. Both aspects will be briefly touched upon before the chapter is concluded.

Token economies in their experimental roots are designed environments. As such, they employ techniques that directly invoke typical digital game elements that in turn get re-contextualised (in the spirit of classical behaviourism) by gamification applications. Tiered progression, often through levels, is a part of the structure of many digital games and is also present in gamification literature (ibid., 75–78; Zichermann and Linder 2010, 34–37; Dignan 2011, 132–134, 151–156). It also appears in token economies, fulfilling a similar function: progression through the rehabilitation program as well as "physical" progression through the ward as such is tiered; access to a privileged status or to additional areas of the ward (e.g. the garden) has to be purchased through tokens (Ayllon and Azrin 1968, 202; Wexler 1973, 104, 105). The psychiatric ward as an already limiting and controlling environment becomes even more restricting to its inhabitants, while at the same time opening up possibilities for new/added agency through participation in the program. Unfortunately, the way the experiments have been documented does not provide the evidence for an in-depth discussion of the way the level-structure actually worked during the experiment and for a comparison to the mechanics of gamification. Besides (or because of) falling back on similar structures, token economies and gamification share a similar problem as well. They either are experiments (in the case of token economies) or put a strong emphasis on the experimental qualities of digital games. As such, they are existentially endangered through all creative approaches in interacting with the rules they present, including (but not limited to) cheating, "power-gaming", and, even, playing. While cheating is usually considered a typical player behaviour that entails a subversion of rules (Consalvo 2007) and as such is inherently threatening to rule-based systems, the extreme optimisation of performance (power-gaming) and playing around with the rules (instead of playing by the rules) are highly problematic as well. Many gamification guides explicitly warn against these unpredictable player behaviours (Zichermann and Linder 2010, 105) and position themselves in a way that suggests that gamification applications are not aimed at players at all, since they obviously try to prohibit core player behaviour.[10] There are similar concerns to be found in the protocols on token economies, albeit not many cases of cheating or playing were actually documented. Ayllon and Azrin underline the importance of attendants for occasional observation through a case of cheating in which the token automatic of a TV set was subverted by inserting a nail file into the token slot (Ayllon and Azrin 1968, 150). The ideas shared by token economies and gamification, automatisation, standardisation and optimisation, are susceptible to play and play-like behaviour. While the question of cheating in gamification applications has already been addressed (Glas 2013), there is still further investigation needed into the relation of gamification and the experimental arrangements it evokes to their players or subjects.

CONCLUSION

It is maintained throughout this paper that, to understand digital games, it is helpful to examine the way they are contextualised in popular media. Specifically, I focus on utopian discourse surrounding digital games in the form of gamification. Gamification guidebooks argue and propose to make use of games in a way that frequently associates digital games with several central qualities. These qualities, among them an emphasis on points and scoring as well as the parallels between games and experimental arrangements, serve to picture games as systems focused on optimisation, automatisation, and standardisation. Through these issues, the measures of gamification can (and have to be) put in a larger context that places them next

---

10 There appear to be some exceptions to this rule, as the case of Foursquare's lenient anti-cheating policy shows. Though some functions of the service are highly restricted and monitored (the mayor-system), it is generally possible (and tolerated by the staff) to perform "false" check-ins and even collect badges and points that way (Glas 2013, 10).

to specific experimental arrangements like token economies. It is necessary to regard digital games not only as contemporary popular cultural artefacts whose techno-cultural evolution is interwoven with digitalisation, but also to question which motives, ideas, and aspirations infuse them. In this case, the analysis reveals the close relationship between gamification and behaviouristic experimental arrangements, as well as the tendency of both to inscribe themselves into the various levels of the structures they are applied to. Thus, it makes sense to describe the way gamification actually takes effect as part of a scoring economy that expands the classical behaviouristic model of token economies through a new focus on competition and self-measurement, while at the same time integrating its core elements into contemporary digital technologies. While this approach entails not focusing on digital games as games per se, it also opens up insights into the fascination with digital games that seems to form the basis of many gamification guidebooks. Digital games appear as phenomena that can be used, their appeal can be made productive, and they can develop a motivational attraction that may be adapted for fields of operation as varied as consulting or marketing. Mere elements of games appear to be capable of transforming mundane structures, systems, and spaces into ludic ones. This view on games opens up a variety of questions that go beyond a critique of gamification, some of which have been touched upon in the article, all of which need to be elaborated further.

One question concerns the circumstances under which digital games are charged with the ideas that have been described and analysed in this article. The conditions under which the assumptions of gamification are made have to be detailed, if we want to understand the mutual interference between digital games and the theories of instrumentalised gaming. To accomplish this, it is necessary to review the games that are cited as examples in the guidebooks, while also considering current developments in mainstream digital gaming such as achievements in an effort to carve out the backdrop of gaming culture against which gamification emerges.

The second, and perhaps more important question, is the problem of players and their position in gamified systems (and in the discourse of instrumentalised gaming in general). Every game and, perhaps even more so, every gamified application carries with it specific assumptions about the player the game is designed for. These assumptions are manifested in design decisions, in code or in hardware architecture, and the physical quality of game elements. They have to be carefully examined and related to actual player practices. In the case of gamification, the implied player is actually not a player at all but instead she or he would be more aptly described as a test subject in the closed and determined experimental arrangement.[11] The chapter already shows that players and their practices can be very problematic for the experimental conditions of gamified environments. It is here that I see the greatest conflict between "classical" (digital) games and gamification: the former can be played with, while the latter cannot. Playing with games, as has been detailed on various occasions (Consalvo 2007; Sicart 2011), always involves a creative, unpredictable moment. This creativity is at odds with the approach gamification exhibits towards games and it is necessary to formulate a critique of gamification that has the player's role in mind.

It is safe to assume that the controversy surrounding gamification and other attempts to instrumentalise games will stay with us for some time to come. Whether we participate in the attempts to make game-transcending use of digital games or not, they will shape the way digital games are perceived, what is thought about, and what is done with them. And regardless of the question whether these developments should be embraced or criticised, in my opinion they offer an excellent opportunity to broaden the scope of game studies as a transdisciplinary approach not only to digital games, but also to the way they are perceived and received as well as to the hopes, ideas, and expectations that take form in the popular utopian discourse surrounding them.

11 While there are rare cases of excellent games like Portal (2007) in which, ironically, player and test subject are one and the same, this cannot be said about gamification and the examples discussed in this chapter.

BIBLIOGRAPHY

AYLLON, TEODORO AND NATHAN AZRIN. 1968. *The Token Economy: A Motivational System for Therapy and Rehabilitation*. New York: Appleton Century Crofts.

BANDURA, ALBERT. 1969. *Principles of Behavior Modification*. New York: Holt, Rinehart and Winston.

BECK, JOHN C. AND MITCHELL WADE. 2004. *Got Game: How the Gamer Generation is Reshaping Business Forever*. Boston: Harvard Business School Press.

BOGOST, IAN. 2011. "Gamification Is Bullshit." *Ian Bogost Blog*, August 8.
http://www.bogost.com/blog/gamification_is_bullshit.shtml.

BOGOST, IAN. 2007. *Persuasive Games: The Expressive Power of Videogames*. Cambridge, MA: MIT Press.

BOGOST, IAN. 2006. *Unit Operations: An Approach to Videogame Criticism*. Cambridge, MA: MIT Press.

CHATFIELD, TOM. 2010. *Fun INC: Why Games are the 21st Century's Most Serious Business*. London: Virgin Books.

CONSALVO, MIA. 2007. *Cheating: Gaining Advantage in Video Games*. Cambridge, MA: MIT Press.

CSIKSZENTMIHALYI, MIHALY. 2008. *Flow: The Psychology of Happiness*. New York: Harper Collins.

DETERDING, SEBASTIAN, RILLA KHALED, LENNART NACKE AND DAN DIXON. 2011. "Gamification: Toward a Definition." Accessed March 27, 2014.
http://gamification-research.org/wp-content/uploads/2011/04/02-Deterding-Khaled-Nacke-Dixon.pdf.

DIGNAN, AARON. 2011. *Game Frame: Using Games as a Strategy for Success*. New York: Free Press.

EDERY, DAVID AND ETHAN MOLLICK. 2009. *Changing the Game: How Video Games are Transforming the Future of Business*. New Jersey: FT Press.

GELLER, E. SCOTT, JOHN C. FARRIS AND DAVID S. POST. 1973. "Prompting a Consumer Behavior for Pollution Control." *Journal of Applied Behavior Analysis* 3(6): 367–376.

GLAS, RENÉ. 2013. "Breaking Reality: Exploring Pervasive Cheating in Foursquare." *Transactions of the Digital Games Research Association* 1(1).
http://todigra.org/index.php/todigra/article/view/4

GRAFT, KRIS. 2011. "GDC 2011: Time to Ditch the Term 'Gamification'?" *Gamasutra*, March 1
http://gamasutra.com/view/news/33315/GDC_2011_Time_To_Ditch_The_Term_Gamification.php

JUUL, JESPER. 2005. *Half-Real: Video Games between Real Rules and Fictional Worlds*. Cambridge, MA: MIT Press.

KAZDIN, ALAN E. 1978. *History of Behavior Modification: Experimental Foundations of Contemporary Research*. Baltimore: University Park Press.

KAZDIN, ALAN E. 1977. *The Token Economy: A Review and Evaluation*. New York: Plenum Press.

KENT, STEVEN L. 2001. *The Ultimate History of Video Games*. New York: Three Rivers Press.

REEVES, BYRON AND J. LEIGHTON READ. 2009. *Total Engagement: Using Games and Virtual Worlds to Change the Way People Work and Businesses Compete*. Boston: Harvard Business Press.

ROBERTSON, MARGARET. 2010. "Can't Play, Won't Play." *Hide & Seek*, October 6.

http://www.hideandseek.net/2010/10/06/cant-play-wont-play/.

SCHELL, JESSE. 2010. "Dice 2010: Design Outside the Box." Accessed March 27, 2014.
http://www.g4tv.com/videos/44277/dice-2010-design-outside-the-box-presentation/.

SICART, MIGUEL. 2011. "Against Procedurality." *Game Studies* 11(3).
http://gamestudies.org/1103/articles/sicart_ap.

SKINNER, BURRHUS FREDERIC. 1948. *Walden Two*. New York: Macmillan.

TWIN GALAXIES. 2013. "About Twin Galaxies." Accessed Dec 17.
https://web.archive.org/web/20050613073727/http://www.twingalaxies.com/index.aspx-?c=17&id=332.

WERBACH, KEVIN AND DAN HUNTER. 2012. *For the Win: How Game Thinking Can Revolutionize Your Business*. Philadelphia: Wharton Digital Press.

WEXLER, DAVID. B. 1973. "Token and Taboo: Behavior Modification, Token Economies, and the Law." *California Law Review* 61(1): 81–109.

ZICHERMANN, GABE AND CHRISTOPHER CUNNINGHAM. 2011. *Gamification by Design: Implementing Game Mechanics in Web and Mobile Apps*. Sebastopol: O'Reilly Press.

ZICHERMANN, GABE AND JOSELIN LINDER. 2010. *Game-Based Marketing*. New Jersey: Wiley.

LUDOGRAPHY

ATTENT. 2013. "Attent with Serios." Accessed December 17.
http://www.seriosity.com/attent.html.

NIKE+. 2006. Nike, Inc.
https://secure-nikeplus.nike.com/plus/.

PORTAL. 2007. Developed by Valve. PC. Valve.

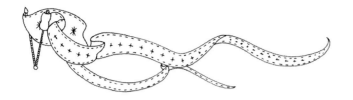

REFRAMING CONTEXT

COMMUNICOLOGY, APPARATUS, AND POST-HISTORY: VILÉM FLUSSER'S CONCEPTS APPLIED TO VIDEO GAMES AND GAMIFICATION

by **Fabrizio Poltronieri**

Among the philosophers who undertook the task of thinking about the status of culture and the key advents of the twentieth century, the Czech-Brazilian Vilém Flusser deserves prominent recognition.

A multifaceted thinker, Flusser produced sophisticated theories about a reality in which man advances towards the game, endorsed by the emergence of a kind of technical device that is dedicated, mainly, to the calculation of possibilities and to the projection of these possibilities on reality, generating a veil that conceals the natural reality and creates layers of cultural and artificial realities.

This technical device, designated by Flusser as "apparatus", being the index of a civilisatory stage where societies are characterised by the fact that they are programmed from discourses that point to a highly abstract shared language exposed through "technical images" which, just like Indian screens, are calculated and projected on the natural reality of the world, hiding and recreating it.

During this brief introduction, we can note the convergence between the main principles exposed by Flusser and that of the field which studies the theories concerned with video games, including the concept of gamification.

Although such connections have yet to be formally established and, in some points, the philosopher himself reaches different and opposing conclusions, the categories created by Flusser, such as apparatuses, technical images, and "projection systems", can be found, analogously, within the field of video game studies.

To conduct part of this process, of reflecting on Flusserian theories applied to video games, is one of the objectives of this text. My current research intends to verify whether the hybrid codes of video games and their syntactical strategies, in which the concept of gamification can be positioned, are suitable for the production of scientific knowledge in a reality that I conceptualise, via Flusser (2011b), as post-historical.

This unease begins mostly from the study of *Does writing have a Future?* (Flusser 2011a), where the author questions if the western alphabetical method of linear writing is still an efficient code for the production of scientific, poetic, and philosophical knowledge, positing that nowadays we are endowed with more efficient codes than the written one.

The change from one code to another brings transformative consequences to previous models used for the production of knowledge and, more importantly, to the way we experience reality around us.

The vital object of this study is, therefore, the understanding of how these codes, particularly the video game one, change what the philosopher Martin Heidegger (1978) called "*Dasein*", altering the way civilisation produces and accumulates knowledge. Heidegger uses the term *Dasein* to label human beings' distinctive way of being. We might conceive of it as Heidegger's term for the distinctive kind of entity that human beings as such are. By using the expression *Dasein*, the philosopher drew attention to the fact that a human being cannot be taken into account except as being existent in the middle of a world among other things (Warnock 1970), that *Dasein*, despite the impossibility to translate the concept, is "to be there" and "there is the world". To be human is to be fixed, embedded, and immersed in the physical, literal, tangible day-to-day world (Steiner 1978). Hence, the present text is an incursion into philosophical concepts such as simulation, representation, and projection, which relate to the philosophy of science, ontology, and communication.

To comprehend how a video game is virtually a suitable apparatus for the likely occurrence of this large-scale change in codes of communication requires, firstly, familiarity with the structure of Flusserian thought, so that his theories concerning connections between apparatuses, technical images, projection, and post-history can be later related to video games and gamification strategies.

It is necessary to immediately stress the principles that guide the proposals of this text, extracted from previous reflections upon Flusser's writings that will be expanded theoretically throughout this paper. It is also important to summarise them, because Flusserian theories leading to a broad understanding of some categories of thought are not always taken into consideration in video game studies.

A video game is an artificial communicational system, which emerges from a cultural scenario where computational apparatuses have become ubiquitous. The video game, as an apparatus, is a system programmed to serve the mediation between the will of larger systems – such as a university, a state, or an industry – and a player or, under Flusserian terms, a "functionary". These systems are dedicated to program and to project a reality on the natural world. As a computational system, the video game archives, processes, and transmits information with the objective of changing human existence in the world and making sure that a person plays symbolically, aiming to distance the player from their awareness of death, as we shall see.

In this respect, gamification is treated as a set of codes that are created from this reality, with the intention of serving as a program implemented through apparatuses seeking to change the way player-functionaries act.

This is a syntactic set that wishes to change the semantic value of human perception of reality, also ontologically changing its existence, thus achieving the status of a set of rules or laws. Flusser, who died in 1991, would probably not be interested in clarifying the concept of gamification. Yet, the author left a considerable legacy regarding the understanding of the gaming theory and the relationship between games and apparatuses.

Based on these elements, we will seek to expand the understanding of the terms beyond their status quo in the available literature, taking advantage of the fact that this is a new and fertile ground. We will seek to understand gamification as programming models that seek to change the world around us. Hence, definitions such as the ones provided by Karl Kapp may appear somewhat reductive.

For Kapp, "gamification is using game-based mechanics, aesthetics and game thinking to engage people, motivate action, promote learning, and solve problems" (2012, 10). This definition, along with others (Zichermann and Linder, 2013; Kumar and Herger, 2013), neglects some aspects that, for Flusser, are crucial in any communication process: modification of being in the world by encoding and decoding codes and the placement of an artificial, programmed, veil on the natural reality.

Lastly, apparatuses and their narrative strategies do not simulate an external reality as some authors tend to describe (Aarseth 2004, Manovich 2001). The processed operation is rather more complex, and Flusser (2011b) calls it "projection". A projection is markedly more abstract than simulation. Simulation, for historical reasons, is nevertheless ever more present in literature than projection.

The act of simulation had an influential effect on the history of Western civilisation, mainly through the artistic activities of the Renaissance (Gombrich 2006), the cradle of modernity, and also being touted as essential in some writings of Aristotle (Reale 2005), where the Greek philosopher conceives it as having an important role for establishing public belief in artistic manifestations such as theatrical narratives, primarily through imitational techniques (Aristotle 2005).

Manovich (2001 and 2008) defines simulation as something that causes a sensation of immersion to one involved within a virtual or real environment. The main question, however, is regarding the fact that Manovich makes assumptions based on the Renaissance's model. When he speaks about computer simulations, he assumes that an apparatus is, still, a window to the external, real, world. Even his concept of image as an interface is based on schemes to control a simulacrum of the objective world, not to create new realities.

What happens in contemporaneity, in Flusser's understanding, is a projection of extremely abstract points calculated within the apparatuses, creating a reality that encompasses the objective and natural world. These points project the Cartesian "thinking thing" on monitors, and "such projections are indistinguishable, as suspected, from the 'things of the world'", as Flusser explains in a letter to Milton Vargas (Flusser 1987, 1). Projections and the world become enmeshed as one thing only.

Flusser, in this way, adopted a position opposite to Baudrillard's, who claims that we live in the culture of simulacrum. For the French thinker, simulation is a "psychosomatic disease, where the patient's pains are quite real and the question whether his illness is also real does not make much sense" (Baudrillard in Bauman 1997, 102). Flusser, unlike Baudrillard, does not adopt an apocalyptical view in relation to the emergence of apparatuses and technical images in contemporary society.

These artificial projections do not simulate reality at all and would never be able to do so, since they are already five degrees of distance from reality, on a scale that Flusser calls a "ladder of abstraction" (figure 1). Any attempt to simulate reality is a frustrated one, semiotically, because the current indexes do not hold any relation to concrete signs. Current indexes are pure projected abstractions that point to the apparatus' interior.

That is the reason why apparatuses such as video games project to the exterior realities that were calculated within it, creating, or at least trying to create, new artificial realities that hide and become symbiotic with the natural world without simulating it. Any attempt at simulation results in the projection of a new reality.

Using different terms, Michael Foucault (2002, 18) had already observed this phenomenon under his archaeology of the human sciences, where he states that a free representation does not answer to facts outside itself, not simulating anything external to it but projecting itself on the world as a reality that envelops it.

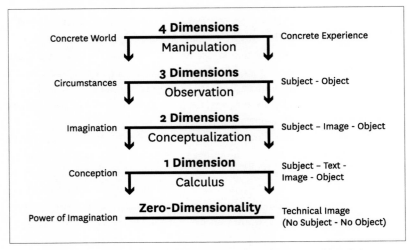

Figure 1: The Flusserian Ladder of Abstraction.

Starting from the concrete world, there follows a negative sequence of abstraction where one reaches a peak, represented by dimensionless calculations and unrelated to the importance of the actual experience. At this step, there are apparatuses dedicated to the calculation of programmed possibilities, such as video games, which project new realities on the natural world.

1 AN INTRODUCTION TO THE THOUGHT OF FLUSSER AND THE CONCEPTS OF COMMUNICOLOGY, APPARATUS, TECHNICAL IMAGE, AND POST-HISTORY

Despite Flusser's vast intellectual output, we shall focus on the most important part to our analysis, namely the field designated by him as "communicology", where the author discusses questions concerned with human communication and language. It is in this field that we find his theories of apparatuses, technical images, and the projection system on reality, all of which are used as arguments that question the validity and role of the written word as the producer of knowledge.

It is important to note that Flusser's communicology changed over the course of his intellectual development. First, communicology was seen as a general theory of humanities (*geisteswissenschaften*), which subsequently was reformulated as a rather broad discipline, positioned in an intermediary field and established on the foundations of humanities and natural sciences (*naturwissenschaften*). Consequentially, this transformation causes a change in his methods, resulting in the incorporation of newer analytical categories, such as the introduction of numbers and concepts of calculus and computation.

For that reason, communicology is a suitable set of theories to be applied to contemporary phenomena such as the discourse presented by video games that, in Flusserian theory, project on reality the results of complex programmed numerical calculations computed by apparatuses.

Unlike other theorists, Flusser's method takes into account not only the punctual changes brought about by these new discourses but also rethinks the way we see apparatuses such as video games, since a change in the communicational method and codes results, necessarily, in a change in the way humans place themselves in the world.

We can define apparatuses as "products of applied scientific texts" (Flusser 2000, 14). Its products, technical images, can be defined as "images produced by apparatuses" (ibid.). These definitions, however simple, hide important consequences. We are dealing with a new type of image here:

> [. . .] in the case of technical images one is dealing with the indirect products of scientific texts. This gives them, historically and ontologically, a position that is different from that of traditional images. Historically, traditional images precede texts by millennia and technical ones follow on after very advanced texts. Ontologically, traditional images are abstractions of the first order insofar as they abstract from the concrete world while technical images are abstractions of the third order: They abstract from texts which abstract from traditional images which themselves abstract from the concrete world. Historically, traditional images are prehistoric and technical ones "post-historic" [. . .] Ontologically, traditional images signify phenomena whereas technical images signify concepts. (Ibid.)

Regarding post-history, we could say that:

> It is concerned with a cultural revolution whose scope and implications we are just beginning to suspect [. . .] When images supplant texts, we experience, perceive, and value the world and ourselves differently [. . .]

And our behaviour changes: it is no longer dramatic but embedded in fields of relationships [. . .] Linear texts have only occupied their dominant position as bearers of critically important information for about four thousand years. Only that time, then, can be called 'history' in the exact sense of the word [. . .] Technical images rely on texts from which they have come and, in fact, are not surfaces but mosaics assembled from particles. (Flusser 2011b, 5)

Thus, a human that plays with apparatuses occupies, ontologically, a different position from the human that does not play. Playing video games is analogous to occupying a post-historical position, as the player now deals with applied scientific concepts, and no longer with the concrete, natural, world. The human panorama is changing, shifting from a procedural behaviour, based on a cause and effect model, to a contextual model of existence, where what we call reality is constantly recalculated by modifications in the context surrounding the player, the one who deals with apparatuses and is embedded in a game composed by mosaics made from scattered particles linked by non-causal relations.

The cultural rearrangement described leads to remarkable modifications in human existence. Flusser points to the fact that communication is always an artificial phenomenon, which aims to be a tool in humanity's struggle against death (ibid.). Adopting a phenomenological method, the artificiality of existence, of *Dasein*, is presented by him as two different perspectives: an internal, subjective one; and an external, objective one.

We should note that existence is linked to communication. In order to exist, humans need to communicate. Video games and its codes function as sophisticated communicational mechanisms that project realities calculated from its interior into the world and, consequentially, alter human existence in its deepest philosophical meaning. Video games are contemporary strategies against death since mankind, according to Flusser, is conscious of its own mortality and that banishes us to a solitary existence (ibid.).

It is in this way that codes, as artificial systems, envelop natural objects, by imposing artificial forms on natural matter, in order to archive acquired information. For Flusser, it is when man becomes aware of the finitude of his experience in the world that he begins projecting an alternative reality, since in his inner self the dream of immortality always remains (ibid.).

From an existential point of view, communicology assumes that every human communication process is an immune and artificial system, built in order to distract us from the acknowledgement of our own mortality. Seen as such, technical images are one of the main antibodies against death, built in order to distract humans from their mortality and working more sophisticatedly and abstractedly than previous codes.

1.1 Functionaries and Freedom

The investigation of human communication methods requires an understanding of cultural historicity, taking into account the various communicational codes currently stacked in layers. Flusser's analysis (2000, 2011a) begins with oral codes, with traditional images – such as petroglyphs – and with texts until it reaches, finally, images produced by apparatuses, produced by a new communicational code, which succeeds texts and inaugurates, as described above, post-history: an age where the process of codification is transferred to outside the body, into the interior of the technical or social apparatus.

The transfer of the codifying capacity to a foreign agent creates a bond of connection between technology and human beings that, according to Flusser (2000), is shown in the figure of the apparatus-functionary complex, which forms a union that cannot be considered separately.

The concept of apparatus-functionary is essential to understand the current cultural situation, since it has reconfigured the relationship between mankind and technology. Flusser defines the functionary as being someone who plays with the apparatus but does not understand how its programming is done and thus cannot have any kind of critical insight into its processes. What remains to the functionary is only to act according to the apparatus.

Historically, the relationship between man and technology occurs in two distinct ways: sometimes technology works for man, sometimes man works for technology (ibid.).

Before the Industrial Revolution, the transformation of nature into culture was executed mainly via technical instruments called tools. In the Renaissance period, at any shoemaker's workshop the production's value resided in the hands of the artisan. The shoemaker's tools were simply variables in his work, working for him. With the industrial revolution and its mechanisation of production, this relation is inverted and man becomes the variable, that is to say, an external agent in a system regulated by machines.

In our first example, the tool is an instrument for freedom while in the second the machine is a mechanism for imprisonment. The novelty of our current situation is the apparent equilibrium between man and technology, when both are merged in unison.

The apparatus is not an instrument, let alone a machine, but rather its synthesis. The machines' trapping annuls the freedom characteristic of the instrument, which in the apparatus is manifested as a phenomenon of thirdness through which both apparatus and functionary are mutually conditioned.

In the case of video games, this mutual conditioning stems from the actualisation of potentialities contained within the programming codes and through the process of interaction between the player and the technical discourse contained in the apparatus.

Murray's definition (1997, 126) regarding agency as "the satisfying power to take meaningful action and see the results of our decisions and choices" is intimately related to the freedom described above. Freedom, in the case of video games, is contained in the symbiosis between apparatus and player-functionary. The player is free to take action to reach desired results as long as these actions are codified in the interior of the apparatus.

The matter of the fact is, in order not to frustrate the player, the apparatuses are programmed in such a way that they are presented as systems capable of projecting infinite possibilities, giving the player the impression that his actions are essentially free. Apparatuses are instruments programmed to codify certain abstract technical concepts into images. The relation between player and system occurs in the agency described above, in Murray's terms, but it can be described better under Flusserian terms in the diagram shown in figure 2.

Technical Text ↔ Apparatus - Functionary ↔ Technical Image

Figure 2: The Relation Between Apparatus and Functionary

A technical text, programmed in the apparatus' interior, virtually contains all the possibilities – alternatives for the player's action – that the system allows. These alternatives, when incited by the player's interaction with the apparatus, are calculated and projected in the form of technical images. The conclusion that Flusser reaches concerning this relationship is that "freedom is playing against the apparatus" (2000, 80).

1.2   Matter, Form, and Probability

It should be borne in mind that technical texts, best represented by computer programming languages and abstract scientific discourse, are articulated through calculations performed in the interior of apparatuses, being the technical images composed of a series of points that, when grouped, appear superficially as an image. They are, therefore, mosaic-like structures. The points composing the mosaic are so small that, in order to be perceived as meaningful forms (gestalten), they need apparatuses that compute and calculate them into a group of images.

With this, the concept of information gains importance, perceived in its probabilistic meaning as an unlikely situation. Communication processes begin to be thought of as a game of probabilities and alternative universes projected via the new images produced by apparatuses. These processes are paths to freedom opened through the arising of unexpected situations.

It is this process that the ladder of abstraction (figure 1) describes, according to Flusser (2011b, 6):

First rung: Animals and "primitive" people are immersed in an animate world, a four-dimensional space-time continuum of animals and primitive people. It is the level of concrete experience.

Second rung: The kinds of human beings that preceded us (approximately two million to forty thousand years ago) stood as subjects facing an objective situation, a three-dimensional situation comprising graspable objects. This is the level of grasping and shaping, characterised by objects such as stone blades and carved figures.

Third rung: *Homo sapiens sapiens* slipped into an imaginary, two-dimensional mediation zone between itself and its environment. This is the

175

level of observations and imagining characterised by traditional pictures such as cave paintings.

Fourth rung: About four thousand years ago, another mediation zone, that of linear texts, was introduced between human beings and their images, a zone to which human beings henceforth owe most of their insights. This is the level of understanding and explanation, the historical level. Linear texts, such as the *Odyssey* (Homer, around 800 BC) and the Bible, are at this level.

Fifth rung: Texts have recently shown themselves to be inaccessible. They don't permit any further pictorial mediation. They have become unclear. They collapse into particles that must be gathered up. This is the level of calculation and computation, the level of technical images.

This is a negative ladder that can also be interpreted as the increasing alienation of existence through artificialisation or as the passage of material culture into the immaterial one, where calculations simulate nothing because they are simply methods to design the zero-dimensional space consisting of scattered points that are united when calculated and projected.

Flusser considers the basis of matter as being an aggregate of aggregates and stuff (*stoff*), a textile. The material world resembles the logic of a Russian doll, in which the starting point of matter is the concrete that can be apprehended by sense, to the extent that thought deepens, matter tends to become increasingly more abstract, less tangible, until effectively disappearing into nothingness, into immateriality.

In this perspective, form appears as an intermediate state of matter (Flusser 2007). At the level of maximum reduction of scale, we reach the zero-dimensionality and there we find only points. In this fluid and ephemeral universe, comprised of relations contaminated with uncertainties, probability calculation appears as the only suitable analytical method.

The fundamental issue regarding this scenario is the dynamics of the shaping of matter, because points are not merely denial, but also locations in potential, that is, potentialities. In the case of theory – science – the issue is the deepening in the direction of more abstract and negative levels creates holes ever more dilated in the fabric of reality; whereas, practice – technique and technology – targets the emergence towards superficiality, that occurs through the projection of probabilities calculation, towards levels ever more concrete and positive, by the filling of holes opened by theory.

Flusser suggests that the post-historical poetic should not begin at the horizons of the real and the fictional but from concepts of abstract and concrete, since the closer and more improbable are the connectedness of points, the denser and more "real" becomes the "sensation" of matter and of image. From this, we could say that the "old real world", objective and represented by the first degree of Flusser's ladder, is devoured by the emergent alternative and projective world, that shapes the universe of technical images.

Flusser expands this idea in the following terms:

> The production of technical images occurs in a field of possibilities: in and of themselves, the particles are nothing but possibilities, from which something accidentally emerges. "Possibility" is, in other words, the stuff of the universe and the consciousness that is emerging. "We are such stuff as dreams are made on." The two horizons of the possible are "inevitable" and "impossible"; in the direction of the inevitable, the possible becomes probable; in the impossible direction, it becomes improbable. So the basis for the emerging universe and emerging consciousness is the calculation of probability. From now on, concepts such as "true" and "false" refer only to unattainable horizons, bringing a revolution not only in the field of epistemology but also in those of ontology, ethics and aesthetics. (Flusser 2011b, 16)

2   VIDEO GAMES, PLAYER, AND POSSIBILITIES

Considering the questions previously discussed, we can observe that video games represent, par excellence, the post-historical era, since they allow a broad hybridisation of cultural codes through the uses of synthetic images and sounds as mediating mechanisms, as well as the inclusion of the player's body as part of the discourse construction process.

Video games are complex representatives of both the game of calculation and the projections processed within the apparatuses and envisaged by Flusser (2011a) as being a real post-historical code. Besides, the methods of production and access to video games' language happen in a non-sequential fashion, as an open hierarchy, in such a way that they present the potential to fulfil, if properly programmed, Flusser's forecast of "future correspondence, science, politics, poetry, and philosophy will be pursued more effectively through the use of these codes than through the alphabet or Arabic numerals" (Flusser 2011b, 3).

In order to produce codes employing the characteristics of post-history, it is necessary to think about post-historical methods that comprehend the phenomena calculated by apparatuses, bearing in mind that the player, ontologically, is modified by the possibilities given by the interior of the apparatuses. His or her being is altered by the projection of a programmed reality.

We should rethink some categories, if we want to examine our culture and more specifically the ideas presented here: the dialogues between post-historical codes and players.

The relationship between player and game begins with the fact that video games do not wish to change the world. As post-historical discourses, they intend to modify human life, since apparatuses do not work, do not take objects from nature, and do not inform them, as instruments and machines do. Apparatuses do not act in the natural world but in the artificial veil that conceals nature, called culture (Flusser 2000).

Although players do not work, they act in the production, handling, and storage of symbols that result in messages whose destiny is to inform culture and other players through their contemplation and analysis. Currently the activity of producing, storing, and manipulating symbols, which is not work but play, is performed through the mediation of apparatuses.

As observed, one of the key characteristics of the apparatuses is the fact that they are programmed. The projections are previously typed within their own boxes. The player who explores a digital game realises some of the possibilities inscribed inside it and obtains the outcome of possible calculations. For a game to be interesting, the number of potentialities should be great but, nonetheless, it is always limited, as it is the sum of all possible interactions made by the player.

Each performed interaction decreases the number of potentialities, of original calculations, and increases the number of projections. The game is ending and at the same time making itself a reality.

For Flusser, the player acts on behalf of the exhaustion of the game and to support the achievement of the universe of the game (ibid.). Or, in other words, the player seeks to modify himself through the playful activity of projecting a reality on the natural world. However, as games become richer, the player strives to discover ignored potentialities. The player manipulates the game, attempting to look into and through it, trying to discover ever-new possibilities.

In touch with the game, the player's interest is focused on the apparatus and the outside world matters only in terms of the programme, since the complex game-apparatus is more

> *"Man plays only when he is in the full sense of the word a man, and he is only wholly Man when he is playing."*
> *– Friedrich Schiller*

concrete than reality. There is no effort to change the world, as the player just obliges the game to reveal its potential.

For that, apparatuses are playthings, and not instruments in the traditional sense. The player does not play with his or her playthings but rather against them. The player attempts to exhaust the programme. Unlike manual workers surrounded by their tools and industrial workers standing next to their machines, players are inside their apparatuses and bound up with them. Yet, "this is a new kind of function in which human beings and apparatus merge into a unity" (ibid., 27).

In their attempt to exhaust the programme, the player fulfils the holes made by the scientific program in the fabric of matter and brings forth, via the act of playing, realities created by the improbable grouping of possibilities contained within the apparatus. While playing, the player reverses the ladder of abstraction and goes from abstraction to projected concreteness.

The activity of projecting games is defined as codifying the theoretical abstract possibilities within the apparatus, taking into consideration the practical act of the player, who calculates such opportunities, returning to the world certain concreteness. The imaginary world merges with the projected one during the act of playing, moved by the imagination of the player, since imagination is a "specific ability to abstract surfaces out of space and time and to project them back into space and time [. . .] It is the precondition for the production and decoding of images" (ibid., 8).

From the players' point of view, to imagine is to fill the gaps left by the designer, as she or he equipped the apparatus with post-historical possibilities, with her or his personal expectations and experiences. We are talking about a game perpetually refilled and exhausted. This continuous game requires a rich program in order to keep the player connected to it. Otherwise it would soon become exhausted, signalling the end of the game. The potentialities contained in the program must exceed the player's capacity to exhaust it. In other words: the act of the player should be only part of the act of the apparatus, in such a way that the program should be impermissible to the player in its totality.

A rich and deep game does not need to be structurally complex but should, instead, be functionally complex. Structurally complex systems can be functionally simple, such as a TV box, in which internal functionality is extremely complex and impermissible but works in a stupid, almost idiotic, manner. The games that challenge creative thought have complex functions despite being structurally simple. Chess (3rd – 6th century AD) is a good example. Tetris (1984) is another one. Both games have simple structures but are, nevertheless, functionally complex, since they hold immense possibilities and are virtually impossible to be exhausted by the player, who is lost in the hidden possibilities allowed by the functionality of the program.

The player cannot ever comprehend functionally complex systems, with virtually infinite possibilities of calculus. That is to say, players cannot exhaust all their possibilities. These programs operate through interchangeable symbols, sets of rules that govern their calculations and that are activated by the players. To work, within the framework of apparatuses, is nothing more than swapping programmed symbols.

It is in this movement of exchange of programmed symbols that lays the aspect of the game in apparatuses. What video games do is to uninterruptedly exchange their rules on the agency of players. Prior to agency, however, it is necessary to codify the rules of permutation subject to calculation.

Flusser affirms that there are apparatuses, such as video games, which can inform and create objects via dynamic projections, calculated in real time. The symbols permutated by these apparatuses are in constant movement, altering the form of the world in an uninterrupted fashion. The game of symbolic permutation envelops the player in such a way that the symbiosis between player and game is fulfilled. The player is emancipated from any kind of work and is free to play. "The tool side of the apparatus is 'done with' and the human being is now only engaged with the play side of the apparatus" (ibid., 29).

There is a broad modification of historical values that become meaningless in this process, since what becomes valid is not the apparatus itself, the hardware, but the set of rules, e.g. the software:

One can see from the softest of the apparatus, e.g. political apparatus, what is characteristic of the whole of post-historical society: It is not those who own the hard object who have something of value at their disposal but those who control its soft program. The soft symbol, not the hard object, is valuable: a revaluation of all values. (Ibid., 30)

Hence, it is the soft, immaterial, abstract, syntactic aspect of game that defines the game of power in post-history that, on the other hand, is held by whoever programs the apparatuses. The game of using symbols is now a hierarchical power game, marking the transition from the industrial era to the current information society and post-industrial imperialism. This shift is linked to the definition of the term apparatus, a complex plaything that doesn't completely reveal itself to those who play against it. Its game is made of uncountable combinations of symbols contained in the interior of its program. Like Ouroboros, the Greek tail-devouring snake, the programs inside the apparatuses were installed by metaprograms and the game results in further programs.

As a symbolic game, the apparatuses surpass machines and are closer to man and, especially, to our intellect. Machines substituted manual labour. Apparatuses projected new mental realities. For that reason, designers and programmers occupy a rather high position in the hierarchy of post-historical societies, since it is up to them to program the possible actions of the apparatuses' games.

With apparatuses, we are dealing with thinking expressed in numbers, as all apparatuses are calculating machines and, in this sense, artificial intelligences. Thinking in numbers overrides linear, historical thinking and allows the overcoming of the Cartesian way of thinking, as since René Descartes we have been subordinating thinking in letters to thinking in numbers. For Flusser, this changes our perception of reality, as only numbers are suited to a process of "bringing thinking matter into line with extended matter" (ibid, 30).

3   GAMIFICATION AND POST-HISTORY

As functionaries of an apparatus, it is clear that the players of video games change, via the agency that they exert over the game, the written possibilities contained and programmed within apparatuses, and their actions consequently project technical images on the world. The act of playing alters the being of the players in their exchange of the symbols with the apparatus. Since any communicational system is artificial and, as such, exists only and solely with the function of distracting mankind from death's certainty, all communication processes are, above all, existential (ibid.).

From this point of view, to think about gamification is to consider it to be a group of language strategies that define the primordial points that should be calculated, with the intention of programming the freedom of players and, consequentially, their position in the world.

As we have seen at the beginning of our discussion, according to this view the concept of gamification is inseparably implicated in the soft, programmatic character of video games and post-historical society. At its most abstract level, the post-historical narrative models are all contaminated with the elements of gamification since the ludic aspect of gaming is found in all images projected over the world. Gamification, therefore, does not wish only to instruct or educate people, let alone make them collect points in fun activities. Its role should be a deeper one, as a communicational and syntactic model, altering the players in an ontological way.

Notwithstanding, the most common discourse regarding the term does not take into account this ontological change. Used extensively as a practical marketing strategy, the deeper implications of the current post-historical society are not taken into account and discourses on the concept are usually heterogeneous, pointing to a society that seems to have realised the cultural importance of playing only after the advent of the video games. Obviously this is not true.

Some definitions regarding gamification in the available literature define the term as a set of strategies to engage customers as never before, align employees, and drive innovation that seemed impossible without the advent of games as a way of reinventing commercial organisations (Zichermann and Linder 2013, xi). Others believe that the concept deals with a previously unspecified group of phenomena. This new phenomenological group would be represented by the use of game elements in non-game contexts (Deterding et al. 2011, 2).

Two arguments in line with the theories presented need to be made:

On one hand, if gamification, as a strategy, distributes throughout society elements and phenomena originated in video games or game design elements, the concept is nothing more than evidence of the Flusserian theory regarding projections. Under this argument, gamification projects on society the calculated reality made within the video game apparatus.

There is no simulation. On the contrary, nothing is simulated but rather projected as new reality, and launched into the world as Flusser foresaw. New signs are projected on the world, originating from programs that compute new realities. There are not, as with simulation procedures, attempts to make one sign impersonate another, aiming to teach strategies, marketing or lifestyle changes. For example, the projection cannot simulate, as it is five steps below, the concrete world. I stress the necessity of new categories for the analysis of contemporaneity.

On the other hand, the current discourse regarding gamification is, somehow, fragile. Paying attention only to more academic conceptualisations of the term (Deterding 2011 et al.; Barden et al. 2013), one can see that there is a great effort on the part of academics in making this field of knowledge be dealt with by newer approaches, when there are already disciplines, such as philosophy, which have observed the issue of games for many centuries.

Video games and their products are elements immersed in culture and language, and to treat them in isolation, as if they were not part of the continuous role of games in the civilisatory process, discards important philosophical accomplishments.

Even if we place games as elements separated from play, it goes against the current scientific and multidisciplinary methods of knowledge production (cf. Kuhn 2012; Feyerabend 2010). Further discussion on this subject is, unfortunately, beyond the scope of this article (see, for example, the in-depth discussion carried out by Gadamer 2011), but it is worth mentioning, especially, a sentence from Schiller (2004/1795, 80): "For, to declare it once and for all, Man plays only when he is in the full sense of the word a man, and he is only wholly Man when he is playing."

As a brief conclusion, in the light of the arguments put forth, the term gamification is undoubtedly a coherent index of the applicability of Flusserian theories, especially in regard to his radical idea of apparatuses' projection on the reality of the world and is also consistent with a philosophical historicity linking the act of playing with every cultural manifestation.

However, I believe that the studies on gamification should take into consideration the existential field of communication processes in order to make the term further integrated within the post-historical structures such as the ones seen throughout this text.

4 CONCLUSION

I have presented a Flusserian theory concerned with the universe of video games as post-historical apparatuses. This theorisation was objectively focused at the presentation of new theoretical underpinnings to the field of game studies that, although recently created, has already some consolidated theories.

This study sought to systematise Flusserian thoughts towards video games, since the points of intersection between these apparatuses and the theories of Flusserian communicology are enormously evident. This is a huge theoretical effort, since this approach had not yet been systematically performed.

The fact that some of the concepts described above may seem overwhelming or controversial is an observation that had been made by the philosopher himself, who claimed that we are witnesses to a complete change in the cultural and civilisational landscape of proportions that are comparable with the invention of writing itself. We are witnessing the rise of a post-historical era and, hence, new categories need to be created and constantly questioned. To open these categories to discussion by a larger audience that research into video games and gamification was a key objective of this text.

Finally, this paper opens some doors that will be explored further in my current research, presenting a theoretical framework that will work to produce a game exploring post-historical codes in knowledge production, especially in the scientific one.

This article is part of a postdoctoral research project conducted between the Pontifical Catholic University of São Paulo (PUC-SP), Brazil, and the Gamification Lab at Leuphana University Lüneburg, Germany. The project has the support of FAPESP, São Paulo Research Foundation.

BIBLIOGRAPY

AARSETH, ESPEN. 2004. "Genre Trouble: Narrativism and the Art of Simulation." In *First Person. New Media as Story, Performance, and Game*, edited by Noah Wardrip-Fruin and Pat Harrigan, 45–49. Cambridge: The MIT Press.

ARISTOTLE. 2005. *A Poética Clássica*. São Paulo: Editora Cultrix.

BARDEN, POLLIE, PAUL CURZON AND PETER MCOWAN. 2013. "Gameful Systems: Play in the Digital Age for Young and Old." Accessed March 31. http://gamification-research.org/wp-content/uploads/2013/03/Barden_Curzon_McOwan.pdf.

BAUMAN, ZYGMUNT. 1997. *Postmodernity and Its Discontents*. Cambridge: Polity Press.

DETERDING, SEBASTIAN, DAN DIXON, RILLA KHALED AND LENNART NACKE. 2011. "From Game Design Elements to Gamefulness: Defining 'Gamification'." In *Proceedings of the 15th International Academic MindTrek Conference: Envisioning Future Media Environments*, edited by Artur Lugmayr, Heljä Franssila, Christian Safran and Imed Hammouda. New York: The Association for Computing Machinery. Accessed March 31. http://85.214.46.140/niklas/bach/MindTrek_Gamification_PrinterReady_110806_SDE_accepted_LEN_changes_1.pdf.

FEYERABEND, PAUL. 2010. *Against Method*. London: Verso Books.

FLUSSER, VILÉM. 2011a. *Does Writing Have a Future?* Minneapolis: University of Minnesota Press.

FLUSSER, VILÉM. 2011b. *Into the Universe of Technical Images*. Minneapolis: University of Minnesota Press.

FLUSSER, VILÉM. 2007. "Forma e Material." In *O Mundo Codificado. Por uma Filosofia do Design e da Comunicação*, edited by Rafael Cardoso, 22–32. São Paulo: Cosac Naify.

FLUSSER, VILÉM. 2000. *Towards a Philosophy of Photography*. London: Reaktion.

FLUSSER, VILÉM. 1987. *Vilém Flusser to Milton Vargas, August 6*. Berlin: Vilém Flusser Archive.

FOUCAULT, MICHAEL. 2002. *The Order of Things. An Archeology of the Human Sciences*. London: Routledge.

GADAMER, HANS-GEORG. 2011. *Truth and Method*. New York: Continuum.

GOMBRICH, ERNST. 2006. *The Story of Art*. London: Phaidon.

HEIDEGGER, MARTIN. 1978. *Being and Time*. Oxford: Blackwell.

HOMER. Around 800 BC. *Odyssey*. Ancient Greece.

KAPP, KARL. 2012. *The Gamification of Learning and Instruction: Game-Based Methods and Strategies for Training and Education*. San Francisco: Pfeiffer.

KUHN, THOMAS. 2012. *The Structure of Scientific Revolutions*. Chicago: The University of Chicago Press.

KUMAR, JANAKI AND MARIO HERGER. 2013. *Gamification at Work: Designing Engaging Business Software*. Aarhus: The Interaction Design Foundation.

MANOVICH, LEV. 2008. "Computer Simulation and the History of Illusion." Accessed February 25, 2014. http://www.manovich.net/DOCS/simulation.doc.

MANOVICH, LEV. 2001. *The Language of New Media*. Cambridge: The MIT Press.

MURRAY, JANET. 1997. *Hamlet on the Holodeck: The Future of Narrative in Cyberspace*. New York: The Free Press.

REALE, GIOVANNI. 2005. *Metafísica. Ensaio Introdutório I*. São Paulo: Edições Loyola.

SCHILLER, FRIEDRICH. 2004/1795. *On the Aesthetic Education of Man*. New York: Dover Publications.
STEINER, GEORGE. 1978. *Heidegger*. Sussex: The Harvester Press.
WARNOCK, MARY. 1970. *Existentialism*. Oxford: Oxford University Press.
ZICHERMANN, GABE AND JOSELIN LINDER. 2013. *The Gamification Revolution: How Leaders Leverage Game Mechanics to Crush the Competition*. New York: McGraw-Hill.

LUDOGRAPHY

CHESS. 3rd – 6th century AD. Probably India and Persia. Board game.
TETRIS. 1984. Developed by Alexey Pajitnov. Electronika 60. Dorodnitsyn Computing Centre.

GAMIFICATION: RETHINKING 'PLAYING THE GAME' WITH JACQUES HENRIOT

by **Thibault Philippette**

INTRODUCTION

Gamification principles are based on the following idea: There is the *game*, and there is the *non-game*. We find it is time for the non-game to take into consideration what works in the game (McGonigal 2011a). The aim of the present article is to question this seemingly clear distinction and to show the limits and the contingence of this premise. Jacques Henriot is the author who inspired this article. He is a well-known philosopher in France where he founded the *Sciences du jeu*[1] research laboratory 30 years ago. Unfortunately, his work is almost unknown to the Anglo-Saxon academic world, which partially stems from the fact that his texts have not been translated. For Henriot, the qualification of an object as a game is arbitrary, since "the thing that I call game right now in the world where I live, was different yesterday, may be different tomorrow. It is probably different elsewhere" (Henriot 1989,

---

1 The term "jeu" in French refers to both English words "game" and "play". This linguistic feature probably has some cognitive consequences, as we shall see.

15).[2] Nevertheless, as he highlights, we must resist a double temptation: on the one hand, considering the game to have no intrinsic reality, something he pointed out with some developmental psychologists; on the other hand, considering the game to be overtaking all parts of our culture (Henriot 1969, 6–15). This means if games have an intrinsic reality, it is perhaps not where it is believed to be.

A CRITICISM ABOUT THE GAME OF GAMIFICATION

"I love playing games." If you identify with this, you probably do too, or at least the subject interests you. But when I say "I love playing games" and you think, "Yes (or no), I (do not) love playing games", are we sure we are talking about the same thing? Maybe I am thinking of strategy games I have played and you are thinking of puzzles or action games. Our idea of games is probably different. Thus the question is: What makes a game a game?

The concept of game in *gamification* is influenced by video games and the success of this industry. The proponents of gamification are mainly interested in a macro-gameplay design principle: the objective-challenge-reward loop (Albinet and Mousson 2010). According to this principle, the game's progression is based on causal relations: a task to accomplish, reward, or failure. The design thus consists of developing a system for reward or punishment in the game (e.g. with badges). Behind terms like "onboarding", "scaffolding", "pathways to mastery" (Coursera 2013), the proponents of gamification infer that a behaviourist stimulus-response-reinforcement process will naturally motivate the player to play. According to one proponent, Gabe Zichermann, this classic game design principle, which can be found in casual games ("average-challenges" games as he calls them), uses what he calls the "dopamine release loop", which is what occurs in our brains when an achievable challenge ends in success (rewarded success, of course) (Zichermann and Linder 2013, 132).

The principle in a reward system, which is only one among others in game design, does not make up the basis of every game. For example, the first video game in history Spacewar! (1962) had three game objects: two missile-armed spaceships and a main star with a gravity well. There was no

2   Henriot's emphasis. All qotations from Jaques Henriot are my translations.

scoring system; two players simply tried to destroy each other's spaceship and avoid crashing into the star. How can we consider this a game since it only has a few rewarding elements? Why is it regarded to be the first video game in history, when examples like Tennis for Two (1958) or Mouse in the Maze (1959) could also claim this status? Game designer Sébastien Genvo gives us an explanation, stating that it was the first video game in history because it was the first game developed as such; the others being software developed with the intention of creating a game (Genvo 2009, 28).

Jane McGonigal, who is credited with being the instigator of gamification with her book *Reality is Broken* (2011a), has recently reacted to the gamification buzz during the Game Developers Conference in a presentation titled "How to Re-Invent Reality without Gamification" (2011b). She admits, like Sebastian Deterding (2010), that points, leaderboards, and challenges do not make a game. She talks about what does make a game – what she calls "gameful design" –, which means "creating the spirit of the gamer". In her keynote talk, while criticising gamification, Jane McGonigal maintains an important idea from her book: There are games and there are non-games, and those who design games can help to improve the non-games. As emphasised by the psychologist Yann Leroux, this is a pleasant discourse in front of a game designers' audience (2011).

Some researchers challenge the separation between game and non-game, considering the game to be an experience rather than a clear system of objects. The game designer Sébastien Genvo uses the term "ludicisation" instead of "ludification" (Genvo 2013) to translate "gamification" into French, just as Ian Bogost criticised the rhetorical "-ify" in the term "gamification" (Bogost 2011), Genvo explains that:

> It is necessary not to maintain inherently playful characteristics and the dimensions of an object, but rather to question how some objects, which were not even considered to be games, gradually started to be designated as such, and how, in doing so, the idea we had of what a game is will change. (Genvo 2013)[3]

---

3   Translation by the author.

Haydée Silva Ochoa points out that gamification is a hybrid word with an English-prefix and a French-suffix, -*fication*, coming from the Latin *facere*, which means "to do / to make". The problem is that it "reinforces the idea of an automatic rather than a problematic transformation of an activity usually excluded from the ludic sphere" (Silva Ochoa 2013).[4] These criticisms draw on the fact that somehow our "language filter" guides our conceptions of things. In English, the distinction between game and play seems to imply that the question should be addressed separately – from the perspective of objects and systems of rules (game) or from the other of the activities of players (play). In French, this distinction does not exist: The free-activity of play or the rule-based game are both found in the same word *jeu*. Unlike other languages, it seems that the distinction is amplified, so the Nordic can "play a play" or "game a game"[5] (Juul 2011, 28–29). This linguistic fact is not neutral. Language, as explained by the semio-pragmatic, is both a way of representing the world, like other symbolic forms, and a way of understanding and interacting with it. By insisting on one aim rather than on another, we reveal how we understand a phenomenon. In this sense, the neologism "gamification" is very clear, and could be translated literally as "make it look like a game". But behind that, there is the idea of making an object (website,

The essence of the game does not lie in the system of objects, but in the relationship that develops between the player and the game.

app, software, or even "reality") look like another (video game). This obviously infers that: 1. games and non-games are clearly identifiable, 2. it is possible to transpose a game to a non-game, and 3. the associated conduct, *play*, will occur, and with it all its positive effects such as engagement, motivation, fun, etc. *Play* is then reduced to "responding to a game". But playing is more than that, as Jacques Henriot explains.

---

4   Translation by the author.

5   In gamification, speaking of "gaming a game" means that players may start cheating the rules of the game that they are supposed to follow. It is considered a gamification risk, or more precisely a risk for the player (in the examples taken) because not following the rules may create a dangerous situation. (Werbach and Hunter 2012, 117–119). For Henriot (see below), it is actually the climax of play, when you play at the extreme limit of the game (Henriot 1989, 92).

THE THEORY OF PLAYING BY JACQUES HENRIOT

In 1969, Jacques Henriot established the foundation for his way of thinking based upon the interwoven themes of obligation, responsibility, and what he calls, the "voluntary condition" in a book simply entitled *Le jeu*. In this book, Henriot explains that: "Le jeu is not in the thing, but in the use made of it" (Henriot 1969, 24).[6] The syntactic definitions of play proposed by authors like Johan Huizinga (2008 / 1938) and Roger Caillois (1992 / 1958) are somewhat unsatisfactory, because they do not allow us to enter the *"pensée du jeu"* or play thinking. For the philosopher, each element proposed in these definitions can be questioned: a "free" activity? Work is equally free, at least in terms of a certain freedom of means – thus, a separate activity? But if separation means "boundary", there are *ad minima* two territories around it, and the other is then also separated – so an "unproductive" activity? When the game produces nothing outside itself; however, to some extent, the player is the result of her or his game – an activity with a "set of rules" then? What behaviour does not follow rules? In that case, a "fictitious" activity? The game can be fake, but it is operational not fictional, it really exists (Henriot 1969, 56–64). Jacques Henriot therefore advocates a pragmatic approach to games:

> A game can probably be defined objectively by the set of rules that give it
> its structure. That allows it to be compared to other games. But in doing
> so, we fail to specify how one game and another are both games. It is im-
> plicitly assumed that any definition of a game begins with the proclama-
> tion of its playful nature [. . .]. We describe the structure, we list the rules,
> but we do not say what makes it a game. (Ibid., 41)

He goes on to argue that the things called games refer to the analysis of playing, which is their principle:

> Any game [. . .] exists if someone invents and reinvents it as such – for
> playing, for being played – and if it offers itself to the *praxis* of someone
> defined as a potential player. (Ibid., 48)[7]

---

6 Henriot's emphasis.

7 Henriot's emphasis.

For him, the essence of the game does not lie for him in the system of objects but in the relationship that develops between the player and the game, explained above with the example of Spacewar! (1962). In this text, Jacques Henriot identifies four criteria characterising the relationship between the player and the game she or he plays (ibid., 73–80):

- Distance: Playing the game remains subjective, no one is ever sure of its reality, not even the player who knows he or she is playing.
- Uncertainty: There is still unpredictability – real or perceived – between the actions and the consequences.
- Duplicity: The player sees her- or himself in a state of "playing" with the assurance that it is just a game.
- Illusion: Entering the game assumes a prior understanding of what the game is. "A playful attitude, like any attitude, is taken" (ibid., 77).

In 1989, according to several published articles (Henriot 2013), Henriot draws a form of synthesis of his reflection: *Sous Couleur de Jouer* (Henriot 1989). As part of an interview with Haymée Silva Ochoa for her PhD (2011), Henriot explains the title of his book:

> It is [in *The Savage Mind* by Levi-Strauss] that I found the phrase *Sous couleur de jouer*. *Sous couleur de jouer*[8] means in reality that we do not play. Basically, we could say that "play" is "the belief that we play". And to believe, it would mean that we bring, in the interpretation we place on behaviour, contents of ideas, ideas that I willingly call metaphysical, because they exceed experience [. . .]. For example, we believe it is possible to introduce into things unpredictability, unexpectability, contingency. And above all, and there is the big word, "freedom"! The player feels free, but is he really? (Brougère 2013)[9]

According to Henriot, there could be a kind of "double illusion" in the act of playing. The first, symbolic or semantic, is due to the status given to the game. It can be called: "the game illusion".

---

8   Wearing the colours of a player, i.e. having a player mentality.
9   Translation by the author.

To play, you must enter the game. To enter the game, you must know that it is a game. There is therefore, from the one who gets to play, a first understanding of the meaning of game. (Henriot 1969, 77)

A *game* in this sense is primarily an idea (Henriot 1989, 15–16). This idea is globally and culturally shared between the people who design the game and the people who accept to play it. Issues of computer-mediated interactions often obscure the role of the cultural conception of the game. Playing video games is seen as a kind of interaction between an object and a user. But the video game is foremost *something designed as a game*, and then it could be seen as a shared idea of playing. In other words, video game designers try, via computer-interactivity, to transmit an idea of how to play this game and players try to understand and in a way *accept* this idea as a game to be engaged in. It is a kind of co-design, as J.P. Gee pointed out (2005). Once this idea is accepted, as described by Caillois, then comes the conduct associated therewith, to conform to the game's forms and the associated illusion ("the play illusion"). If the first step, for Henriot, is necessary for the second, both are ontologically related:

> [. . .] I do not think that the two English words game and play refer to two different types, one with rules, and the other without. Rather, they characterise two different aspects, but complementary ones, of any act of playing. There is no playing without a requirement of rationality, without an obligation that we ourselves impose, without respecting some kind of rule; there is no game if the structure remains empty and purely formal, if it is not referred to as an instrument of possible play.
> (Henriot 1989, 107–10)

Jacques Henriot explains that a game is actually the representation of a kind of conduct in relation to a situation's shape (ibid., 216). To be played, the situation should allow for it, and the subject in the situation should have the capacity to perceive and imagine the situation as a game. "Taken separately, neither the situation nor the mental attitude is enough to make it a game" (ibid.). Jacques Henriot uses the concept of "*jouabilité*" to describe a situation conducive to play. "I propose to theorise as '*jouabilité*' that which, on a purely structural level, makes a potential game out of a situation." (ibid., 217).

The French term *jouabilité* could be translated as "playability" in English. Playability, as user experience, generally refers to methods used to assess the quality of a game's design (Bernhaupt, Eckschlager and Tscheligi 2007, Nacke et al. 2009). As Regina Bernhaupt noted: "Terms like fun, flow and playability are most often used to explain user experience in game design" (Bernhaupt, Eckschlager and Tscheligi 2007, 309). In practice, the concept is difficult to pin down:

> [. . .] more research is needed to create a coherent set of playability heuristics that can be used to evaluate all kinds of digital games in all kinds of different settings and environments [. . .]. (Nacke et al. 2009, 2)

In this sense, the purpose of the playability approach is to determine a matrix of indicators that can be applied to video game products to help assess the quality of the play experience each one offers. This approach is interesting for comparing products between each other. But these approaches fail, at one level, to say in which way it is a "playable experience" and in which way it is not. They do not allow us to determine why situations are suitable or not to be played, and furthermore why situations, which were not considered playable, are now considered, at least semantically, to fall within the *game* family.

Gonzalez Sanchez and colleagues consider playability to be "the degree to which specified users can achieve specified goals with effectiveness, efficiency and especially satisfaction and fun [. . .]" (2012, 1038). They do conceptual work around identified relational forms (and not purely constitutive) in the study of a corpus of video games. It shows that there are different facets of playability (ibid., 1042):

- Intrinsic: playability of the game's design (mechanisms, rules, etc.)
- Mechanical: playability of the software (communication system, fluency, etc.)
- Interactive: playability of the user interface (controls, dialogues, etc.)
- Artistic: the aesthetic playability (visual graphics, music, storylines, etc.)
- Intrapersonal: the subjective outlook produced by the video game in each player
- Interpersonal: the group awareness that arises when playing the game

Even with this differentiation, we maintain an approach that seeks to identify indicators to assess the quality of objects; although, Sanchez and colleagues do point out that video games are games, of course, and software ("good games can be bad software or vice versa"), and communication tools, and artistic works, but their results especially demonstrate that variability comes from the subjective and facets related to shared experience (ibid., 1049). However, based on the framework outlined here following Henriot, the *jouabilité* of a game, what Jesper Juul describes as the "pull" or desire to play the game (Juul 2010, 2–5), must be considered on a different level, and the game objects and mechanisms highlighted by the proponents of gamification are just one of those levels. A situation becomes playable when the situation inspires the game to "come to mind". The idea of the game seems to come from both intrinsic object characteristics (rules, interface, graphics, etc.) and the player's previous personal experience. As Juul noted in his study on casual gamers (ibid., 127), there are several "frames" to consider regarding the playability of a game: the first is related to the game as an object ("the goal orientation and the desire to win"), the following is related to previous experience ("the game as an experience and the desire to participate in an interesting game"), and finally there are the relationships allowed by the game ("the game as a social event and the desire to manage social situations"). As Alain and Frédéric Le Diberder say: "Video games are not a solitary practice that is occasionally shared. It is rather a common practice often played alone" (1998, 171).[10]

Following Jacques Henriot, when a game is identified as playable, a specific conduct must be adopted.[11] He calls this conduct *le jouer*. What characterises this conduct is that it is based on both obligation and uncertainty (Henriot 1989, 114–115). The obligation does not come from the structure of the game, but from the obligation that is imposed on the player as she or he agrees to play the game. The obligation is not only placed upon the goal, but also upon the means to achieve it (ibid., 235). He calls the obligation an "arbitrary theme" in the sense that it is an individual decision and not a

---

10 Translation by the author.

11 Henriot prefers the term "conduct" to "behaviour", as it refers to a voluntary act and not a conditioned one.

transcendent order, even when rules are given by a system, since these rules are only mandatory for the person who wants to play during the time period she or he plays (ibid., 229).

If the essence of any game lies its completion, the path to accomplishment is paved with uncertainty. For Henriot, this uncertainty may be due to different things: the lack of information available to the player, her or his intellectual faculties or position within the situation (ibid., 237). This uncertainty is then subjective and irreducible. In this context of uncertainty, playing is decision-making unaided by rigorous logical deduction. "Playing is always *deciding under uncertainty*" (ibid., 239).[12] He calls this arrangement of means under uncertainty "random patterns" in the sense that players do not often have the resources needed to achieve their project and must "tinker" to do so (ibid., 236).

At least, *playing a game* for Jacques Henriot is the relationship established between the appropriate object and the playful conduct. The foundation of this relationship can be expressed as a metaphor:

> The player lives on two levels. He does what he does and at the same time he plays. He plays in doing what he does. His playing is due to the distance he puts and tries to maintain between what he does and what he does when he is doing. (Ibid., 256)

The metaphor is related to both the game and the play illusion, in the sense that the situation is first interpreted as a game, which is itself the result of a metaphorical process. It is a shift in meaning or a second-degree activity: "what characterizes the game is a diversion, a transformation of denotation" (Brougère 2005, 44).

In summary, Jacques Henriot considers that to be taken as a game, a situation must exhibit some characteristics that make it identifiable. But at the same time, none of those characteristics, taken separately or together, are sufficient to make it a game without any mediation. The "idea of game" must come to someone, and this can only happen, in fact, if the person is able to transcend the situation but also to identify the conduct he adopts (playing)

---

12 Henriot's emphasis.

as relative to the game. In other words, it is necessary for the person to arrive at the idea that she or he is actually "playing a game" (Henriot 1989, 292–295).

THE FALLACIES OF GAMIFICATION

The serious games designer Olivier Mauco sees a triple fallacy in gamification:
1. The *digitisation* fallacy: There are no new objects or practices, but rather the adoption of other marketing practices like loyalty coupons: "It is only a change of medium."
2. The *behaviourist* fallacy: Studies in media sociology show that the importance of local cultural practices and devices do not condition individuals because they belong to a social space.
3. The *aesthetic* fallacy: Gamification adopts the arcade persona but only at a visual level. From the ludic side, game is mostly a competition between a player and a system (Mauco 2012, 9–12).

For Mauco, the use of gamification as a marketing technique must be interpreted in the context of the "attention economy". In a society over-saturated with information, the problem is not the information, but the attention of the public. As he says: "Gamification is the rationalization of the attention's problem by the use of behavioral techniques." (ibid.).[13]

Nevertheless, the first fallacy of gamification is simply the *game fallacy*. A game structure, as good as it may be, is not enough to make a game. As Jacques Henriot says, if a "playable" structure is necessary, the game only exists if the idea of game comes to someone's mind. A game is a game first because someone has been able to communicate *it* through a system of objects and rules; but second because this structure becomes *a game for someone else* through the evolution of its understanding, appropriation, maybe diversions, and surely the sharing of this idea. In brief, when it is played.

"Think like a game designer" (Coursera 2013) is the slogan of gamification's proponents. Jacques Henriot might say, "No! Think like a player". When we think like a player, we think of game situations that were exciting and others that we did not like even though people said they were great games. We think about games that occupied us for hours and then we passed

---

13 Translation by the author.

on to others. We think of tips and tricks that allowed us to circumvent a step that we regarded as boring or for which we did not want to spend the extra hours. And mostly, we think of times when we did not want to play at all. So long as it merely represents a set of proven techniques, gamification will still not guarantee that people will play the game (or the game you think they must play) or that the success will immediately come from the situation. You can dream of Foursquare (2009), World of Warcraft (2004) or Candy Crush (2012) successes, but they are probably more cultural than technical. You can mimic their structures without having the same success. We certainly cannot determine when it's game on… and when it's game over.

BIBLIOGRAPHY

ALBINET, MARC AND PIERRE MOUSSON. 2010. *Concevoir un jeu vidéo*. Limoges: Fyp.

BERNHAUPT, REGINA, MANFRED ECKSCHLAGER AND MANFRED TSCHELIGI. 2007. "Methods for Evaluating Games: How to Measure Usability and User Experience in Games?" In *ACE '07 Proceedings of the International Conference on Advances in Computer Entertainment Technology*, 309–310. New York: ACM.

BOGOST, IAN. 2011. "Persuasive Games: Exploitationware." *Gamasutra*, May 3.
http://www.gamasutra.com/view/feature/134735/persuasive_games_exploitationware.php?page=2.

BROUGÈRE, GILLES. 2013. "Jacques Henriot et les sciences du jeu ou la pensée de Villetaneuse." *Sciences du jeu* 1.
http://sciencesdujeu.univ-paris13.fr//index.php?id=279.

BROUGÈRE, GILLES. 2005. *Jouer / Apprendre*. Paris: Economica.

CAILLOIS, ROGER. 1992 / 1958. *Les jeux et les hommes*. Paris: Gallimard.

COURSERA. 2013. "3.2 Think Like a Game Designer." Accessed May 1, 2014.
https://class.coursera.org/gamification-003/lecture/32.

DETERDING, SEBASTIAN. 2010. "Pawned: Gamification and Its Discontents." Accessed May 1, 2014.
http://fr.slideshare.net/dings/pawned-Gamification-and-its-discontents.

GEE, JAMES PAUL. 2005. "Learning by Design: Good Video Games as Learning Machines." *E-Learning* 2(1): 5–16.

GENVO, SÉBASTIEN. 2013. "Penser les phénomènes de ludicisation à partir de Jacques Henriot". *Sciences du jeu* 1.
http://www.sciencesdujeu.org/index.php?id=243.

GENVO, SÉBASTIEN. 2009. *Le jeu à son ère numérique: Comprendre et analyser les jeux vidéo.* Paris: L'Harmattan.

GONZALEZ SANCHEZ, JOSÉ LUIS, FRANCISCO LUIS GUTIÉRREZ VELA, FRANCISCO MONTERO SIMARRO AND NATALIA PADILLA-ZEA. 2012. "Playability: Analysing User Experience in Video Games." *Behaviour & Information Technology* 10(31). 1033–1054.

HENRIOT, JACQUES. 2013. "Traces d'un cheminement." *Sciences du jeu* 1.
http://sciencesdujeu.univ-paris13.fr//index.php?id=214.

HENRIOT, JACQUES. 1989. *Sous couleur de jouer.* Paris: Jose Corti.

HENRIOT, JACQUES. 1969. *Le jeu.* Paris: PUF.

HUIZINGA, JOHAN. 2008/1938. *Homo ludens: Essai sur la fonction sociale du jeu.* Paris: Gallimard.

JUUL, JESPER. 2011. *Half-Real: Video Games Between Real Rules and Fictional Worlds.* Cambridge, MA: The MIT Press.

JUUL, JESPER. 2010. *A Casual Revolution: Reinventing Video Games and Their Players.* Cambridge, MA: The MIT Press.

LE DIBERDER, ALAIN AND FRÉDÉRIC LE DIBERDER. 1998. *L'univers des jeux vidéo.* Paris: La Découverte.

LEROUX, YANN. 2011. "Les illusions de la gamification." *Psy et Geek*, September 21.
http://www.psyetgeek.com/les-illusions-de-la-Gamification.

MAUCO, OLIVIER. 2012. "Sur la gamification." *Game in Society.* January 19.
http://www.gameinsociety.com/post/2012/01/19/Sur-la-gamification2.

MCGONIGAL, JANE. 2011a. *Reality Is Broken: Why Games Make Us Better and How They Can Change the World.* London: Vintage.

MCGONIGAL, JANE. 2011b. "How To Re-Invent Reality without Gamification." Accessed May 1, 2014.
http://www.gdcvault.com/play/1014576/We-Don-t-Need-No.

NACKE, LENNART E., ANDERS DRACHEN, KAI KUIKKANIEMI, JOERG NIESENHAUS, HANNU J. KORHONEN, WOUTER M. VAN DEN HOOGEN, KAROLIEN POELS, WIJNAND A. IJSSELSTEIJN AND YVONNE A. W. DE KORT. 2009. "Playability and Player Experience Research." Accessed May 1, 2014.
http://www.digra.org/digital-library/publications/playability-and-player-experience-re-search-panel-abstracts/.

SILVA OCHOA, HAYDÉE. 2013. "La 'gamification' de la vie: Sous couleur dejouer?" *Sciences du jeu* 1.
http://www.sciencesdujeu.org/index.php?id=55.

SILVA OCHOA, HAYDÉE. 2011. "Poétiques du jeu. La métaphore ludique dans la théorie et la critique littéraires françaises au XXe siècle." PhD diss. Université Sorbonne Nouvelle - Paris 3

WERBACH, KEVIN AND DAN HUNTER. 2012. *For the Win. How Game Thinking Can Revolutionize Your Business.* New York: Wharton Digital Press.

ZICHERMANN, GABE AND JOSELIN LINDER. 2013. *The Gamification Revolution: How Leaders Leverage Game Mechanics to Crush the Competition.* New York: McGraw-Hill Education.

LUDOGRAPHY

CANDY CRUSH SAGA. 2012. Developed by King. Browsergame. King.

FOURSQUARE. 2009. Dennis Crowley and Naveen Selvadurai. http://www.foursquare.com.

MOUSE IN THE MAZE. 1959. Developed by Massachusetts Institute of Technology. TX-0. Massachusetts Institute of Technology.

SPACE WAR! 1962. Developed by Steve Russel, Martin Graetz and Wayne Wiitanen. DEC PDP-1. Massachusetts Institute of Technology.

TENNIS FOR TWO. 1958. Developed by William Higinbotham. Oscilloscope. Brookhaven National Laboratory.

WORLD OF WARCRAFT. 2004. Developed by Blizzard Entertainment. Windows, OS X. Blizzard Entertainment.

TO PLAY AGAINST: DESCRIBING COMPETITION IN GAMIFICATION

by **Gabriele Ferri**

1 TOWARDS A SEMIOTIC PERSPECTIVE ON GAMIFICATION

This paper presents a set of categories to interpret the field of gamification by examining different features that emerge in the competition between players and adversaries. To do so, notions from the disciplines of semiotics, narratology, and philosophy will be adapted to describe gamified experiences.

Within the relatively new sector of game studies, gamification is an even more recent development. Many current perspectives have their roots in marketing, business communications, and advertising, as gamification attracts significant attention and economic investments from corporate entities. However, more theoretical approaches can also bring concrete benefits to this market-oriented area.

At the same time, the reception of gamified apps within videogame culture has often been controversial. Opposed to enthusiastic proponents such as Priebatsch (2010), other game scholars and designers have stressed how limited the current concept of gamification is (Robertson 2010). The overall consumer response to gamified apps seems to mirror this division as, on one hand, products like Foursquare (2009) or Nike+ Running (2006) attracted a significant user base but, on the other hand, influential magazines and opinion leaders have criticised this phenomenon (Poole 2011).

Moving on from these premises, it is interesting to discuss from a theoretical perspective how gamification relates to other types of games by analysing their competitive features. To do so, semiotic and narratological categories will be adapted to describe the logical opposition of subjects and adversaries, and this will allow us to distinguish between different modes of competition in various types of gamified apps.

2 A COMPLEMENTARY MODEL TO QUANTITATIVE APPROACHES

Today, most studies on gamification are entrenched in market-specific contexts and aim towards immediate objectives – with a majority of quantitative approaches to marketing, customer loyalty, or employee motivation. Instead, the approach discussed here is rooted in semiotics and narratology, and complements existing models that draw from game design, human-computer interaction, informatics, marketing, and business communication. As the study of gamification is making its first steps, it will benefit from more detailed methodology to describe gamified activities in relation to games, narratives, and other significant everyday events. Without being in contrast with other methodologies, a semiotic view contributes to this field by introducing more abstract categories and by allowing more general comparisons between different gamified and non-gamified activities.

Let us begin this discussion by introducing some of the lenses through which gamification will be examined in these pages. The relation between gamified activities and other associated experiences has not been satisfyingly described yet: the one between advergames and gamification will be considered here as a first step to exemplify the benefits brought by semiotic categories. In general, advergames are simple video games used for advertisement purposes: they usually elaborate on popular game genres such as puzzles, racing, or platform games; they make use of simple and widely available technologies such as Adobe Flash and they are closely coordinated with the public image of the brand they promote. Similarly to the field of gamification, advergaming is rapidly gaining relevance, as testified by the wide distribution of titles like Magnum Pleasure Hunt (2011). Consumers often distinguish in an instinctive way between advergames, conventional advertisements, video games, linear narratives, and other everyday practices (Bogost 2007; Cauberghe and De Pelsmacker 2010; Smith and Just 2009; IAB Game Committee 2010) without elaborating on their specific differences. Here, the main reason for comparing advergames with gamified apps is that they share the persuasive and pragmatic objective of attracting and retaining customers.

The forms and the degrees of competition between players, and against the computer system, are the second lens through which gamification will be studied in these pages. As argued above, the relation between gamified apps and other games is complex and not yet fully studied. Video games and gamified apps appear to share the same medium, but also to diverge in their ways of competing against players. Structured video games are often characterised by some degree of competitive attitude, but gamified apps seem to promote different agonistic forms – such as a generally softer competition, often lacking defeat conditions, and strong computer-generated antagonists. All this makes competition a promising parameter for producing more detailed analyses and comparisons.

2.1   A Field in Need of a More Formal Methodology

Several meaningful differences between ordinary games, advergames, gamified activities, and other everyday activities have been intuited by many users – often with the more passionate players arguing against gamified apps being *proper games* – but have not yet been featured prominently in scholarly discussion. In some respects, such blurring among different fields might be beneficial, with marketing campaigns intuitively playing with the ambiguity between what is ludic and what is not, or what is competitive and what is not. However, the lack of formal categories makes it difficult for researchers and content producers to reflect on gamification past a certain intuitive level, and weakens both theory and practical design.

To progress after the current stage, research in this field will benefit from a better typology of gamified practices. Moving towards it, this contribution investigates how a semiotic approach might be used to describe the presence, the absence, and the relative weight of competition in gamified applications. The proposed model is based on abstract logic relations and, thus, easier to generalise and adopt for comparing artefacts and experiences across different domains (e.g. gamified products versus everyday practices, or versus unilinear advertising). This aims at two beneficial effects:

1. A more detailed understanding of the internal boundaries in the field, distinguishing different types of gamification
2. More effective comparisons with non-gamified artefacts or experiences, made possible by adopting shared, general descriptive categories

2.2 Using Semiotic Categories

In this context, a categorisation based on the semiotic notion of an actant contributes to the resolution of the above-mentioned current shortcomings. Programmatically, the semiotic categories that will be proposed in this work aim at being:

1. Abstract and logical, favouring the deep semantic structures underlying the analysed artefact rather than its specific figurative qualities: In other words, they look beyond the single example and its particular characteristics and they concentrate on finding more general similarities and differences across a wide corpus.
2. Technologically agnostic: semiotic categories – especially the most abstract ones such as actants and their disposition on a semiotic square – remain the same, independent from the specific medium considered. Complementing other media-specific approaches, this particular method allows evaluations across different media and accounts for the pervasiveness of certain gamified activities.
3. Scalable, allowing the description of simple or complex activities regardless of their size or of the number of players taking part in them.
4. Generative, capable of giving useful insights to practitioners: While they are not directly intended as design tools, semiotic categories can inspire practitioners, highlighting relevant differences and points of view.

As the majority of the semiotic approaches, this contribution is mainly descriptive and aims at complementing prescriptive design methodologies. Well-articulated analyses can facilitate the understanding of gamified activities, their assessment beyond quantitative / economical parameters, their evaluation, and their comparison. The overall objective is to open an interdisciplinary dialogue with a common metalanguage that could facilitate, in a longer perspective, a selection of best practices and shared examples in the field of gamification.

3   TOWARDS A MODEL FOR GAMIFICATION: A SEMIOTIC FRAMEWORK

This contribution on gamified activities draws from the logical categories of narration to describe the abstract schemas at work in the competitive aspects of gamification, and situates itself in the tradition of general semiotics.

In the most general terms, semiotics refers to a systematic study of signs, their possible uses, their classification, and their role in social contexts. Umberto Eco (1976) distinguishes between specific semiotics, describing the organisation of particular systems such as linguistics, proxemics or iconography, and general semiotics, a more philosophical approach concerned with the emergence of meaning. Semiotics is largely a descriptive discipline but specific semiotics is also, in some respects, prescriptive and predictive – as it aims to analyse and foresee how a typical interpreter would react to certain stimuli given some contextual rules. General semiotics, on the other hand, constructs schemas and shared categories to describe heterogeneous phenomena. This paper will adopt the broader point of view of general semiotics, constructing a framework that links gamification with deeper logical categories and that is not limited to the specific textual types of games.

To have a clearer view, a model based on the notions of actant, actor, and automata will be adopted – rooted in the tradition of the Paris school of narrative semiotics (Greimas and Courtés 1979). The semiotic model constituted a mainstream contribution to the past decades of European narratology, from Tesnière (1959) and Barthes (1966) to recent developments in cognitive sciences (Herman 2009; Herman 2013). Since its first steps in the 1960s, narrative semiotics has deemed it necessary to take distance from the empirical author and related psychological issues and to favour, instead, qualitative analyses through interdefined notions. While early semiotics was mostly concerned with signs and texts, current theoreticians have extended its scope to include also computer games and interactive practices. In this context, the generative trajectory (Greimas 1970; Greimas 1983; Greimas and Courtés 1979; Bertrand 2000) provides a skeleton for understanding how different, concrete texts emerge from deep, abstract structures. In brief, the generative trajectory traverses different layers: abstract semantic values (e.g. good vs. evil) are converted in narrative structures (e.g. a protagonist desires to obtain a precious object, but an antagonist fights back) and, finally, into discursive structures with concrete, figurative, and thematic elements (e.g. a virtuous knight, with a white and blue armour and a white horse, is searching for a magical gem, but an evil wizard with a dark cape tries to prevent it). In this minimal case, meaning emerges from a trajectory across many levels: for example, the abstract notion of *being evil* flows into the role of the antagonist and then is made more concrete with the *dark cape*. This is not an interpretive schema – as it does not describe the hypotheses formulated by specific subjects or how interpretation is guided by the text – but it is a general guideline for understanding how abstract concepts are articulated in concrete texts: for example, it would be possible to trace the distribution of a semantic oppositions such as young vs. old, or local vs. foreign, in its many narrative or ludic expressions across a whole novel, or in a set of advertisements, or in a computer game.

3.1 Keeping an Open Dialogue with Ludology

In a preliminary review of the impact of semiotics in this field, the ludology versus narratology debate cannot be ignored. In the past decade, the discussion centred on whether games constituted a class of their own, requiring a specific methodology for analysis and criticism, or if they should be understood in relation to non-ludic and non-digital media. The discipline of ludology strongly argued against narrative-based approaches to games (Aarseth 2001; Eskelinen 2001; Juul 2001; Frasca 1999, 2003) and for the autonomy of that field from disciplines such as media studies, film studies, or literary criticism. The proponents of this new approach advocated a strong specificity of rules, playfulness, interactivity, and agency to video game experiences, as opposed to narrative interpretation. They aimed at describing game systems with formal categorisations like Järvinen's (2007) – with categories such as elements, mechanics, goals, ability sets, and emotions. Over the course of the years, the distance between ludology and other analytical approaches to games has diminished and interdisciplinary methods have been introduced, as exemplified by Aarseth proposing a "Narrative Theory of Games" (Aarseth 2012) as a possible synthesis.

While this is not the place to discuss such debate, it is necessary to specify that the approach proposed here is not specifically narrative but, more broadly, semiotic. A semiotic perspective on games obtained international visibility in 2009 with *Computer Games Between Text and Practice* (Coppock and Compagno 2009). Its editors sum up a possible definition for a semiotics of games as:

> [. . .] a strictly formal analytical (or descriptive) methodology, independently of any of the more specific characteristics of the actual objects and other phenomena it was supposed to be applied to [. . .] A semiotic plane or level of analysis does in fact exist; it is intuitively easy to isolate, since it is precisely this analytical sphere in which both Narratology and Ludology operate. (Ibid., 2)

In other words, following the direction taken by Compagno and Coppock, this contribution will not attempt to make games and other gamified activities fit in the mould of verbal narratives. Instead, it will aim at adopting general, abstract categories encompassing different fields.

3.2 Competition

If we adopt a point of view rooted in narrative categories, the competition between user and system might be, at first, difficult to position in such theoretical approach. While the presence of persuasive or manipulatory components in many texts, such as advertising, is well known and well described, a first humanistic reading might find it anomalous that videoludic experiences also deploy competitive strategies against the player. When considering that video games play against their users, it is important to stress that it is quite literally a pragmatic activity and not simply a textual strategy. Written texts remain static and do not actively interfere with their reader, even in the case of texts specifically designed to be ambiguous or misleading (e.g. murder mystery novels often contain decoys and other strategies to keep readers guessing) or art pieces whose open interpretation is part of the intended experience. The focus, instead, is on systems that actively contrast the player's actions: in other words, while a verbal text might be difficult to interpret while still being static, a video game may be difficult as its components react pragmatically to the player's actions. Of course, ludology has dealt with these specific characteristics of games, described as simulated challenges and their canonical form involves at least two subjects in mutual competition, each one enacting strategies and actions against an adversary (Järvinen 2007). In this context, electronic games are never completely solitary activities, as even single-player games require computer-generated antagonists or some kind of system or environment or set of rules to keep a certain level of competition.

Differently from what it might appear to be at a first glance, a general semiotic approach is well suited to explore the components constituting the competitive instances of electronic games. A first step in this direction is to recognise that players have indeed some authorial properties in video game experiences – at minimum whether a session actually takes place and, in general, the overall outcome of a session – and gameplay practices show both competitive and cooperative traits at the same time. It would be a mistake to consider such competitive and cooperative parts in mutual conflict as both participate in creating a fully videoludic experience. They are cooperative as users are required at least not to produce aberrant behaviours – such as refusing to play, or deliberately killing their own avatar – and competitive thanks to the agonistic nature of games. While this may be taken as granted in a certain sense, a satisfactory study of gamification should be based on a more complete understanding of the interaction between a game and its player. In this sense, games demand to be played, they challenge players and they teach them how to play through different codified strategies.

3.3 Narrativity, Actors, Actants, Automata

This premise allows us to introduce a semiotic view on competition as an effective contribution, as structuralist semiotics has already developed theoretical models to describe the conflict between characters in fictional and narrative settings and the same models have more recently been adapted for the description of social activities and situated contexts (Landowski 1989). In the next parts of this article, a semiotic polemico-contractual model (Greimas 1970; Greimas and Courtés 1979) analysing competition between a subject and one or more antagonists will be applied to gamified contexts. Structuralist and poststructuralist semiotics adopt the notion of narrativity as the deepest, most general and abstract identifiable level of any text and as a common layer for any meaningful artefact regardless of the medium adopted. In this sense, narrativity is intended as the logic baseline of every form of expression, and can be described in highly abstract terms – as detailed in the works of Greimas (1966) and subsequent evolutions. In this case, narrativity does not refer to *having a narrative* or *being a narrative* in the ordinary or literary sense of the term, but is defined as the quality of every text to be formalised as a network of semantic opposition and of actantial roles that change over time following a canonical schema. As Coppock and Compagno remark:

> [. . .] every meaningful artifact or activity is then narrative in this abstract theoretical sense, and all cultural productions specify the way in which they determine how a interpreter is able to understand and respond to them (thus integrating these interpretations into his/her prior cultural knowledge base). If we agree on this notion of narrativity, then computer games cannot but be narrative. (Coppock and Compagno 2009, 2)

In the following paragraphs, the basic elements of these definitions will be explored and, then, this model will be applied to the categorisation of gamified activities.

Actants are part of a general narrative grammar (Greimas and Courtés 1979) and – in the most accepted version of the model – are described as mutually defined positions to be filled during the course of a narrative. The labels used to identify them (subject, object, sender) are rooted in narratology, but today their use has been generalised and is not limited to traditional narrations. An actor occupies a subject actantial position when it is characterised by agency, competences, desires; it occupies an object position when it is acted upon; and a sender actantial position is defined by the transfer of knowledge, aims, and tasks to a subject. While actants are positions in an abstract network, actors are concrete entities occupying them: this way, actors are defined figuratively and thematically, as well as situated in specific narrative programs. The notion of automata, already present in classical Greimasian semiotics as a tool to analyse scientific discourses, gains further relevance when adapted for studying interactive objects such as digital media. In this specific context, I argue that the original definition of automata as neutral subjects should be extended and brought up to date with interactive technologies as autonomous actors with an algorithmic programming capable of reacting to outer stimuli, such as a user's behaviour.

Competition enters the semiotic model through polemico-contractual relations (Greimas 1970; Greimas and Courtés 1979): instead of distinguishing between a protagonist and an antagonist, mature narrative semiotics

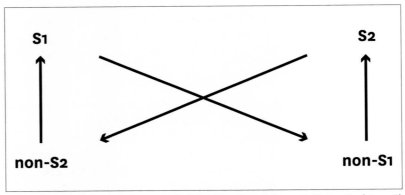

Figure 1: A Semiotic Square Articulating Two Generic Semantic Categories (s1 vs. s2)

adopts a general schema where many actants (a subject and one or more anti-subjects) compete for an object. From a logical point of view, subject and anti-subject are equivalent and try to achieve the same goal from different starting points: a dual actant similar to the classical ludic situation in which two players struggle for a ball. The subject vs. anti-subject opposition may be unpacked further by positioning each piece in a semiotic square. Derived from Aristotelian logic, the square articulates the constituent relationships of a category in terms of contrariety, contradiction and complementarity or implication. Its underlying principle requires the development of a semantic category (s1 vs. s2) through the negation of each component (non-s1 vs. non-s2) – in this case, constructing a square between subject, anti-subject, non-subject (non-s), and non-antisubject (non-as).

By expanding the dichotomy between subject and anti-subject, it is possible to obtain a more fine-grained distinction. To understand the mechanisms at work in the subject vs. anti-subject semiotic square in a linear narration, let us consider, for example, the final part of the movie *Star Wars Episode VI: Return of the Jedi* (Lucas 1983). Luke Skywalker, the protagonist, surrenders and is brought to Vader and the Emperor, the two main villains. Luke and Vader engage in a duel, Vader's hand is severed, and the Emperor tempts Luke, asking him to kill Vader and take his place. As Luke refuses, the Emperor attacks him, but Vader takes pity and slays the Emperor. Mortally wounded, Vader removes his mask and lets Luke finally see that there was

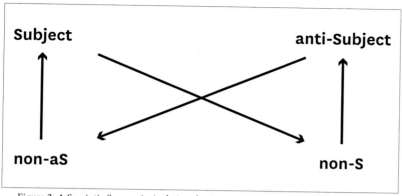

Figure 2: A Semiotic Square Articulating the Opposition Between a Subject Actant and an Anti-Subject Actant

still good left in him. These narrative developments are structurally complex and benefit from a schematisation based on a semiotic square. In the beginning, Luke occupied the subject position while Vader and the Emperor were anti-subjects. As Luke surrendered, he moved from subject (the active protagonist of the story) to non-subject (suddenly passive in front of the antagonist); then he is tempted to move towards anti-subject when the Emperor invited him to join his cause. However, it was Vader who chose the opposite movement – from anti-subject (actively opposing Luke), to non-antisubject (the active opposition stops), and to subject together with Luke (killing the Emperor).

Drawing from this narrative logic will allow us to produce a mapping of actantial competitive stances in games continuing research initiated – and then interrupted – by David Myers (1991) to discuss more in-depth the different competitive situations in gamified activities.

4 DIFFERENTIATING COMPETITION IN GAMIFIED APPLICATIONS

Several points of view on gamification have been recently formulated – from scholars (Deterding et al. 2011), practitioners and enthusiastic proponents (Zicherman 2011; Bunchball 2013), or critics (Robertson 2010; Mosca 2012). However, competition has not yet been proposed as an analytical lens to understand gamified activities. Instead, a preliminary exploration shows that they feature different types and intensities of agonistic activity among players or between players and computer-controlled automata. To map such possibilities, it will be particularly useful to track which kinds of actors enter the role of anti-subjects and, thus, compete against players. To do so, they will now be subdivided in three sets, whose characteristics will be modelled and described using actantial analysis and narrative semiotic categories. The nature of actors opposed to players is, indeed, instrumental in determining which type and intensity the competition will exhibit.

As a first distinction, it is possible to isolate three general categories of actors contrasting the players' actions:

1. Other human participants
2. Contextual elements
3. Computer-controlled automata

More specifically, the first category may be further complicated by considering the social and logical distance between a player and other competitors. Human competitors might be friends using the same gamified app, or they may be part of a wider social network to which the gamified app is linked, or even complete strangers taking part in the same activity. As an extreme case, players might be even competing against their own previous performances – as it happens, for example, if an athlete attempts to beat his or her own best performance.

Foursquare is a canonical example for the first category, where a bland agonistic activity takes place among human actors. Foursquare users compete principally by accumulating and comparing points on a leaderboard accessible from within the app and its scoreboard is not exported to wider social networks such as Facebook. Other systems, for example Nike+ Running, favour the second option and allow their users to compete both on in-app leaderboards against their friends and also to share their performances on general social networking sites. Further fitness-oriented apps explore approaches that are even more competitive: for instance, Runno combines a GPS activity tracker with other mechanics similar to the traditional, open-air game "capture the flag".

Different gamified practices might also select contextual elements to occupy anti-subject positions; this is the case, in other words, for apps and initiatives that ask players to avoid or to prefer certain actions, or objects, during their activities. Motivational and feedback systems that increase or reduce the users' score whenever they carry out a task – or refrain from doing so – are suitable examples for this category. The EpicWin app (2010) is a well-known example, but it is possible to include also car insurance policies rewarding customers for driving safely, or credit card companies giving bonuses to clients paying their balance on time.

Finally, computer-controlled automata explicitly competing against players are not common in gamified activities; whereas, they appear much more frequently in related genres that are closer to everyday computer games. Advergames are a fitting example of this category, where non-interactive ads, e.g. a visual advertising in newspapers, are translated into very simple games. Advergames often deploy the exact same mechanics of regular video games in smaller, simpler pieces where competition is generally between a single human player against computer-controlled adversaries and dangerous environments.

To synthesise the different types of actors occupying the position of anti-subject actant:

1. Human competitors, player's acquaintances inside the gamified app
2. Human competitors, from the player's social network (e.g. Facebook), even if they do not explicitly use the gamified app
3. Human competitors, even complete strangers
4. The player's own actions and other contextual circumstances in the case of motivational and self-help apps
5. Software automata, even though such category rarely appears in gamified apps while it is more common in ordinary computer games and advergames

This shortlist shows a variety of different elements entering the competition against players. For a more detailed view of their characteristics, it could be productive to come back to the subject versus anti-subject dichotomy articulated on a semiotic square, producing a more fine-grained logical view. The logical opposition between subject (s) and anti-subject (as) is expanded by finding two intermediate positions (non-s and non-as) acting as mediators and identifying competitive tendencies.

The Runno app is a fitting example of a system where adversaries occupy the proper anti-subject position. It is a fitness tracker where users claim territories by running around a specific area and then use in-game currency to fortify it. Other runners might attack the player's lands using mechanics similar to the famous Risk board game (1957). The combat is resolved automatically by the system and ends with a clear victory or defeat. Each player is an anti-subject for the others, the competition is clearly represented, and intermediate positions are not possible. As a secondary example, we might recall that the majority of advergames feature automata in the anti-subject positions – either anthropomorphic characters or, more generically, a hostile environment opposing the player's progression.

A semiotic approach helps us to describe the presence, the absence, and the relative weight of competition in gamified applications.

Other actantial positions, non-s and non-as, appear in different proportions in other gamified applications in which the competitive stance is problematised. The next three examples – EpicWin, Foursquare, and Nike+ Running – will be used for mapping how such positions are used in practice. In general, non-s and non-as are seldom separated and, together, articulate non-burdening, playfully competitive situations. It is possible to identify non-s competition with the cases in which a player challenges himself or herself to do (or not to do) certain actions: it is not a concrete adversary to play against but a component of the player's own activity. Non-as adversaries represent a complementary approach and appear in the situations where competition is blurred, amicable, and the other participants are not fully opposing the player's actions. To understand better what has been briefly presented here, let us now consider three examples showing how non-s and non-as positions are concretely articulated.

User experience in EpicWin and similar apps is fundamentally different from the Runno app (2013), as there seem to be no actors or automata actively contrasting the player's actions. EpicWin is a gamified to-do list that allows the user to create their avatars as if they were characters of a fantasy-themed massively multiplayer online game; the system encourages users to rephrase mundane tasks on the to-do list (e.g. washing the dishes) into more heroic quests (e.g. banishing the grease monster). EpicWin, finally, rewards its users by assigned experience points and virtual treasures for completing tasks, fostering some kind of competition among players. Within the logical framework outlined before, no concrete actors appear to occupy the anti-subject position as nothing inside the system actively opposes the subject. In concrete terms, users of this type of gamified motivational apps are

214

more in conflict with their own actions (or lack thereof) rather than with other actors. For this reason, the adversarial role is more focused on the non-s position on the semiotic square rather than on anti-subject.

In addition, the Foursquare system does not feature any anti-s actant opposing the users' actions but, differently from the previous example, relies on the non-as position. The user experience of these gamified apps involves collecting a score on a shared leaderboard "against" other participants – who might be more or less connected to the player's social network depending on the implementation. For example, it is certainly possible to "win" a weekly competition in Foursquare by accumulating the largest amount of points, but it constitutes a weak agonistic activity that has little impact on the overall experience. In the Foursquare example, the role of opponents is situated in the non-as actantial position and not in the anti-subject because the game-play experience lacks any strong sense of victory: typical Foursquare users are more engaged in an urban experience than in a fight against any competitor.

Finally, Nike+ Running and the Nike+ ecosystem in general emerge as a synthesis of the above-mentioned positions, as the actors taking part to its experience might transit through all the actantial roles detailed so far. An actual competitive challenge between two runners would see one of them in the subject position and the other as anti-subject. Its use by a single person trying to beat his or her own best performance would position that simulacrum in the non-s role and, finally, using it as a sort of social network for tracking the other's activities in a low-key competition would refer to a non-as position.

5 DIFFERENT CATEGORIES FOR GAMIFICATION

By definition, gamification blends ludic mechanics with non-ludic activities or objects and it is often experienced in contexts that are not usually considered playful. For this reason, gamified activities and applications seem to be inextricably intertwined with everyday practices and several descriptions have been proposed for this overlapping. Famously, Seth Priebatsch, founder and CEO of SCVNGR – a creative studio operating in the field of gamification – opened his TED-Boston speech in July 2010 claiming that through his company's products he was "fairly determined to try and build a game layer on top of the world" (Priebatsch 2010). Priebatsch's intuitive idea of game

215

layer seems to adhere to the gamification practice of using ludic mechanics to make non-game products more ludic, but it is possible to trace its roots to the tension between being in a magic circle and, on the opposite end, to being pervasive. While these concepts have been widely discussed in game studies and media studies, we might benefit from developing a more formal and logical framework for mapping different experiences. In the conclusion of this article, I will argue that using the anti-subject actantial position as a marker for different types of gamification may lead to a better understanding of their ludic qualities and social situation.

In 1938, cultural theorist Johann Huizinga gave a definition of the ludic context that has become influential in contemporary game studies:

> All play moves and has its being within a play-ground marked off before-hand either materially or ideally, deliberately or as a matter of course. Just as there is no formal difference between play and ritual, so the "consecrated spot" cannot be formally distinguished from the play-ground. The arena, the card-table, the magic circle, the temple, the stage, the screen, the tennis court, the court of justice, etc, are all in form and function play-grounds, i.e. forbidden spots, isolated, hedged round, hallowed, within which special rules obtain. All are temporary worlds within the ordinary world, dedicated to the performance of an act apart. (Huizinga 1955, 10)

In Huizinga's view, the magic circle delimits the real world from ad hoc, non-permanent fictional worlds created for playing. Current game studies have imported such a notion through the work of Katie Salen and Eric Zimmerman who, at first, operationalised this concept, describing gameplay as surrounded by physical or metaphorical boundaries remarking the subdivision of ludic space from everyday life. However, Salen and Zimmerman's simplification had mostly didactic purposes and the authors themselves later note how, while games are in the most cases formal, defined, rule-based entities, the act of playing remains inevitably fuzzy:

> [T]he boundary between the act of playing with the doll and not playing with the doll is fuzzy and permeable. Within this scenario, we can identify concrete play behaviours, such as making the doll move like a puppet. But there are just as many ambiguous behaviours, which might or not be play,

such as idly kneading its head while watching TV. There may be a frame
between playing and not playing, but its boundaries are indistinct. (Salen
and Zimmerman 2004, 94)

On the other end of the spectrum, pervasive games seem to defy the idea of
magic circle. In research published in 2009, Markus Montola, Jaakko Stenros,
and Annika Waern described playful pervasive practices as having in common one or more salient features that expand the contractual magic circle of
play spatially, temporally, or socially. The three scholars note:

> The contracts of pervasive games are different from the contracts of tradi-
> tional, non-expanded games. The magic circle is not an isolating barrier
> distinguishing the ludic from the ordinary, but a secret agreement mark-
> ing some actions as separate from the ordinary world. While all human
> actions are real, those that happen within the contract of a game are given
> a special social meaning. In conclusion, we can see that there is a twofold
> dynamic between the playful and the ordinary that provides pervasive
> games a reason to exist: Both play and ordinary life can benefit from the
> blurring of the boundary. (Montola, Stenros and Waern 2009, 21)

This dichotomy intersects productively the theme of gamification, understood either as the addition of "a game layer" on top of other activities or
other texts (Priebatsch 2010) or "the use of design elements characteristic
for games in non-game contexts" (Deterding et al. 2011). In other words, a
gamified situation seems to be composed by a first-order activity or object
(e.g. entering a train station) and a second-order one, having some component derived from game-design (e.g. checking-in using Foursquare at the
train station, to improve one's own score on the leaderboard but also – in
the case of advergames – experiencing an advertisement as a platform game
rather than as a non-interactive billboard). Some gamified activities emerge
as interstitial and can easily take place at the same time as other actions,
sharing their time, space and cognitive resources – they are, in brief, fit to be
experienced while undertaking other tasks. The second type of gamified activities, instead, is exclusive – as they demand the player's attention and they
cannot share the same space and time with other everyday practices. In this
analytical dimension, *interstitial gamification* will refer to gamified activities

that take place in parallel with other activities that do not require the user's full attention and that complement existing social practices. Foursquare and other similar apps are good examples of this category, as they coexist with other activities. Exclusive gamification is at the opposite end of the continuum and refers to games that require the user's concentration and that are difficult to play while doing other tasks. The proposal of an interstitial / exclusive continuum for gamified practices has its roots in – on one side – the classic notion of magic circle, widely adopted in game studies to theorise a separation between ludic and non-ludic activities, and – on the other – in the genre of pervasive games.

Insights from the analysis of actantial positions related to competition can be used together with other descriptive categories to construct a continuum from interstitial to exclusive practices and to map the blending (or lack thereof) between gamified experiences and their users' ordinary everyday activities. Using categories that are more abstract allows us to formalise the difference between the gamification of practices (weak anti-s, often in shifted positions on the square) and the gamification of texts and discourses (strong anti-s, usually in advergames). By examining the anti-subjects, their positions on the semiotic square, the kind of strategic actions the undertake, and the general victory conditions of the system, we can understand better the degree of flexibility and porousness of several types of gamification: weak anti-subject positions allow less-competitive gamified activities to be interstitial practices that can be easily paired with other everyday actions without much interference. Vice versa, a strong anti-subject with effective tactics generates an openly agonistic situation that may be quite engaging for the user, but might be more difficult to seamlessly blend the game into different other behaviours: to compete against a tough opponent requires concentration and strategic planning that risk subtracting cognitive resources from other parallel activities.

Among the abstract variables that can be considered while positioning examples on the interstitial/exclusive continuum, we can include:

Which actantial position is occupied by the adversaries in a semiotic square (anti-subject, non-s, non-as) during gameplay, as described in the previous section.

The type of actions the competitors undertake and the strategies they follow in relation to the user. Do the adversaries actively try to contrast the player's actions, or do they simply act independently? This point is determined, in the case of software automata, by their algorithmic programming and, if the opponents are human actors, by the instructions or priming they have received from the system.

The presence, or absence, of victory and defeat conditions. In other words, whether the experience might potentially proceed indefinitely, or if it will end at one point with a win or a loss. If win/lose conditions are present, it is also important to assess their rigidity or flexibility describing, for example, if players are able to set their own victory conditions, or if they win or lose relatively to other players' performances, or if there is an absolute criteria for determining the outcome of a session.

These descriptive parameters help us to formalise the difference between interstitial and exclusive gamification at an abstract, logical level that does not depend on technological and contextual-specific characteristics. In other words, this type of approach aims at being technologically agnostic, generalisable, and potentially future-looking, not depending on specific characteristics of any implementation. On one side of the continuum, interstitial gamified practices like Foursquare feature a weak competitive situation where opponents do not occupy the anti-subject actantial position but rather the non-s or non-as ones. Adversaries in interstitial gamified activities do not generally enact specific strategies to hinder the player's activity. In addition, the victory conditions for this type of apps are usually quite flexible, without specific objectives that – once obtained – cause the end of the experience. Vice versa, exclusive gamification – such as, for example, an advergame like the well-known Magnum Pleasure Hunt – feature opponents in a strong anti-subject position which actively oppose the players and that are characterised by clear victory and defeat conditions.

6 DISCUSSION AND CONCLUSIONS. RESEARCH TRENDS AND FUTURE WORK

In these pages, a semiotic model for competition has been introduced using the notions of actants, automata, and semiotic square. In synthesis, why should a new methodology complement existing quantitative views? This approach provides the means for comparing different design strategies within the field of gamification, and also between gamified apps and other objects. The two results may be summarised as follows:

Adopting a semiotic square to articulate the opposition between subject and anti-subject allows us to examine more clearly different modes of competition. These preliminary results need further validation, but less competition seems so far to be correlated to a better flexibility inside a social context and to a higher compatibility with other activities at the same time: this mode could be named interstitial gamification. Vice versa, more intense competition seems to require a separation between the act of playing and other events – a mode that could be called "exclusive gamification".

Subdividing the antagonists between those occupying the anti-subject position and those in intermediate collocations such as non-subject or non-antisubject allows us to contrast gamified apps with other ludic activities. Advergames, among other genres, were chosen here for comparison because their persuasive ends are close to those of gamification. In brief, initial observation suggests that gamified apps usually do not pit players against strong computer-controlled anti-subjects; whereas, advergames – and many other ludic activities – often do so.

Formulating design principles is not the main objective of semiotic analyses but, in conclusion, some tendencies can be sketched. Future gamified apps could explore other modes of competition and different actantial positions: this research suggests that new ways to automatically adjust the relation between the intensity of competition in relation to the social context (proposing harder challenges only at the right moments) could be beneficial for new products. Finally, by examining how the subject position is articulated, it emerges that only few titles collocate several players in subject positions as collaborators; thus, more cooperative and team-based gamified apps might be welcome additions to the field. These possible tendencies, along with further theoretical and comparative exploration, suggest a considerable expressive potential and will need more attention in the future from scholars and practitioners alike.

BIBLIOGRAPHY

AARSETH, ESPEN. 2012. "A Narrative Theory of Games." In *Proceedings of the International Conference on the Foundations of Digital Games* (FDG '12), edited by Magy Seif El-Nasr, Mia Consalvo and Steven Feiner, 129–133. New York: ACM.

AARSETH, ESPEN. 2001. "Computer Game Studies, Year One." *Game Studies* 1(1). http://www.gamestudies.org/0101/editorial.html.

BARTHES, ROLAND. 1966. "Introduction à l'Analyse Structurale des Récits." *Communications* 8: 1–27.

BERTRAND, DENIS. 2000. *Precis de Semiotique Litteraire.* Paris: Nathan.

BOGOST, IAN. 2007. *Persuasive Games.* Cambridge, MA: MIT Press.

BUNCHBALL, 2013. "What is Gamification?" Accessed December 17. http://www.bunchball.com/gamification.

CAUBERGHE, VEROLINE AND PATRICK DE PELSMACKER. 2010. "Advergames: The Impact of Brand Prominence and Game Repetition on Brand Responses." *Journal of Advertising,* 39(1): 5-18.

COPPOCK, PATRICK AND DARIO COMPAGNO. 2009. "Computer Games Between Text and Practice." Accessed March 31, 2014. http://www.ec-aiss.it/monografici/5_computer_games.php.

DETERDING, SEBASTIAN, DAN DIXON, RILLA KHALED AND LENNART NACKE. 2011. "From Game Design Elements to Gamefulness: Defining Gamification". In *Proceedings of the 15th International Academic MindTrek Conference,* edited by Artur Lugmayr, Heljä Franssila, Christian Safran, Imed Hammouda, 9-15. New York: ACM.

ECO, UMBERTO. 1976. *A Theory of Semiotics.* Bloomington: Indiana University Press.

ESKELINEN, MARKKU. 2001. "The Gaming Situation." *Game Studies* 1(1). http://www.gamestudies.org/0101/eskelinen/.

FRASCA, GONZALO. 2003. "Ludologists Love Stories, Too: Notes From a Debate That Never Took Place." In *Level Up: Digital Games Research Conference Proceedings,* edited by Marinka Copier and Joost Raessens. Utrecht: University of Utrecht. Accessed March 31, 2014. http://www.ludology.org/articles/frasca_levelup2003.pdf.

FRASCA, GONZALO. 1999. "Ludology Meets Narratology: Similitudes and Differences Between (Video)Games and Narrative." Accessed March 31, 2014. http://www.ludology.org/articles/ludology.htm.

GREIMAS, ALGIRDAS JULIEN. 1983. *Du Sens II. Essais Sémiotiques.* Paris: Seuil.

GREIMAS, ALGIRDAS JULIEN. 1970. *Du Sens.* Paris: Seuil.

GREIMAS, ALGIRDAS JULIEN. 1966. *Sémantique Structurale: Recherche de Méthode.* Paris: Larousse.

GREIMAS, ALGIRDAS JULIEN AND JOSEPH COURTÉS. 1979. *Sémiotique. Dictionnaire Raisonné de la Théorie du Langage.* Paris: Hachette.

HERMAN, DAVID. 2013. *Storytelling and the Sciences of Mind.* Cambridge, MA: MIT Press.

HERMAN, DAVID. 2009. *Basic Elements of Narrative.* Oxford: Wiley-Blackwell.

HUIZINGA, JOHANN. 1955. *Homo Ludens: A Study of the Play-Element in Culture.* Boston: The Beacon Press.

IAB Game Committee. 2010. "Video Game Interactive Advertising Platform Status Report." Accessed March 31, 2014.
  http://www.iab.net/guidelines/508676/1488/GamesPlatform.
Järvinen, Aki. 2007. "Introducing Applied Ludology: Hands-on Methods for Game Studies." In *Proceedings of DiGRA 2007 Conference: Situated Play*, edited by Baba Akira, 134–144. Tokyo: University of Tokyo.
Juul, Jesper. 2001. "Games Telling Stories? A Brief Note on Games and Narratives". In *Game Studies* 1(1).
  http://www.gamestudies.org/0101/juul-gts/.
Landowski, Eric. 1989. *La Société Réfléchie: Essais de Socio-Sémiotique*. Paris: Seuil.
Lucas, George. 1983. *Star Wars Episode VI: Return of the Jedi*. Directed by Richard Marquand. Los Angeles: 20th Century Fox.
Myers, David. 1991. "Computer Game Semiotics." *Play & Culture* 4: 334–345.
Montola, Markus, Jakko Stenros and Annika Waern. 2009. *Pervasive Games: Theory and Design*. Burlington: Morgan Kaufmann Publishers.
Mosca, Ivan. 2012. "+10! Gamification and deGamification." *GAME* 1(1).
  http://www.gamejournal.it/plus10_gamification-and-degamification/#.UrcXj4sXVI8.
Poole, Steven. 2011. "Nil Point." *Edge Online*, March 25.
  http://www.edge-online.com/features/nil-point/
Priebatsch, Seth. 2010. "The Game Layer on Top of the World." Accessed March 31, 2014.
  http://www.ted.com/talks/seth_priebatsch_the_game_layer_on_top_of_the_world.html.
Robertson, Margaret. 2010. "Can't Play, Won't Play." *Hide and Seek*, October 6.
  http://www.hideandseek.net/2010/10/06/cant-play-wont-play/.
Salen, Katie and Eric Zimmerman. 2004. *Rules of Play: Game Design Fundamentals*. Cambridge, MA: MIT Press.
Smith, Jonas Heide and Sine Nørholm Just. 2009. "Playful Persuasion: The Rhetorical Potential of Advergames." *Nordicom Review* 30(2): 53–68.
Tesnière, Lucien. 1959. *Éléments de Syntaxe Structurale*. Paris: Klincksieck.
Zicherman, Gabe. 2011. "A Long Engagement and a Shotgun Wedding: Why Engagement is the Power Metric of the Decade." Accessed March 31, 2014.
  http://de.slideshare.net/gzicherm/g-summit-opener.

LUDOGRAPHY

EpicWin. 2010. Supermono.
  http://www.rexbox.co.uk/epicwin/.
Foursquare. 2009. Dennis Crowley and Naveen Selvadurai.
  http://www.foursquare.com.
Magnum Pleasure Hunt. 2011. Developed by Lowe Brindfors. Adobe Flash. Unilever.
Nike+ Running. 2006. Nike, Inc.
  https://secure-nikeplus.nike.com/plus/.
Risk. 1957. Developed by Albert Almorice. Board game. Parker Brothers.
Runno. 2013. ePlinovo AB.
  http://www.runno.me.

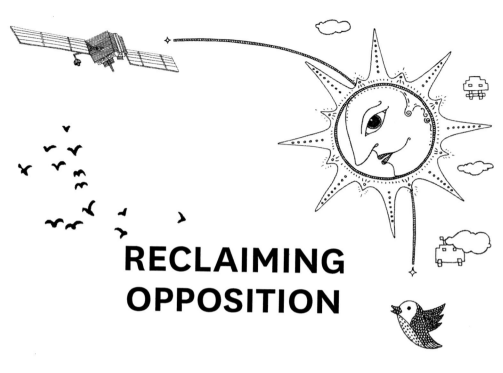

RECLAIMING
OPPOSITION

COUNTER-GAMIFICATION: EMERGING TACTICS AND PRACTICES AGAINST THE RULE OF NUMBERS

─────────

by **Daphne Dragona**

1 INTRODUCTION

Social media are ruled by numbers. Counts of friends and followers, scores of "likes", views, and shares play a central role in defining what is on view and what is not, in a constantly evolving info stream. As every move is measured and every post awaits feedback, a particular ground for action is being set up. Images, links, videos, and thoughts constantly compete with each other for attention. The number of friends a user has, the time he chooses to upload a post, and the number of responses she or he gets are all decisive for her or his online presence. The social media world is a competitive world with scores dependent on networks' algorithms on one hand and on users' promptness and virtuosity on the other; it is part of a new gameful reality, which – based on machinic modes of counting – continuously tracks and processes networked human moves and interactions.

But is this then a new form of a gamespace? As users constantly consider what their next "move" should be while checking the scores of others, they very much seem to be acting like players. But what looks like a game is actually not such. It is rather the ultimate convergence of the real world with the online realm where real data is being used in a new peculiar game system (Dragona 2014, 98). What happens in the web is one of the many facets of the phenomenon of gamification which opens the way not only to opportunities for gameful interaction, but also to new modes of exploitation, capitalisation, and control. As McKenzie Wark puts it, there seems to be "a sort of enclosure of the world" within what he famously called "gamespace", "where the logics of the game become the general patterns of organization". And this happens thanks to the contemporary game like media, "the allegories of our times" (Wark 2013a).

2 THE EMERGENCE OF GAMIFICATION

Gamification can be described as a trend (Gartner, Inc. 2013), a buzzword (Kumar 2013, 528), a method (de Neef 2013, 4), a process (Huotari and Hamari 2012, 19; Zicherman and Linder 2013, xii), or a strategy (Pradeep Kumar and Addagada 2013, 47). It relates to a vast array of activities to which game features are added, assigning a gameful character to people's daily rhythm. Nowadays, for instance, someone could compete with his friends while jogging using Nike+ Running App (2006), gain or lose points while following a diet on Lose It! (2011), create a more engaging website with Bunchball, form a more productive work environment with Gameffective, and learn some new foreign language with Duolingo (2011). These are only some of the known gamification platforms that allow the inclusion of badges, points, progress bars, and leaderboards in non-game environments with the aim to challenge people to continuously improve their performance and to compete for better outcomes.

Described as "the application of a game layer on top of the world" (Priebatsch 2010), "the use of game design elements in non-game contexts" (Deterding et al 2011) or "the penetration of our society with methods, metaphors, values and attributes of games" (Fuchs 2012), gamification seems to have made an appearance which cannot be ignored, highlighting a new era for the role of games in culture and society. Although the idea behind gamification is not new – in certain areas, like the military or education, the use of game elements was always present – what happens today is something ultimately different as it also becomes clear from the controversies and discussions about it.

see also
Fuchs
p. 119–140

Gamification's origins are not to be found necessarily in games. Even though the word itself appeared back in 1980 when Richard Bartle named gamification the process of "turning something that is not a game into a game" (Werbach and Hunter 2012, 25), the term only started being used in 2010 after it was reintroduced by the technology company Bunchball as a new form of game-based marketing strategy (Ionifides 2012, 8). According to the company, game mechanics and dynamics started then being introduced into a "site, service, community, content or campaign", in order to "drive participation", to "teach, motivate and persuade people" (Bunchball 2010), or else as Zichermann and Linder put it, "to serve business purposes" (2010, 20). For this reason, gamification was confronted with hesitation by scholars mainly from the game studies field doubting its aims and values. Ian Bogost has referred to gamification as "exploitationware", purposefully recalling practices of software fraud such as malware or adware (Bogost 2011). Chaplin described it as a "tactic employed by repressive authoritarian regimes" (2011) while Chorney argues that gamification "pacifies" players in order to generate revenue (2012, 9), and Man similarly claims that "value is created for the corporations while its citizens are playing games and kept happy" (2011). At the same time, its very connection to the world of games has been negated. Several scholars have claimed that gamification actually uses the least important element of games (Robertson 2010, Bogost 2011) in order exactly to invite the user to behave like being in a game (de Neef 2013, 4), and become more active, engaged, and motivated. For this reason, gamification was ironically characterised as "pointsification" by Robertson while it has also been argued that the fiction, ambiguity, and uncertainty found in games are also purposefully absent (Roberson 2010; Bogost 2011; Mosca 2012). But this is how it is perhaps meant to be as, according to Huotari and Hamari, the goal of the process is no other but to support the overall value creation by the users themselves. And this is done simply by offering to them affordances for gameful experiences (Huotari and Hamari 2012).

On the other hand and taking into consideration this line of thought, several game developers and games enthusiasts have asserted that, if used properly, game elements can still become an integral and positive part of life. In particular, it has been argued that gamification can be "smart", creating compelling experiences (Kin 2011), or "meaningful" by offering inner motivations, developing engaging habits, and taking into consideration users' needs and goals (Nicholson 2013, Rapp 2013). It might not need to follow the marketing strategy necessarily, but rather one of gameful design, which pays attention to positive emotions, and purposes, which can ultimately bring changes to daily life (McGonigal 2011).

As it becomes clear, the spectrum of the gamification discourse is wide and so are its applications and uses, which might or might not be directly connected to the market. What all sides agree on, however, is the fact that the whole process did not appear unexpectedly. It rather followed what Raessens has framed as the "ludification" of culture, which emerged with the rapid development in the fields of computer games, mobile telecommunications, and the Internet (2006, 52). The serious and persuasive games, the pervasive and alternate games, as well as the use of games as services have all been aspects of this continuum, which set the stage for gamification to appear along with new possibilities offered by constant connectivity and availability of mobile devices. However, what was still unclear when ludification just became apparent was the direction that would be followed given the ambiguity of the term itself. Would it mean "an increase of playful activities" or rather a "transformation of perspective" using "play as a metaphor" for entities and domains that might not be necessarily playful (Frissen, de Mul and Raessens 2013, 82)? Ludification was an outcome not only of the adoption of a game logic penetrating different sectors of life, but also of the playfulness that these technologies encouraged. And what one could confidently now argue is that society was gamified at times when the lusory attitude, that is the game-like attitude according to Bernard Suits' term, was on a high level (Fuchs 2012). This gameful shift in the behaviour and the perception of the many seems to have been a precondition for today's gamified world.

3   GAMIFICATION IN SOCIAL MEDIA

Social media entered gamification after a quite discrete period of ludification. It is actually possible, as it will be explained in this section, to even refer to a *gamified* and a *ludified* web, which respectively followed the early – now almost forgotten – playful web of the 90s.

Since the appearance of the social web in the middle of the previous decade, social networking platforms were based on technological structures which embraced different game and play elements, encouraging users to have a lusory attitude when interacting within them. One can recall, for example, the period when YouTube had a star voting system for videos, MySpace had a top friends rank, and Facebook offered its users the possibility to send virtual gifts to each other. The two spaces of social networks and games seemed back then to actually have quite a lot in common. Based on voluntary participation, encouraging sociability, allowing users to play with their identities, and providing a particular context of action, social networking platforms just like games were inviting users to bring in their disposal and skills in order to freely interact with others.

The passage from ludification to gamification happened when certain elements started becoming apparent. These included the introduction of progress bars in users' profiles, the addition of social buttons (e.g. the *like*, *share*, or *check-in* button) enabling measurement on users' posts and interactions, the connection of various external gamification applications to social networking platforms to (e.g. Nike+; Starbucks reward card, 2014), and the emergence of social games especially designed to be played within social networks. The ludified space of the web was now being formed into a new, gamified one, not only because of the already game-like attitude of the users within it, but mostly because the web's development greatly enabled this change and this can possibly be associated to the following two aspects:

First, when the above elements appeared, at the end of the previous decade, the numbers of users and respectively of friends' networks on social networking sites had significantly augmented. As networks are systems, just like games, this meant that a great territory was opening up that could possibly accelerate and intensify interaction. And what could have been more convenient for social media companies than to use growing active and vivid systems to apply a strategy like gamification? If, as Salen and Zimmerman have argued, games can be defined as "systems in which players engage in an artificial conflict, defined by rules, that results in quantifiable outcome" (2004, 80), then one easily realises that all gamification needed was the construction of this artificial conflict in order to bring about quantifiable outcomes that would prove to be especially useful for the networks.

Second, gamification reached users in the era of a data-driven economy and culture, when new forms of measurement, capitalisation, and valorisation started to emerge. The social media are, of course, a great resource of data. As users constantly exchange information within them, an amazing wealth of data is collected, analysed and re-organised. This "datafication", as Mayer-Schonberger and Cukier name the process (2013, 73), not coincidentally, emerged at the same time as gamification, and the two of them, as will be explained further below, serve and support one another. And it is not only companies and governments that are interested in the power of data. It is the very users themselves that are becoming more and more dependent on emerging forms of measurements and data structures. Phenomena such as the "quantified self/self knowledge by numbers" movement need to be taken into consideration in order to realise that a new trend and a new way of thinking now exist which see self improvement in the continuous self tracking of everything.

To conclude this point, it could therefore be argued that the earlier game-like or else ludified social networks were developed into gamified systems thanks to the very structure of the networks, the wealth of data circulating within them, and the lusory attitude of users, which was strengthened with the growing importance of online scores and numbers. While the emergence and application of gamification in the case of social networking sites might seem "light" compared to other gamified contexts, it is of a special interest as it can greatly capture the reasons that made this overall process feasible, while also revealing its goals and outcomes.

4 FROM LUDIFICATION TO GAMIFICATION: LOCATING THE CHANGES OF THE TRANSITION

In the section that follows, the transition from ludification to gamification is discussed, locating the game elements being introduced on one hand and the way users are being affected on the other. The changes are presented through different examples in relation to a) the online profile, b) the network of friends, and c) users' networked interactions within the urban environment.

4.1 The Gamified Profile

When web 2.0 emerged, a user's online profile very much resembled an online avatar. The way users choose images and attributed features to their profiles was not far from the process of identity-building for the characters of the online gaming worlds. Identities were often re-invented and the networked spaces seemed open to diversity and multiplicity. Many profiles on Friendster or MySpace were fictional and playful, and the social network seemed to be a new stage for social interaction and identity performance. As has been explained by different scholars, new, disembodied, mediated, and controllable spaces were offered where users could actually create their own staging and setting for performances based on their social and affective needs and skills (Cover 2012; boyd 2006; Pearson 2009).

With the empowerment of subsequent social networking platforms like Facebook, Linkedin, or Google+, however, and especially with the appearance of status updates, progress bars, and social buttons, a different form of gameful interaction appeared. The online self started more and more to be fed by data and numbers; it became measurable and started resembling a Sims character or a Tamagotchi toy that needed to be taken care of in order to remain "alive" (Dragona 2014, 101). If no new data was given, the online identity might be forgotten and be off the stage. And this is how, unavoidably, a shift occurred. A user-generated gamified data body replaced the playful performative online identity and gave way to a stronger connection to reality and to the logging of more data on the networks' databases.

4.2 The Gamified Network of Friends

For many users, the network of friends on a social networking site is their informal daily audience. As boyd puts it, it was the actual collection of friends that provided space for people to engage in identity performance (2006). It needs, however, to be taken into consideration that the number of friends for an average user in the early days of social media was much smaller compared to today, reflecting only a sample of a person's real-life friends and acquaintances. Some of the networks were presenting a high ranking of friends, chosen by the user as the "top ones", and in general a high number of connections was not necessarily seen positively. The ones with superficial friends were often called names, and in the case of Friendster they have even been called "whores", as Donath and boyd write (2004, 80).

As the number of users in social media significantly increased, the importance of friends for an online profile changed. Not only did it become indicative for a user's real or fictitious sociability, it also started playing a decisive role for her or his overall score of influence. Within this context, aggregating platforms such as Klout or ProsKore appeared, developed especially with the aim to measure users' influence and to assist them in improving their score. This brought about a new form of exponential growth of social capital for the networks and a new kind of alienation for the users, an alienation from their own data. At the same time, a new class of friends appeared, the "high quality" ones as Andrejevic calls them (2011), describing as such the people of special interest, the influential nodes of the networks, that users connect to in order to raise their social or professional status. As for the "top friends", they were replaced – for instance on Facebook – by the friends the user interacts with the most, depicted automatically by the network's algorithm. The new scores therefore brought along not only different metrics of power and status, but also different metrics of friendship.

4.3 Gamified Urban Interactions

Location-based social networking services were designed with the aim to facilitate users' communication and especially coordination in the urban space. Just like on standard social networking sites, early location-based ones like DodgeBall offered opportunities not only for sociability in the physical space, but also for identity performance and "cataloguing" according to their preferences and tastes (Humphreys 2007, 355). Users were associating themselves with venues and were meeting up with friends, but as they were using an SMS-based system – in the case of DodgeBall – check-ins and shouts were "manual" and regulated by them. Game elements were therefore hardly present while at the same time a different field, location-based games, was emerging, highlighting the potentiality of gaming on the streets of a city.

In the era of datafication, things changed. When urban interactions became traceable and quantified, new game-like experiences became apparent. The map became a territory for exploration, socialisation, and gameful interaction, as users' moves and preferences became connected to check-ins, badges, rewards, and leaderboards. In platforms like Foursquare (2009), city inhabitants were now offered moments of sharing, meeting up, and playing, but interactions were no longer regulated by the users; even if the venues were created by the users "manually", they would in any case be datafied. Either used to locate friends, to express themselves, or to play with others (Cramer, Rost and Holmquist 2011), in all cases a wealth of geo-locative data and metadata was generated within these networks, without users really being aware of it. It seems like people were being challenged and rewarded to explore the city and be social – if we follow McGonigal's (2011) line of thought – but in reality, more data was becoming vulnerable to exploitation and control.

5 SITUATING THE OUTCOMES AND OVERALL IMPACT

When discussing the gamification of the online self, online sociability, or mediated city interaction, one thing becomes clear. It is the users' data that is at stake and the mechanisms of gamification have come to facilitate access by the networks and other third parties to this very data. Social media networks sit "on an enormous treasure chest of datafied information that, once analysed, will shed light on social dynamics at all levels", Mayer-Schonberger and Cukier clarify (2013, 94). The question, however, is at what cost. On social networking sites, as Andrejevic frames it, "every image we write, every video we post, every item we buy or view, our time-space paths and patterns of social interaction all become data points in algorithms for sorting, predicting and managing our behaviour" (Andrejevic 2010). And if our networked algorithmic culture has already entered this path, the introduction of game elements makes particular processes connected to data collection, organisation, and analysis easier today. These processes could briefly be described as follows:

First, gamification assists in narrowing identity down to identification. As de Lange specifically argues, online social media platforms are coded spaces that define users by their personal taste and attributes (2010, 172). The inclusion of progress bars, the standardised questions, and the rapid flow of status updates demand information, which needs to be real and often updated. The user-generated data bodies created are based on one hand on the personal data the users willingly fill in – such as their date of birth, their relationship status, their religious views, etc. – and on the other on the information they provide regarding their interests and preferences. From this perspective, game mechanics assist in the formation of what Richard Rogers calls "post-demographics", that is the demographics which are being shaped by online profiles based on joined groups, accepted invitations, and installed apps, and not on race, ethnicity, age, income, and educational level, like the traditional ones (Rogers 2009, 30).

Second, gamification succeeds in applying new forms of *measurement* and *capitalisation*. Gerlitz and Helmond particularly discuss how data and numbers today have gained performative and productive capacities, how "they can generate user affects, enact more activities, and thus multiply themselves" (2013, 13). Different forms of affective responses are translated as "likes". They become productive while also opening the way to advertisements, merely through their placement on web pages. Additionally, Evans specifically explains how a giant resource is formed for platforms like Foursquare by the check-ins of the users, who are not only checking in somewhere, but also work for the particular places, creating the entries themselves (Evans 2013, 196). And finally, at this point, one should not forget that that it is not only data, but also metadata which are constantly generated. Data's value does not diminish. On the contrary it can be processed and again constitute an open resource for the future (Mayer-Schonberger and Cukier 2013, 101).

Third, taking into consideration the aforementioned points, as identities are logged and behaviours can be predicted, processes of *homogenisation* and *normalisation* are also facilitated. As Grosser argues, "the more one's personal details are shared with the world, the harder it is to retrieve or change them without others noticing [...]" (2011). Accordingly, Mayer-Schonberger and Cukier note that "measure leaves little room for change in a person's life" (2013, 167). Being limited to lists of shares and likes, users learn to "cycle through trends" (Dean 2013, 137). Online friendships are based on sameness, while datafied and gamified urban interactions accordingly seem to be limiting unexpected encounters and spontaneous city exploration (Dragona 2011). In the social media world, as Dean argues, in the era of post-disciplinary societies, there are no more normative expectations or institutional norms imposed by the school, the church, or the family (ibid.). The new norm is now rather defined by an audience, a network of users one feels that she or he presents oneself to. And this is unavoidably dependent on metrics, algorithms, and social software.

What options are users left with to oppose gamification, when quantification governs an increasing part of their lives?

Gamification came in at a time when "software is the invisible glue that ties it all together" (Manovich 2013, 8), when it is software that "regulates and disciplines" (Kitchin and Dodge 2011, 133). Within this context, little possibility for any counter-action seemed to be an option. After all, this can only be possible "if an application's underlying calculative algorithms and communicative protocols are encoded to support such actions" (ibid.). So what options are today's users left with? Does data govern an increasing part of their reality? To what extent are current game-like structures responsible for pacifying citizens? Gamification is the mode, the way used to enable exploitation and control. Networks can rule "through freedom" (Rose in Arvidsson 2007) while users might not even realise that they are playing by the rules of a gamified system. They might be in a state of unaware gaming, as Fuchs puts it, recalling Montola and Waern (Fuchs 2012).

Game mechanics therefore appear to have assisted the formation of new contemporary apparatuses, of mechanisms that have the capacity "to capture, orient, determine, intercept, model, control, or secure the gestures, behaviors, opinions or discourses of living beings", to follow Agamben's definition (2009, 14). They came to contribute to the process of datafication and to facilitate the sovereignty of algorithmic control. With game elements that might not be directly perceived as such – as there are often no leaderboards, no winners and losers – and with the application of rules and modes of control, which in networks are "light" and "soft" (Terranova 2004, 100) – as users are never told how data is collected and processed and for whom – gamification in the case of the social networking sites is a practice that goes hand in hand with the market's practices and interests.

6 DEFINING AND LOCATING COUNTER-GAMIFICATION

Is the current gamified condition irreversible? Enabling processes of identification, capitalisation, and normalisation, play became "functional" (Wark 2013a), rendering personal information traceable, social relationships exploitable, and behavioural patterns recognisable as expected in a progressively datafying world. And like it is often said in relation to different fields of the post-fordist society, there seems to be no outside. These processes cannot be undone; they can only progressively be developed into something else, possibly more controlled and centralised. danah boyd, when discussing the future of gamification, argues that it will seep into even more aspects of life without people even acknowledging it (Anderson and Rainie 2012, 15). Susan Crawford, on the other hand, disagrees; "[. . .] there have to be ways to explore, invent, create, and avoid – it can't be that we'll be adding up points for every salient element of our lives", she says (Crawford in ibid., 16). But which are these ways? How can the processes of gamification and datafication be disrupted or rendered non-valid or non-reliable? How can the expropriation of users' data based on the new mechanisms of capturing and quantifying stop? How can users be empowered? Do such modes of resistance exist and how would a notion like counter-gamification be defined?

Etymologically, the prefix *counter* denotes opposition, retaliation, or rivalry. It has been used by philosophers and scholars in order to express different forms of resistance, highlighting the importance of the power to against the power over. Gilles Deleuze introduced the term "counter-actualisation" to describe the possibility of one becoming the actor of her own events (1999, 155, 161) while Hardt and Negri have framed as "counter-empire" the potentiality of multitude for resistance (2000). Respectively, addressing resistance within the networks, Castells names as "counterpower" the possibility – lying in collective action – to introduce new codes or to alter the existing codes (2009, 38) while Galloway and Thacker argue that counterprotocological practices can be found when power differentials within the system are located and exploited (2007, 13). But, interestingly, it is Agamben's approach on the "counter-apparatus" which seems to be of special interest when addressing resistance within gamified and datafied systems. Opposition against mechanisms of power equals de-activation or profanation for Agamben, and this property can only be found in the element of play. Apparatuses need to be played, he claims, in order to not only abolish and erase the separations existing within them, but also to reverse and change their use (Agamben 2009).

So what if ultimately the network needs to be played, as Dmytri Kleiner impulsively also argued when discussing forms of resistance at the Transmediale festival in Berlin in 2013? What if the current gamespace – that is the ways with which data regulate today's world – can be redesigned as Wark also suggests, through play (2013a)? This does not mean that play itself can become a form of resistance; it cannot be. But if elements of game can facilitate exploitation, capitalisation, and control, on this same ground elements of play can assist in activating mechanisms of counter-gamification, revealing the functioning of network structures and raising awareness.

Such an approach brings of course the old battle between *game* and *play*, between *ludus* and *paidia* as Caillois famously addressed the two notions as two opposing poles (2001, 13), back to the foreground while at the same time offering an opportunity for their redefinition and a re-framing of their use in present time. With one word, this could be framed ambiguously as *datenspiel* in German, and be translated as the *game* of data, but also playing with *data* or else *dataplay* in English. And while the game of data refers to a new form of infinite and asymmetrical game algorithmically controlled, *dataplay* comes to express the potentiality of resistance against the rule of numbers and the power of the algorithm.

The fact that there is no outside does not mean that there is no room to move within the structures of the networks. One only needs to imagine the "emerging gaps and cracks", as Wark says; good play is still possible when the "internal tensions, ambiguities and possibilities within systems" are discovered: "The time for the hack or the exploit is at hand" (Wark 2013b).

Counter-gamification therefore can be described as a form of opposition to the increasing use of game elements within non-game systems, which aims to disrupt the processing and exploitation of users' data; it calls for a gaming with the system, for a disruptive play with its rules and content while being within it. For this reason, this form of resistance seems to be very close to hacking. Its actors might be artists, programmers, and very often skilful users who purposefully apply rules in unexpected ways, ignoring and surpassing the ones imposed by the platforms. They know that there might be no outside and no undoing. They know that there is no winning and losing in these systems. But they do move towards a changing and a re-designing of the system. They are the ones that Jan Rune Holmevick calls "electrate" inventors, as contemporary bricoleurs that use ad hoc strategies while also building a discourse around them (2012, 2–5, 23–25). Perhaps they could rather be addressed as "critical engineers" instead of artists (Oliver, Savicic and Vasiliev 2011). But at the same time, one can not ignore that they are equally connected to a long tradition of art based on "dismeasure" and "disproportion" (Virno 2012), on a revolt "against the rule of the number" (Caffetzis 2005, 100), confronting enclosures, commodification, and capitalism.

In the following section, different practices and tactics are discussed as acts of creative and playful opposition which aim to stop, confuse, subvert, or change the processes of gamification in order to enhance users' understanding and empower resistance. An attempt for their categorisation is made following different strategies that have been developed by various scholars.

6.1 Obfuscation

Obfuscation is a term introduced by Helen Nissenbaum and Finn Brunton, used to describe a form of vernacular resistance, which is based on the idea of providing misleading, false, or ambiguous data in order to make data gathering less reliable and therefore less valuable. As a counter-logic, it is proposed as an ad hoc strategy, a weapon for the weak, a practice potentially beyond moral codes with the mission to protect the privacy of the individual. Some well-known examples the writers refer to are Tor, TrackMeNot, and Facecloack (Brunton and Nissenbaum 2011). Turning to events and projects initiated by creators, it is worth mentioning the CryptoParties that invite users to learn how to defend their right to anonymity, pseudonymity, and privacy, or the work conducted by the Unlike Us network and particularly the *Unlike Art* project (2012). Playful and humorous extensions have been developed such as the *John Smith Extension*, for example, which transforms any users in Facebook and Google+ to John Smith, the most common name in the social media.

6.2 Overidentification

Overidentification is a form of resistance based on the appropriation of the sovereign ideology in order to criticise it. It is an aesthetic strategy that was initiated first back in the late 80s by the band Laibach and the art collective Neue Slowenische Kunst in Ljubljana (Pasquinelli 2010). Slavoj Žižek has explained how the particular practice, or rather in this case strategy, "frustrates" the system not as its ironic imitation, but rather by over-identifying with it, by bringing to light the obscene superego underside of the system (Žižek 1999).

In social networking platforms, creators have often used similar tactics of appropriation to oppose the system in an ironic way. Such an example is the work of the artist Tobias Leingruber. In February 2012, he set up a *Social ID Bureau* in Berlin, which would print Facebook ID cards for people interested in it. Setting up a fake office, appropriating the aesthetics of Facebook for the production of the card, and playing himself the Facebook person, the artist purposefully identified with the sovereign network, in order to underline the power of control it possesses and imply its connection to any government and third parties with interests.

6.3 Desertion – Exodus

Desertion, connected to exodus and nomadism, stands for the evacuation of places of power. Hardt and Negri have defined desertion as a contemporary form of resistance, which followed sabotage that was an act of opposition for the disciplinary society (2000, 212), whereas Galloway and Thacker, going even further, see it as resistive act for the future, which will follow what subversion was for the society of control (2007, 101). The challenge is one of "existence without representation" (ibid., 138). In times when everything can be aggregated and measured, an act of desertion signifies leaving a space of control.

Two famous applications that can be related to this act were *Seppukoo* by Les Liens Invisibles and *Web 2.0 Suicide Machine* by Moddr, which co-incidentally developed similar software at the same time in 2009 enabling users to delete their accounts from social networking sites. Gathering testimonials from the suiciders and – especially in the case of *Seppukoo* – encouraging competition among them, the creators of both platforms playfully introduced the idea of an online suicide as a social experience that can ultimately free users and their data. It is important to note that the two projects were initiated in a period when Facebook users were only able to de-activate and not to delete their accounts. Following the appearance of such projects and users' demands, the option for users to delete an account and consequently their data was added.

6.4 Hypertrophy

In this case "the goal is not to destroy technology in some neo-Luddite delusion but to push technology into a hypertrophic state", Galloway and Thacker explain, while introducing a notion of resistance that actually encourages acts of mismeasurement (Galloway and Thacker 2007, 98). "Allowing to be measured now and again for false behaviours, thereby attracting incongruent and ineffective control responses, can't hurt", they clarify (ibid., 136). Sean Dockray, in his *Suicide Facebook (Bomb) Manifesto*, similarly writes: "If we really want to fight the system we should drown it in data, we should catch as many viruses as possible; click on as many Like buttons as possible; join as many groups as possible; request as many friends as possible [. . .] Become a machine for platforms and engines" (Dockray 2010).

241

On Facebook, users have been playing with tagging and linking from the start in order to confuse the system and to break the productivity chain for the profit of the market. On Foursquare also, users have been found acting similarly when they repeatedly check-in into their home for instance, or when they name uncommon check-in places and therefore confuse the system (Cramer et al. 2011). Artist and researcher Benjamin Grosser, however, went a step further. He created *Reload the Love* (2011), a project that automatically and fictitiously inflates the notification numbers of a user's profile, playing with the value lying behind them for the user and for the network.

6.5 Exposure of Game Mechanics

Another tactic embraced by creators is the exposure of the gamefulness of the system. In this case, the game mechanics and dynamics involved are being appropriated and used in a new context, possibly a platform, a game, or an application. Such projects do not have as a goal to over-identify with the networks, but rather to imitate and ultimately reveal their game-like structures, highlighting the impact they have on users' behaviour.

An early example of this direction is the *Folded-In* game by Personal Cinema & the Erasers, created in 2008. Based on YouTube video wars, Folded-In highlighted the rating system of the videos and the competitiveness found within the popular video platform. A more recent example is Ian Bogost's *Cow Clicker* (2010), an application developed for Facebook, which invited people to click on a Farmville-like cow every six hours, simply to gain more clicks. Commenting on social games, clicktivism, and the monetisation of simple game-like interactions, Bogost made a successful satire about the "numerical socialization", as he says, of our times (Dragona 2012).

6.6 De-Gamification

De-gamification is a term introduced by Margaret Robertson in her critique of gamification where she argues that the latter unavoidably also means the former. For her, when fictional elements of games vanish, the game itself also vanishes (Robertson 2010). But, interestingly, this idea can also equally express the negation of gamification, the will that is to remove the game mechanics and dynamics added. Such is the position of game designer Holly Gramazio, who supports the idea of removing points, leaderboards, and game elements added to non-game contexts, that force people to be competitive in game-like contexts (2010).

The *Facebook Demetricator* (2012) is a project that seems to be embracing Gramazio's logic. It is a web browser extension by Benjamin Grosser that removes all metrics from the platform connected to a user's performance and sociability. The demetricator invites people to experience how a non-quantified reality may be, how motivations and interests would change, and respectively how the market could be affected. The demetricator therefore both de-gamifies and de-datafies, one could say.

6.7 Re-Appropriation / Devaluation

This category is proposed to be included as one that can reflect practices and tactics embraced by creators who wish to render the algorithmic processes and the network structures visible and understandable to the users. If gamification works by applying game elements on datafied social networking platforms and by facilitating the processing of data, this practice is rather a form of reverse engineering. It invites people to get involved in networks' obscure mechanisms and become aware of how data is really used.

Such examples are the following projects. *Commodify.us* (2012) allows users to export their data from the social media, to view them, inspect their contents, and create a new account where their data is verified and anonymised. They are invited to explore and understand how their information looks to "potential licensors" of data and social media companies while also deciding how to license their data and leverage their monetary and creative potential. A similar approach is followed by the creators of the *Data Dealer* (Averintsev et al. 2013) game, which allows users to become data vendors and "build up their assets by trading in personal information", capturing the entire population in a database.

7 CLOSING THOUGHTS

"Gamification is the latest and most sophisticated strategy of the vectoral class, its aim being on one hand to manage networks and extracting data on the other", Wark (2013c, 74) writes in a single phrase summarising the main arguments behind gamification critique and highlighting the differentiations of power between those who own the means of producing and valorising information and the ones, the users that is, who produce data. Locating and quantifying relationships, interests, and desires, gamification does indeed seem to be market's current weapon of choice as it greatly facilitates processes of identification, capitalisation, and normalisation. But what about the intentions, the effects, values, virtues, and aspirations lying behind these processes, one could ask. When discussing the impact of phenomena such as gamification, we should also consider those elements, as Sebastian Deterding (2012) argues. If game mechanics are only brought in to serve the market, what is left for the users? And how perceivable is this profound asymmetry? Aiming to highlight the urge for critical awareness and understanding, the paper presented different practices and tactics developed today by creators who wish to render control impossible, to re-appropriate content and disrupt the strategy of gamification. Empowering cryptography, embracing anonymity or pseudonymity, exposing networks structures and functions while also impeding metrics and building awareness, the aforementioned examples can be considered as emerging modes of counter-gamification, which play with the data and the networks' rules. Perhaps they are "allusions" – a notion political philosopher Paolo Virno (2012) uses to refer to contemporary forms of disobedience – in relation to what real resistance could be. But yet their existence is crucial as they highlight the potentiality users have to act and think differently while being within the gamified contexts. Changes can happen when dynamic elements, which are playful – rather than gameful – are introduced in order to disrupt predicted expectations and reinforce free movement within networked systems.

Despite the increasing datafication, gamification, and capitalisation of our times, there is always something that cannot be captured, which is yet to come. "The spark of invention becomes what the data does not say. This is something that no amount of data can ever confirm or corroborate since it has yet to exist", as Mayer-Schonberger and Cukier write (2013, 196). The excess, uncertainty, and potentiality for change are the elements that can be found within what can be defined as counter-gamification today. And possibly its creators – whether they are artists, programmers, or skilful users – are the "datapunks" that Wark claims we are in need of (2013d); the ones that, while playing "from within", will discover the gamespace's "internal tensions, ambiguities and possibilities" and possibly "redesign" it beyond systems of control (ibid.).

Acknowledgement
This research has been co-financed by the European Union (European Social Fund – ESF) and Greek national funds through the operational programme "Education and Lifelong Learning" of the National Strategic Reference Framework (NSRF) – research funding programme: Heracleitus II. Investing in knowledge society through the European Social Fund.

BIBLIOGRAPHY

AGAMBEN, GIORGIO. 2009. *What is an Apparatus and Other Essays.* Stanford: Stanford University Press.

ANDERSON, JANNA AND LEE RAINIE. 2012. "The Future of Gamification." *PewResearch Internet Project*, May 18, 2012.
http://www.pewinternet.org/Reports/2012/Future-of-Gamification.aspx.

ANDREJEVIC, MARK. 2011. "Social Networking Exploitation." In *A Networked Self: Identity, Community, and Culture on Social Network Sites*, edited by Zizi Papacharissi, 82–101. New York: Routledge.

ANDREJEVIC, MARK. 2010. "Surveillance and Alienation in the Online Economy." *Surveillance & Society* 8(3): 278–287.

ARVIDSSON, ADAM. 2007. "Creative Class or Administrative Class? On Advertising and the Underground." *Ephemera* 7(1): 8–23.

BOGOST, IAN. 2011. "Persuasive Games: Exploitationware." *Gamasutra*, May 3.
http://www.gamasutra.com/view/feature/6366/persuasive_games_exploitationware.php.

BOYD, DANAH. 2006. "Friends, Friendsters and Top 8: Writing Community into Being on Social Networking Sites." *First Monday* 11(12).
http://firstmonday.org/htbin/cgiwrap/bin/ojs/index.php/fm/article/view/1418/1336.

BRUNTON, FINN AND HELEN NISSENBAUM. 2011. "Vernacular Resistance to Data Collection and Analysis: A Political Theory of Obfuscation." *First Monday* 16(5).
http://firstmonday.org/article/view/3493/2955.

BUNCHBALL. 2010. *Gamification 101: An Introduction to the Use of Game Dynamics to Influence Behavior*. Accessed March 27, 2014.
http://www.bunchball.com/sites/default/files/downloads/gamification101.pdf.

CAFFENTZIS, GEORGE. 2005. "Immeasurable Value? An Essay on Marx's Legacy." *The Commoner* 10: 87–114.

CAILLOIS, ROGER. 2001. *Man, Play and Games*. Chicago: University of Illinois Press.

CASTELLS, MANUEL. 2009. *Communication Power*. New York: Oxford University Press.

CHAPLIN, HEATHER. 2011. "I Don't Want To Be a Superhero." *Slate*, March 29.
http://www.slate.com/articles/technology/gaming/2011/03/i_dont_want_to_be_a_super-hero.html.

CHORNEY, ALAN IVAN. 2012. "Taking the Game out of Gamification." *Dalhousie Journal of Interdisciplinary Management* 8(1).
http://ojs.library.dal.ca/djim/article/view/2012vol8Chorney.

COVER, ROB. 2012. "Performing and Undoing Identity Online: Social Networking, Identity Theories and the Incompatibility of Online Profiles and Friendship Regimes." *Convergence: The International Journal of Research into New Media Technologies* 18(2): 1–17.

CRAMER, HENRIETTE, MATTIAS ROST AND LARS ERIK HOLMQUIST. 2011. "Performing a Check-In: Emerging Practices, Norms and 'Conflicts' in Location-Sharing Using Foursquare." In *Proceedings of the 13th International Conference on Human Computer Interaction with Mobile Devices and Services*, 57–66. New York: ACM.

DEAN, JODI. 2013. "Whatever Blogging." In *Digital Labor, The Internet as a Playground and a Factory*, edited by Trebor Scholz, 127–146. New York: Routledge.

DE LANGE, MICHIEL. 2010. "Moving Circles, Mobile Media and Playful Identities." PhD diss., Erasmus Universiteit Rotterdam.

DELEUZE, GILLES. 1999. *The Logic of Sense*. New York: Columbia University Press.

DE NEEF, RIANNE. 2013. "Bread and Games: Pacifying Rewards in Gamified Systems." Accessed March 27, 2014.
http://www.academia.edu/2129229/Bread_and_Games_Pacifying_Rewards_in_Gamified_Systems.

DETERDING, SEBASTIAN. 2012. "What Your Designs Say About You" *Ted*, May 31.
http://www.ted.com/talks/sebastian_deterding_what_your_designs_say_about_you.html.

DETERDING, SEBASTIAN, DAN DIXON, RILLA KHALED AND LENNART NACKE. 2011. "From Game Design Elements to Gamefulness: Defining Gamification." In *Proceedings of the 15th International Academic MindTrek Conference: Envisioning Future Media Environments*, 9–15. New York: ACM.

DOCKRAY, SEAN. 2010. *Suicide Facebook Bomb Manifesto*. Accessed March 27, 2014.
http://spd.e-rat.org/writing/facebook-suicide-bomb-manifesto.html.

DONATH, JUDITH AND DANAH BOYD. 2004. "Public Displays of Connection." *bt technology Journal* 22(4): 71–82.

DRAGONA, DAPHNE. 2014. "Can Someone Pause the Counting Please? Encountering the New Gamified Reality of our Times." In *The Act of Reverse Engineering*, edited by Günther Friesinger and Jana Herwig, 97–114. Bielefeld: transcript.

DRAGONA, DAPHNE. 2012. "Ian Bogost." *Neural* 41: 42–45.

DRAGONA, DAPHNE. 2011. "Fremde, Ferngesteuerte Spielumgebung. Freundschaft und der Prozess der Gamifizierung." *Springerin* 4: 38–42.

EVANS, LEIGHTON. 2013. "How to Build a Map for Nothing: Immaterial Labour and Location Based Social Networking." In *Unlike Us Reader: Social Media Monopolies and Their Alternatives*, edited by Geert Lovink and Miriam Rasch, 189–199. Amsterdam: Institute of Network Cultures.

FRISSEN, VALERIE, JOS DE MUL AND JOOST RAESSENS. 2013. "Homo Ludens 2.0: Play, Media and Identity." In *Contemporary Culture, New Directions in Arts and Humanities Research*, edited by Judith Thissen, Robert Zwijnenberg and Kitty Zijlmans, 75–92. Amsterdam: Amsterdam University Press.

FUCHS, MATHIAS. 2012. "Ludic Interfaces. Driver and Product of Gamification." *GAME* 1(1). http://www.gamejournal.it/ludic-interfaces-driver-and-product-of-gamification/

GALLOWAY, ALEXANDER AND EUGENE THACKER. 2007. *The Exploit. A Theory of Networks*. Minneapolis: University of Minnesota Press.

GARTNER. 2013. "Gamification." Accessed November 10. http://www.gartner.com/technology/research/gamification/.

GERLITZ, CAROLIN AND ANNE HELMOND. 2013. "The Like Economy: Social Buttons and the Data Intensive Web." *New Media & Society* 15(8): 1348–1365.

GRAMAZIO, HOLLY. 2010. "The Degamification of Everything, Including Games." *Hide and Seek*, October 6. http://hideandseek.net/2010/10/06/the-degamification-of-everything-including-games-please/.

GROSSER, BENJAMIN. 2011. "How the Technological Design of Facebook Homogenizes Identity and Limits Personal Representation." Accessed March 27, 2014. http://bengrosser.com/blog/how-the-technological-design-of-facebook-homogeniz-es-identity-and-limits-personal-representation/.

HARDT, MICHAEL AND ANTONIO NEGRI. 2000. *Empire*. Cambridge, MA: Harvard University Press.

HOLMEVIK, JAN RUNE. 2012. *Inter/vention. Free Play in the Age of Electracy*. Cambridge, MA: The MIT Press.

HUMPHREYS, LEE. 2007. "Mobile Social Networks and Social Practice: A Case Study of Dodgeball." *Journal of Computer-Mediated Communication* 13(1): 341–360.

HUOTARI, KAI AND JUHO HAMARI. 2012. "Defining Gamification: A Service Marketing Perspective." In *Proceeding of the 16th International Academic MindTrek Conference*, edited by Artur Lugmayr, Heljä Franssila, Janne Paavilainen and Hannu Kärkkäinen, 17–22. New York: ACM.

IONIFIDES, CHRISTOS. 2012. "Gamification: The Application of Game Design in Everyday Life." MA thes., University of Copenhagen.

KIN, AMY. 2011. "Smart Gamification: Seven Core Concepts for Creating Compelling Experiences." Accessed March 27, 2014. http://www.youtube.com/watch?v=F4YP-hGZTuA.

KITCHIN, ROB AND MARTIN DODGE. 2011. *Code/Space, Software and Everyday Life*. Cambridge, MA: The MIT Press.

KLEINER, DMYTRI. 2013. *Presentation by Dmytri Kleiner: Disrupting the Bureaucracy, Re-thinking Social Networks*. Accessed March 27, 2014. http://www.transmediale.de/content/presentation-by-dmytri-kleiner-disrupting-the-bu-reaucracy-rethinking-social-networks.

KUMAR, JANAKI. 2013. "Gamification at Work: Designing Engaging Business Software." In *Design, User Experience, and Usability. Health, Learning, Playing, Cultural, and Cross-Cultural User Experience*, edited by Aaron Marcus, 528–537. Heidelberg: Springer.

247

MAN, PHILLIP. 2011. "Playing the Real Life: The Ludification of Social Ties in Social Media.
"Accessed March 27, 2014.
http://www.scribd.com/doc/53189712/Man-Playing-the-Real-Life.

MANOVICH, LEV. 2013. *Software Takes Command*. New York: Bloomsbury Academic.

MAYER-SCHONBERGER, VIKTOR AND KENNETH CUKIER. 2013. *Big Data: A Revolution that Will Transform How We Live, Work and Think*. New York: Hodder & Stoughton.

MCGONIGAL, JANE. 2011. "How to Re-Invent Reality without Gamification." Accessed March 27, 2014.
http://www.gdcvault.com/play/1014576/We-Don-t-Need-No.

MOSCA, IVAN. 2012. "+10! Gamification and deGamification." *GAME* 1(1).
http://www.gamejournal.it/plus10_gamification-and-degamification/#.UwTfbXna9d0.

NICHOLSON, SCOTT. 2013. "A User-Centered Theoretical Framework for Meaningful Gamification." Accessed March 27, 2014.
http://scottnicholson.com/pubs/meaningfulframework.pdf.

OLIVER, JULIAN, GORDAN SAVICIC AND DANJA VASILIEV. 2011. "The Critical Engineering Manifesto." Accessed January 8.
http://criticalengineering.org/.

PASQUINELLI, MATTEO. 2010. "Communism of Capital and Cannibalism of the Common: Notes on the Art of Over-Identification." Accessed March 27, 2014.
http://kruzok.files.wordpress.com/2011/05/pasquinelli_communism_of_capital1.pdf.

PEARSON, ERIKA. 2009. "All the World Wide Web is a Stage: The Performance of Identity in Online Social Networks." *First Monday* 14(3).
http://www.firstmonday.org/htbin/cgiwrap/bin/ojs/index.php/fm/article/view/2162/2127.

PRADEEP KUMAR, SAM FELIX AND TEJASVI ADDAGADA. 2013. "Leading Transformation through Gamification." *Infosys Lab Briefings* 11(3): 47–54.

PRIEBATSCH, SETH. 2010. "The Game Layer on Top of the World". *Ted*, August 30.
http://www.ted.com/talks/seth_priebatsch_the_game_layer_on_top_of_the_world.html

RAESSENS, JOOST 2006. "Playful Identities, or the Ludification of Culture." *Games and Culture* 1(1): 52–57.

RAPP, AMON. 2013. "Beyond Gamification: Enhancing User Engagement Through Meaningful Game Elements." Accessed March 27, 2014.
http://www.fdg2013.org/program/doctoral/dc10_rapp.pdf.

ROBERTSON, MARGARET. 2010. "Can't Play, Won't Play." *Hide & Seek*, October 6.
http://hideandseek.net/2010/10/06/cant-play-wont-play/.

ROGERS, RICHARD. 2009. "Post-Demographic Machines." In *Walled Gardens*, edited by Annet Dekker, and Annette Wolfsberger, 29–39. Eidhoven: Lecturis.

SALEN, KATIE AND ERIC ZIMMERMAN. 2004. *Rules of Play. Games Design Fundamentals*. Cambridge, MA: The MIT press.

TERRANOVA, TIZIANA. 2004. *Network Culture. Politics for the Information Age*. London: Pluto Press.

VIRNO, PAOLO. 2012. "The Dismeasure of Art: An Interview with Paolo Virno." In *Being an Artist in Post-Fordist Times*, edited by Pascal Gielen and Paul De Bruyne, 19–46. Rotterdam: NAi publishers.

WARK, MCKENZIE. 2013a. "A Ludic Century." *Public Seminar*, November 22.
http://www.publicseminar.org/2013/11/a-ludic-century/#.UrP-dYXj_QI.

WARK, MCKENZIE. 2013b. "#Celerity, A Critique of the Manifesto for an Accelerationist Politics." Accessed March 27, 2014.
http://syntheticedifice.files.wordpress.com/2013/06/celerity.pdf.
WARK, MCKENZIE. 2013c. "Considerations on a Hacker Manifesto." In *Digital Labor, The Internet as a Playground and a Factory*, edited by Trebor Scholz, 69–75. New York: Routledge.
WARK, MCKENZIE 2013d. "Accelerationism." *Public Seminar*, November 18.
http://www.publicseminar.org/2013/11/accelerationism/#.UqNPGoXj_QJ.
WERBACH, KEVIN AND DAN HUNTER. 2012. *For the Win: How Game Thinking Can Revolutionize Your Business*. Philadelphia: Wharton Digital Press.
ZICHERMAN, GABE AND JOSELIN LINDER. 2013. *The Gamification Revolution: How Leaders Leverage Game Mechanics to Crush the Competition*. New York: McGraw-Hill Professional.
ZICHERMANN GABE AND JOSELIN LINDER. 2010. *Game-Based Marketing: Inspire Customer Loyalty Through Rewards, Challenges and Contests*. Hoboken: John Wiley & Sons.
ŽIŽEK, SLAVOJ. 1999. "The Interpassive Subject." Accessed March 27, 2014.
www.lacan.com/zizek-pompidou.htm.

LUDOGRAPHY

DUOLINGO. 2011. Luis von Ahn.
https://www.duolingo.com.
FOURSQUARE. 2009. Dennis Crowley and Naveen Selvadurai.
http://www.foursquare.com.
LOSE IT! *2011,* FitNow, Inc.
https://www.loseit.com.
NIKE+ RUNNING APP. 2006. Nike, Inc.
https://secure-nikeplus.nike.com/plus/.
STARBUCKS. 2014. "My Starbucks Rewards." Accessed February 20.
https://www.starbucks.com/card/rewards.

ARTWORKS

AVERINTSEV, IVAN, WOLFIE CHRISTL, PASCALE OSTERWALDER AND RALF TRAUNSTEINER. 2013. *Data Dealer*. Game on Facebook.
https://datadealer.com.
BOGOST, IAN. 2010. *Cow Clicker*. Game on Facebook.
COMMODIFY, INC. 2012. *Commodify.us*. Web application.
http://commodify.us/.
GROSSER, BENJAMIN. 2012. *Facebook Demetricator*. Web application.
http://bengrosser.com/projects/facebook-demetricator/.
GROSSER, BENJAMIN. 2011. *Reload the Love*. Web application.
http://bengrosser.com/projects/reload-the-love/.

LEINGRUBER, TOBIAS. 2012. *Social ID bureau*. Performance at Supermarkt, Berlin, March 2. http://socialidbureau.com/.

LES LIENS INVISIBLES. 2009. *Seppukoo*. Web application. http://www.seppukoo.com/.

MODDR. 2009. *Web 2.0 Suicide Machine*. Web application. http://suicidemachine.org/.

PERSONAL CINEMA & THE ERASERS. 2008. *Folded-In*. Web application.

UNLIKE US. 2012. *Unlike Art*. Workshop at TrouwAmsterdam, Amsterdam, March 8. http://networkcultures.org/unlikeart/.

GAMED AGENCIES: AFFECTIVELY MODULATING OUR SCREEN- AND APP-BASED DIGITAL FUTURES

by **Matthew Tiessen**

In other words: the internet, like a pack of cigarettes or lots of cocaine, lets you just sit in a room and repeatedly trigger reward chemicals that, back in the environment of our evolution, you could trigger only with more work and only less frequently. That's why an internet habit, like a cocaine habit, can reach dysfunctional levels [. . . W]hat the internet does is take lots of things that natural selection designed us to find gratifying and make them much easier to get. (Wright 2012)

Imagine waking up on Monday morning with your web-connected alarm clock awarding your "Early Bird" account 175 points for getting out of bed in less than a minute. Imagine slowly shuffling to the kitchen anticipating that your refrigerator will reward you 55 "Health Superstar" points if you choose the low-fat organic yoghurt as a topping for your breakfast granola. Your shuffling immersion into digital forms of distraction continues when you swipe the finger-grease covered screen of your smartphone to check for messages – the government reminds you that digitally geo-tagging "suspicious activity" on your commute to work will lead to refunds come tax time.

Suddenly, your smartphone vibrates and you anxiously check the status of your Facebook page to see if your comments recommending Google's latest wearable technologies on a friend's "Wall" have received any "Thumbs Up" votes – not to mention whether Google's web-crawlers have credited your bank account given your positive comments about their products (Kalwar et al. 2012; Weidman et al. 2012). Having finished your yoghurt and granola, you trundle to the bathroom to brush your teeth with your digitally-enabled BeamBrush toothbrush[1], which you know will add "Sparkly Smile" badges via your smartphone to your online account if you brush for a solid three minutes. But your favourite part of your morning ritual is your commute to the office in your new hybrid automobile. You experience such a profound thrill watching the digital readouts of your Ford Fusion Hybrid playfully depict growing virtual plants on your instrument panel as a digital reflection of your attempts to drive as efficiently as possible (Zichermann and Cunningham 2011, 78). The fact that driving this way is better for the environment is also a bonus. Upon arriving at your job for a Web 3.0 venture-capital supported startup, you feel great about your morning, about your contributions to society, about games well played, and about your chances of success in your office's new Worker Incentivisation Challenge… (Heisler 2012; Meister 2012).

This hypothetical vignette of future morning rituals gives us a glimpse of a not too distant world in which everyday activities are overrun by digitally mediated gamification – a world in which the embedding of game-like logics and game-like mechanics into the screens and digital devices that mediate between us and our everyday routines adds "value" and a layer of quantification-derived incentives to previously non-game contexts. This is a digitally and visually mediated world in which intrinsic values aren't quite valuable, profitable or affectively desirable enough and so are overcoded and re-coded by icons, graphs, statistics, points, and badges, all in pursuit of access, privileges, productivity, prestige, and feelings of satisfaction. This is a world in which the awarding, redeeming, gifting, and trading of credits, digital achievements, and virtual trophies has become an end in itself.

---

1   See: www.beamtoothbrush.com (accessed May 6, 2014).

Increasingly, gamification software applications are embedding digitally and virtually readable metrics into people's everyday lives (Anderson 2012; Juul 2010; Kohler 2010) in order, for instance, to encourage individuals to:

1. Embrace repetitive chores
2. Complete customer surveys
3. Promote socially desirable behaviour (Greitemeyer and Osswald 2010; Harris 2010)
4. Engage more deeply with social media and company websites (Curran 2012)
5. Achieve fitness and health goals (Read and Shortell 2011; Lin et al. 2006; Woods 2012)
6. Contribute to e-learning contexts (Kapp 2012; Tannahill, Tissington and Senior 2012)
7. Support desirable financial behaviour (Shin and Shin 2011; Yamakami 2012)
8. Even make crowd-sourced scientific discoveries (Cooper et al. 2010)

Indeed, the increasing role being played by visual and digital representations of quantified success finds emerging and market-driven modes of digital discipline, such as gamification, encroaching upon and colonising new areas of life that presumably require "added value" in order to be meaningful. Consider the number of "likes" you get on Facebook, the number of followers you have on Twitter, not to mention your salary, your credit score, your investment returns as examples of "values" in a valueless world. This is the very type of meaning making that Nietzsche once diagnosed as typical for our valueless and nihilistic era. For Nietzsche, nihilism was in part a disheartening product of his historical moment, one in which he diagnosed humanity to have become corrupt insofar as it had lost "its instincts". As Nietzsche explains it, a species becomes corrupt "when it loses its instincts, when it chooses, when it prefers, things that will harm it" (Nietzsche 2005, 6). In Nietzsche's view, a life full of value and health must manifest "an instinct for growth, for endurance, for the accumulation of force, of power" since "when there is no will to power, there is decline" (ibid.). Nietzsche, then, was compelled to announce to all who would hear that "nihilistic values, values of decline, have taken control under the aegis of the holiest of names" (ibid.).

While Nietzsche's bombastic admonitions that we have lost our instincts can be regarded as ever so slightly extreme, are they not also illuminating for us as we live through this era of gamified toothbrushes and algorithmically driven online dating platforms?

A future overrun by gamification – whether we deem it nihilistic or not – won't be one in which the rules, conditions, and incentives of the "games" – and of our gamed lives – remain static; rather, by layering high-speed computational capacities on top of digitally enabled everyday objects, context-bound information is able to be fed to game-players in real time, creating adaptive game-spaces capable of modulating gamer behaviour in milliseconds by providing game-based inputs based on the game-player's outputs. In other words, in the hypothetical total-game-space of the future, it won't be us creatively adapting to our games, but our games creatively adapting to us (in real time). Drawing on high-speed algorithmic techniques already at work in the financial world, the gamification of the future is being developed today. The goal of this capital-obsessed development: to develop new forms of digital distraction and sensory stimulation capable of overcoding self-reflexive and, as Nietzsche might say, "instinctual" ways of negotiating life's challenges and choices (Martin 2002).

GAMIFICATION'S PREHISTORY

In the face of the burgeoning gamification explosion, my objective here is to develop a more critical understanding of the affective dimensions of our increasingly mobile and screen-based economy by interrogating some of the social, political, and expanding economic implications of gamification. More specifically, I want to objectify and critically examine two ways gamification is reshaping everyday social relations between humans (and machines):

First, the ways game-like apps and game-based modes of incentivisation are affecting relations between humans and other humans, humans and nonhumans, and even nonhumans and nonhumans as they become an increasingly prominent phenomenon in our digitally mobile and wireless world, infiltrating the realms of business, education, health, public policy, and "global governance" (Pearce 2009; Schreiner 2008).

Second, the idea that while the gamification of everyday life affords societies, businesses, institutions, and communities the ability to encourage and support socially, politically, and economically "desirable" behaviour

(Deterding et al. 2010; Whitson and Dormann 2011), the desirability of organisations attempting to use real-time managerial control in a deliberate attempt to direct "dividualized" (Deleuze 1992) behaviour through affectively charged modulations of desire (Dormann and Biddle 2008) and point-based modes of incentivisation and quantification might not be so desirable after all.

Of course, attempts to control, train, coerce, and compel populations using seductively designed new media platforms are not by any stretch new. We recall that in the 1920s, modern propaganda's founding father Edward Bernays seized on the power of what was the "new media" of the time in order, in his words, to "manipulate" and to "mould" public opinion. Bernays understood then what gamification's proponents are mobilising today – the idea that, through the "mass distribution of ideas" using new media platforms, public opinion could be "moved, directed, and formed" (Bernays 1928, 971). Moreover, Bernays understood that to appropriately "move" people, you needed to define, activate, and in turn fulfil the public's yearnings and desires – their (apparent) longings for success, achievement, recognition, and so on. As he explained:

Public opinion can be moved, directed, and formed by such a technique. But at the core of this great heterogeneous body of public opinion is a tenacious will to live, to progress, to move in the direction of ultimate social and individual benefit. He who seeks to manipulate public opinion must always heed it. (Ibid., 971)

For Bernays, those wishing to control the individuals within the mass had to gain access to the "great basic motivations" which he described as: "self-preservation, ambition, pride, hunger, love [. . .] imitativeness, the desire to be a leader, [and] love of play". "[T]hese and others", he wrote, "are the psychological raw materials of which every leader must be aware in his endeavour to win the public to his point of view" (Bernays 1935, 83). They are also, of course, the targets of gamification's designers, practitioners, and boosters. Indeed, it's interesting just how apparently natural and intuitive this logic of affectively modulated control and persuasion is to gamification's practitioners whose ideas and strategies could be regarded as being at the forefront of current academic thought insofar as they are, in many respects, premised on thinking "the human" as a potential cyborg (Hayles 1999), as an affectively motivated "desiring machine" (Deleuze and Guattari 1987), and as one agential actor among others (Latour 2005; Thrift 2008).

Later on, Marshall McLuhan echoed Bernays' promise of mediated publics in his famed Playboy interview from 1967 when he noted that through the use of a pre-iPhone screen-based technology the public could be manipulated and affectively modulated through the power of sensorial – primarily visual – stimulation. As McLuhan explained: "There's nothing at all difficult about putting computers in the position where they will be able to conduct carefully orchestrated programming of the sensory life of whole populations" (McLuhan 1969, 19).

Similarly, in the early 1990s Deleuze was warning us of the dark side of digital quantification. In his "societies of control" article, he warned us that future modes of discipline and control would be, at once, more focused on targeting the individual (consider, for instance, your debt score or credit rating) and more capable of dividing us up into numerical strata – of dividualizing us. As he explains:

> The disciplinary societies have two poles: the signature that designates the individual, and the number [. . .] that indicates his or her position within a mass. This is because the disciplines never saw any incompatibility between these two, and because at the same time power individualises and masses together, that is, constitutes those over whom it exercises power into a body and molds the individuality of each member of that body. (Deleuze 1992, 5)

For Deleuze, digital forms of dividualising quantification would offer "power" the means to control subjects using a light – almost imperceptible – touch. Digital "control mechanisms" – as he called them – would form a system of "variable geometry the language of which is numerical". These control mechanism would work using modulation, they would be responsive to subtle changes, to invisible variations. He explains that the controlling mechanisms of the future (of our present) would operate almost intuitively, "like a self-deforming cast that will continuously change from one moment to the other, or like a sieve whose mesh will transmute from point to point" (ibid., 4).

More recently, in the late 1990s, techno-sceptics like the artist/activist group the Critical Art Ensemble were feverishly warning us of the dangers of our post-visual data-bodies and the ways they will – in the future – begin to define what our fleshy selves are capable of. As they explained in 1997:

> With the virtual body came its fascist sibling, the data body – a much more highly developed virtual form, and one that exists in complete service to the corporate and police state [. . .] What brought the data body to maturity is the technological apparatus. With its immense storage capacity and its mechanisms for quickly ordering and retrieving information, no detail of social life is too insignificant to record and to scrutinize. From the moment we are born and our birth certificate goes online, until the day we die and our death certificate goes online, the trajectory of our individual lives is recorded in scrupulous detail [. . .] The desire of authoritarian power to make the lives of its subordinates perfectly transparent achieves satisfaction through the data body. Everyone is under permanent surveillance by virtue of their necessary interaction with the marketplace. Just how detailed data body information actually may be is a matter of speculation, but we can be certain that it is more detailed than we would like it to be, or care to think [. . .] But the most frightening thing about the data body is that it is the center of an individual's social being [. . .] We are powerless to contradict the data body. Its word is the law [. . .] The corporate intention for deploying this technology (in addition to profit) is so transparent, it's painful. The only possible rejoinder is: 'Have you ever been at a work station... 24 hours a day, 365 days a year? You will'. Now the virtual sweat shop can go anywhere you do! (Critical Art Ensemble 1997, 145–146)

For the Critical Art Ensemble, the emergence of the "virtual" digital platform created the conditions for the immaterial expansion of capital-driven ways of being, thinking, and doing. The Internet, in their view, would emerge as a computerised tool for the powers that be who were – as they are now – intent on maintaining, quite literally, business as usual. In their view, "the most significant use of the electronic apparatus is to keep order, to replicate dominant pancapitalist ideology, and to develop new markets" (ibid., 141). In the face of this imminent future (our NSA-surveilled present [Gellman, Soltani and Peterson 2013; Risen and Poitras 2013]), they urged anyone who would listen that the "need for Net criticism certainly is a matter of overwhelming urgency". Critical Art Ensemble acknowledges that "a number of critics have approached the new world of computerised communications with a healthy amount of scepticism". They fear that "their message has been lost in the noise and spectacle of corporate hype – the unstoppable tidal wave of seduction has enveloped so many in its dynamic utopian beauty that little time for careful reflection is left" (ibid., 139). Their hyperbolic observations might even give us pause by encouraging us to ask: If that was then, what about now?

Well, for one thing we could observe that social media platforms, the touch screens and mobile technologies that help enable them, and emerging gamification protocols and databases are valuable not because they involve data, statistics, tweets, and desires expressive of the general experience of being alive, but because this data produces a useful resources for organisation whose professional interest is in surveilling us once we "go public", as Greg Elmer (2013) has observed. Moreover, as is increasingly becoming clear, once we've rendered ourselves transparent to the digital apparatus, our desires are parsed before being fed back to us in a virtuous – and seemingly benign – loop of desiring rewards and rewarding desires.

GAMIFICATION HYPE-NOSIS

But let's look a bit more closely at gamification today – as a market, a promise, a quasi-religion, an incentivisation tool, a way to manufacture "better" human beings... Over the past few years, gamification has been taking the digital – and especially the mobile – world by storm, promising at once to increase bottom lines, promote healthy behaviour, while extending and deepening social as well as virtual relationships. The hype surrounding gamification has generated a certain level of debate about its merits, its relationship to gaming-culture more generally, whether it works at all, etc. Indeed, "real" gamers – those who use consoles like the just released Xbox One or PlayStation 4 – are embarrassed by the gamification upstarts who want to associate with them. But whether or not gamification lives up to the hype, its strategists and proponents persist in their attempts to embed game-based logics into more and more of the screens and devices that define our everyday (digital) lives.

But the hype surrounding gamification was – and is – certainly real, and occasionally breathless. For example, gamification guru Jane McGonigal has insisted that "reality is broken" and that digital games can "save the world" (2011). Similarly, game designer Jesse Schell wondered in a recent TED talk whether using "game-like external rewards" can "make people lead better lives?" (2010). The scale of today's gamification industry is enormous and growing; for example, in 2011 the profits from social gaming company Zynga – which recently held its initial public offering (IPO) – made up 12% of Facebook's entire revenue stream prior to Facebook's own controversial IPO (i.e. of Facebook's $3.71 billion in sales in 2011, Zynga contributed $445 million) (Geron 2012). Indeed, gamification-based companies such as Bunchball.com, Badgeville.com, and Bigdoor.com are helping global corporations like Adobe, eBay, Intel, ABC, CBS, ESPN, NBC, CISCO, Microsoft, Toyota, and Ford connect digitally with their customers through mobile communication technologies (smartphones, tablets, laptops, etc.), "Corporate Game Design" and "Emotion Hacking" by embedding game-driven incentives into, for example, employee training programs, financial services websites, shopping websites, enhanced loyalty programmes, social networks, e-surveys, call-centre protocols, and market research. Other gamification companies such as Strava and Fitocracy (more about Strava later) turn fitness into a game by encouraging users to upload GPS data onto the web from their mobile devices where it is data-mined and quantified in order to provide users with feedback and graphs that not only contain information about their individual athletic performances and newly "quantified selves" (Wolf 2010), but help place their performances among an athletic hierarchy of digitally equipped athletes. Additionally, e-learning companies such as the Canadian company Desire2Learn are applying game-based strategies to the field of learning management systems, embedding digital technologies into "real" and "virtual" classrooms, and enabling instructors at, for example, the University of Waterloo, to make "data-driven decisions" in order to design, customise, develop, and deliver online "social learning" experiences capable of catering to students at a "granular" level across mobile platforms by allowing them to collaborate virtually while being data-mined and assessed by their teachers (Desire2Learn 2011).

The basic strategic motivation driving gamification's designers is to provide rewards for repetitive tasks at regular and random intervals in order

Will we live in a "gamocracy" where we're the ones being played? to allow for the perception of constant improvement, thus providing an *addictive motivation* for gamers to keep playing the game (Wills 2009). Essentially, the thinking goes, if gamification can provide the right set of data-driven and sensorial stimuli, our brains will treat software-based digital representations like a drug, potentially resulting in the Pavlovian responses marketers dream about. The potential result of the gamification of everyday life is that, over time, more and more daily events and professional activities will develop a sort of virtual "achievement layer" that primarily reflects gamers' abilities to fulfil their desire to click buttons, remain distracted, follow guidelines, achieve top scores, and make it to the next level. Indeed, the ideal gamification scenario, we might say, would result not so much in gamers playing games as it would in gamers being played by their games. It would also result, let's not forget, in digital metadata pertaining to the patterns of everyday life to be uploaded and instrumentalised in new and powerful ways, resulting in the creation of yet more information-driven markets capable of absorbing the seemingly endless flows of liquidity flowing from central bank "printing presses".

As I've already suggested, given the unrelenting process of gamifying everyday life, gamification has its critics. For instance, Ian Bogost, a prominent game-theorist, describes game-based digital strategies – particularly those designed to sell merchandise and manipulate customers – as "exploitationware" (Bogost 2011) due to the ways these games prey on affective and emotional needs for quantifiable achievement and re-value "play" as a mere product promotion strategy. Moreover, Bogost – also an object-oriented ontology philosopher (Bogost 2012) – cautions us about the potential for life in a future gamocracy to become one in which the relationship between human, machine, and digital agency becomes increasingly blurred. As he explains: "When people act because incentives compel them toward particular choices, they cannot be said to be making choices at all" (Bogost 2010).

Indeed, it is this "beyond the human", or posthuman (Barad 2003; Braidotti 2013; Hayles 1999), dimension of gamification that is perhaps most interesting and will become increasingly worthy of critical examination, particularly as attempts at algorithmic and digitally modulated control intersect with social, legal, moral, and ontological conventions that regard the so-called "human" as the locus for agency, decision-making, and desire.

As has already been demonstrated and critiqued, 21st-century digital algorithms and computational capacities are increasingly being used to analyse and represent complex streams of what's known as "big data" in order to attempt to pre-emptively modulate, customise, and control the (actual and virtual) world before we encounter it (Andrejevic 2011; Best 2010; Bratich 2006; Crang and Graham 2007; Elmer 2003; Elmer and Opel 2006; Fuchs et al. 2012; Lyon 2001; Lyon 2003; Massumi 2007). Gamification, then, has the potential to short-circuit or pre-empt our desires by being better and faster at being contextually aware of a world increasingly overlayed with – and determined by – the data we generate as we go about our lives (not to mention the data that has already been accumulated and mined from the past). That is, the persistent extension of gamification and achievement-driven metrics of value has the potential to result in a corresponding decrease in the once "inherent" value of things like health, education, friendship, and community-building insofar as they will become increasingly obscured or replaced by quantified metrics and credits such that the act of choosing and making everyday decisions is pre-emptively short-circuited or modulated (Deleuze 1992) by not only extra-subjective motivations, but also by nonhuman algorithms whose secret "understanding" (Tiessen and Seigworth 2012) of desires is perpetually being discerned and translated into computer-readable binary code and other virtual quanta (Galloway 2004; Munster 2011).

OVERCODING THE OUT OF DOORS: MOUNTAIN BIKING, ROAD CYCLING, AND STRAVA

At this point, in the spirit of peering into the darker sides of the digital, I want to shift gears a bit to focus on some of the very tangible effects of the overlaying of gamified logics onto previously non-game contexts, namely mountain biking and road cycling. I want to focus on these sporting activities and some of the ways they intersect with a gamification-facilitating web platform named Strava, in order to examine what can happen when digital data comes to overcode the immersive continuity of what, in this case, we might describe as the thrill-seeking pursuit of flow, adrenalin, speed, and encounters with "nature". Indeed, as an avid mountain biker, the implications of the digital overcoding of the woods, mountains, and trails is a topic that is of great interest to me.

As you may know, mountain biking is usually an activity that allows us to encounter the beauty of our natural environments while, at the same time, seeking out spills, thrills, physical challenges, and – when done with others – social camaraderie. This changes on the race course, but this description is fairly comprehensive. This bucolic bubble, however, is increasingly being burst by the adoption by mountain bikers of mobile GPS units that allow them to visually map their ride and digitally data-mine their adventures before uploading the metadata generated by the ride to websites like Strava.com (2009) where this data is pooled with the data – the heart-rates, the distances, the speeds, the caloric output, the number of rides, times, and biometric data – of other riders. The experience of mountain biking, then, is increasingly being quantified – and overcoded. This quantification, in turn, has led to measurement and measurement, in turn, has led to comparison, and comparison has led to competition where it didn't exist before. Competition is then catalogued, represented, and shared by Strava, which gives riders the ability to transform even solo rides into "social" – as in, social media – experiences. The thing is, though, riders are finding that the virtual and digital social spaces created by Strava are feeding back into the analogue spaces of the mountain bike trails in not so desirable ways. Indeed, increasingly riders are commenting that their rides are becoming less bucolic, less social, less sensorially immersive and satisfying as those riders pursuing virtual trophies or seeking to become "KOMs" (Kings of the Mountain on Strava) in order to impress their online followers and "friends", holler at fellow riders to "Get outta the way! Strava! Strava!" as they ride past at a pace that turns the once immersive and flow-centric experience into nothing but a statistically focused blur. As Tom Vanderbilt recently wrote in Outside Magazine, Strava has led to the quantified self-equipped cyclist having to ask herself or himself: "Is the unexamined ride worth riding?" (Vanderbilt 2013).

According to Strava's "About" page, the website and gamification platform grew out of the needs of its digitally connected designers to create quasi-social athletic experiences in the face of their professional lives which were exceedingly busy and usually only allowed for solo cycling excursions. They explain:

> We missed the sense of camaraderie and friendly competition that drove us to achieve our best through training with others. We envisioned Strava

as the means to put our workouts and races into context. We call that *social fitness.* Today, Strava lets athletes all over the world experience social fitness – sharing, comparing and competing with each other's personal fitness data via mobile and online apps. Currently focused on the needs of avid cyclists and runners, Strava lets you track your rides and runs via your iPhone, Android or dedicated GPS device to analyze and quantify your performance. Strava makes fitness a social experience, providing motivation and camaraderie even if you're exercising alone. (Strava 2013)

Obviously, the intentions of Strava's designers are more or less straightforward and noble ones. But like gamification itself, Strava's infiltration of cycling's ranks – not to mention its disturbance of the once less competitive and more casual and flow-centric thrill-seeking of mountain biking – has been the target of some unsubtle critique by those with a pulpit in the mountain biking world. Author Seb Kemp's rant from *Bike Magazine* – an influential mountain bike publication – sums up the situation without pulling any punches. In his view:

The Strava app helps you become more and more of a desperate loser by creating an imaginary world where every moment on your bicycle can be turned into a race. Not against yourself, but against other people. Other imaginary people. Each part of your ride becomes a series of timed sections where you compete with the virtual world for the title of KOM (King Of the Mountain). It is sort of like internet gaming except the people that play Strava actually go outside.
Anyway, Strava has become very popular in a very short amount of time, which goes to show that not that many people actually ever enjoyed riding their bike. Strava gave internet [surfers] a reason to grin and bare the drudgery of riding because now they could be in contact with their internet friends and, better still, compete with them for an imaginary title. (Kemp 2012)

But Strava's gamified effects on non-digital space and time go beyond its ability to transform random stretches of road or trail into time-trail-like segments of a quasi-virtual or quasi-actual race course. In fact, Seb Kemp's commentary in Bike Magazine is a response to another story involving, in this case, Strava, virtual competition, and death – what has become known as "Stravacide". The virtual recognition afforded by Strava is a gamified reward in recognition of the speed cyclists can achieve while passing through given sections of road and trail. The faster, the better! To paraphrase media theorist Paul Virilio: "In the world of Strava, speed is power" (Virilio 2006). Of course, KOM (King of the Mountain) recognition does not only go to those with the best climbing speeds, it also gets bestowed upon those capable of the quickest descents. For one cyclist – William K. Flint, Jr. – the overlay of digital incentives onto his everyday life while out for a ride in the hills above Berkeley, California proved fatal (Darlington 2013). Flint, an avid Strava user, twitterer, and computer coder, died on a descent after running into a car at the intersection of Grizzly Peak Blvd. and South Park Drive. It seems Flint's King of the Mountain time on that stretch had just been beaten by some other unnamed and faceless virtual nemesis, and in an attempt to reclaim the crown he crashed into a sport utility vehicle driven by a mother and her daughter and met his demise (McLaughlin 2012).

But what's perhaps most interesting about this tragic situation – this tragic conflagration of virtual and actual environments and desires – is what happened next: Flint's parents decided to sue Strava – which they claimed had developed a sort of nonhuman agency in excess of that of its user, William K. Flint – and was now at fault for "failing to warn cyclists competing in KOM challenges that the road conditions were not suited for racing" and "encouraging dangerous behaviour" (Bicycle Retailer 2012). According to Flint's parents, Strava failed "to host a safe competition" (ibid.). By extension, the Flints' legal argument can be seen as representing the nascent emergence among an increasingly digitally and algorithmically modulated public of what will become a more widespread – and ontologically significant (Bennett 2010; Bogost 2012; Pickering 1995) – notion: that when faced with the right digital and algorithmic architecture, humans will be unable to resist its plans for them. In this case, of course, the plan was to go faster and farther at any cost. What this case objectifies and even foreshadows, is that popular understandings of the lines that distinguish between human agency and the "agency" of computer code and digital devices will increasingly become blurred and destabilised in the popular imagination in the not too distant future, giving rise to ontological and existential questions and complexities that will increasingly challenge legal, political, and philosophical paradigms –

all thanks to the affectively enticing lure of online achievements and the perpetual pursuit of virtual supremacy and digitally designed deliverance.

The author wishes to acknowledge the support of the Social Science and Humanities Research Council of Canada (SSHRC).

BIBLIOGRAPHY

ANDERSON, JANNA. 2012. "Gamification and the Internet: Experts Expect Game Layers to Expand in the Future, with Positive and Negative Results." *Games for Health Journal* 1(4): 299–302.

ANDREJEVIC, MARK. 2011. "The Work That Affective Economics Does." *Cultural Studies* 25(4–5): 604–620.

BARAD, KAREN. 2003. "Posthumanist Performativity: Toward an Understanding of How Matter Comes to Matter." *Signs: Journal of Women in Culture and Society* 28(3): 801–831.

BENNETT, JANE. 2010. *Vibrant Matter: A Political Ecology of Things*. Durham: Duke University Press.

BERNAYS, EDWARD. 1935. "Molding Public Opinion." *Annals of the American Academy of Political and Social Science* 179: 82–87.

BERNAYS, EDWARD. 1928. "Manipulating Public Opinion: The Why and The How." *American Journal of Sociology* 33(6): 958–971.

BEST, KIRSTY. 2010. "Living in the Control Society: Surveillance, Users and Digital Screen Technologies." *International Journal of Cultural Studies* 13(1): 5–24.

BOGOST, IAN. 2012. *Alien Phenomenology, or, What It's Like to Be a Thing*. Minneapolis: University of Minnesota Press.

BOGOST, IAN. 2011. "Persuasive Games: Exploitationware." *Gamasutra*, May 3. http://www.gamasutra.com/view/feature/6366/persuasive_games_exploitationware.php.

BOGOST, IAN. 2010. "Persuasive Games: Shell Games." *Gamasutra*, March 3. http://www.gamasutra.com/view/feature/132682/persuasive_games_shell_games.php.

BRAIDOTTI, ROSI. 2013. *Posthuman*. Cambridge: Polity.

BRATICH, JACK. Z. 2006. "Nothing is Left Alone for Too Long: Reality Programming and Control Society Subjects." *Journal of Communication Inquiry* 30(1): 65–83.

COOPER, SETH, FIRAS KHATIB, ADRIEN TREUILLE, JANOS BARBERO, JEEHYUNG LEE, MICHAEL BEENEN, ANDREW LEAVER-FAY, DAVID BAKER, ZORAN POPOVIĆ AND FOLDIT PLAYERS. 2010. "Predicting Protein Structures with a Multiplayer Online Game." *Nature* 466: 756–760.

CRANG, MIKE AND STEPHEN GRAHAM. 2007. "Sentient Cities: Ambient Intelligence and the Politics of Urban Space." *Information, Communication & Society* 10(6): 789–817.

CRITICAL ART ENSEMBLE. 1997. *Flesh Machine*. New York: Autonomedia.

CURRAN, KEVIN AND ROISIN LAUTMAN. 2012. "The Rise of Gaming on Social Networks." *International Journal of Social Networking and Virtual Communities* 1(1). http://iaesjournal.com/online/index.php/VirCom/article/view/477.

DARLINGTON, DAVID. 2013. "The Strava Files." *Bicycling* November: 60–70, 86–91.

DELEUZE, GILLES. 1992. "Postscript on the Societies of Control." *October* 59: 3–7.

DELEUZE, GILLES AND FELIX GUATTARI. 1987. *A Thousand Plateaus: Capitalism and Schizophrenia*. Minneapolis: University of Minnesota Press.

DESIRE2LEARN. 2011. "News." Accessed December 1. http://www.desire2learn.com/news/2011/Desire2Learn-Announces-Release-of-Newest-Enhancements-to-Desire2Learn-Learning-Suite/.

DETERDING, SEBASTIAN, STAFFAN BJORK, STEPHAN DREYER, AKI JARVINEN, BEN KIRMAN, JULIAN KUCKLICH, JANNE PAAVILAINEN, VALENTINA RAO AND JAN-HINRIK SCHMIDT. 2010. *Social Game Studies: A Workshop Report*. Accessed March 27, 2014. http://socialgamestudies.org/report.

DORMANN, CLAIRE AND ROBERT BIDDLE. 2008. "Understanding Game Design for Affective Learning." In *Future Play 2008: Proceedings of the 2008 Conference on Future Play: Research, Play, Share*, 41–48. New York: ACM.

ELMER, GREG. 2013. "IPO 2.0: The Panopticon Goes Public." *MediaTropes* 4(1): 1–16.

ELMER, GREG. 2003. "A Diagram of Panoptic Surveillance." *New Media & Society* 5(2): 231–247.

ELMER, GREG, AND ANDY OPEL. 2006. "Surviving the Inevitable Future. Preemption in an Age of Faulty Intelligence." *Cultural Studies* 20(4): 477–492.

FLINT, WILLIAM, K. AND KATHLEEN B. FLINT. 2012. "William K. Flint et al vs. Strava, Inc." Accessed March 27, 2014. http://www.bicycleretailer.com/sites/default/files/downloads/article/StravaSuit.pdf.

FUCHS, CHRISTIAN, KEES BOERSMA, ANDERS ALBRECHTSLUND AND MARISOL SANDOVAL, eds. 2012. *Internet and Surveillance: The Challenges of Web 2.0 and Social Media*. New York: Routledge.

GALLOWAY, ALEXANDER. R. 2004. *Protocol: How Control Exists After Decentralization*. Cambridge: MIT Press.

GELLMAN, BARTON, ASHKAN SOLTANI AND ANDREW PETERSON. 2013. "How We Know the NSA Had Access to Internal Google and Yahoo Cloud Data." *Washington Post*, November 4. Accessed December 1, 2013. http://www.washingtonpost.com/blogs/the-switch/wp/2013/11/04/how-we-know-the-nsa-had-access-to-internal-google-and-yahoo-cloud-data/.

GERON, TOMIO. 2012. "Zynga Makes up 12% of Facebook's 2011 Revenue." *Forbes*, January 2. http://www.forbes.com/sites/tomiogeron/2012/02/01/zynga-makes-up-12-of-facebooks-2011-revenue/.

GREITEMEYER, TOBIAS AND SILVIA OSSWALD. 2010. "Effects of Prosocial Video Games on Prosocial Behavior." *Journal of Personality and Social Psychology* 98(2): 211–221.

HARRIS, JONATHAN DANIEL. 2010. "The Zynga-Haiti Controversy: A Tale of Two Campaigns." *HuffingtonPost.com*, May 4. Accessed December 1, 2013.
http://www.huffingtonpost.com/2010/03/04/the-zynga-haiti-controver_n_485919.html.

HAYLES, N. KATHERINE. 1999. *How We Became Posthuman: Virtual Bodies in Cybernetics, Literature, and Informatics*. Chicago: University of Chicago Press.

HEISLER, KATHERINE. 2012. "Let's Play: To Keep Gen Y Staffers, Gamify Their Work." *Forbes*, August 5.
http://www.forbes.com/sites/ciocentral/2012/07/03/lets-play-to-keep-gen-y-staffers-gamify-their-work/.

JUUL, JESPER. 2010. *A Casual Revolution: Reinventing Video Games and Their Players*. Cambridge, MA: MIT Press.

KALWAR, SANTOSH KUMAR, KARI HEIKKINEN AND JAN PORRAS. 2012. "Conceptual Framework for Assessing Human Anxiety on the Internet." *Procedia – Social and Behavioral Sciences* 46: 4907–4917.

KAPP, KARL M. 2012. *The Gamification of Learning and Instruction: Game-Based Methods and Strategies for Training and Education*. New York: John Wiley & Sons.

KEMP, SEB. 2012. "Strava, Sexy Botnets, and Suicide Cycling." *Bike Magazin*.
http://www.bikemag.com/news/news-of-the-tweet-virtually-real/.

KOHLER, CHRIS. 2010. "Farm Wars: How Facebook Games Harvest Big Bucks." *Wired*, May 19.
http://www.wired.com/gamelife/2010/05/farm-wars/all/1.

LATOUR, BRUNO. 2005. *Reassembling the Social: An Introduction to Actor-Network-Theory*. Oxford: Oxford University Press.

LIN, JAMES, LENA MAMYKINA, SILVIA LINDTNER, GREGORY DELAJOUX AND HENRY STRUB. 2006. "Fish'n'Steps: Encouraging Physical Activity With an Interactive Computer Game." In *UbiComp 2006: Ubiquitous Computing. Lecture Notes in Computer Science*, edited by Paul Douris and Adrian Friday, 261–278. Berlin: Springer.

LYON, DAVID. 2003. *Surveillance as Social Sorting: Privacy, Risk, and Digital Discrimination*. New York: Routledge.

LYON, DAVID. 2001. "Facing the Future: Seeking Ethics for Everyday Surveillance." *Ethics and Information Technology* 3(3): 171–180.

MARTIN, RANDY. 2002. *Financialization of Daily Life*. Philadelphia: Temple University Press.

MASSUMI, BRIAN. 2007. "Potential Politics and the Primacy of Preemption." *Theory & Event* 10(2).
http://muse.jhu.edu/login?auth=0&type=summary&url=/journals/theory_and_event/v010/10.2massumi.html.

MCGONIGAL, JANE. 2011. *Reality is Broken: Why Games Make Us Better and How They Can Change the World*. New York: Penguin Press.

MCLAUGHLIN, ERIN. 2012. "Negligence Suit Filed Against Cycling Website Over Accidental Death." *ABC News*, June 19. Accessed December 1, 2013.
http://abcnews.go.com/US/family-suing-website-cyclists-death/story?id=16605785.

MCLUHAN, MARSHALL. 1969. "The Playboy Interview: Marshall McLuhan." *Playboy Magazine* March.
http://www.cs.ucdavis.edu/~rogaway/classes/188/spring07/mcluhan.pdf.

Meister, Jeanne. 2012. "Gamification: Three Ways To Use Gaming For Recruiting, Training, and Health & Wellness." *Forbes*, May 21.
http://www.forbes.com/sites/jeannemeister/2012/05/21/gamification-three-ways-to-use-gaming-for-recruiting-training-and-health-amp-wellness/.

Munster, Anna. 2011. "From a Biopolitical 'Will to Life' to a Noopolitical Ethos of Death in the Aesthetics of Digital Code." *Theory, Culture & Society* 28(6): 67–90.

Nietzsche, Friedrich. 2005. *The Anti-Christ, Ecce Homo, Twilight of the Idols*. New York: Cambridge University Press.

Pearce, Celia. 2009. *Communities of Play: Emergent Cultures in Multiplayer Games and Virtual Worlds*. Cambridge, MA: MIT Press.

Pickering, Andrew. 1995. *The Mangle of Practice: Agency and Emergence in the Sociology of Science*. *The American Journal of Sociology* 99(3): 559–589.

Read, J. Leighton and Stephen M. Shortell. 2011. "Interactive Games to Promote Behavior Change in Prevention and Treatment." *JAMA: The Journal of the American Medical Association* 305(16): 1704–1705.

Risen, James and Laura Poitras. 2013. "NSA Report Outlined Goals for More Power." *The New York Times*, November 22. Accessed December 1, 2013.
http://www.nytimes.com/2013/11/23/us/politics/nsa-report-outlined-goals-for-more-power.html.

Schell, Jesse. 2010. "When Games Invade Real Life." *TED*, April.
http://www.ted.com/talks/jesse_schell_when_games_invade_real_life.html.

Schreiner, Keri. 2008. "Digital Games Target Social Change." *IEEE Computer Graphics and Applications* 28(1): 12–17.

Shin, Dong-Hee and Yoon-Joo Shin. 2011. "Why Do People Play Social Network Games?" *Computers in Human Behavior* 27(2): 852–861.

Strava. 2013. "About Us." Accessed December 1.
http://www.Strava.com/about.

Tannahill, Nick, Patrick Tissington and Carl Senior. 2012. "Video Games and Higher Education: What Can 'Call of Duty' Teach our Students?" *Frontiers in Educational Psychology* 3.
http://www.frontiersin.org/Journal/10.3389/fpsyg.2012.00210/full.

Thrift, Nigel. 2008. *Non-Representational Theory*. New York: Routledge.

Tiessen, Matthew and Gregory Seigworth. 2012. "Mobile Affects, Open Secrets, and Global Illiquidity: Pockets, Pools, and Plasma." *Theory, Culture & Society* 29(6): 47–77.

Vanderbilt, Tom. 2013. "How Strava Is Changing the Way We Ride." *Outside*, January 8.
http://www.outsideonline.com/fitness/biking/How-Strava-Is-Changing-the-Way-We-Ride.html.

Virilio, Paul. 2006. *Negative Horizon: An Essay in Dromoscopy*. London: Continuum.

Weidman, Aaron C., Katya C. Fernandez, Cheri A. Levinson, Adam A. Augustine, Randy J. Larsen and Thomas L. Rodebaugh. 2012. "Compensatory Internet Use Among Individuals Higher in Social Anxiety and its Implications for Well-Being." *Personality and Individual Differences* 53(3): 191–195.

Whitson, Jennifer R. and Claire Dormann. 2011. "Social Gaming for Change: Facebook Unleashed." *First Monday* 16(10).
http://firstmonday.org/ojs/index.php/fm/article/view/3578/3058.

Wills, David and Stuart Reeves. 2009. "Facebook as a Political Weapon: Information in Social Networks." *British Politics* 4: 265–281.

Wolf, Gary. 2010. "The Data-Driven Life." *The New York Times*, April 28. Accessed December 1, 2013.
  http://www.nytimes.com/2010/05/02/magazine/02self-measurement-t.html.

Woods, Dan. 2012. "Gamification Grows Up to Become a CEO's Best Friend." *Forbes*, May 14.
  http://www.forbes.com/sites/danwoods/2012/05/14/gamification-grows-up-to-become-a-ceos-best-friend/.

Wright, Robert. 2012. "Why We All Have 'Internet-Addiction Genes.'" *The Atlantic*, September 7.
  http://www.theatlantic.com/health/archive/2012/09/why-we-all-have-internet-addiction-genes/262112/.

Yamakami, Toshihiko. 2012. "Gateway Analysis of Nine Success Factors in Mobile Social Games: Lessons From Mobile Social Game Business." In *Human Centric Technology and Service in Smart Space, Lecture Notes in Electrical Engineering*, edited by James J. Park, Qun Jin, Martin Sang-soo Yeo, and Bin Hu, 129–136. Dordrecht: Springer Netherlands.

Zichermann, Gabe and Christopher Cunningham. 2011. *Gamification by Design: Implementing Game Mechanics in Web and Mobile Apps*. Sebastopol: O'Reilly.

LUDOGRAPHY

Strava. 2009. Strava.
  http://www.strava.com.

REMODELLING
DESIGN

WHY FUN MATTERS: IN SEARCH OF EMERGENT PLAYFUL EXPERIENCES

by **Sonia Fizek**

GAMIFICATION AFTER BULLSHIT

In his article, which became the cornerstone for vehement critique of gamification, Ian Bogost boldly claims that:

> [...] gamification is marketing bullshit, invented by consultants as a means to capture the wild, coveted beast that is videogames and to domesticate it for use in the grey, hopeless wasteland of big business. (Bogost 2011b)

Indeed, much discussion, especially with marketing background, has been focused on taming the beast and closing it within reproducible score-based structures. The phenomenon has been scrutinised predominantly from the perspective of the mechanical and iterative capacity of gamified systems, which rely on the adaptation of game mechanics to daily activities in order to influence the individual's behaviour and drive engagement (Gartner Inc. 2011; Radoff 2011; Zichermann and Linder 2010 and 2013; Zichermann and Cunningham 2011; Tkaczyk 2011). And the latter are believed to be achieved by implementing the elements of challenge and competition. These require the winning condition, which in most cases translates to a point system

Gabe Zichermann is a vehement advocate of. In his Google Tech Talk, promoting "Game-based Marketing" (2010), Zichermann mentions the gamification loop, a mechanism based on the allocation of points through creating challenges, win conditions, leaderboards, badges, and social networking, which in turn lead to the achievement of status. Those simple game mechanics elements form the essence of gamification also for Gamify, a San Francisco based technology company, whose official mission is to achieve business goals and influence the customers' behaviours by means of gamified systems implementing levels, badges, quests, rewards and more (Gamify 2014).

The rhetoric around gamification seems to be predominantly structured around accumulation and pointsification.[1] Whereas, as Bogost vehemently notices, "games or points isn't the point" (2011a). He also encourages researchers critical of the marketing usage of gamification, to stop using the word entirely and replace it with exploitationware or develop innovative approaches to the use of games in different contexts (ibid.). Despite those fervent reactions in the academic and game designer communities, neither the term nor the gamified "Viagra for engagement dysfunction" (Bogost 2011b) have disappeared from the digital horizon. Game designers, gamers, and researchers all seem to have agreed that gamification is bullshit, and yet they still keep stumbling upon it. In 2014 the Gamification World Championship takes place (Gamify 2014). It is enough to take a look at the event's partners to notice the major worldwide business players, among them Amazon Web Services, Deloitte Digital, and Badgeville. Numerous marketing prognoses still portray a bright and profitable future covered with billions of dollars (Corry 2011, Gartner Inc. 2011). However, if gamification refuses to complement its hype factor with more than easily predictable repetitive reward structures, it may as well considerably slow down or even "[. . .] fail to deliver" (Fleming 2012).

The question remains: What will the post-bullshit era of gamification concentrate on once a simple replication of points and badges loses its initial impact? The answer may be found in Gamify's CEO and Co-founder's re-

---

1 "Gamification is the wrong word for the right idea. The word for what's happening at the moment is pointsification" (Robertson 2010).

sponse post to Bogost's "Gamification is bullshit" (2011b). Nathan Lands, whose company's official slogans still promise its customers effective point-based solutions to engagement, when confronted with harsh criticism, puts a more friendly face to the profit-driven marketing machine. He might not have realised what a simple and powerful message was delivered when he emphasised the importance of playfulness and fun, defining gamification as "re-imagining experiences with fun in mind" and "an amazing opportunity to experiment with creating a more fun world" (ibid.).[2]

It seems that the most powerful driver for player's engagement is not based on quantification methods artificially imposed onto every possible context, but indeed on fun. And fun, as Sebastian Deterding notices, is neither about extrinsic motivation powered by rewards nor about adding game features to random products (2012). If the recipe towards meaningful engagement is contained within three simple letters, why is it so difficult to successfully implement it and why does it seem so scarce in existing gamified practices? In order to address this question, I propose to embrace the seemingly ungraspable concept of fun through the lens of *emergent playfulness*, which may guide researchers and practitioners in explaining the fun-driven mechanism of successfully gamified activities. The concept describes the experience of fun as an activity deriving from gameplay and allowed by a system "[. . .] flexible enough for players to inhabit and explore through meaningful play" (Salen and Zimmerman 2004, 165).

PLAYFUL VERSUS PLAYABLE

It is not an easy task to define the ephemeral concept of fun, even when narrowing it down to the medium of games. Taking into consideration all the varied video game genres and player typologies (Bartle 1996, Yee 2004), it becomes even more challenging. Jesper Juul voices his concerns about delineating the enjoyable ingredients of games by emphasising that:

> [. . .] there is ultimately no one-sentence description of what makes all games fun; different games emphasize different types of enjoyment and

---

2 Land's reply may be found under Bogost's blog entry: http://www.bogost.com/blog/gamification_is_bullshit.shtml (accessed May 6, 2014).

different players may even enjoy the same game for entirely different reasons. (Juul 2005, 19)

see also
Schrape
p.24–25

Despite the complexity of the phenomenon and the multitude of game genres, most gamified applications seem to be relying on a simple point-based structure, which is believed to provide enjoyment in all possible contexts. To gamification evangelists such as Zichermann the formula is simple: "If air-trafficking can be fun, anything can be fun" (Zichermann 2010). He transferred this rule to Livecube, one of the latest gamified inventions by Dopamine, a creative agency co-founded by himself. Livecube is a gamified environment, the aim of which is to trigger maximum audience engagement during a live event. This may be achieved by incorporating game mechanics and linking it with a social interaction tool. As the creators emphasise, "we use the latest engagement technology to motivate the audience with points, badges and real-world rewards" (Livecube 2014). Yet again, the proposed tool reveals Zichermann's grammar of a successfully gamified experience, based on the point system, which ultimately leads to the achievement of status. And status, according to another gamification leader, is everything. Similarly to Dopamine's solutions, Badgeville has developed its Behavior Platform (2014), on an intricate scoring system. The cloud-based tool may be adapted to the brand's digital ecosystem and performs four basic functions: it rewards the users, elevates their status, provides social proof, and analyses the brand's success. The platform's creators emphasise its innovativeness in comparison to other score-based systems by assuring they are "[. . .] leaving rudimentary point, badge and leaderboard systems in the dust" (Badgeville 2014). However, the only new approach they seem to be adding to an already proven model is a personalised point distribution system they wittingly and enigmatically refer to as contextual game mechanics.

The above examples very accurate illustrate what Robertson refers to as pointsification (2010) and Bogost as exploitationware (2011a). They seem to derive from a formal notion of what constitutes games and playing, concentrating on reapplying proven game mechanics to different scenarios. The design of the gamified experiences certainly makes them playable. But are they playful? Playfulness, after all, is a much more complex and volatile state and may not be easily transplanted by predictable iterative structures.

In order to pin down this slippery phenomenon, I will turn to Eric Zimmerman's gaming literacy, which explains "how playing, understanding, and designing games all embody crucial ways of looking at and being in the world" (Zimmerman 2009, 30). His research contributes to my understanding of *emergent playfulness*, a concept developed in a later section of this article and attempting to shed more light into what makes games fun.

GAMING LITERACY

According to Zimmerman literacy has been formulated as "[. . .] the ability to understand, exchange, and create meaning through text, speech, and other forms of language" (2009, 23). However, as he emphasises, diverse forms of media, including images, films, music, and television among others, require a new set of competences in order for them to be produced and understood. The situation becomes even more complex when we think about games (including video or electronic games), constituting elaborate systems, which may include all the above phenomena. Games in all their shapes have already left the safe confinement of the magic circle and no longer seem to stand outside ordinary life or within the boundaries of time and space. They are now, more than ever before, used in a myriad of contexts (learning, medicine, marketing) and have become the tools for creating meaning outside of their self-contained systems. According to Zimmerman, an important question to ask in the light of the current status of games is not "What does gaming look like? but instead: What does the world look like from the point of view of gaming?" (ibid., 24). And the latter question seems to be partially answered by the current examples of gamified every day practices, such as participating in events (Livecube, 2014), prioritising e-mails (Attent, 2014), reading books (ReadSocial App, 2014), or even brushing teeth (Kolibree, 2014). All the above examples seem to be turning daily activities into games. However, experiencing the world via gaming is not only about upward movement, rewards, scoring, ranks, and the achievement of status displayed in corresponding social platforms. The process of "[. . .] assigning a new game-like character to people's daily rhythm" (Dragona 2013, 1) does not have to be defined solely by points and rewards. It may be a little bit more fun to play with.

Interestingly, when referring to the playful world in which "the way we live and learn, work and relax, communicate and create, will more and more resemble how we play games", Zimmerman does not even mention the term gamification (Zimmerman 2009, 30). Whether he did it consciously, or whether the term was not yet such a popular buzzword at the time of shaping the concept, the phenomenon he describes to a certain degree seems to be illustrated by gamified practices. But only partially. Gaming literacy explains those practices and creates a meaningful framework, which surpasses the point-based structure and focuses equally on the importance of play and meaningful contextual design.

The concept involves three interweaving phenomena – systems, play and design – which demand a new set of cognitive, creative, and social skills from the participants (ibid., 25). Being systems literate is the ability to understand the world in terms of dynamic structures formed out of changing elements. This way of understanding cultural texts in their broad sense, is very much useful with reference to games, which are systemic constructs based on sets of rules. When those very same rules are put into action and interacted with, the concept of play emerges. As Zimmerman emphasises, "[j]ust as games are more than their structures of rules, gaming literacy is more than the concept of systems. It is also play." (ibid., 26). Rules are fixed and rational, whereas the activity of play may be subversive and improvisational. Play may be understood as a "free movement within a more rigid structure" (Salen and Zimmerman 2004, 304) or it may as well refer to play within or with that very same structure. Zimmerman supports this observation with the examples of players modding games, engaging in playful discourse between games, and developing whole cultures around certain game titles (2009, 27).[3] Systems are crucial for the proper understanding of gamified practices, but without the play component, they do not make much sense. As Zimmerman rightfully notices, systemic literacy centres on games whereas playful literacy shifts the focus towards the very action of playing and players who are at its core. It diverges from structures of rules towards structures of human interaction (ibid.). The third component focuses on creating meaning through game design. It differs from system design in that it refers to a particular social and cultural context. Not only is it based on

---

3 Such creative practices and shadow economy surrounding games have been extensively discussed by James Newman in *Playing with Videogames* (2008).

logic and rules, more importantly it demands the understanding of culture and entertainment environment in general.

TOWARDS EMERGENT PLAYFULNESS

Being game literate equals being playful, which translates into "[. . .] a ludic attitude that sees the world's structures as opportunities for playful engagement" (Zimmerman 2009, 27). In accordance with Zimmerman's concept, in order for engagement to appear, one needs not only a system of rules, but also human interaction with it and culturally significant design. Playfulness then does not reside solely within the systemic infrastructure of games, but seems to be a quality deriving from the very interaction with the system. Following this observation, I propose the following definition of fun with reference to games: an enjoyable emotional reaction deriving from the capacity to engage in playful behaviour, which emerges out of the interaction with the game. This may be achieved in numerous ways, for instance conditioned by the implemented rules, and/or as a result of autonomous player's actions not directly predicted by the system.[4] In the case of the first scenario, the player's satisfaction is achieved only through the actions performed in accordance with the strict and fixed rules of a given ludic system. The latter one points towards all the unexpected activities that happen in and around the game, creative interpretation of rules, modding, shadow economy (Newman 2008), or to go back to Zimmerman's concept, play within and play with the game (Zimmerman 2009). It is this second component, which is not as easily replicable as the intended interaction with the system itself. Fun, defined in this way, seems to be relying on play as "[. . .] a voluntary activity" (Huizinga 1950/1938, 7), providing the player with a certain amount of autonomy (Deterding 2012), which in turn creates space for playful behaviour. This free movement within a given structure ultimately leads to what I refer to as *emergent playfulness*.

---

4   For Raph Koster, for instance, fun emerges as a result of the mental mastery of a task, and is specifically related to the learning scenario (Koster 2005, 2012). He supports his claim with Chris Crawford's remark on fun as "[. . .] the emotional response to learning" (in Koster 2005, 228).

The concept bears noticeable terminological affinity to emergent gameplay, which describes a basic game structure combining simple rules to produce large numbers of variations (Juul 2002 and 2005). Emergence as such may also indicate a general term for player behaviours that have not been predicted by game designers (Smith 2001). It is a phenomenon arising "[...] out of complexity [and . . .] unplanned patterns appearing from within a system" (Salen and Zimmerman 2004, 152). Juul juxtaposes games of emergence to games of progression (2005, 67). To him, both present the players with different types of challenges. In the first case, the challenge is set up by means of interacting rules. The latter one requires each challenge to be presented consecutively, as it is done in classic adventure games. It is also important to emphasise that "many games can be found on a scale between emergence and progression" (ibid., 71). Emergent playfulness draws from the above understandings of emergence, and links them with the idea of fun as a process originating from the more open design allowing for some level of improvisation on the part of the player.

How will gamification look like in the post-bullshit era? The improvisational quality of play, as demonstrated in the previous paragraph, is also a crucial component in Zimmerman's gaming literacy.

However, it should be noticed here that emergent playfulness, unlike emergent gameplay, is not understood in a strictly design-focused way and does not have to refer to a gameplay style or to a structural way of providing challenges. It designates a joyful activity, which is the result of meaningful gameplay. Just as Zimmerman shifts his focus from systemic literacy occupied with game structures to playful literacy referring to playing, I propose to look at playfulness as a quality emerging from play rather than a framework describing a certain design schema. In the case of emergent playfulness the space of possibility (Salen and Zimmerman 2004, 165) or landscape of possibilities (Juul 2005, 73), do not have to be exclusively tied to the patterns of emergence. The rewarding experience may result from the enjoyment of rules (emergence) or fictional worlds and storylines (progression) or both (emergence with progression components or progression with emergence components), but more importantly it does not have to be tied to strictly defined design frameworks. The concept detaches the notion of fun from a systemic understanding and elevates it to a more general quality expressed by gaming literacy.

The above reasoning may help us understand why such applications as the previously mentioned Attent and Kolibree do not translate the world's structures into playful interactions but more so into well thought through fixed game structures. Let us have a closer look at the two examples and their mechanics keeping emergent playfulness and gaming literacy as reference points.

Attent is a simple tool, the purpose of which is to develop more cautious behavioural patterns of e-mail distribution. The main function of the application is to facilitate the prioritisation of sent messages. This simple quantification mechanism is based on the Serios currency, which enables the users to attach value to distributed information. The allocation process needs to be considerate as the number of points is finite. The systemic solution offered by Seriosity may greatly influence communication efficiency within a corporation. However, its relation to games seems far-fetched and disguises a marketing strategy to increase product sales. The company claims that their currency solutions are inspired by multiplayer online games. This simple currency exchange rule, however, does not turn reading e-mails into a game or an inherently playful experience.

see also Razcowski p. 154–155

Zicherman claims to be able to change the behaviour and motivational patterns by gamification loop where the point system consists of six elements: challenges, win conditions, leaderboards, badges, social networks, and status. The creators of Attent selected points as the only means of gameness, resigning from leader boards, badges, status, or win conditions. And such a simplified solution may be a perfect choice to deal with information overload. It should be, however, taken for what it really is, a well-designed pointsification system, not a game, and certainly not one allowing for emergent playfulness. Juxtaposing Attent with the three concepts forming gaming literacy (see figure 1), further exposes its simplicity.

The core of Attent is its currency allocation system, which constitutes a simple structure devoid of the mechanism that would further contextualise the activity. There seem to be no apparent challenges, winning conditions, or rewards. The closed design of the system does not allow for any improvisation. Furthermore, the action of e-mail prioritisation has not been embedded in any storyline scenario. Lack of those elements makes playfulness difficult to achieve, if not impossible. The user neither plays within nor with the system, but rather interacts with a familiar interface structure,

System	Play	Design
• Dynamic Structures Involving Constituent Parts	• Play within Structure • Play with Structure	• Taking into Account Social and Cultural Context • Not Only Based on Rules and Logic

Figure 1: Gaming Literacy and Its Components (based on Zimmerman 2009)

attaching points to the outgoing messages. Attent does not provide any win conditions and rewards for the challenge of witty point management. The user may of course try to create a meaningful game-like scenario for the application and in that sense play with the lack of imagination on the part of its designers. The main goal may be the attempt to win the attention of the receiver by allocating the right number of points. Such a perspective still does not turn Attent into a game, but rather creates potential for a non-existent meaningful ludic scenario.

The gameness of Seriosity's first gamified application may be questionable. However, the company's aspirations to design their products as ludic experiences have been articulated in black and white. In their blog post devoted to games and work, Seriosity refers to Byron Reeves, a professor at the Department of Communication at Stanford University, who emphasises that highly engaging features of games may become ingredients, recombined in different scenarios to make them more game-like (Reeves 2011). As one of the participants at the Business Innovation Factory-7 Summit, Reeves was wondering how to combine gaming with work, so that a boring interface incites a similar level of excitement to a World of Warcraft (2004) session. Maybe, if the creators of Attent turned directors or managers into guild masters, and applied reward conditions for or a possibility to trade Serios among the employees, they could be successful in creating a game-like experience. However, a simple point distribution system does not turn e-mail boxes into a World of Warcraft gameworld.

Points are not inherently bad, but gamified practices devoid of emergent playfulness and meaningful design in favour of raw pointsification systems, may seem futile and a little less, if at all, fun to play with. In order for play to take place, a certain level of improvisation is needed (Zimmerman 2009, 26). Let us see whether Kolibree, a gamified teeth-brushing experience, fosters emergent playfulness and enables the shift from systemic interaction towards player-centred involvement and meaningful design. Kolibree is a new product by a French start-up, which is launching its Kickstarter campaign in the summer of 2014. If successful, it will be one of the first attempts to deliver a smart toothbrush with an integrated gamified smartphone application. The device and the corresponding software will track long-term progress and analyse brushing habits, moves, and frequency. The results will be displayed on scoring scales and assigned to a personalised account, which may incorporate up to five users/players. The brushing progress will be rewarded with points where each score corresponds to a certain brushing accomplishment. The scores will ultimately be translated into rewards and badges, and the overall performance will be shared via social networks.

If we removed the name of the product from the above description, it could certainly refer to most gamified applications available on the market. Similar to Attent, Kolibree operates on the systemic level. The interaction with the device incorporates progress measurement and score-based reward system, which ultimately may lead to the achievement of status in social networks. This rule-driven design seems to correspond very accurately with Zicherman's gamification loop (challenges, win conditions, leaderboards, badges, social networks, status). However, when juxtaposed with the three concepts underlying gaming literacy, Kolibree fails to integrate the aspects of playfulness and meaningful design. Again, the constrained rule-based structure does not create space for improvisation. The big question remains. How to go beyond points and purely systemic features of games, and move the experience onto the remaining two levels of gaming literacy that might lead to emergent playfulness?

The Brusheads (2014) concept proposed by PA Consulting seems to be addressing the above concern. Most importantly, the game-like properties of Brusheads start at the level of its design. The prototype comes in five different versions, modelled as cartoon characters. As Ahmad Bitar, PA expert in product design, explains, children identify with their character and the personified toothbrush influences their behaviour in playful ways. The toy toothbrush has a built-in microphone, so if the child does not complete a two-minute brushing cycle, a pre-recorded voice of the character could encourage them to finish the otherwise mundane task. The characters may be further brought to life in a corresponding smartphone or computer application, which enables the competition between friends. Each account is assigned to a selected toothbrush character. On the level of the system, PA Consulting's gamified application does not seem to differ from the previous example. However, by placing the activity of brushing teeth in a wider context, building storyline and fostering emotional attachment to characters, the Brusheads concept creates ample space for playful behaviours, also literally outside of the provided structure. For instance, the design of the toothbrush makes it possible for the child to take it outside of the bathroom scenario. The brush is encapsulated in a handy portable structure resembling a marker pen, and has a suction cup underneath, so it may be applied to different surfaces.

The Brusheads case emphasises the fact that a game design process involves not only a formal rule-based system, it should also incorporate playful experience set in a socio-cultural context. I would like to conclude this section with the definition of a meaningful game design as understood by Zimmerman:

> Game design involves math and logic, aesthetics and storytelling, writing and communication, visual and audio design, human psychology and behavior, and understanding culture through art, entertainment, and popular media. (Zimmerman 2009, 29)

After all, design is a holistic process and only when it is kept as such, emergent playfulness has the chance to develop. Reapplying a uniform well-tailored point system to all possible contexts does not create enough space for fun to arise.

CONCLUSIONS: FUN IS THE FUTURE

The broad importance of playfulness as a socio-cultural concept was raised as early as in 1938 by Johan Huizinga (*Homo Ludens*). However, as this article demonstrates, almost a century later it continues to be a highly disputed topic in game studies. Fun, although originally deriving from the ludic system, remains an aspect of play, which is not easily encapsulated within and replicated by rigid structures. Additionally, various genres of gamified practices may implement different strategies leading to emergent playfulness. Thanks to Zimmerman's understanding of what any game should comprise of, this ephemeral quality becomes translatable to practical design hints, which take into consideration the complexity of ludic entertainment. In order to make more engaging gamified experiences, it is crucial to understand the phenomenon of game-related fun not only as a quality deriving from their systemic nature, but equally importantly from the playful engagement with that very system. If fun is the future as Gabe Zichermann assures us (2010), it should become apparent that successful and fun-driven gamification can no longer be the result of a simple replication of the standard point-based structure in accordance with the one-size-fits-all rule. Weather it is described as a voluntary activity (Huizinga 1950/1938, 7), an autonomous experience (Deterding 2012) stemming from games of emergence (Juul 2002 and 2005), play with or within the system (Zimmerman 2009), or emergent playfulness, fun is a quality which should inform the post-bullshit era of gamification and pave the way towards more meaningful and enjoyable design. The path may be a little more serpentine than the marketing gamification gurus expect. After all, drafting emergent playfulness requires a mind-set of an artist, not necessarily that of a craftsman.

BIBLIOGRAPHY

BADGEVILLE. 2014. "Game Mechanics." Accessed March 21.
  http://badgeville.com/products/gamification.

BARTLE, RICHARD. 1996. "Hearts, Clubs, Diamonds and Spades: Players Who Suit MUDs."
  Accessed April 7, 2014.
  http://www.mud.co.uk/richard/hcds.htm#1.

BOGOST, IAN. 2011a. "Persuasive Games: Exploitationware." *Gamasutra*, May 3.
  http://www.gamasutra.com/view/feature/6366/persuasive_games_exploitationware.php.

BOGOST, IAN. 2011b. "Gamification Is Bullshit! My Position Statement at the Wharton
  Gamification Symposium." *Ian Bogost Blog*, August 8.
  http://www.bogost.com/blog/gamification_is_bullshit.shtml.

CORRY, WILL. 2011. "Games for Brands Conference, Launching in London on October 27th."
  TheMarketingblog Extra, September 13.
  http://wcorry.blogspot.de/2011_09_11_archive.html.

Deterding, Sebastian. 2012. "Paideia as Paidia. From Game-Based Learning to a Life Well
  Played." Accessed April 7.
  http://www.pinterest.com/pin/471118810989035304/.

DRAGONA, DAPHNE. 2013. "Counter-Gamification. Emerging Forms of Resistance in Social
  Networking Platforms." Accessed April 7.
  http://projects.digital-cultures.net/gamification/files/2013/05/Daphne-Dragona-_-
  rethinking-gamification.pdf.

FLEMING, NIC. 2012. "Gamification: Is It Game Over?" *BBC*, December 5. Accessed March 14,
  2014.
  http://www.bbc.com/future/story/20121204-can-gaming-transform-your-life.

GAMIFY. 2014. "Gamify." Accessed January 24, 2014.
  http://gamify.com.

GARTNER INC. 2011. "Gartner Predicts Over 70 Percent of Global 2000 Organisations Will
  Have at Least One Gamified Application by 2014." Accessed April 7, 2014.
  http://www.gartner.com/newsroom/id/1844115.

HUIZINGA, JOHAN. 1950/1938. *Homo Ludens: A Study of the Play Element in Culture*. New
  York: Roy.

JUUL, JESPER. 2005. *Half-Real: Video Games Between Real Rules and Fictional Worlds*. New
  York: The MIT Press.

JUUL, JESPER. 2002. "The Open and the Closed: Games of Emergence and Games of Progression." Accessed April 7, 2014.
  http://www.jesperjuul.net/text/openandtheclosed.html.

KOSTER, RAPH. 2012. "Theory of Fun 10 Years Later." Accessed April 7, 2014.
  http://www.gdcvault.com/play/1016632/A-Theory-of-Fun-10.

KOSTER, RAPH. 2005. *Theory of Fun for Game Design*. Phoenix: Paraglyph Press.

LIVECUBE. 2014. "Home." Accessed January 24.
  http://www.livecube.co.

NEWMAN, JAMES. 2008. *Playing with Videogames*. New York: Routledge.

RADOFF, JON. 2011. *Game On: Energize Your Business with Social Media Games*. Indianapolis:
  Wiley.

REEVES, BYRON. 2011. "Work Is a Serious Game." Accessed April 7, 2014.
  http://www.businessinnovationfactory.com/iss/video/bif7-byron-reeves.

ROBERTSON, MARGARET. 2010. "Can't Play, Won't Play." *Hide and Seek*, October 6. http://hideandseek.net/2010/10/06/cant-play-wont-play/.

SALEN, KATIE AND ERIC ZIMMERMAN. 2004. *Rules of Play: Game Design Fundamentals*. Cambridge: MIT Press.

SMITH, HARVEY. 2001. "The Future of Game Design: Moving Beyond Deus Ex and Other Dated Paradigms." Accessed April 7, 2014. http://legacy.igda.org/articles/hsmith_future.

TKACZYK, PAWEŁ. 2012. *Grywalizacja: Jak Zastosować Mechanizmy Gier w Działaniach Marketingowych*. Gliwice: Hellion.

YEE, NICK. 2004. "Through the Looking Glass: The Daedalus Project." Accessed April 7, 2014. http://www.nickyee.com/daedalus/archives/print/000755.php.

ZICHERMAN, GABE. 2010. "Fun is the Future: Mastering Gamification." Accessed April 7, 2014. http://www.youtube.com/watch?feature=player_embedded&v=6O1gNVeaE4g.

ZICHERMANN, GABE AND CHRISTOPHER CUNNINGHAM. 2011. *Gamification by Design: Implementing Game Mechanics in Web and Mobile Apps*. Sebastopol: O'Reilly Media.

ZICHERMANN, GABE AND JOSELIN LINDER. 2013. *The Gamification Revolution: How Leaders Leverage Game Mechanics to Crush the Competition*. New York: McGraw-Hill.

ZICHERMANN, GABE AND JOSELIN LINDER. 2010. *Game-Based Marketing: Inspire Customer Loyalty Through Rewards, Challenges, and Contests*. Hoboken: Wiley.

ZIMMERMANN, ERIC. 2009. "Gaming Literacy. Game Design as a Model for Literacy in the Twenty-First Century." In *The Video Game Theory Reader* 2, edited by Mark J. P. Wolf and Bernard Perron, 23–32. New York: Routledge.

LUDOGRAPHY

ATTENT. 2014. Seriosity. http://www.seriosity.com/products.html.

BEHAVIOR PLATFORM. 2014. Badgeville. http://badgeville.com/products/behavior-platform.

BRUSHEADS. 2014. PA Consulting Group. http://www.paconsulting.com/our-thinking/meet-the-brusheads.

KOLIBREE. 2014. Kolibree. http://www.kolibree.com.

LIVECUBE. 2014. Gabe Zicherman, Aaron Price and Justin Schier. http://www.livecubeapp.co.

READSOCIAL APP. 2014. Travis Alber and Aaron Miller. http://readsocialapp.com.

WORLD OF WARCRAFT. 2004. Developed by Blizzard Entertainment. Windows, OS X. Blizzard Entertainment.

EXPLORING THE ENDGAME
OF GAMIFICATION

by **Scott Nicholson**

———

Gamification is the application of gameful or playful layers to motivate involvement within a specific context. Most current applications of gamification focus on offering points and rewards to motivate users. This reward-based gamification takes only a small part of gaming – a scoring system – and uses it to create the same type of loyalty system that has been in existence for decades.

These systems are designed around the concept of a core currency, such as a "point". The name of this currency may be different. It may be *gold* or *experience* or *happiness*, but for purposes of simplification in this article, the word *point* will be used to represent the basic unit of exchange that players earn for taking on certain behaviours. The underlying concept of reward-based gamification is simple – offer points to manipulate players.

CONSIDERING THE POINT

Motivating players through points is no different than motivating people through other forms of incentives like money or grades; people are used to doing things for a reward. Using a virtual reward like points is less expensive than using a tangible reward, and can, at least in the short term, have the same effect. Many citizen science projects, where researchers use game mechanisms to allow players to perform a task that moves a large-scale research project forward, are thin veneers of narrative, points, and other virtual rewards used to motivate people to do work that is traditionally done by students in a lab for a stipend or extra credit.

From a game design perspective, points are used to manipulate the actions of a player. Players are offered points or other in-game awards for taking certain actions and receive punishments (which, according to Kohn [1999, 50], are the same as rewards) for taking other actions. Video game design used to be about taking "lives" from the player as a punishment, but now many games just take time from the player's real life as the player has to repeat a section of the game. Few gamification systems employ the punishment aspects of game design, and focus mainly on the reward.

Since gamification is based upon game design elements, the concept of points being used to control behaviour is not surprising. But what are points used for? In many loyalty programs, points are good for tangible rewards, but to avoid giving out tangible rewards, gamification designers focus more on virtual rewards. The mechanics of massively multiplayer online roleplaying games (MMORPGs) have served as an inspiration for many reward-based gamification systems.

THE GRIND OF MMORPGS

Many MMORPGs follow a uniform pattern of rewarding and motivating players:

- Experience Points – Players earn points for taking on challenges in a game. In many MMORPGs, the highest number of points per hour of play are awarded through combat, and more difficult combats award more points. Some games award experience points for exploration, for using craft skills to create new objects, or for helping others. More recently developed games better balance experience points for these different types of activities so that players can do what they find most enjoyable and meaningful.

- Levels – As players reach a certain number of experience points, they go up to a new level. New levels provide players with additional skills and higher status in the game. The level structure is designed so that, as players advance, it takes progressively more points to move from level to level. Players must then take on more difficult challenges and play for longer periods of time before reaching a new level. This system is designed to get players addicted to the excitement of achievement early by providing them with new abilities frequently. Then, as the player advances, it becomes increasingly harder to reach additional levels.

- Items – Another form of rewards in MMORPGs is item distribution. By defeating enemies, players can gain items and earn in-game currency that can be used to purchase more powerful items that make their character stronger so that they can take on more difficult challenges. The games are designed around a player having an appropriate number of these items for his or her level in order to defeat monsters.

This combination of points, levels, challenges, and items creates a style of play that is known as "grinding". In most MMORPGs, a monster reappears a short time after it is defeated. In addition, in-game locations are designed with a certain level in mind, so that players do not run into challenges that are too easy, and therefore reward few experience points, or challenges that are far too hard. Players remain in one area of the virtual world until they finish the storyline in that area through quests. They might also find out that fighting monsters offers little reward and then move on to a new location. Since the monsters continually re-appear on the map, the player can grind simply by hunting and killing the same monster types again and again until he or she has gained enough experience to move on.

As the player progresses from level to level, grinding becomes more time-consuming and tedious, as each level requires more points to achieve than the previous level. Sometimes monsters will randomly drop a specific item that a player wants, so the player must repeatedly hunt and kill the same monster type (frequently while other players are doing the same thing) with the hope of finding that rare item. What keeps the players going is the promise of new abilities, continuing the storyline, and new areas to explore. This grinding process is shown in figure 1.

In recent years, MMORPGs have added achievements and badges to their offerings of virtual rewards. Achievements are specific tasks that may or may not also give the player other rewards in the game. Badges are public displays of accomplishments. Sometimes to earn an achievement or a badge, the player has to go against the normal paths to get points, which creates new experiences for the player.

This system came into existence because many MMORPGs charge a monthly fee. Because of this, the designers of these games need to develop a

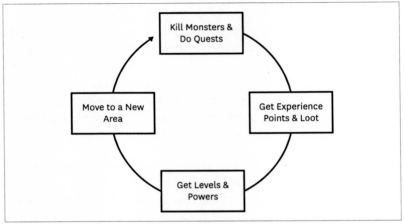

Figure 1: The Grind in a Traditional MMORPG

game system that encourages players to continue playing (and subscribing) without a "game over" feature. Traditional digital role-playing games have a similar structure where players move from one location to another, but these journeys are designed with a finish line in mind as soon as the narrative comes to an end. With the MMORPG structure, the game company needs the players to continue paying each month even after players have finished the main storyline. While players are interacting with the current game world, the designers are creating additional content to keep them engaged. As a result, players will engage with an MMORPG game for years and years, long after other standalone digital games they purchased at the same time have been retired to the shelf.

THE GRIND OF GAMIFICATION

Many gamification systems have been developed around traditional MMORPG concepts, so much so that I coined the term BLAP for reward-based gamification focused on badges, levels and leaderboards, achievements, and points (Nicholson 2012a). Users perform actions determined by the designer to earn points and badges. These may be used to rank players on a leaderboard and may also be converted to levels. Achievements

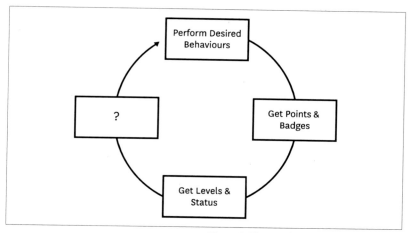

Figure 2: The Grind in a Gamification System

encourage the player to explore the game in different ways. Badges are used as public indicators of accomplishments. This is shown in figure 2.

But what about the new powers and skills granted by an MMORPG? In theory, this is where the real-world setting for gamification comes into play. The user makes purchases, does chores, gains knowledge, or does whatever activity is worth points in the system, and in doing so, changes himself or herself or the world in some way. The gamification system can help the player realise when he or she has levelled up in life by acknowledging when a new skill has been mastered. This concept of mastery is one of the three key elements of self-determination theory, which is a theory that explains how people develop a positive self-image (Deci and Ryan 2004).

There is an element of the MMORPG model that is missing in many gamification structures: the concept of moving to a new area. Without this element, players grow weary of a grind with no end in sight. Some gamification systems create new areas by providing different types of content. For example, Codecademy (2014) is a gamified system where users can learn how to program. After users grind in one area, they can move into a different area and learn more complex tasks. Foldit (2008) is a citizen science project where users first explore puzzles and end up developing new protein sequences to meet specific needs; the best sequences are synthesised, which is said to have led to real-world advances in scientific research (Burke 2012).

Sometimes, reward systems can be appropriate. If the system is designed to bring about a short-term goal, such as marketing an event, then rewards can be a simple way to do this. Even with a marketing goal, however, focusing on building longer-term loyalty for engagement with an organisation can be more beneficial in the long term than continually bribing participants with rewards. Pink (2011) argues that rewards raise performance if the task requires no creativity or personal engagement. Some successful reward-based gamification systems are developed as short-term systems to teach a specific skill where the utility of being able to use that skill is greater than the value of waiting to be rewarded to use the skill. However, if the goal of the gamification involves a long-term change or work that involves creativity, a basic reward-based system can fail to keep users engaged (ibid.).

There are several problems with using a basic reward-based system for long-term change. Once a user becomes accustomed to receiving a reward for an activity, the intrinsic motivation to perform that activity is replaced with extrinsic motivation. This means that the gamification system will have to run forever to keep the user engaged (Zichermann and Cunningham 2011). In addition, users will grow weary of one reward level and will expect the reward to change or increase over time to keep their interest. If the goal is to move users into the real-world setting without a continued reliance on the gamification system, then something has to be changed from the traditional BLAP-based system to engage users in a different way.

THE ENDGAME OF MMORPGS

There is a point in MMORPGs where a player reaches the end of the grind. This usually happens when he or she has reached the highest level that the game designers have planned for. The player can continue to fight monsters and take on quests, but the experience points gained are now meaningless. This creates a design challenge – how does a designer keep players interested when the grind that they have been engaged with for months or years has come to an end? This concept is known as the "endgame" and represents a different way that the player now engages with the game.

In some ways, this can be quite the existential challenge for a player. He or she has come to the game every day to earn more points and levels in order to defeat bigger monsters so that they can earn more points and levels. Then, with a final flash of light and "level up" message, the player's primary way of tracking accomplishments is over. Some want to settle back into the comfort of the grind and start a new character. Many MMORPGS have different races, factions, and character classes, each with different stories to explore. In these cases, this becomes a valid path of exploration. Many of the games allow players to pass money, items, or other benefits on to their new characters to reduce the typical penny-pinching grind found in the early stages of many MMORPGS.

Another way the games continue to engage players is by replacing one grind for another. In World of Warcraft (2004), for example, once players hit the level cap, they begin to focus their grind for specific items. These items may complement their play-style or may be upgrades to things they already have. Many of these rare items will be dropped at random from a specific monster, so some players will then fight the same monster again and again until they get the item. There are activities that can be done once per day that give awards of various currency, so players at their level cap will find the game can become one of doing the same set of things every day in order to build up their character.

There are two main reasons players want to build up their characters: to engage in battles with other players or to engage in the most challenging endgame content. Many MMORPGs encourage players to battle with others during the grind to level cap, and some of them will allow players to raise in levels just as effectively through player vs. player activities as they do if they engage with the main storyline of the game. But once players reach the top level, they must then get more powerful items if they wish to be competitive with other players at the highest level in the game.

Another method for keeping players engaged after they reach the highest level in the game is to provide them with content designed specifically for them, which is known as endgame content. This content is designed for small or large groups of players to work together in order to overcome significant challenges. In many cases, these challenges introduce new types of obstacles and risks that the players did not face during the grind to the level cap. For example, in World of Warcraft, some of the original endgame content had teams running from place to place to avoid ground-based obstacles while fighting a large boss. As the designers increased the level cap, this old content originally designed for the endgame became part of what players could do while levelling up, and so the challenge of ground-bases obstacles became more commonplace. Designers then had to come up with more complex endgame challenges to go up against higher level characters. This cycle has resulted in extremely complex team-based challenges requiring players to study video strategy guides and spend hours to prepare for a short, but intense, combat. This also has resulted in a much tighter community-based structure, as players come together from different guilds to share strategies on how to defeat these challenges.

Many players participate in all of these endgame activities: player vs. player, team-based challenges, and grinding through the levels as they move toward the endgame. Well designed MMORPGs provide them with a multitude of choices to play the game, and then funnel players together for a shared endgame experience. Poorly designed MMORPGs do not have different storylines or well developed endgame content and end up losing players once they work through the storyline, as there is nothing left to challenge them in the game world.

One important aspect of MMORPGs that keeps players in the game is something that designers cannot control: the social aspect. Some players engage in MMORPGs with current friends or acquaintances from a previous stage in their lives. The game can serve as an activity that people share with friends from around the globe or across the street. In this way, playing with others turns it into a chat room built around a shared activity. Another social aspect is engaging with online friends. Many MMORPGs use the concept of guilds that provide the players with an opportunity to meet a specific group of other players. The guilds may schedule activities and expect players to perform a specific role when working together to take on challenges in the game. People who are part of the same guild can become friends after taking on challenge after challenge together.

In this way, the MMORPG constitutes a community of practice, which may be defined as a "group of people who share a concern or passion for something they do and learn how to do it better as they interact regularly" (Wenger-Trayner 2006, 1). By their design, MMORPGs are cloaked in mystery. Many aspects of the game are not explained through rules. Instead, the players must work together to figure out the different subsystems in the game, and communicate through chat within the game and on external forums attempting to figure out how the game works. Guilds form sub-communities who come together to share resources, plan ahead of time, and meet at a specific time to attempt to complete the game's challenging endgame content. A player who is immersed in an MMORPG community is more likely to return and engage with others than a player who is working through the game by himself or herself.

Each MMORPG is working to create alternatives to the grind and endgame model. EVE Online (2003) does not use levels; but rather is based upon skill development, so players can always continue to work to develop their character. Guild Wars 2 (2012) provides a continuing chain of special events, and allows players to join any group working on an event, so players can always be involved in something different instead of repeating the same task. Tabletop RPGs do not have grinding issues because a game master's task is keeping the adventure new for each play session. This concept is challenging for a game with millions of players, but will serve to provide players with an alternative to grinding.

THE ENDGAME OF GAMIFICATION

What is the endgame of gamification? The endgame of an MMORPG occurs when the user is no longer involved with the grind, and, instead, moves into other ways to engage with the game. If the goal of gamification is to engage a user in a non-game setting, then the endgame of gamification is the process by which the user is moved from the gamification reward-based grind into the non-game setting. This matters most when the gamification is focused on long-term change, such as losing weight, exercising, making better financial choices, or brand loyalty. Without a planned endgame, the users are trapped within an ongoing grind that requires a continual outlay of rewards (Zichermann and Cunningnahm 2011).

Looking at different alternatives to the grind in MMORPGs can provide gamification designers with different paths to keep users engaged with their gamification system. Before players tire of earning the basic points in the gamification system, designers need to provide players with other ways to engage with the real-world setting. For a robust gamification system, the designers should provide players with a wide variety of activities to choose from instead of creating linear paths to follow (Nicholson 2012a).

The different design concepts used by MMORPGs for endgame content are useful in thinking about different ways of creating post-reward gamification activities that can move people from the reward-based grind into deeper engagement with the real world.

Creating a Different Grind – The easiest way to move players out of one grind is to give them another grind. This starts the cycle again and can keep people engaged for a longer period of time, but the same problem will come up once they reach the end of or tire of the new grind. Theoretically, once the user has worked through the first grind, they have some knowledge and expertise that can be tapped in order to make the next grind more transparent in connecting it with the real-world situation. The user may be more ready to take on information and grind more directly toward the real-world benefit than they were at the beginning. In addition, as the user understands more about the real-world setting, he or she can be given more meaningful choices about the goals of the new grind.

Nike+ (2006) uses this model. When users start, they are just collecting points as they do activities. As they get into the gamification system, they are given a chance to set their own fitness goals and grind toward those goals. The overall points are still being counted in the background, but they are less important than the goals that the user sets for himself or herself.

One way to do this is to value new experiences and activities. Many gamification systems have a single system, so that players who are experienced are seeing the same challenges as they saw when they started. To add variety, designers can develop different types of challenges and create mini-grinds around each challenge. The users will be more likely to stay engaged because of the novelty effect. SuperBetter (2012) does this by presenting a continuous stream of new challenges and ties in the information about why these challenges matter. By creating moments of information and reflection, designers can raise the chance for players to find their own connection to the real world context.

Creating Larger Challenges – Another approach to creating the gamification endgame is to present users with larger-scale challenges. Players will either need to tap significant expertise or work with others to accomplish these difficult goals. If these large-scale challenges are more directly tied into the needs of the real world, then this can serve as a segue to move players from a focus on the gamification system to a focus on the real world.

The aforementioned Foldit does exactly this. Users grind through challenges and puzzles in a game-like setting, but as they do so, they are gaining the knowledge and expertise needed to then engage with real research problems with unknown answers. The result is that the researchers have training and motivated research partners who are engaged in real-world problem solving.

In *The Multiplayer Classroom* (2011), Sheldon has used a similar model in his gamification of the classroom. Throughout the class, the students grind through challenges and quests. After the students acquire knowledge and skills, the class has to come together to work against a "boss fight", which is a greater challenge that requires cooperation. This works to bring students out of the daily grind and into larger challenges that can be more meaningful.

As grinding for points loses its lustre, meaningful gamification moves players to strive for the rewards of the real world.

Creating Competition between Users – Another route is to let the users create challenges for one another. In many games, after players have spent many hours working through challenges and improving their characters, they are eager to see how their characters stack up against those controlled by other players. In a gamification system, the designer could create competitive challenges where users work alone or with others to compete over real-world goals.

Foldit uses this method to keep expert users of the system engaged. While users are given real world challenges, only the most promising proteins created by users are synthesised and tested. It is important to note that this level of competition is only tapped once users have become confident with the tools. If users are put into a competitive space too early and are quickly crushed, it can be a disincentive to continue. This is one of the problems with leaderboards; while they can motivate those at the top, they can demotivate those at the bottom.

Another scenario where this model makes sense is where there is already competition, such as a sales force in a company. When participants are already used to competition and rewards, adding a game layer to help track more nuances of the competition can enhance the existing structures.

MAKING GAMIFICATION MEANINGFUL

The larger concept that all of these ideas play into is what I call meaningful gamification. The concept of meaningful gamification is that it focuses on using game design elements to help users find a meaningful connection to the real-world setting. It reduces the emphasis on or avoids rewards, and, instead, focuses on the non-reward based aspects of game design (Nicholson 2012b).

In order to help designers consider alternatives to point-based rewards, I created a framework known as the RECIPE for Meaningful Gamification (Nicholson 2012c), where the letters of the word RECIPE spell out different ways of using game design elements to build meaning:

- *Reflection* – creating situations where users reflect to discover personal connections with the real-world setting
- *Exposition* – using narrative and user-created stories to create deeper connections to the real-world setting
- *Choice* – allowing the user to select paths and develop goals within the real-world setting that are more meaningful to him or her
- *Information* – providing the user with information about the connections between the gamification activities and the real-world setting
- *Play* – creating a safe space and set of boundaries where the user can choose how he or she wishes to engage with different gamification activities in the real-world setting
- *Engagement* – using the gamification system to connect users to a community of practice that surrounds the real-world setting

By thinking about the endgame of gamification, designers can create systems that may start with rewards, but are designed to bring players into more meaningful connections. By doing this, chances are that the user will find a connection into the real-world setting and will no longer require the gamification system for engagement. The gamification system could be developed as a short-term activity, as shown in figure 3. It could be hoped that as a result of this users will make differences in the real world instead of just trying to earn one more point.

The goal of gamification is to motivate people to engage in a context. In the short-term, using rewards like points, levels, and badges can be used as the sole motivational tool to bring about this engagement. But if the purpose

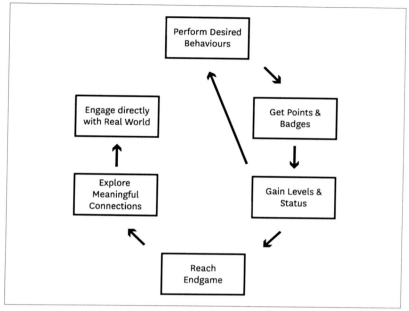

Figure 3: Bringing Together BLAP and Meaningful Gamification

of the system is to bring about long-term change, these shallow rewards are not enough to maintain the interest of most users, and can even do harm to someone's pre-existing motivations (Deci & Ryan 2004). Some gamification systems allow players to earn real-world rewards and benefits, and this can serve as an ongoing motivational tool; however, this can be a costly long-term proposition.

For long-term change, the gamification designer needs to create a system that is designed to engage someone in an authentic manner directly with the real-world setting. This means that the gamification system is designed to help people get engaged with existing communities and information resources that already surround the real-world context. As the player becomes more of an expert user of the gamification system, there is less and less of the system to engage with and more of the real-world context. The eventual goal is to help the player find the aspects of the real world that are meaningful and to diminish the role of gamification, until the player is left in the real-world context. Instead of trapping users in a reward-based grind, using these concepts allows designers to create a gamification journey, where the end of the journey leaves the user immersed in and connected to the real world.

BIBLIOGRAPHY

BURKE, KATIE. 2012. "Behind the Scenes of Foldit, Pioneering Science Gamification." Accessed May 7, 2014.
http://www.americanscientist.org/science/pub/behind-the-scenes-of-foldit-pioneering-science-gamification.

DECI, EDWARD AND RICHARD RYAN. 2004. *Handbook of Self-Determination Research*. Rochester: University of Rochester Press.

KOHN, ALFIE. 1999. *Punished by Rewards: The Trouble with Gold Stars, Incentive Plans, A's, Praise, and Other Bribes*. Boston: Houghton Mifflin.

NICHOLSON, SCOTT. 2012a. "Strategies for Meaningful Gamification: Concepts Behind Transformative Play and Participatory Museums." Accessed March 27, 2014.
http://scottnicholson.com/pubs/meaningfulstrategies.pdf.

NICHOLSON, SCOTT. 2012b. "A User-Centered Theoretical Framework for Meaningful Gamification." Accessed March 27, 2014.
http://scottnicholson.com/pubs/meaningfulframework.pdf.

NICHOLSON, SCOTT. 2012c. "A RECIPE for Meaningful Gamification." Accessed March 27, 2014.
http://www.youtube.com/watch?v=f4qikCx_SSc.

PINK, DANIEL. 2011. *Drive: The Surprising Truth About What Motivates Us*. New York: Riverhead Books.

SHELDON, LEE. 2011. *The Multiplayer Classroom*. Stamford: Cengage Learning.

WENGER-TRAYNER, ETIENNE. 2006. "Communities of Practice: A Brief Introduction." Accessed March 27, 2014.
http://wenger-trayner.com/theory/.
ZICHERMANN, GABE AND CHRISTOPHER CUNNINGHAM. 2011. *Gamification by Design: Implementing Game Mechanics in Web and Mobile Apps.* Sebastopol: O'Reilly Media.

LUDOGRAPHY

CODECADEMY. 2014. "Codecademy." Accessed February 20.
http://www.codecademy.com/de.
EVE ONLINE. 2003. Developed by CCP Games. Windows, OS X. CCP Games.
FOLDIT. 2008. Developed by Center of Games Science and Department of Biochemistry. Windows, OS X, Linux. University of Washington.
GUILD WARS 2. 2012. Developed by ArenaNet. Windows, OS X. NCsoft.
NIKE+. 2006. Nike, Inc.
https://secure-nikeplus.nike.com/plus/.
SUPERBETTER. 2012. Jane McGonigal.
https://www.superbetter.com.
WORLD OF WARCRAFT. 2004. Developed by Blizzard Entertainment. Windows, OS X. Blizzard Entertainment.

EUDAIMONIC DESIGN, OR: SIX INVITATIONS TO RETHINK GAMIFICATION

by **Sebastian Deterding**

1   INTRODUCTION

In his seminal book *Flow: The Psychology of Optimal Experience*, Mihaly Csikszentmihalyi writes: "Mowing the lawn or waiting in a dentist's office can become enjoyable provided one restructures the activity by providing goals, rules, and the other elements of enjoyment" found in games (1990, 51). This idea – that game design holds valuable principles for making even the most mundane activity more engaging – has a long history in human-computer interaction, design, and education, regularly re-emerging under names like funology, ludic design, serious games, game-based learning, or playful inter-action (Deterding forthcoming a). Its most recent iteration has come to be known as "gamification": using game design elements in non-game contexts (Deterding et al. 2011).

The title of this volume invites us to rethink gamification, and this is indeed a timely demand. A mere four years ago, in 2010, the main challenge was to *think* gamification, to talk and think and act it into being as a *thing* to begin with. There was no shared *gestalt* yet, no established set of experien-tial and discursive reference points what we talk about when we talk about gamification – not even agreement whether to use that very word (Deterding forthcoming a).

Things have changed. Today, the main challenge has become to work against the grain of existing preconceptions of gamification (be they apocalyptic or utopian), established by evangelists, critics, industry practices, and mass media reporting. Many have rightfully questioned whether gamification is anything more than a marketing ruse to sell the next digital snake oil (Juul 2011). The current field is certainly littered with shallow interpretations and implementations – essentially incentive and customer loyalty programs repackaged with a superficial "gamy" veneer as software services that disregard decades of research on the limited effectiveness and manifold unintended consequences of such systems. In addition, these forms dominate the collective imagination: If one were to elicit the prevalent framing of gamification in industry, design, academia, or mass media today, it would presumably be something like "driving any desired activity by tracking it and adding a feedback layer of points, badges, leaderboards, and incentives ontop" – the blueprint established in 2009 by the social, mobile, local application Foursquare (Deterding forthcoming b).

The main task of rethinking gamification today is to rescue it from the gamifiers.

And that is worrisome. For one, this prevalent conception of gamification doesn't even begin to engage with the psychology and sociology of game enjoyment, let alone realise the promise of translating its insights into other fields (Deterding forthcoming b). Instead, current gamification evangelists have turned away many with troublesome ethics and a disregard for the complexities of design and motivation. And as their overwrought promises will inevitably fail to realise, they risk leaving scorched earth behind.

However, cases like the Quest to Learn schools demonstrate that the very notion and promise of gamification far surpasses the confines of its currently dominant form, and that this promise can be realised (Salen et al. 2011). Thus, the main task of rethinking gamification today is to rescue it from the gamifiers: to provide a positive vision of gamification that addresses the valid criticism it has received, and realises the actual promise of learning from game design as a holistic, systemic practice. Or put differently: to try and establish an alternative, more promising framing of gamification before discourses and institutions have fully solidified.

To this end, this article presents six critiques of the currently dominant rendition of gamification, and six invitations to rethink it. The empirical basis for this critique I draw from previous analyses of gamification rhetoric (Deterding forthcoming a) and gamification design literature (Deterding forthcoming b). I suggest expanding the remit of gamification (1) from the structuring of objects to the framing of contexts, and (2) from game design elements to motivational affordances. In its current form, gamification presents an additive, atomistic and deterministic conception of experience design. Truly learning from game design, I suggest, means to adopt a (3) relational account of experience, and (4) an emergent-systemic method of experience design. When it comes to the ethics and aspirations of gamification, I invite designers to move (5) from avoiding harm and coercion to facilitating the good life, and (6) from the instrumental perfection of existing orders to their critical transformation. A rethought, positive vision of gamification, then, is that of a critical, transformative, socio-technical systems design practice for motivational affordances in the service of human flourishing – in a word, eudaimonic design.

2. FROM OBJECTS TO CONTEXTS: RETHINKING THE SCOPE OF GAMIFICATION

What is the first thing that comes to your mind when you hear the word "video game"? Likely, it will be a box, some square screen, some interface tied to a piece of hardware running a piece of software. That is, you are thinking of a game as a designed object. There is nothing to say against that: It is a lasting achievement of game studies to have demonstrated in detail how the design of games makes and breaks their experience and potential effects – and we are still far from understanding these matters fully.

Still I would argue that this box is what currently most limits our thinking about games and gamified systems, because it disregards what happens outside of it: the specific ways and contexts in which people come to interact with games. Simply put, it ignores that people are usually *playing* them. For although games are certainly designed to be played with, there is no necessary connection between the two. We can do very many things with games – we can build, test, debug, review, analyse and play them, and we can work in them, as gold farming demonstrates. Likewise, there are many things we can play with – our hands, sticks and stones, passing cars on a long highway drive, games, even work assignments.

Is this a trivial point? Well, a growing number of games scholars urge us to extend our attention "from content to context" (Squire 2006), towards the broader "ecology of games" (Salen 2008), to the many ways games are being played, and to the way both, games and playing, interact to create the unique affordances of fun, motivation, learning that we are hoping to make use of (Taylor 2009; Hung 2011; Sicart 2011). When it comes to gamification, there are at least three crucial ways in which the context mediates the effects of any gamified system: autonomy, situational norms, and embarrassment.

2.1 "The Electronic Whip": Autonomy

In a recent news story in the LA Times, journalist Steve Lopez (2011) has chronicled the use of gamification by Disney: In the basement floors of the Disneyland hotels, large flat screens showed leaderboards pitching the working speeds of the laundry workers against each other. However, instead of the device spurring fun competition – as standard gamification logic would suggest – workers reported that they felt pressured and controlled by this "electronic whip" of their management.

This little story points to a crucial feature of gameplay often overlooked in gamification: As scholars from Johan Huizinga (1955 / 1938) onwards have stressed, playing games is a voluntary activity. And the voluntariness of gameplay is mainly constituted by its social context: to what extent others coerce an individual to do something, and to what extent the individual, in light of such actions of others, comes to define said activity as autonomous, self-determined or not.

Growing empirical evidence suggests that situational autonomy support indeed poses an issue for serious games and gamification: Forced serious game play is less enjoyable and effective (Heeter et al. 2011). When workers do not consent to games at their workplace, their use decreases positive affect and performance (Mollick and Rothbard 2013). Having to play games as part of one's profession is generally described as less enjoyable and less engaging by practitioners, and comes with more frequent unpleasant experiences of being controlled (Deterding 2013).

Why is that? A rich literature in psychology has demonstrated that autonomy – the sense of acting with volition, willingness, and in congruence with one's own goals, needs, values, and identity – is a basic psychological need and core part of intrinsic motivation: What makes activities feel enjoyable or worth pursuing for their own sake is that they satisfy basic psychological needs like autonomy, relatedness, or competence (Deci and Ryan 2012). Conversely, research indicates that a person's sense of autonomy can be thwarted by attaching material rewards or punishments to an activity – or even just verbal admonitions that evoke internalised controlling voices of guilt, shame, or social pressure. If a child is already intrinsically motivated to read, for instance, paying or reprimanding it to read may paradoxically reduce its overall motivation: It adds some extrinsic motivation (a monetary incentive and guilt), but reduces some pre-existing intrinsic one by the same token (Deci, Koestner and Ryan 1999).

Importantly, the controlling, autonomy-thwarting quality of environmental events – their "functional significance" – results from an active interpretation. Take a supervisor's feedback on worker performance: How that feedback impacts motivation depends on whether the worker understands it as informational ("the supervisor is helping me see how I can improve"), which supports an experience of competence and relatedness, or as controlling ("the supervisor tells me what I ought to do"), which thwarts autonomy (Ryan and Deci 2002).

We typically think that games are so enjoyable that people play them voluntarily. But to a certain extent, the causal arrow points in the opposite direction: Because gameplay is a voluntary activity – something we can choose to do and cease doing – it satisfies our need for autonomy, and that satisfaction we experience as "enjoyment". Several studies have found evidence that playing video games is motivating because (among other things) it delivers strong experiences of autonomy: In games, we can choose who to be, what goals to pursue, and how to pursue them (Przybylski, Rigby and Ryan 2010). Even more fundamentally, playing a game is an autonomous act in itself: Playing games – especially single-player games – is an activity we typically feel we do following our own interest, where we decide what to play, when, how, and how long, with no social or material pressures or consequences affixed (Deterding 2013).

In sum, if gamified systems are deployed for activities happening within mandatory and consequential contexts (such as work or formalised education), they run the risk of being perceived as "electronic whips" that effectively reduce rather than enhance motivation, enjoyment, and performance.

2.2 Gamespersonship and Gaming the System: Situational Norms

Every society has social norms and conventions how to understand what is happening within different types of social situations, and how to behave "appropriately" in them. Sociologist Erving Goffman (1986) has called these clusters of understandings, norms, and practices around types of situations "frames". In the "doctor's visit" frame, for instance, it is considered appropriate when a patient gets undressed in front of a doctor and understood to be "for medical purposes": whereas the same person getting undressed in front of the same doctor in a public bus would appear absurd and inappropriate.

The same holds for the "playing games" frame (Deterding 2013), which among other things is characterised by a "bracketed morality" (Shields and Bredemeier 1995). In competitive sports and playing games, we are allowed and in fact expected to act as strategic actors single-mindedly focused on maximising our individual payoff – winning. To not overtly care about and try to win characterises the half-hearted spoilsport. The cold-blooded bluffing, double-talking, and out-manoeuvring that is positively valued as "good gamespersonship" in Poker (first half of 19th century) or Diplomacy (1959) would earn us the label "Machiavelli" or "psychopath" if enacted in everyday conversation with friends and colleagues. However, even in playing games, there is a limit: The allowed and valued egocentrism is "bracketed" in a larger care for fair play and the enjoyment of others. If a game player focuses too myopically on winning and their own enjoyment, ignoring her impact on the enjoyment of others, she becomes a "munchkin" (Gribble 1994). This larger bracket of fair play and collective enjoyment is enforced not so much by the rules of the game as by the constant monitoring, enactment, and sanctioning of the "play community" (DeKoven 2013).

Which brings us to the frequently raised gamification issue of "gaming the system" (Werbach and Hunter 2012): Devise a game system of rules and goals, the standard version goes, and some of your users will find a way to exploit any rule loophole and min-max their way through. But following the notion of frames, this is not so much a moral failing of individual users as a systemic issue endemic to the very process of adding rules and goals:

By specifying goals and rules and explicit, quantitative forms of feedback, a gamified system creates social signals that the thus-gamified activity is to be taken as a "gaming" situation, where myopic min-maxing is allowed and expected. Without a play community enacting bracketing values of harmony and fair play, game-like systems on their own exert a strong pull towards strategic action that ignores any "negative externalities" not explicitly internalised in or outlawed by the rule system. And since – following Wittgenstein – no rule can ever fully specify how to be enacted (Stueber 2005), relying on more rules to prevent gaming the system instead of the lived values of the enacting community is a losing proposition: It merely generates more opportunities for gaming (Deterding 2012b).

The opposite is likewise possible: Information systems research has demonstrated the lasting impact of "technological frames" – that is, prevailing organisational understandings, practices, and norms – on the adoption and usage of new technologies (Orlikowski and Gash 1994). Often enough, if these technical frames are not changed, they just absorb new technologies into "business as usual": new, different ways of doing things offered by the technology are never realised. The entailed manifest risk for gamification is that it becomes absorbed by companies as yet another customer loyalty or employee incentive programme, with slightly different language and visuals – rather than an actual transformation of business practices.

2.3 Acting Out of Bounds: Embarrassment

For Goffman and many after him, the central mechanism by which situational norms and conventions are reproduced is embarrassment: Early in our socialisation, we learn from parents and peers how to behave properly in all kinds of situations, and are scolded by them if we misbehave. Over time, this instils an internalised view of others in us: Acting in any situation, we think about how others would think about us if they saw us – if they would approve or disapprove. Pride, in this logic, is the emotional experience of imagined approval of others, and shame of imagined disapproval. Socialised adults observe and regulate themselves in order to act situationally appropriate and avoid feelings of shame or embarrassment (Scheff 2003).

The ramifications for serious games and gamification are obvious: Both by definition take games and game design into "serious", non-gaming contexts, expecting people do playfully and/or gamefully engage with them.

However, if the situational norms of those non-gaming contexts – work, for-malised education, politics, public spaces, etc. – do not entail "playing" as appropriate, engaging in play ought to be shunned because it would induce embarrassment. And indeed there is evidence for this. Installing a simple exergame that motivates users to do pull-ups in a public tram, Toprak and colleagues (2013) found that people would not use the game because people found it embarrassing to play-exercise in a public tram.

2.4 Gamification as Socio-Technical Systems Design

Autonomy (and its subjective construal), situational and technical frames (and the communities enacting them), embarrassment: all these point to the importance of the contextual framing of a gamified system. Maybe more importantly, all can be intentionally designed for: Supervisors can do much to create an autonomy-supporting atmosphere even around mandatory work activities (Reeve 2006). Community building and change management acknowledge and entail the change of lived values, practices, narratives, frames, and mental models (Todnem By 2005). And every clown, comedian, or workshop facilitator worth her salt knows how to establish a trusting at-mosphere where play is perceived as welcomed and non-embarrassing.

All of these practices operate outside the box of current gamification, which is narrowly understood as the design of (software) systems and inter-faces. Thus, rethinking the remit of gamification entails expanding it from the mere re-structuring of activity through (largely software-based) rule systems towards re-framing activity as a specific type of situation (playing games) entailing specific norms, conventions, and understandings, using so-cial signals and actors modelling, enacting, and sanctioning this framing. A good practical example can be seen in the playful performative interventions by former mayor of Bogota, Antanas Mockus, aimed at rebuilding the Bogo-ta's civic culture, by the time of his taking office a city with one of the highest rates of violence and traffic fatalities.

One such intervention involved mimes controlling traffic, helping pedestrians across streets, and mocking misbehaving, aggressive drivers. Instead of harsher rules and fines, the mimes signalled vulnerability and appealed to the drivers' self-esteem as good citizens. They reframed traffic as a realm of civic-mindedness – more than halving the number of traf-fic fatalities as a result (Singhal and Greiner 2008). Understood as such – a unified whole of restructuration and reframing – gamification is a holistic socio-technical systems design practice (Withworth and Ahmad 2013), one that understands humans interacting with technology as assemblages, activity systems, or ecologies of heterogeneous and intertwined actors.

3 FROM USING GAME DESIGN ELEMENTS TO MOTIVATIONAL DESIGN: RETHINKING THE GOAL OF GAMIFICATION

Current conceptions of gamification are not only problematic in the object of design they make out, but also in their design goal. They typically frame gamification as the application of elements, patterns, or "mechanics" of game design to motivate desired end-user behaviours (Deterding forthcoming b).

3.1 Experiences Not Elements

The first issue with this framing is conceptual. As many authors have pointed out, it is impossible to clearly identify and distinguish "game design elements" from other design elements, or to identify a gamified system by their presence: Many design patterns commonly sold as part of gamification platforms – such as notification streams – are not game design patterns to begin with (Björk and Holopainen 2005), but rather originate from social software (Crumlish and Malone 2009). Conversely, game designers frequently criticise that core game design concerns and patterns such as interestingly hard challenges and meaningful choices are not even part of standard gamification practice (Robertson 2010, Deterding forthcoming b). Furthermore, it is problematic to make sense of "patterns of source domain X in target domain Y" in general, because patterns and pattern languages are domain-bound and system-bound. It is always a kind of analogy, like speaking of the "anatomy" of a house with a "brain", "lungs", "arteries", and so on. There can be direct morphological or functional symmetries between houses and bodies, and it is sometimes helpful to tease those out to help understanding or provide inspiration. But even if you would build, say, a ventilation system in the direct, immediate image of a human lung, you would not call this the "anatomy design element" of the house. You would call it ventilation, and it would serve a ventilation function. In the same way, it is just nonsensical to speak of the game design pattern "deadly traps" (Björk and Holopainen 2005, 74–75) instantiating the function of "damage" in the context of a mobile e-commerce app.

313

Finally, many design patterns core to games and gamification have iso-morphic counterparts in other social domains that existed long before the rise of gamification: Goal-setting and quantitative feedback are pervasive in business and education, for instance. Yet isomorphisms across domains do not influences make. Else, we would have to relabel grading systems at schools or targets and key performance indicators in organisations "gam-ification". In fact, much popular gamification writing engages in this sort of facile retro-fitting, describing existing popular application and services (such as LinkedIn, Quora, or OkCupid) as gamification, with no solid ev-idence whether (a) the "identified" design elements actually produce the proclaimed engagement effects through the proclaimed causal routes, nor whether (b) the designers at the point of design were actually and intention-ally taking inspiration from games.

In response to these issues, several scholars have suggested delineating gamification (or gameful design) via the design goal of affording gameful experiences – that is, experiences characteristic for gameplay – rather than through an ill-defined bundle of design patterns (Deterding et al. 2011; Huotari and Hamari 2012; Werbach forthcoming). Yet whereas this does present a conceptual advancement, it remains unsatisfying in its narrow, tactical focus.

3.2   Gameful and Playful Experiences

In his book *Man, Play, and Games*, philosopher Roger Caillois (2001 / 1958) distinguished between two poles of play: *paidia* and *ludus*. Paidia captures the free-form, exploratory, autotelic recombination of behaviors, actions, and meanings prototypically found in children's pretend play, whereas ludus denotes the rule-bound, goal-directed overcoming of challenges. Gamifica-tion in its current form has focused squarely on the ludic: it almost invariably constitutes an addition of structure, of goals and rules to a given activity in order to afford gameful experiences of challenge and competition (Deterding forthcoming b). This focus is apt when competence or recognition are the main targeted motivations, and when the main design problem is that the given activity is poorly structured to afford these motivating experiences – that is, when it lacks clear goals, clear and immediate feedback, a good scaf-folding of challenge, etc. Yet this focus also misses out on the paidic pole of playful experiences, which has been the focus of a significant body of work in human-computer interaction (see ibid. for a review). Such playful experiences are of utmost relevance when one wishes to tap into motivations like curiosity, or design for exploration, transgression, creativity, or innovation (Bateson and Martin 2013). Conceptually, framing gamification as design supporting gameful experiences may be sound, but practically, it is hard to justify why one would leave such a vast field of learnings and insights from game design untapped. This is why colleagues and I early on spoke of gameful *and* playful design (Deterding et al. 2011).

3.3 Motivational Experiences

Now following the majority of gamification design literature, gamification practitioners are not interested in creating gameful or playful experiences per se, but in motivating end user behaviours (Deterding forthcoming b). Thus, gameful and playful design describes a subset of *motivational design* (Zhang 2008), which in turn can be understood as a subset of *persuasive design* – for motivation is typically yet another proximate means towards the ultimate goal of some targeted change of behaviour in some targeted audience (Deterding 2012a). However, gameful and playful experiences are only a small subset of desired, enjoyable, motivating experiences (Desmet 2012, Hassenzahl, Diefenbach and Göritz 2010). Many more things (de)motivate human action (Reeve 2009), and many more factors affect human behaviour than motivation (Michie, van Stralen and West 2011).

Thus, relevant as creating playful and gameful experiences is to toy and game designers, and inspiring as it may be for motivational design, even gameful and playful design ultimately remain *tactics*. There is no principled reason – no persistent design problem – for "gamifying" things. The persistent, principled design challenge gamification addresses is motivating users. By the same token, graphic designers can learn a lot from architecture when it comes to spatial drawing or negative and positive space for example. But nobody would expect there to exist an "architecturalisation expert", because "taking design tactics from architecture" or "architecturalising graphics" is no ultimate design goal for graphic design: "communicating and idea" is. This is why gamification in its current form – defined via game design elements or gameful experiences – is destined to be a temporary *gestalt*, whereas motivational design (and/or persuasive design) have the potential to stay: For only the latter articulate a lasting, well-defined, domain-spanning strategic goal. And just as importantly, if motivating user behaviour is one's goal, it is practically nonsensical to limit the space of possible tactics and solutions to gameful (or playful) experiences. If a designer discovers that fears about the security of an online banking service is the main issue keeping people from signing up – and the most cost-benefit efficient way to fix this is adding trust indicators to the interface –, it would simply be poor design to instead make the experience of the service more gameful or playful. Approaching every motivational design challenge with gamification is a solution in search of a problem: fine for marketers selling said solution, but poor practice for any designer trying to find the best solution to her design problem.

4 FROM STIMULUS-EFFECT DETERMINISM TO AFFORDANCES: RETHINKING "GAMEFUL EXPERIENCES"

Speaking of experiences and design, the existing gamification design literature showcases an additive-deterministic notion of experience design reminiscent of the first generation of serious games. These "edutainment" games were predominantly grounded in behaviourist theories, assuming that instrumental activities like learning or work entail certain inherently unpleasant and games certain inherently enjoyable elements (Egenfeldt-Nielsen 2007). By analogy, sugar has inherent chemical features that, when imbibed by a living being with the respective dispositions (taste receptors, etc.), will infallibly result in the experience of sweetness. The resulting design paradigm has been called "chocolate-covered broccoli" (Bruckman 1999): A presumed-inherently unenjoyable activity (learning) is made appealing by adding presumed-inherently enjoyable gameplay. This is precisely the model of current gamification: It assumes that game design can be broken down into isolatable atomic units ("elements", "patterns", "mechanics"), whose addition reliably produces one and only one motivational effect across users.

However, based on years of research and failing applications, game-based learning has largely abandoned the additive-deterministic paradigm. Instead, the current third generation of serious games subscribes to emergent theories of game enjoyment (Egenfeldt-Nielsen 2007, Squire 2006). By analogy, whether a piece of pastry tastes good or not does not depend on its sugar content, but on the specific mixture and preparation of all the ingredients, and how the resulting whole suits the sensitivities of the specific person eating it. This aligns well with current views of user experience as subjective, holistic, emergent, situated, and dynamic, afforded by and realised in the interaction of specific, situated human beings with the systemic whole of a designed artefact in its socio-material environment (Hassenzahl 2010, 6–31).

Now what does this mean applied to gamification? First, the motivational valence (or "functional significance", cf. Ryan and Deci 2002) of a stimulus or design element depends on its situationally appraised meaning. Paying a waiter at a restaurant is proper and motivating, paying your friends for cooking you dinner at their home is a social affront. One and the same dollar bill can evoke different, situationally negotiated and appraised meanings: I might angrily smack down a dollar bill as tip and signal social disapproval, and the waiter may or may not pick up on that (Benkler 2006, 92–99).

Second, one and the same stimulus or design element can have multiple different motivational functions. As Antin and Churchill (2011) outline, the seemingly straightforward design pattern "badges" can tie into at least five possible different motivational processes. There is no deterministic one-to-one relationship between design elements and motivational effects (though there can be tendencies, see Hassenzahl 2010, 4–8). Vice versa, one and the same motivational process can be supported by very many different design elements: Quests, badges, leaderboards, high score lists etc. all can (but need not) be functionalised for goal-setting by a user.

Third, any motivational valence emerges from the relation between the object's properties and the actor's dispositions. This relationality is enshrined in the ecological concept of *affordance* (Gibson 1986, Chemero 2009), today widely used in human-computer interaction, communication research, and sociology to model the interaction of humans and technology. An affordance is not an objective feature of a design element, but a relational quality of both object and subject. Relative to my skills, a Sudoku puzzle affords frustration or competence experiences. Relative to my current level of satiety, a slice of cake looks like the most delicious thing in the world, instilling a strong motivational pull, or induces sickness because I am currently overfed (Deterding 2011).

Fourth and finally, such motivational affordances emerge not from a single stimulus or design element, but the total animal-environment system. Whether slamming down a dollar bill on a table constitutes a rage-inducing insult or an unintentional slip of the hand depends on the total chain of previous and following interactions and social signals in which the slamming is embedded. How satisfying beating a boss monster in a game is depends on the number of previous failed attempts and the actual challenge of beating the boss monster, which again is an emergent quality of the relation of player skills and monster difficulty, etc.

In sum, (motivational) experiences are emergent properties afforded (not determined) by the relation of actors and their total environment, arising from situated, subjectively appraised valences relative to multiple motivational processes. And yet, the majority of gamification design literature claims or implies that one and the same game design element deterministically produces one (and only one) kind of motivational experience across users and contexts (Deterding forthcoming b).

5 FROM PATTERNS TO LENSES: RETHINKING GAMIFICATION DESIGN

The obvious conclusion from an emergent, relational, systemic affordance view of motivation is that motivational design should revolve around designing whole systems for motivational affordances, not adding elements with presumed-determined motivational effects. And yet, this is today's standard operating procedure in gamification. Instead of outlining motivational processes, the currently available gamification design literature largely consists in the cataloguing of patterns like "points", "achievements", "leaderboards", etc., and portrays gamification as the choice and customisation of pre-existing patterns (Deterding forthcoming b). The following quote is exemplary: "Putting all these [game] elements together is the central task of gamification design, and having knowledge of these game elements will make your gamification project compelling" (Werbach and Hunter 2012, 81). In essence, current gamification design literature recommends a pattern-based design approach (Seffah and Taleb 2011) – which as we have seen is at odds with an affordance perspective on motivation or experience more generally.

So what to do instead? It turns out that a promising answer is right before our eyes: game design. Rethinking gamification design means taking game design as a practice seriously. For game design has long acknowledged the emergent, systemic quality of experience, formalised in the MDA model (Hunicke, LeBlanc and Zubek 2004): A game's *mechanics* – the rules specifying possible player actions – together form a system that players interact with, giving rise to interactional *dynamics*, which in turn give rise to experiential *aesthetics*. And game design has answered to this systemic quality with a series of methods and tools that can fruitfully inform gamification, two of which are worth calling out (see Deterding forthcoming b for a fuller account).

The first are *design lenses*. Initially developed by Jesse Schell (2009) for game design, this concept was quickly adopted in interaction design, specifically to transfer concepts from game design (Scott 2010). Lenses provide general guidance in generating and evaluating design in a manner that design patterns do not. Design patterns articulate proven solutions to reoccurring problems – yet as such, they are ultimately prescriptive, with little room for innovation or context-sensitivity (Seffah and Taleb 2011).

Furthermore, as we have seen patterns are domain-bound, system-relative elements, often meaningless and non-functional outside this context: Just as it is nonsensical to speak of the game design pattern "deadly traps" (Björk and Holopainen 2005, 74–75) in the context of a mobile app, just adding a "deadly trap" to any given game (like Scrabble, 1948 or Poker) does not automatically make sense or generate a desired experience either.

In contrast, a design lens articulates a single design perspective in a form that is both inspiring and guiding. As Schell puts it, a lens is "a way of viewing your design" (2009, xxvi). Practically, a lens combines (a) a memorable name, (b) a concise statement of a general design principle, including a rationale for that principle, and (c) a set of focusing questions that allow the designer to take on the "mental perspective" of the lens, "illuminating issues that may have been invisible before" (Scott 2010). By focusing a specific quality of a total system, design lenses avoid the decontextualised, additive-deterministic design paradigm of contemporary gamification. By binding together said quality or principle with a rationale and focusing questions, they become self-contained, and thus easy to transfer from game design into other design disciplines.

The second game design method worth calling out is "playcentric design" (Fullerton 2008): A designer starts with specifying a target experience for a target audience. In an abductive process, she then ideates first systems of mechanics that might generate the desired experience. But because of the double emergence of player-system dynamics and resultant aesthetics, results cannot be reliably predicted. Instead, the designer creates and tests functional prototypes of the total system as quickly as possible to observe what dynamics and aesthetics actually emerge. Based on their evaluation and analysis of how and why these diverge from the intended experience, she then ideates promising design changes and revises and tests the prototype again, repeating this process until the delta between desired and actual experience is satisfactorily closed.

Summarising once more, if the re-envisioned scope of gamification are socio-technical systems, if its re-envisioned goal is motivational experiences, and if motivational experiences are systemic, emergent affordances, then a promising re-envisioned gamification design method would entail formalising desired motivational experiences in the form of design lenses, using these lenses to analyse target activities, and then engage in iterative experiential prototyping until the total prototyped socio-technical system affords the targeted motivational experiences (Deterding forthcoming b).

6   FROM AVOIDING HARM TO LIVING WELL: RETHINKING GAMIFICATION ETHICS

Almost from day one, gamification has been criticised as inherently manipulative, exploitive, or coercive (Bogost 2011, Rey forthcoming). On the one hand, given the statements of some gamification evangelists, this backlash is warranted. But on the other, it reveals a narrow conception of design ethics. As communication scholar Paul Watzlawick once put it, "one cannot not communicate" (Watzlawick, Beavin Bavelas and Jackson 1967, 51). In much the same way, one cannot not influence others: Any communication (and non-communication), any action (and inaction), and any shaping (and non-shaping) of the environment affects ourselves and others. Intentionally or not, every designer is "materializing morality" (Verbeek 2006): Every designed object makes certain actions and experiences easier or harder to realise, communicates certain ways of being as normal or good, and opens or closes certain realms of being to ethical deliberation and decision-making. Gamification is therefore not inherently "more" unethical or even "more" ethically relevant: Its overt persuasive intent simply brings the ethical unconscious of all design to the fore.

And indeed, gamification designers (like persuasive designers) have found themselves compelled to engage in a constant (legitimising) ethical discourse around their practice (Berdichevsky and Neuenschwander 1999;

Fogg 2003; Zichermann 2012). This is to be welcomed. However, both condemning and legitimising voices typically frame design ethics in a bound, defensive, other-centred fashion: Acting ethically is construed as avoiding coercion or harm on others. Thus, gamification (and persuasive design) are ethical if they do not produce negative effects for users, and come with informed consent (Fogg 2003; Zichermann 2012). The prototypical expression of this view is Thaler's and Sunstein's "libertarian paternalism," which "tries to influence choices in a way that will make choosers better off, as *judged by themselves*" (2008, 5).[1]

Against this stands a wider, positive framing of the morality of design grounded in Aristotelian virtue ethics and its contemporary descendants (Aristotle 2002, May 2010; Hursthouse 2013). Virtue ethics start not with the question what we owe to the other (be that a god or our fellow human beings), but with the self and the question: What constitutes the ultimate goal of all our action? What is it that we do for its own sake, and everything else in the sake of it? According to Aristotle, this ultimate *telos* of human beings is not hedonistic sense pleasure, but *eudaimonia*, "the good life": flourishing, bringing to full fruition and refinement our capacities as human beings (and modern virtue ethical interpretations allow for wide individual and cultural differences in what that entails). In this framing, we treat others well because as social animals, we could neither survive nor flourish without them: Living well with others is a condition and component of living well ourselves.

Viewed through this lens, "the ethical" is not a bounded domain of "negatively impinging on others", but an all-pervasive, positive dimension of life: *Every* human act and object is ethical because it partakes in life, and can be performed or made in a way that realises fruition, refinement, excellence, *eudaimonia*: an act or thing done well for its own sake. Ethical gamification (as any other design practice) would thus mean (a) being a potential tool for "positive design" (Desmet 2013) actively supporting human flourishing, (b) a practice performed virtuously, excellently in itself, (c) something that realises, furthers, or is at least congruent with living a good life with others.

---

1   Thaler's and Sunstein's emphasis.

7 FROM INSTRUMENTAL PERFECTION AND TOKENISM TO CRITICAL TRANSFORMATION: RETHINKING GAMIFICATION'S PURPOSE

Minimally, any such ethical design practice involves (a) deliberating what constitutes the good life, and (b) understanding how design has an impact on it. Contemporary gamification has been criticised for doing neither: Whereas many art and persuasive games emerge from and facilitate the critical reflection of values, ideally opening a space for the exploration and transformation of human practice (Bogost 2007; Raphael et al. 2009), current gamification merely promises technical solutions to achieve the given goals and perfect the given procedures of businesses, governments, and other institutions (Deterding forthcoming a). And instead of actually addressing the root cause of an issue, it presents a tokenist exercise in "virtualpolitik" (Losh 2009) that merely signifies taking action, coolness, hipness, etc. (Bogost forthcoming).

A perfect case in point: the PlayPump (1994), a contraption for water supply in developing nations popularised by retired advertising executive Trevor Field (Borland forthcoming). The pump replaces traditional pumping mechanics with a roundabout for kids to play with. Water would be pumped easy as child's play, and advertising billboards on the reservoir tower would pay for the pumps. The images of happy African kids playing on a roundabout made for good media both in popular and design press. Thus, Field managed to get a commitment of 60 million US dollars in aid for installing PlayPumps. But in 2009, problems started to surface: The pump was more costly and less efficient than existing solutions. It required maintenance by specially trained and approved PlayPump mechanics, resulting in many being left defunct once they broke. Advertisers interested in rural African populations did not materialise. One calculation showed that children would have to operate the pump 27 continuous hours to pump the daily water demand of an average rural African village. Thus, women ended up working on the inefficient roundabouts, resulting in strained backs because they had to constantly bow down to operate a child-sized roundabout. In a word, the main purpose and success of the PlayPump was media attention and good feelings in the developed nations, while the pump was an utter failure for the actual people having to use it in developing nations (ibid.). This illustrates not only gamification as *virtualpolitik* in full bloom, but also that successful design interventions require a deep understanding of and continued engagement with the actual people, sites, and systems they target – with the help of tools and frameworks for participatory design, sustainability, and systems thinking.

In an early classic of design ethics, Victor Papanek's *Design for the Real World* (1971, 47), one finds an interesting diagram. It is a plain pyramid with a little horizontal line that separates a small tip from a vast body. The tip of the pyramid Papanek labeled "the designer's share", and its body, "the *real* problem". Over the course of several pages, Papanek reapplies this diagram again and again to demonstrate how designers typically focus their energy and time on trivial matters: on what their clients want, not what their users need; on what a small, privileged consumer class wants, not what the whole population of their country needs; on the first world problems of their country, not the global challenges of hunger, war, inequality, or global warming. To this list we can add: on alleviating the symptoms of a societal issue, not eliminating its root causes. Rethinking the ethics of gamification, then, means seeing the whole pyramid: distancing ourselves from the day-to-day in order to work through, on all of these levels, what we as designers and scholars understand and aspire our vision of the good life, "the real problem", and our share in solving it to be.

8   CONCLUSION: TOWARD EUDAIMONIC DESIGN

If there has been one recurring theme of the preceding pages, it was to move outside the literal and figurative box: to abandon a narrow, atomistic, decontextualised notion of gamification as the implementation of technical design elements, and take into view the wider systems and contexts in which designed objects and their features are indexically embedded and implied: social situations, frames, meanings, norms, and practices; affordances as actor-environment relations; whole systems of game mechanics giving rise to gameplay dynamics that, in turn, give rise to experiential aesthetics; our individual and collective notions of the good life; our understanding of the root causes thwarting its realisation; and our moral share in striking at these roots.

So how would a rethought, positive vision of gamification look? It would aspire to critically understand, reflect, and transform the goals and systems of our society to facilitate human well-being, targeting motivation as its main strategic lever. Well-aware of the situated, socio-material quality of human motivation and action, it would take into view objects and people and their interactions, paying as much attention to the structuring of the material environment as to the framing of social contexts. Cognizant of the emergent quality of motivational experiences, it would use design lenses and iterative prototyping to design these total socio-technical systems for motivational affordances. One might call this re-envisioned, positive gamification eudaimonic design.

In closing, let us return to Paul Watzlawick once more: "These are two types of change: one that occurs within a given system which itself remains unchanged, and one whose occurrence changes the system itself [...] Second-order change is thus change of change" (Watzlawick, Weakland and Fish 1974, 10). If anything, this article has been attempting to reframe gamification – on any level of theory and practice – from a first-order to a second-order change practice.

Now in one sense, this is what current gamification already engages in. "Traditional" serious game design deployed games as interventions within existing contexts like educational institutions to convey attitudes, knowledge and skills, hoping and praying that these learnings might transfer into a different, final context of application: using condoms, being an active citizen, noticing and counteracting discrimination, etc.

In contrast to this stands the recent line of reasoning in policy and design circles heavily informed by behavioural economics that goes under names like persuasive technology, choice architecture, or nudging (Thaler and Sunstein 2008; Deterding 2012a). It argues that traditional measures in health communication, civic engagement, and consumer education have seen only limited success not so much because people do not learn, or learning does not transfer, but because emotion, habit, cognitive biases and material environments strongly shape and bound our conscious action and decision-making. In other words, we do not necessarily do better just because we know better. Instead, proponents of persuasive technology argue that we should try to affect decisions and actions directly when and where they are happening, operating on the level of emotions, habits, cognitive biases, and material environments (Deterding 2012a).

This is exactly what current gamification attempts: It implements features of games that are presumably conducive to desired actions right where these occur: Instead of building a simulation game about personal budgeting to improve financial literacy, provide a personal financial management tool informed by good game design to make it fun. Thus, gamification is already a move from change in the system to change *of* the system: from designing games as interventions deployed within certain contexts to designing contexts as interventions, informed by game design.

Again, there are legitimate doubts as to whether this strategy is ultimately effective and sustainable on its own: Should we not empower people to reflect on and self-regulate their own conduct, rather than making them ever more dependent on technological environments "nudging" them? There is evidence that the abundant use of outer measures of control forestalls the development of people's ability to autonomously self-regulate (Deci and Ryan 2012). Then again, embodiment and distributed cognition have taught us that thinking, learning and acting always already involve tools – done well, gamification "just" improves the tools at our disposal. As Heath and Anderson (2010) suggest, for us humans to get anything done at all, we always did and always will rely on the "extended will" provided by social and material devices like to-do lists and public commitments. Ideally, gamification not only "offloads" self-regulation, but helps us to develop the skills to self-regulate and enrol the tools our environment provides in the course. As such, gamification would immediately support a good life as understood by virtue ethics: For realising *eudaimonia* crucially requires the *virtues* to act in accordance with reason – that is, the trained, acquired habits or dispositions necessary to perform deliberate, planned, goal-directed, self-determined action even against our impulses (May 2010).

On the one hand, then, gamification is *conceptually* a move towards second-order change in support of human flourishing. On the other, current gamification very much remains an exercise in change in not of the system: Calling key performance indicators and targets "experience points" and "levels" and tracking and displaying them via a new software-as-a-service platform to increase "employee engagement", as so many business gamification initiatives do, merely deploys a novel technical system for a given purpose in a given institution, instead of taking into view and re-designing the larger socio-technical system itself. It uncritically fits itself into and is co-opted by standing goals and procedures in businesses, governmental and educational institutions. Instead of transforming society through and in the image of play, it instrumentalises play – and this is anathema to *eudaimonia*.

Following Aristotle, *eudaimonia* is the autotelic, self-determined exercise and perfection of one's innate capacities for its own sake and "proper pleasure" – in a sense, play is the prototypical realisation of *eudaimonia*. But more importantly, if such autotelic pursuit of excellence is the good life, then as long as we work for the sake of play, or play for the sake of work, as long as we instrumentalise one for the other, rather than cherish each for the excellence we find in it, we are living the false life. We realise the good life to the precise extent that we are able to transform whatever situation we find ourselves in into a self-determined pursuit where we find some measure of excellence, some focus on mastery and joy, some connection to our goals, needs, and values – as if it were a game we chose to play.

BIBLIOGRAPHY

ANTIN, JUDD AND ELIZABETH F. CHURCHILL. 2011. "Badges in Social Media: A Social Psychological Perspective." Accessed April 10, 2014. http://gamification-research.org/chi2011/papers.

ARISTOTLE. 2002. *Nicomachean Ethics.* New York, Oxford: Oxford University Press.

BATESON, PATRICK AND PAUL MARTIN. 2013. *Play, Playfulness, Creativity and Innovation.* New York: Cambridge University Press.

BENKLER, YOCHAI. 2006. *The Wealth of Networks: How Social Production Transforms Markets and Freedom.* New Haven: Yale University Press.

BERDICHEVSKY, DANIEL AND ERIK NEUENSCHWANDER. 1999. "Toward an Ethics of Persuasive Technology." *Communications of the ACM* 42(5): 51–58.

BJÖRK, STAFFAN AND JUSSI HOLOPAINEN. 2005. *Patterns in Game Design.* Boston: Charles River Media.

BOGOST, IAN. Forthcoming. "Why Gamification Is Bullshit." In *The Gameful World: Approaches, Issues, Applications,* edited by Steffen P. Walz and Sebastian Deterding. Cambridge, MA, London: MIT Press.

BOGOST, IAN. 2011. "Exploitationware." *Gamasutra,* May 3. http://goo.gl/jK1VR.

BOGOST, IAN. 2007. *Persuasive Games: The Expressive Power of Videogames.* Cambridge, MA, London: MIT Press.

BORLAND, RALPH. Forthcoming. "The PlayPump." In *The Gameful World: Approaches, Issues, Applications,* edited by Steffen P. Walz and Sebastian Deterding. Cambridge, London: MIT Press.

BRUCKMAN, AMY. 1999. "Can Educational Be Fun?" In *GDC* 1999, 75–79. San Jose, CA: Game Developer's Conference.

CAILLOIS, ROGER. 2001/1958. *Man, Play, and Games.* Urbana, Chicago: University of Illinois Press.

CHEMERO, ANTHONY. 2009. *Radical Embodied Cognitive Science.* Cambridge, MA, London: MIT Press.

CRUMLISH, CHRISTIAN AND ERIN MALONE. 2009. *Designing Social Interfaces: Principles, Patterns, and Practices for Improving the User Experience.* Sebastopol: O'Reilly.

CSIKSZENTMIHALYI, MIHALY. 1990. *Flow: The Psychology of Optimal Experience.* New York: Harper and Row.

DECI, EDWARD L. AND RICHARD M. RYAN. 2012. "Motivation, Personality, and Development within Embedded Social Contexts: An Overview of Self-Determination Theory." In *The Oxford Handbook of Human Motivation,* edited by Richard M. Ryan, 85–107. New York: Oxford University Press.

DECI, EDWARD L., R. KOESTNER AND RICHARD M. RYAN. 1999. "A Meta-Analytic Review of Experiments Examining the Effects of Extrinsic Rewards on Intrinsic Motivation." *Psychological Bulletin* 125(6): 627–668.

DEKOVEN, BERNIE. 2013. *The Well-Played Game: A Player's Philosophy.* Cambridge, London: MIT Press.

DESMET, PIETER. 2013. *Positive Design.* Delft: TU Delft.

DESMET, PIETER. 2012. "Faces of Product Pleasure: 25 Positive Emotions in Human-Product Interactions." *International Journal of Design* 6(2): 1–29.

DETERDING, SEBASTIAN. 2013. "Modes of Play: A Frame Analytic Account of Video Gaming." PhD diss., Hamburg University.

DETERDING, SEBASTIAN. 2012a. "Persuasive Design." In *Depletion Design: A Glossary of Network Ecologies*, edited by Carolin Wiedemann and Soenke Zehle, 115–119. Amsterdam: Institute of Network Cultures.

DETERDING, SEBASTIAN. 2012b. "Ruling the World: When Life Gets Games". Accessed April 10, 2014.
http://codingconduct.cc/Ruling-the-World.

DETERDING, SEBASTIAN. 2011. "Situated Motivational Affordances of Game Elements: A Conceptual Model." Accessed April 10, 2014.
http://gamification-research.org/chi2011/papers.

DETERDING, SEBASTIAN. Forthcoming a. "The Ambiguity of Games: Imaginaries, Histories, and Discourses of a Gameful World." In *The Gameful World: Approaches, Issues, Applications*, edited by Steffen P. Walz and Sebastian Deterding. Cambridge, MA, London: MIT Press.

DETERDING, SEBASTIAN. Forthcoming b. "The Lens of Intrinsic Skill Atoms: A Method for Gameful Design."

DETERDING, SEBASTIAN, DAN DIXON, RILLA KHALED AND LENNART E. NACKE. 2011. "From Game Design Elements to Gamefulness: Defining 'Gamification.'" In *MindTrek '11 Proceedings of the 15th International Academic MindTrek Conference: Envisioning Future Media Environments*, 9–15. New York: ACM Press.

EGENFELDT-NIELSEN, SIMON. 2007. "Third Generation Educational Use of Computer Games." *Journal of Educational Multimedia and Hypermedia* 16(3): 263–281.

FOGG, B.J. 2003. *Persuasive Technology: Using Computers to Change What We Think and Do.* Amsterdam: Morgan Kaufmann.

FULLERTON, TRACY. 2008. *Game Design Workshop: A Playcentric Approach to Creating Innovative Games.* Amsterdam: Morgan Kaufman.

GIBSON, JAMES J. 1986. *The Ecological Approach to Visual Perception.* Hillsdale: Lawrence Erlbaum.

GOFFMAN, ERVING. 1986. *Frame Analysis: An Essay on the Organization of Experience.* Boston: Northeastern University Press.

GRIBBLE, NATHAN. 1994. "Munchkin Examined." *Interactive Fantasy* 2: 101–108.

HASSENZAHL, MARC. 2010. *Experience Design: Technology for All the Right Reasons.* San Rafael: Morgan and Claypool.

HASSENZAHL, MARC, SARAH DIEFENBACH AND ANJA GÖRITZ. 2010. "Needs, Affect, and Interactive Products – Facets of User Experience." *Interacting with Computers* 22(5): 353–362.

HEATH, JOSEPH AND JOEL ANDERSON. 2010. "Procrastination and the Extended Will." In *The Thief of Time: Philosophical Essays on Procrastination*, edited by Chrisoula Andreou and Mark White, 233–252. New York: Oxford University Press.

HEETER, CARRIE, YU-HAO LEE, BRIAN MAGERKO AND BEN MEDLER. 2011. "Impacts of Forced Serious Game Play on Vulnerable Subgroups." *International Journal of Gaming and Computer-Mediated Simulations* 3(3): 34–53.

HUIZINGA, JOHAN. 1955 / 1938. *Homo Ludens: A Study of the Play Element in Culture.* Boston: Beacon Press.

HUNG, AARON CHIA YUAN. 2011. *The Work of Play: Meaning-Making in Video Games.* New York: Peter Lang.

Hunicke, Robin, Marc LeBlanc and Robert Zubek. 2004. "MDA: A Formal Approach to Game Design and Game Research." In *Papers From the 2004 AAAI Workshop 'Challenges in Game Artificial Intelligence'*, edited by Dan Fu, Stottler Henke and Jeff Orkin, 1–5. Menlo Park: AAAI Press.

Huotari, Kai and Juo Hamari. 2012. "Defining Gamification – A Service Marketing Perspective." In *Proceedings of The 16th International Academic Mindtrek Conference*, 17–22. New York: ACM Press.

Hursthouse, Rosalind. 2013. "Virtue Ethics." Accessed April 10, 2014. http://plato.stanford.edu/archives/fall2013/entries/ethics-virtue.

Juul, Jesper. 2011. "Gamification Backlash Roundup." *The Ludologist*, April 2. http://www.jesperjuul.net/ludologist/gamification-backlash-roundup.

Lopez, Steve. 2011. "Disneyland Workers Answer to 'Electronic Whip'." *Los Angeles Times*, October 19. Accessed April 10, 2014. http://articles.latimes.com/2011/oct/19/local/la-me-1019-lopez-disney-20111018.

Losh, Elizabeth. 2009. *Virtualpolitik: An Electronic History of Government Media-Making in a Time of War, Scandal, Disaster, Miscommunication, and Mistakes*. Cambridge, MA: MIT Press.

May, Hope. 2010. *Aristotle's Ethics: Moral Development and Human Nature*. London, New York: continuum.

Michie, Susan, Maartje M. van Stralen and Robert West. 2011. "The Behaviour Change Wheel: A New Method for Characterising and Designing Behaviour Change Interventions." *Implementation Science* 6(42). http://www.implementationscience.com/content/6/1/42/.

Mollick, Ethan and Nancy Rothbard. 2013. "Mandatory Fun: Gamification and the Impact of Games at Work." Accessed April 10, 2014. http://ssrn.com/abstract=2277103.

Orlikowski, Wanda J. and Debra C. Gash. 1994. "Technological Frames: Making Sense of Information Technology in Organizations." *ACM Transactions on Information Systems* 12(2): 174–207.

Papanek, Victor. 1971. *Design for the Real World: Human Ecology and Social Change*. New York: Pantheon Books.

Przybylski, Andrew K., C. Scott Rigby and Richard M. Ryan. 2010. "A Motivational Model of Video Game Engagement." *Review of General Psychology* 14(2): 154–166.

Raphael, Chad, Christine Bachen, Kathleen-M. Lynn, Jessica Baldwin-Philippi and Kristian A. McKee. 2009. "Games for Civic Learning: A Conceptual Framework and Agenda for Research and Design." *Games and Culture* 5(2): 199–235.

Reeve, Johnmarshall. 2009. *Understanding Motivation and Emotion*. Hoboken: John Wiley and Sons.

Reeve, Johnmarshall. 2006. "Teachers as Facilitators: What Autonomy-Supportive Teachers Do and Why Their Students Benefit." *The Elementary School Journal* 106(3): 225–236.

Rey, P. J. Forthcoming. "Gamification and Post-Fordist Capitalism." In *The Gameful World: Approaches, Issues, Applications*, edited by Steffen P. Walz and Sebastian Deterding. Cambridge, MA, London: MIT Press.

Robertson, Margaret. 2010. "Can't Play, Won't Play." *Hide & Seek*, October 6. http://hideandseek.net/2010/10/06/cant-play-wont-play/.

Ryan, Richard M. and Edward L. Deci. 2002. "An Overview of Self-Determination Theory: An Organismic-Dialectical Perspective." In *Handbook of Self-Determination Research*, edited by Edward L. Deci and Richard M. Ryan, 3–36. Rochester: University of Rochester Press.

Salen, Katie. 2008. "Toward an Ecology of Gaming." In *The Ecology of Games: Connecting Youth, Games, and Learning*, edited by Katie Salen, 1–20. Cambridge, MA: MIT Press.

Salen, Katie, Robert Torres, Loretta Wolozin, Rebecca Rufo-Tepper and Arana Shapiro. 2011. *Quest to Learn: Developing the School for Digital Kids*. Cambridge, MA, London: MIT Press.

Scott, Bill. 2010. "Designing with Lenses." UX Booth, April 6.
http://www.uxbooth.com/articles/designing-with-lenses/.

Scheff, Thomas J. 2003. "Shame in Self and Society." *Symbolic Interaction* 26(2): 239–262.

Schell, Jesse. 2009. *The Art of Game Design: A Book of Lenses*. Amsterdam: Morgan Kaufman.

Seffah, Ahmed and Mohamed Taleb. 2011. "Tracing the Evolution of HCI Patterns as an Interaction Design Tool." *Innovations in Systems and Software Engineering* 8(2): 93–109.

Shields, David Lyle Light and Brenda Jo Light Bredemeier. 1995. *Character Development and Physical Activity*. Champaign: Human Kinetics.

Sicart, Miguel. 2011. "Against Procedurality." *Game Studies* 11(3).
http://gamestudies.org/1103/articles/sicart_ap.

Singhal, Arvind and Karen Greiner. 2008. "Performance Activism and Civic Engagement Through Symbolic and Playful Actions." *Journal of Development Communication* 19(2): 43–53.

Squire, Kurt. 2006. "From Content to Context: Videogames as Designed Experience." *Educational Researcher* 35(8): 19–29.

Stueber, Karsten R. 2005. "How to Think About Rules and Rule Following." *Philosophy of the Social Sciences* 35(3): 307–323.

Taylor, T.L. 2009. "The Assemblage of Play." *Games and Culture* 4(4): 331–339.

Thaler, Richard H. and Cass R. Sunstein. 2008. *Nudge. Improving Decisions About Health, Wealth, and Happiness*. New Haven, London: Yale University Press.

Todnem By, Rune. 2005. "Organisational Change Management: A Critical Review." *Journal of Change Management* 5(4): 369–380.

Toprak, Cagdas Chad, Joshua Platt, Hsin Yang Ho and Florian Floyd Mueller. 2013. "Cart-Load-O-Fun: Designing Digital Games for Trams." Accessed April 10, 2014.
http://www.fdg2013.org/program/papers/paper17_toprak_etal.pdf.

Verbeek, Peter-Paul. 2006. "Materializing Morality: Design Ethics and Technological Mediation." *Science, Technology and Human Values* 31(3): 361–380.

Watzlawick, Paul, Janet Beavin Bavelas and Don D. Jackson. 1967. *Pragmatics of Human Communication: A Study of Interactional Patterns, Pathologies and Paradoxes*. New York: W.W. Norton and Company.

Watzlawick, Paul, John Weakland and Richard Fish. 1974. *Change: Principles of Problem Formation and Problem Resolution*. New York: W.W. Norton.

Werbach, Kevin. 2014. "(Re)Defining Gamification: A Process Approach." *Persuasive* 2014: 266–272.

Werbach, Kevin, and Dan Hunter. 2012. *For the Win: How Game Thinking Can Revolutionize Your Business*. Philadelphia: Wharton Digital Press.

WHITWORTH, BRIANM AND ADNAN AHMAD. 2013. "Socio-Technical System Design." In *The Encyclopedia of Human-Computer Interaction,* edited by Mads Soegaard and Rikke Friis Dam. Aarhus: The Interaction Design Foundation. Accessed May 6, 2014. http://www.interaction-design.org/encyclopedia/socio-technical_system_design.html.

ZHANG, PING. 2008. "Motivational Affordances: Reasons for ICT Design and Use." *Communications of the ACM* 51(11): 145–147.

ZICHERMANN, GABE. 2012. "The Code of Gamification Ethics." *Gamification.co,* December 10. http://www.gamification.co/2012/12/10/code-of-gamification-ethics/.

LUDOGRAPHY

DIPLOMACY. 1959. Developed by Allan B. Calhamer. Board game. Self-published.

PLAYPUMP. 1994. Developed by Roundabout Outdoor. Playground water pump. Trevor Field and Playpumps International.

POKER. First half of 19th century. United States. Board game.

SCRABBLE. 1948. Developed by Alfred Mosher Butts. Board game. James Brunot.

AUTHORS

Sebastian Deterding
Dr. Sebastian Deterding is a researcher and designer working on gameful and playful experiences and their wider social ramifications. He is currently a visiting Assistant Professor at Rochester Institute of Technology's School for Interactive Games and Media and Laboratory for Media, Arts, Games, Interaction and Creativity (MAGIC) in New York, USA. He is an independent designer and associate of the international design studio Hubbub. He lives online at codingconduct.cc.

Daphne Dragona
Daphne Dragona is a media arts curator and researcher living and working in Athens and Berlin. Her interest lies in the fields of network-based art, game-based art, commons based peer production and emerging forms of collaborative creativity embracing critical awareness and resistance. She is a PhD candidate in the Faculty of Communication and Media Studies of the University of Athens, Greece.

Gabriele Ferri
Dr. Gabriele Ferri, Postdoctoral Researcher at Indiana University, holds a PhD in Semiotics from the University of Bologna, Italy. He is currently involved in the Intel ISTC Social initiative, where his research focuses on the interaction between digital media and narrative, critical, satirical, and political discourses. He is an editor for G|A|M|E Journal and an independent urban game designer. He can be reached at gabferri@indiana.edu and gabrieleferri.com.

Sonia Fizek
Dr. Sonia Fizek is a Postdoctoral Researcher at the Centre for Digital Cultures at Leuphana University Lüneburg, Germany, where she joined the Gamification Lab. She completed her PhD in 2012 at the School of Creative Studies and Media at Bangor University, UK. In her doctoral thesis she developed a method for the study of the player character in offline computer role-playing games. Her current academic interests include: gamification, games for change, and playful interfaces, with an emphasis on the audio game genre.

Maxwell Foxman
Maxwell Foxman is a second year PhD candidate in Communications at Columbia University in New York, USA. His research interests include gamification, internet culture and the effects of digital media on everyday life and memory.

Mathias Fuchs
Prof. Dr. Mathias Fuchs studied Computer Science in Erlangen and Vienna (Vienna University of Technology), and Composition in Vienna (Universität für Musik und darstellende Kunst Wien) and in Stockholm (EMS, Fylkingen). In 2010 Mathias Fuchs received his Doctor title by Humboldt University of Berlin for a PhD thesis on the meaning of sounds ("Sinn und Sound"). He has pioneered in the field of artistic use of games and is a leading theoretician on game art and games studies. He is an artist, musician, media critic, and Professor at the Centre for Digital Cultures at Leuphana University Lüneburg, Germany. He is also Director of the Leuphana Gamification Lab.

Scott Nicholson
Dr. Scott Nicholson is Associate Professor at Syracuse University School of Information Studies in New York, USA and Director of the Because Play Matters game lab.

Thibault Philippette

Thibault Philippette is a researcher at the Catholic University of Louvain (UCL) in Belgium within the Research Center in Communication Sciences. He is member of the "Groupe de Recherche en Médiation des Savoirs" (GReMS) and the "Observatoire des Mondes Numériques en Sciences Humaines" (Omnsh).

Fabrizio Augusto Poltronieri

Dr. Fabrizio Augusto Poltronieri holds a PhD in Semiotics from the Pontifical Catholic University of São Paulo (PUC-SP), Brazil, with a thesis on the role of chance in computer art. Currently, his research efforts are engaged in understanding how the post-historical codes founded in video games could be used in the production of knowledge.

Felix Raczkowski

Felix Raczkowski is currently working on his PhD thesis on the instrumentalisation of games with a special focus on serious games and gamification. He is an affiliated scholarship holder at the Institute for Media Studies at Ruhr University Bochum, Germany. Among his other research interests are transmedia phenomena, convergence- and fan-cultures as well as theories on games, play, and toys. He can be reached at felix.raczkowski@rub.de.

Joost Raessens

Prof. Dr. Joost Raessens holds the chair of Media Theory at Utrecht University in the Netherlands. He was the conference chair of the first Digital Games Research Association (DiGRA) conference Level Up in Utrecht (2003), and is on the editorial board of *Games and Culture* (SAGE). Raessens' current research concerns the "ludification of culture" focusing in particular on the playful construction of identities, on applied, serious and persuasive gaming, and on the notion of play as a conceptual framework for the analysis of media use. Raessens is the scientific director of GAP: the Center for the Study of Digital Games and Play (gamesandplay.nl).

Paolo Ruffino

Paolo Ruffino is a Research Associate at the Gamification Lab, Centre for Digital Cultures (Leuphana University Lüneburg, Germany). He is also completing a PhD at Goldsmiths, University of London and works as Lecturer at the Game Cultures programme at London South Bank University. His PhD research involves a study of the concepts of consumer and producer in video games, the history of the medium of the video game and phenomena such as "modding", independent gaming, open engines and game art. He is a member of the art collective IOCOSE. Paolo lives and works in London, UK. paoloruffino.com/.

Niklas Schrape

Dr. Niklas Schrape is a Postdoctoral Researcher at the Centre for Digital Cultures at Leuphana University Lüneburg, Germany. He holds a double position at the Gamification Lab and at the Institute for Advanced Study in Media Cultures of Computer Simulation (MECS). Between 2007 and 2011, Niklas finished his PhD thesis in Media Studies at Film and Television University Potsdam-Babelsberg (HFF). His current research interests encompass the consequences of gamification on our understanding of social reality and the relationship between simulation and gamification.

Matthew Tiessen

Dr. Matthew Tiessen is an Assistant Professor in the School of Professional Communication (ProCom) and a Research Associate at the Infoscape Research Lab in the Faculty of Communication and Design (FCAD) at Ryerson University in Toronto, Canada. His research and teaching focuses on digital and visual communication and culture and is supported by a Social Science and Humanities Research Council of Canada (SSHRC) Insight Development Grant.

INDEX

A

achievement 290, 292
actant 204–205, 208–220
advergame 202–203, 213, 217–220
advertising 22–23, 322
agency 54–61, 66, 174, 180–181, 209, 264
alea 102, 123–127, 134–136
app (see Attent, Codecademy, Duolingo, EpicWin, Foursquare, Kolibree, Livecube, Lose It!, Nike+, NikeFuel, ReadSocial App, Runno, Strava, SuperBetter)
    gamified app 201–220
apparatus 165–184, 257–258
artwork 62–67, 240–243
automation 148–149
Attent (app) 154–155, 281–283

B

badge 291–293, 317
Badgeville (company) 259, 274, 276
big data 30–34, 41–42, 124, 261
Bigdoor (company) 259
biopolitics 38–39
bonus programme 31
brand loyalty (see loyalty)
Bunchball (company) 22, 24, 26, 32, 211, 228–229, 259

C

Candy Crush Saga (game) 198
cheating 76, 145, 155–156, 190
Chess (game) 180
choice architecture 21, 34–38, 42, 324
Codecademy (app) 293
communication 72–73, 84–87, 166–175, 182–184
communicology 13, 170–173, 184
competition 75, 77, 79, 80–87, 203, 207–220, 299
complexity 276, 280, 285
control 22, 28, 39–40, 42, 255–256, 260–261
creativity 50, 56, 64, 67
cybernatisation 31–32
cybernetics 59–60

D

data 231–244
    data body 233, 257
    datafication 14, 231, 234, 237, 244
    datafied information 235
    dataplay 239
death 167, 172–173, 241, 257, 264
Der allezeit fertige Menuetten- und Polonaisencomponist (game) 125
Der Frommen Lotterie (game) 123–124
desertion 241
design 290–302, 305–307, 312–325
    design lenses 318–320, 324
    eudaimonic design 307, 323–324
    meaningful design 282–283
    playcentric design 319
    socio-technical systems design 312–313, 320, 324–325
Diplomacy (game) 310
dividualising 256
Dopamine (company) 276
Duolingo (app) 228

E

Einfall, einen doppelten Contrapunct in der Octave von sechs Tacten zu machen
    ohne die Regeln davon zu wissen (game) 126
emergence 280, 285
engagement 47–48, 55–58, 62
EpicWin (app) 213–214
ethics 56, 123, 306–307, 320–325
European Commission 37
EVE Online (game) 397
exploitation 72, 106, 228, 234, 239
exploitationware 51–52, 229, 274, 276

F

Facebook 71, 75, 86, 95, 98, 105, 212, 213, 230, 233, 234, 240–243, 252–253, 259
feedback 21, 30, 33, 42–43, 212, 259, 306, 309, 314
film (see O Brother, Where Art Thou?, Up in the Air, Slumdog Millionaire, Star Wars)
    puzzle film (see Lola rennt, Lost Highway, Memento)
fitness (see social fitness)
flow 56–57, 143–144, 261–263, 305
Foldit (game) 293, 299
Foursquare (app) 71–88, 156, 201, 212, 214–215, 217–219, 234–236, 242, 306
frequent flyer programme 25–35, 42, 149
fun... 273–285
funology 305

G

game

    board game (see Chess, Diplomacy, Risk)

    endgame 294–300

    game art 62–67, 240–243

    game-based learning 305

    game design .... 50, 52, 121, 188, 278, 284, 290–300 , 305–307, 313–319, 324–325

    game fallacy 197

    game show (see TV game show)

    massively multiplayer online role playing game (see World of Warcraft)

    non-game 22, 104, 187, 190, 216

    persuasive game 52, 230, 322

    serious game (see Foldit, SPENT)

    video game (see Candy Crush Saga, EVE Online, Guild Wars 2, Mouse in the Maze, Portal, Space War!, Tennis for Two, Tetris, World of Warcraft)

gamification (etymology) 8, 189–190, 229–230

gamification

    … of cleaning 308

    … of communication 104

    … of killing 133–135

    … of labour 154–155

    … of learning 132–133, 312, 314, 324

    … of lifestyle 131–132

    … of music 124–128

    … of magic arts 129–130

    … of marketing 28, 34

    … of religious practice 122–124

    … of television 98

    … of water supply 322

gamification company (see Bunchball, Badgeville, Bigdoor, SCVNGR)

    counter-gamification 237–239, 244

    de-gamification 242–243

    exclusive gamification 218–220

    interstitial gamification 217, 220

    meaningful gamification 299–301

gaming literacy 109, 277–283

gamocracy 260

George Clooney 23–27

gift culture 81–83

Gioco filarmonico, o sia maniera facile per comporre un infinito numero di minuetti e trio anche senza sapere il contrapunto (game) 126–127

governmentality 21, 38–43

grinding 151, 270–271, 291, 296–297

Guild Wars 2 (game) 297

H

Hasard (game) 131

history

    post-history 167, 170–173, 178, 181–184

    predigital history of gamification 122–135, 95, 103

I

identity 24, 27–29, 232–235

identification 235, 240, 244

improvisation 98, 102, 280–283

incentivisation 252, 255, 258

item 147, 291, 295

J

jouabilité 193–195

K

killing 133–135, 208, 291

Kolibree (app) 277, 281, 283

L

lawsuit 264

level 290–291

L'Hombre (game) 131

libertarian paternalism 21, 34–36, 321

life 48–50, 54–67

LinkedIn 233, 314

Livecube (app) 276–277

Lola rennt (film) 97

Lose It! (app) 228

Lost Highway (film) 97

loyalty 22–28, 32, 124, 289–290, 294, 297

ludicisation 189

ludic turn 96, 100, 103, 109–111, 127

ludification 95–98, 103–104, 120–124, 230–232

ludoliteracy 105, 109–110

ludology 73, 206–207

ludus 98, 102, 120, 238, 314

M

Magnum Pleasure Hunt (game) 202, 219

magic circle 73, 83–88, 216–218, 277

materiality 54, 57–61

measurement 146, 153–155, 231–235

media

    media studies 91–92, 97–100

    new media 97–99, 106

    social media 71, 74–75, 230–236, 240, 243, 258, 262

Memento (film) 97

Memory-Builder (game) 132–133

motivation

    intrinsic motivation 294, 309

    extrinsic motivation 275, 294, 309

motivational affordances 307, 317–320, 324
Mouse in the Maze (game) 189
Musikalisches Würfelspiel (game) 125–126
N
narrative 203–212
narratology 202, 206–207
network (see social network)
New York City 72, 78
Nike+ (app) 49, 59, 154, 201, 212, 214–215, 228, 231, 298
NikeFuel (app) 48, 61
nonhuman 254, 261, 264
non-place 29
normalisation 49, 148, 236–237, 244
O
obfuscation 240
O Brother, Where Art Thou? (film) 24
OkCupid 314
opposition (see counter-gamification)
P
paidia 98, 102, 120, 238, 314
panopticon 40–41
persuasion 22–23, 143, 255
Pharo (game) 131
playability 106–110, 194–195
playbor 79–80
playfulness 275–285
PlayPump 322
point 141–156, 235–237
pointsification 229, 274, 276, 281–282
point system 27, 150, 273, 276, 281, 284
Poker (game) 310, 319
Portal (game) 158
potlatch 81–84
proceduralism 143
projection 165–170, 176–180, 183
proximal communication 73, 84–87
psychiatric experiment 146–151
punishment 30, 33, 42, 188, 290, 309
Q
quantification 236, 252, 255–256, 262
quantification of movement 48–49
Quantified Self movement 9, 154, 232, 262
Quora 314
R
ReadSocial App (app) 277
RECIPE 300
reward 289–291, 294, 297–302
rhetorics 22

Risk (game) 214
Runno (app) 212–214
S
Scrabble (game) 319
SCVNGR (company) 215
Second Life (game) 62–64
second-order change 324
self-governance 9
simulacrum 168–169
simulation 166, 168–169, 183
semiotics 205–209
semiotic square 204, 210–215, 218–220
Slumdog Millionaire (film) 92–93, 106
social
... fitness 263
... media 71, 74–75, 230–236, 240, 243, 258, 262
... network 84–86, 212–215, 232
Spacewar! (game) 188
Starbucks 231
Star Wars (film) 104, 210
status 24–29, 33, 41, 43, 274, 276–277, 281, 283, 290
Strava (app) 261–264
SuperBetter (app) 49, 59, 136, 298
T
technology 173–174, 176
Tennis for Two (game) 189
Tetris (game) 180
time 61–62
token economy 146–147, 149, 150–155
TV game show 92
U
Up in the Air (film) 26
W
Who Wants to Be a Millionaire (TV game show) 92
World of Warcraft (game) 108, 198, 282, 295
Y
YouTube 97–98, 102, 104, 230, 242

ACKNOWLEDGEMENTS

We would like to thank all the participants of the 2013 Rethinking Gamification Workshop that motivated this book project, Fabian Lehmann for the editorial work and great project management, Laleh Torabi for the wonderful design and artwork, Jacob Watson for being a thorough proofreader and editorial consultant, Ingrid Leonie Severin and Piet Simon for help with the final proofreading, Christopher Borgmann for legal advise, Tina Ebner for valuable help with budget, and all our colleagues from the Centre for Digital Cultures (CDC) and the Institute for Advanced Studies on Media Cultures of Computer Simulation (MECS) for being a tremendous inspiration.

We would also like to express our gratitude to Claus Pias and Timon Beyes for making the Gamification Lab possible in the first place.

Lightning Source UK Ltd.
Milton Keynes UK
UKOW04f0322070515

251039UK00001B/5/P